Developing Government Bond Markets

A Handbook

THE WORLD BANK

INTERNATIONAL
MONETARY FUND

Library of Congress Cataloging-in-Publication Data

Developing government bond markets : a handbook.
    p. cm.
  Includes bibliographical references.
  ISBN 0-8213-4955-4
  1. Government securities — Handbooks, manuals, etc. 2. Bond market — Handbooks, manuals, etc. I. World Bank.

HG4715 .D48 2001
332.63'232—dc21

                                                     2001026281

Cover Design: Rock Creek Publishing Group.

Photo Credit: Salomon Brothers Fixed Income Trading Floor, New York, USA, circa 1997.

Contents

Preface

This handbook is designed to serve as a reference source for two distinct user groups involved in the development of government bond markets: (i) senior government officials responsible for the development of the government bond market (i.e., senior officials in ministries of finance, central banks, and securities regulatory and banking supervisory institutions) and (ii) individuals responsible for guiding the market development process at the operational level, and who have a substantial need to understand the policy issues involved. The handbook is structured as follows. Chapter 1 provides an overview of certain policy considerations relevant to the development of a government bond market. This overview considers key issues, but at a level of generality appropriate for senior government officials responsible for making key strategic decisions. The remaining eleven chapters present more detailed discussions of key policy issues, including substantive considerations relating to implementation. The handbook's primary emphasis, however, focuses on the policy dimension of developing medium- and long-term bond markets. It is not intended as a technical manual for use by individuals engaged in day-to-day implementation or operations. The handbook also provides bibliographic and website references for those interested in pursuing further the issues covered. A comprehensive glossary of terms related to securities markets appears at the end of the handbook.

In planning the structure and content of the handbook, the authors were mindful of existing literature on the subject which addresses specific elements of government bond markets, both with respect to their creation as well as their functioning. However, it was determined that a gap existed with respect to a reference publication that comprehensively covers a wide range of relevant elements in one volume. The handbook is intended to address this need. It presents an integrated view of the government bond market in a manner that will enable policymakers and operational staff to better understand how different elements related to developing such a market are linked, and how they can best be sequenced to achieve the desired result—an efficient and liquid market for government securities.

The handbook, therefore, covers a wide range of topics, including: the linkages with money markets and monetary policy operations; the policies needed to develop an issuance strategy and debt management considerations to build credibility; and the reforms necessary to promote institutional investment. Although by design the handbook covers considerable ground, it remains focused throughout on policy considerations, which are the essential building blocks for reform. The policy discussion is based on the experiences and views of practitioners drawn from both the public and private sectors around the world. Their experiences helped shape the recommendations regarding the best way to achieve the desired objectives notwithstanding the existence of various external and internal constraints.

In preparing the handbook, it became clear that there was no single-best way to sequence the chapters. As such, it was decided to follow a sequence most conducive to achieving a better understanding of the government bond market development process, starting with the key linkages with other essential processes such as money market and monetary policy operations, then turning to the essential market participants (issuers and investors), followed by the basic market operations (secondary markets), and finally considering the fundamental infrastructure needed to operate the market (legal and regulatory framework and settlement and depository facilities). The handbook's two final chapters consider the important linkages between the government bond market and two strategic emerging segments of the domestic securities markets, namely the subnational and the private sector securities markets.

There are three additional considerations worthy of note. First, the reader will find some overlap among the chapters. This was done to highlight the interrelationship among the different elements and to present the subject of securities market development in all its complexity. Second, when considering the target audience from a country perspective, the intent was to make it especially relevant to those countries that are more effectively engaged in the process of extending the term structure of their markets beyond the money market segment. Third, the handbook should be viewed in the nature of work-in-progress, and as an ongoing effort of the World Bank and the IMF to provide countries with a comprehensive reference source for the development of government bond markets. The handbook will be reviewed and revised over time to take into account the latest developments and emerging trends in government bond markets, as well as new perspectives on these markets.

Clemente L. del Valle

Foreword

There is a consensus between the World Bank and the International Monetary Fund that the development of domestic bond markets deserves high priority on the financial sector development agenda. On the one hand, bond markets are essential for a country to enter a sustained phase of development driven by market-based capital allocation and increased avenues for raising debt capital. On the other hand, the central position occupied by domestic bond markets in markedly increasing the resilience of a country's financial system and insulating it against external shocks, contagion and reduction of access to international capital markets is established.

Since the recent eruption of wide-spread financial crises in 1997, the World Bank and the International Monetary Fund have dedicated substantial human and financial resources to efforts geared towards restructuring the financial sector and reducing financial vulnerability. A key component in our efforts has been strengthening capital markets, in particular domestic bond markets. This Handbook spearheads our work in this area.

The importance of government bond markets in catalyzing the growth of overall bond markets is recognized and accepted. A survey of the world's major developed bond markets reveals diverse paths of development. While there is no general development philosophy which can be applied to developing domestic bond markets, the task is too important not to tackle head-on. There are many insights, lessons and strategies which can be gleaned from the market development experience of the developed and emerging markets, and this handbook attempts to capture them to help policy makers and market participants.

As national economies become increasingly open and interlinked with a market-oriented global financial architecture, it is imperative that the domestic financial sectors become market-based as well. Many economies which suffered during the Asian financial crisis were borrowing from international debt markets, but were running semi-controlled local financial sectors. This weakness cost them dearly.

We would like to signal our increased focus on the development of government bond markets by the publication of this Handbook, and look forward to working together with member countries to delve deeper into specific market development issues. The Handbook will be revised over time to reflect comments and suggestions from national authorities and market participants.

Manuel Conthe
Vice President,
Financial Sector
World Bank

Stefan Ingves
Director,
Monetary & Exchange Affairs Dept.
International Monetary Fund

Handbook Team and Acknowledgments

This Handbook was prepared by a group of experts from the World Bank Group and the International Monetary Fund, and coordinated by Clemente del Valle of the World Bank.

The core group in the World Bank Group, led by Clemente del Valle, included Noritaka Akamatsu, Jose Antonio Alepuz, Juan Costain, Sonsoles Gallego, Tomas Glaessner, Yongbeom Kim, Jeppe Ladekarl, Jeong Yeon Lee, Michel Noel, Dimitri Vittas, David Willey, David Wilton, Xin Zhang, and Tadashi Endo (IFC). They received invaluable support from Pedro Martinez Mendez and David Willey who served as external consultants to this project. The core group in the IMF, led by Piero Ugolini, included Peter Dattels, Jennifer Elliott, George Iden, Robert Price, Jodi Scarlata, Charles Siegman, Mark Swinburne, Howell Zee, and Mark Zelmer.

The core group was ably assisted in the World Bank by Mueen Batlay, Maria Gabriela Gonzalez, Mari Kogiso, and Peter Taylor (IFC), who conducted background research, compiled and analyzed data, prepared tables and graphs, and provided general support in the development of the Handbook. Additional research and guidance was provided by Dafna Tapiero and the Financial Sector Help Desk's Neesham Kranz and Zeynep Kantur. Invaluable administrative support was provided by Noemi Dacanay.

The team benefited from comments from numerous individuals: special thanks are due to those who provided guidance, substantive input and other constructive suggestions with respect to the development of the Handbook. These included Sarah Calvo, Gerard Caprio, Patrick Conroy, Manolo Conthe, Frederick Jensen, Kenneth Lay, Larry Promisel, and Graeme Wheeler in the World Bank, and Alison Harwood in the IFC. The team also benefited from comments from Laura Burakis, Elizabeth Currie, Gregorio Impavido, Anjali Kumar, Rodney Lester, P.S. Srinivas, C.K. Teng, Antonio Velandia in the World Bank, and Mamta Shah and Jack Glen in the IFC.

From the outside, the Private Sector Advisory Committee, which included Ignacio Garrido (Council of Europe Social Development Fund), Robert Grey (Hongkong Shanghai Bank), Sir Andrew Large (Barclays Bank), Jose Perez (Banco Bilbao Bizcaya Argentaria), Claude Rubinowicz (private consultant), Jeffrey Shafer (Salomon Smith Barney), and Ernest Stern (JP Morgan) offered valuable guidance. The project also benefited from a select group of OECD-area government debt managers (Paul Malvey from the U.S Treasury, Paul Mills from the UK Debt Office, J.T. M Hammers from the Dutch Debt Office, Ove Steen Jensen and Lars Jensen from the Danish Debt Office in the Danish Central Bank, Paul Tucker from the Bank of England, Isabel Ucha from the Portuguese Debt Office (IPDP), Maria Cannata from the Italian Treasury, Ambroise Fayolle from the French Treasury, Carlos San Basilio from the Spanish Treasury and Hans Blommestein from the OECD Secretariat. Loretta Wong and Arthur Yuen from the HongKong Monetary Authority also provided useful comments. In the preparation of the Handbook, important feedback sessions with private sector practitioners were organized in relation to selected chapters. Participants in these sessions included Michel Adler (Columbia University), David Cohen (Goldman Sachs), Frank Fernandez (Securities Industry Association), Robert Kowit (Federated), Douglas Metcalf (Nomura), Michael Pettis (Bear Sterns), Kenneth Telljohann (Lehman Brothers), and Francisco Ybarra (Citicorp). The Handbook team members also received important insights and material from their participation in various workshops and conferences (Second OECD/World Bank Workshop, Development of Fixed-Income Securities Markets in Emerging Market Economies: Enhancing Liquidity and Demand in Emerging Fixed-Income Markets, 24-26 January 2000, Washington DC; Tenth OECD Workshop on Government Securities Markets and Public Debt Management in Emerging Markets, 29-30 May 2000, Warsaw; ADB Conference on Government Bond Market and Financial Sector Development in Developing Asian Economies, 28-30 March, 2000, Manila; ASEM Government Bond Market Conference, August 2000, Singapore; and the Regional Seminar on Public Debt Management, October 18-20, 2000, Santiago, Chile).

Finally, the World Bank and International Monetary Fund teams are indebted to Charles Siegman for his substantial editing and polishing of this text .

Developing a Government Bond Market: An Overview

1.1 Introduction

The need to develop domestic securities markets has, following the recent international financial crises, increasingly attracted the attention of national and international policymakers.[1] This has resulted in the issuance of a number of policy recommendations by various organizations, such as the Asia-Pacific Economic Cooperation (APEC) collaborative Initiative on Development of Domestic Bond Markets. The issue of government debt management is intrinsically linked to government securities market development. Work is currently under way on this issue at the International Monetary Fund (IMF) and the World Bank, where guidelines have been developed to guide government actions as an issuer, thereby steering development of the government securities market.[2] This handbook on government securities market development seeks to fill an existing gap between specific technical studies about securities market microstructure and publications that offer general policy recommendations about securities market development. The handbook integrates these two perspectives by outlining important issues confronting senior strategic policymakers or those implementing policies to support development of a government securities market.

---

1. The Working Group on Capital Flows, one of three working groups established in 1999 by the Financial Stability Forum (FSF), highlighted the importance of both debt management and the related issue of securities market development as part of efforts to strengthen risk management and governance in the public sector (see Financial Stability Forum 2000).

2. See IMF and World Bank 2001.

1

Developing a government securities market is a complex undertaking that depends on the financial and market system development of each country. For many governments, this involves immense challenges, as the problems that inhibit securities market development run deep in the economy. For example, some governments rely on a few domestic banks for funding, which makes competition scarce and transaction costs high. In addition, a proliferation of government agencies issuing securities can fragment national government securities markets. Absence of a sound market infrastructure may make specific actions to develop a government securities market premature. A paucity of institutional investors, low domestic savings rates, and lack of interest from international investors can result in a small, highly homogeneous investor group, contrary to the heterogeneity needed for an efficient market. Furthermore, economic instability, often fed by high fiscal deficits, rapid growth of the money supply, and a deteriorating exchange rate, can weaken investor confidence and increase the risks associated with development of a market for government securities. This overview of the handbook on developing a government securities market examines some of the policy questions that arise for policymakers seeking to address these and other problems.

1.2　Benefits of Developing a Bond Market

Bond markets link issuers having long-term financing needs with investors willing to place funds in long-term, interest-bearing securities. A mature domestic bond market offers a wide range of opportunities for funding the government and the private sector, with the government bond market typically creating opportunities for other issuers. In this handbook, the market for government securities is defined as the market for tradable securities issued by the central government. The primary focus is on the market for bonds, which are tradable securities of longer maturity (usually one year or more). These bonds typically carry coupons (interest payments) for specified (for example, quarterly) periods of the maturity of the bond. The market for Treasury bills (securities with a maturity of less than a year) and other special securities is considered here in the context of developing a long-term bond market.

Table 1.1. Composition of Domestic Debt Markets in Selected Countries
(outstanding amount, September 2000)

	All issuers US$ billions	Public sector	Financial institutions (percentage share)	Corporates
United States	14,335.8	56	28	17
Japan	6,329.0	76	13	12
Germany	1,603.4	43	56	1
Italy	1,213.3	77	21	1
France	1,005.7	59	30	11
United Kingdom	851.5	49	32	19
Spain	306.1	82	10	8
Brazil	306.7	83	16	1
South Korea	304.4	28	33	40
China	261.3	66	31	2
Argentina	83.7	31	69	0
Mexico	68.5	81	6	13
Turkey	47.5	100	0	0
Hong Kong, China	41.5	40	49	11
Poland	30.5	100	0	0
Czech Republic	20.9	78	12	11
Singapore	22.3	39	0	9
Hungary	14.9	97	0	3
Russia	8.8	100	0	0

Source: BIS Quarterly Review (March 2001).

Government bonds are the backbone of most fixed-income securities markets in both developed and developing countries, as can be seen from Table 1.1. They provide a benchmark yield curve and help establish the overall credit curve. Government bonds typically are backed by the "faith

1

and credit" of the government, not by physical or financial assets. In the private sector, however, mortgage financing often relies fully or partially on bonds backed by mortgages. Similarly, bonds securitized by receivables of various types, including bonds issued to finance infrastructure projects, constitute an important component of the bond market.

Bond markets worldwide are built on the same basic elements: *a number of issuers* with long-term financing needs, *investors* with a need to place savings or other liquid funds in interest-bearing securities, *intermediaries* that bring together investors and issuers, and an *infrastructure* that provides a conducive environment for securities transactions, ensures legal title to securities and settlement of transactions, and provides price discovery information. The *regulatory regime* provides the basic framework for bond markets and, indeed, for capital markets in general. Efficient bond markets are characterized by a competitive market structure, low transaction costs, low levels of fragmentation, a robust and safe market infrastructure, and a high level of heterogeneity among market participants.

Development of a government bond market provides a number of important benefits if the prerequisites to a sound development are in place (see Section 1.3 below). At the macroeconomic policy level, a government securities market provides an avenue for domestic funding of budget deficits other than that provided by the central bank and, thereby, can reduce the need for direct and potentially damaging monetary financing of government deficits and avoid a build-up of foreign currency–denominated debt. A government securities market can also strengthen the transmission and implementation of monetary policy, including the achievement of monetary targets or inflation objectives, and can enable the use of market-based indirect monetary policy instruments. The existence of such a market not only can enable authorities to smooth consumption and investment expenditures in response to shocks, but if coupled with sound debt management, can also help governments reduce their exposure to interest rate, currency, and other financial risks. Finally, a shift toward market-oriented funding of government budget deficits will reduce debt-service costs over the medium to long term through development of a deep and liquid market for government securities.

At the microeconomic level, development of a domestic securities market can increase overall financial stability and improve financial intermediation through greater competition and development of related financial infrastructure, products, and services. Development of a securities market can help change the financial system from a primarily bank-oriented to a multilayered system, where capital markets can complement bank financing. As government and related private sector securities markets develop, they force commercial banks to develop new products and to intermediate credit more competitively. The development of securities and credit markets and a related benchmark yield curve enables the introduction of new financial products, including repurchase agreements (repos), money market instruments, structured finance, and derivatives, which can improve risk management and financial stability. Finally, development of a securities market entails creation of an extensive informational, legal, and institutional infrastructure that has benefits for the entire financial system.

1.3 Basic Prerequisites for Successful Development of Government Securities Markets

It is not always necessary for a country to develop a government securities market. Even some mature economies do not have one, either because the government has not run budget deficits requiring funding through securities issues or because the country is not large enough to support the necessary infrastructure. Depending on the availability of alternative financing channels for the public and the private sectors, the size of the economy, and the maturity of the financial sector, better options might include private placements of securities, development of retail markets, or even regional solutions.

Government securities market development must be viewed as a dynamic process in which continued macroeconomic and financial sector stability are essential to building an efficient market and establishing the credibility of the government as an issuer of debt securities. Prerequisites for establishing an efficient government domestic currency securities market include a credible and stable government; sound fiscal and monetary policies; effective legal, tax, and regulatory infrastructure; smooth and secure settlement arrangements; and a liberalized financial system with competing intermediaries. Where these basics are lacking or very weak, priority should be given to adopting and implementing a stable and credible macroeconomic policy framework, reforming and liberalizing the financial sector, and ensuring the proper pace of liberalization in different areas (for example, financial sector versus capital account measures).

1

Both domestic and foreign investors will be reluctant to purchase government securities, especially medium- and long-term instruments, when there are expectations of high inflation, large devaluations, or high risks of default. Working toward a macroeconomic policy framework with a credible commitment to prudent and sustainable fiscal policies, stable monetary conditions, and a credible exchange rate regime is therefore important (see Annex 1.A). Such steps will reduce government funding costs over the medium to long term, as the risk premia embedded in yields on government securities fall.

From the perspective of government securities market development, management of fiscal policies must aim at increasing the incentives of both domestic and foreign investors to invest in government securities. If a country is seen as not having the ability to manage its public expenditures or collect tax revenues, or if it has built up substantial explicit or implicit domestic or foreign debt obligations, investors will perceive a high default risk and the cost of financing government securities will rise.

Inflationary expectations will feed directly into longer-term nominal government securities yields and affect not only government funding costs, but also, in countries with volatile monetary conditions, the government's ability to extend the yield curve beyond very short maturities. Thus a credible commitment to contain inflation is critical for government securities market development. A coordinated approach to a monetary/fiscal program via appropriate information sharing will be important in this respect. The availability of the necessary information to analyze such a program and to use the information effectively in the formulation of sound monetary and debt management policies will also be essential. As most governments have their primary account with the central bank, day-to-day operational coordination between the monetary authorities and the Treasury will be important in establishing an orderly market where liquidity balances can be forecast with a minimum of uncertainty.

Exchange rate and capital account policies have important implications for the development of government securities markets, especially for their ability to attract foreign investors in many countries. Foreign investors have played a major role in the development of government securities markets and in catalyzing development of the necessary infrastructure by infusing new competition into otherwise stagnant markets. Foreign investors will consider the yield on domestic government securities in light of international interest rates, a time-varying exchange rate risk premium reflecting the expected rate of exchange rate depreciation or appreciation, and a default risk premium. Exchange rate and capital account policies can affect each of these risks in combination with fiscal and monetary policies, and inappropriate policies can result in increased interest rate and exchange rate volatility. Such volatility hinders development of government securities issues with long maturities and can hurt secondary market liquidity when there are no complementary markets that investors can use to protect against the risk of price movements. The risk of contagion from external crises places a large premium on pursuing macroeconomic policies that maintain a prudent and sustainable level, structure, and rate of growth of government debt and international reserves. Sound fiscal policy, in combination with proper overall debt and reserve-asset management, can help to substantially lessen the extent to which a country will be subject to contagion when economic shocks occur.[3]

The soundness of the banking system also has important implications for development of the government securities market. Domestic and foreign investor concerns about the soundness of the banking system will adversely affect the ability of the government to roll over or issue new debt. At another level, lack of financially healthy intermediaries will cause secondary market liquidity and efficiency to fall. A banking system in crisis will further complicate development of a government securities market because important related markets, such as those for interbank and repurchase agreement transactions, are unlikely to function properly. Significant liquidity shortages, therefore, are likely to arise (see Annex 1.B).

The structure of the financial system and its links to macroeconomic policies must be given careful consideration early rather than late in the reform process.[4] Financial sector liberalization must be preceded by important actions to strengthen information infrastructure, supervision, and regulation, and in many cases modify the definition of the safety net. The process to adopt in undertaking domestic financial sector liberalization is not independent of leverage present in the financial system and the corporate sector as well as the overall macro policy stance. In addition, phasing

---

3. Ironically, a more liquid and developed government securities market can increase the possibility of contagion when foreign investors treat emerging markets as one asset class. Even with sound fundamentals, a country with liquid markets may see foreign investors sell its securities as general uneasiness spreads about emerging market risk.

4. See Dooley 1998a and 1998b.

in capital account deregulation after domestic financial sector liberalization is increasingly seen as the preferred course of action.

The many challenges involved in providing the appropriate macroeconomic and financial framework needed to develop a government securities market should not deter authorities from embarking on such an endeavor, as the potential benefits to the government and the economy are considerable. In its role as regulator of the market and, in many cases, the primary issuer, the government is a central player in the government securities market. The central bank, in implementing monetary policy, will also influence market structure. Such official actions will inevitably influence the way the market develops. Given the involvement of several government entities in the process of market development, it may be critical to designate a coordinating body to guide the way forward. A high level committee on which all relevant government sectors are represented, and which interacts with the private sector, may be a useful tool to spearhead market development efforts. The following sections provide an overview of the principal strategic policy questions and associated initiatives that may help government securities markets to develop. The sections are based on the content of the different chapters of the handbook and follow its chapter sequence.

1.4   Money Markets and Monetary Policy Operations

An active money market is a prerequisite for government securities market development. A money market supports the bond market by increasing the liquidity of securities. It also makes it easier for financial institutions to cover short-term liquidity needs and makes it less risky and cheaper to warehouse government securities for on-sale to investors and to fund trading portfolios of securities. Where short-term interest rates have been liberalized, development of money and government securities markets can go hand in hand. When a money market has materialized and the government securities market is ready to take hold, coordination with monetary policy operations becomes essential for sound market development. Monetary policy operations are the responsibility of the monetary authorities and have increasingly been left solely to the purview of the central bank. There are, however, some overlapping areas requiring coordination between the government securities market and the money market. There are a number of questions with which policymakers should be concerned. Are add-ons to Treasury bill auctions the appropriate instrument for monetary policy implementation? How can coordination between monetary authorities and debt managers be enhanced? How can predictions of the liquidity effects of the government's expenditure and revenue flows be improved (see Chapter 2)?

Most countries are moving from the use of direct monetary policy tools, such as interest rate controls and credit ceilings, to the use of indirect monetary policy instruments, such as open market operations. Indirect monetary policy instruments have the advantage of improving the efficiency of monetary policy by having financial resources allocated on a market basis. In addition, growing financial market integration has made direct monetary controls increasingly ineffective as agents have found it easier to circumvent them. Government securities are particularly important instruments to implement indirect monetary policy operations. In most countries, these securities are the most liquid securities in the market.

The central bank's accommodation policy, which temporarily supplies reserve money to the market when changes in money market conditions are particularly tight for particular banks, influences the development of the money market. If accommodation policy makes it easy and cheap for banks to obtain funds from the central bank, banks will transact less with each other. A money market will not readily develop under such conditions.

The ability of the central bank to maintain the level of excess reserves very close to that desired by the banking system as a whole will induce individual banks to use the interbank market to fulfill their specific liquidity needs. In addition, by reducing the likelihood of a large surplus or shortage of reserves through close liquidity management, the central bank will reduce volatility of interest rates. As high volatility tends to result in one-way markets, a reduction in volatility will also support further development of the interbank money market.

Where government securities are already in circulation and financial markets are thin, using the same instrument for both the Treasury's funding operations and the central bank's monetary policy operations can avoid market fragmentation. In countries where a range of market intervention instruments has not yet been developed, add-ons to the Treasury bill auction are the main instrument for liquidity management. For purposes of monetary policy implementation, the central bank adds Treasury bills in addition to those sold to meet the government's funding needs. Add-ons

1

may confuse the market, since participants may not be aware of what portion of the tender will be used for implementing monetary policy and what portion to financing the government. Transparency needs to be ensured by announcing the amount of central bank add-ons. Explicit and well-defined arrangements should be made to ensure that the proceeds from the sale of add-ons should not be available for financing of government expenditure and for the cost sharing in relation to the interest costs of the add-ons. Without such arrangements, central bank/Treasury coordination of add-ons can become a source of misunderstanding and discord.

An alternative to add-ons more under the central bank's control is for the central bank to issue bills or accept deposits, which are employed, like add-ons, as a market intervention instrument. These obligations can substitute for Treasury bills where there is not yet a working Treasury bill auction. Central bank securities can be traded in the market, helping to facilitate development of a secondary market. Where there is a Treasury bill market, however, central bank bills may fragment demand, especially if Treasury bills and central bank bills carry similar maturities.

Coordination is required to avoid conflicts between the government's debt/cash management and the central bank's open market operations. In particular, the timing and amounts of government securities issuance will not always coincide with the needs of the central bank's monetary policies. The government may wish to issue securities at a time when the market is illiquid. The central bank must then choose whether or to what extent it will provide additional liquidity to the market to correct this condition. At a minimum, coordination requires that the issuer inform the central bank of its intentions to raise funds in the market. In addition, the government may be able to adjust the timing and amount of borrowing to better conform to conditions in the money market.

Government debt and cash management can coordinate with monetary policy by moderating the effect of government expenditures and receipts on the banks' cash balances and by keeping the central bank informed in a timely manner of government cash flows. In order to achieve an accurate forecast of the government's funding requirements, it is necessary to develop day-by-day forecasts for revenues and expenditures for items being received or paid by the government. The only transactions that need to be forecast as a part of improved coordination with monetary policy are those that cause a shift of funds between an account at the central bank and an account at a commercial bank, since those are the only transactions that affect the government's net position at the central bank. However, full cash forecasting can be important for the government's own purposes, for good cash management can result in cost savings for the government through lower transaction balances and fewer payment errors. Improving the government's cash balances forecast requires good communication among government departments and between the Treasury and the central bank.

1.5   Government Securities Issuance Strategy and Market Access

The government securities issuance process influences the government securities market development. Credibility in offering securities takes time to acquire, and must be built, or the market will not develop. In this context, a number of questions arise for policymakers. What are the appropriate objectives for government debt management? What is the most efficient way for the government to access the credit market? What are the benefits and drawbacks of using primary dealers to issue government securities? What are the optimal characteristics of government securities issues? Should the government establish benchmark securities? Should the government use more advanced debt management tools such as reopening issues, debt buybacks, debt/equity swaps, and exchange offers (see Chapters 3, 4, and 5)?

1.5.1   Government Securities Issuance Strategy and Debt Management[5]

A market-oriented government funding strategy is one of the essential pillars supporting development of a domestic securities market. Such a strategy includes the government's adherence to basic market principles of broad market access and transparency, a commitment to finance itself through the market, and a proactive approach in developing the necessary regulatory framework to support market development.

---

5. See IMF and World Bank 2001.

1

Governments need to improve market access and transparency by providing high-quality information about debt structure, funding needs, and debt management strategies to market participants and the public at large. They must solicit investors' and market makers' views on the current strategy and plans for change. In this way, the government will better understand the sources of demand for its instruments and have the ability to act to remove barriers obstructing investment in them. The government can demonstrate its commitment to borrow through the market by early acceptance that debt instruments must be priced at market rates, even though this may increase debt servicing costs in the short run. Finally, a proactive approach to market development requires governments to develop a comprehensive strategy in consultation with the central bank, relevant regulatory agencies, and market participants.

A sound and prudent debt management operation is also central to the government's credibility as an issuer. The principal components of sound debt management in many countries are based on the importance of having clear debt management objectives, proper coordination between debt management and monetary and fiscal policy, a prudent risk management framework, an effective institutional framework, and a strong operational capacity enabling efficient funding and sound risk management practices. A consensus is evolving in which the main objective for public debt management is "to ensure that the government's financing needs and its payment obligations are met at the lowest possible cost over the medium to long run, consistent with a prudent degree of risk."[6] Development of the domestic debt market is also often included as a prominent government objective. This objective is particularly relevant for countries where short-term debt, floating-rate debt, and foreign currency debt are, in the short run at least, the only viable alternatives to extensive borrowing from the central bank.

A strong organization capable of attracting and retaining a professional staff to the debt management area is also vital for a sound debt management operation. Access to appropriate analytical and information tools will be essential to the day-to-day efficiency of debt management operations and the development of debt management strategies. To further increase credibility of debt management, a sound governance arrangement

---

6. See IMF and World Bank 2001.

and operating relationships in the Ministry of Finance and between fiscal and monetary authorities need to be established. As outlined in the *Guidelines for Public Debt Management*,[7] a clear legal framework, well-specified organizational arrangements, and public disclosure and auditing procedures are key elements of an effective governance structure for public debt management.

As part of developing and maintaining a well-functioning government securities market, authorities will have to provide clear and timely information about the structure of the public debt and Treasury operations, including amortization schedule, issuing calendar, description of outstanding securities, schedule for buybacks or reopenings where relevant, and Treasury cash balances. There should also be disclosure of essential budget information and simple presentations of balance sheets by the central bank and fiscal authorities.

1.5.2 Government Securities Instruments and Yield Curve

The development of government benchmark securities is an essential element of a well-functioning government securities market. By concentrating new issues of government securities in a relatively limited number of popular, standard maturities, governments can assist the development of liquidity in those securities and thereby lower their issuance costs. Markets, in turn, can use such liquid issues as convenient benchmarks for the pricing of a range of other financial instruments. In addition, spreading the relatively few benchmark issues across a fairly wide range of maturities—building a "benchmark yield curve"—can facilitate more accurate market pricing of financial instruments across a similar maturity spectrum.

Governments need to take a variety of actions to ensure that the government securities market cannot be easily manipulated and that it has sufficient liquidity. Steps will be needed to reduce government securities market fragmentation by consolidating, under national issuance, what would otherwise be issues by many public entities and by issuing uncomplicated securities such as Treasury bills and bonds. Policymakers will have to weigh the advantages of longer-term benchmark issues against the possibility of higher cost associated with longer-term benchmark bonds,

---

7. See IMF and World Bank 2001.

the concentration of refinancing risk that comes with focusing on maturities, and the needs of government debt financing and benchmark development. Governments, in the nascent stages of a government securities market, may have to rely on floating or adjustable rate instruments to increase the average maturity of the government debt to deal with refinancing risk.

The various types of securities used by governments in the domestic market have typically different characteristics in terms of maturity, coupon (interest rate), method of interest setting, and use of embedded options. The dominant ones have historically been nominal fixed-interest instruments, with coupon rates close to market rates at the time of issue. This type of bond offers standardization and simplicity. Typical benchmark maturities in the domestic markets are 10, 5, and 2–3 years. A number of countries have also issued fixed-interest, 30-year bonds. Treasury bills dominate the short end of the government securities market, with maturities normally less than one year. These bills are typically issued as zero-coupon instruments.

Floating rate notes and bonds with variable interest rates have, in some countries, historically played an important role in extending the maturity of government debt. In most of the Organization for Economic Cooperation and Development (OECD) countries, however, floating rate bonds are no longer used as primary issues. More prominent in recent years have been longer-term bonds linked to an inflation index.

For most countries, the simplest choice of funding instruments will be the appropriate one. Standard marketable Treasury bonds will often be the main funding instrument. Special purpose bonds, including nonmarketable instruments, should generally be issued with caution, since they will fragment the market and, if certain receipts are earmarked to pay the bond, complicate budget management. Furthermore, governments should strive to have as few public issuers as possible. Many entities issuing securities in the name of the government will fragment the market and make a consolidated strategy for market development difficult to implement.

1.5.3 Primary Market Structure and Primary Dealers

Selling and distributing government securities to investors efficiently involves the choice of sales procedure (auctions, retail schemes, tap sales, and/or syndication) and the possible use of primary dealers. In return for meeting the obligations for being designated a primary dealer, governments grant primary dealers some privileges, often including exclusive access to the auctions.

Auctions are the common method for the sale of government securities in most domestic markets, following the pattern of Treasury bill auctions and requiring a number of independent bidders. Some countries have also used tap sales, either in combination with auctions or as the sole sales method, but the latter is rare. Syndication is increasingly being used in Euro-zone countries to launch new products or benchmark issues or reach new investors in the region. Syndicates can be a useful alternative to auctions in the nascent stages of market development, where too few participants can easily destroy the competitive outcome of an auction procedure. Where there is not an active, liquid secondary market, making the government uncertain about the price it will achieve for a new bond issue, syndication (or other underwriting arrangement) can be used to minimize placement risk and ensure allocation. The use of the Internet also opens new possibilities for the government to build a broader investor base. The most important policy objective in choosing a securities issuance technique is usually to maximize potential competition in the primary market. This might require the use of different sales techniques over time to achieve the optimal result.

Another element of government securities market design relates to the use of primary dealers. Primary dealers are financial intermediaries selected by the government, typically to promote investment in government bonds and activity in the government securities market. Having a group of primary dealers to buy and distribute government securities entails advantages and risks. Setting up a primary dealer system can facilitate the change to a market-based funding environment. It may also improve the government's ability to tap potential investors and develop market liquidity. In addition, in countries where the technological infrastructure is not strong and where the potential investor base can only be accessed via intermediaries, the use of primary dealers may initially be needed. Some governments, through regularly scheduled meetings and ongoing discussions with actual and potential primary dealers, have also used the primary dealer system to generate interest in government securities markets. If a primary dealer system is chosen, objective criteria for entry and exit of participants, limits on amounts of securities any individual dealer is allowed to hold, and the capital requirements to qualify to be a primary dealer must be set and observed. Standards governing dealers' trading practices and disclosure to clients and issuers will also be important.

1

The use of primary dealers, especially in countries with a small financial sector, may pose the risk of collusion. Despite limitations on the amount of securities any one dealer can hold and safeguards built into the auction design, small markets can be squeezed or cornered, seriously limiting the attractiveness to the government of a primary dealer system.[8] Even in the absence of collusion, the installation of primary dealers in a small market may unnecessarily limit competition. Primary dealer systems may also be difficult to implement in markets which do not provide liquidity generating tools such as repos.

Some governments have successfully issued securities and developed secondary markets through a wider group of dealers. A primary dealer system should not impede development of efforts over time to distribute government securities directly to wholesale or retail investors, onshore or offshore.

Before policymakers embark on development of a full-fledged primary dealer system, they should carry out an extensive review of the most effective way to sell and distribute government securities. The review should consider (i) the structure of the wholesale and retail investor base, offshore and onshore; (ii) the level of development of the financial system and the role of banks and the soundness of intermediaries; (iii) how technology might be used to create other avenues for distributing government securities more directly to end investors; and (iv) the accounting framework for fixed-income portfolios. The objective should be to balance the benefits of having a dedicated group of intermediaries to assist in market development with the decrease in (potential) competition that follows from limiting the number of primary dealers. It must also consider the extent to which dealers will have the instruments and techniques to manage the risks that they take in carrying an inventory of fixed-income securities.

---

8. Irrespective of whether a primary dealer system is used and as a way to break collusive practices, the government at times may have to threaten buyers with the prospect of being forced to take issues or of changes in the method of marketing. It might also reject bids or cancel auctions in the extreme case where collusion is evident. Even the most liquid markets have experienced squeezes, with the so-called "Salomon incident" in the United States in 1991 providing a good example. Having learned from this experience, the U.S. Treasury now offers approaches to auction design and other procedures aimed at preventing collusive practices (see U.S. Department of the Treasury 1992).

1.6 Investor Base for Government Securities

Reliance by governments on captive sources of funding whereby financial institutions are required to purchase and hold government securities, often at below-market interest rates, is diminishing in many countries. Instead, countries are developing a diversified investor base for their government securities. Investors in developed government securities markets can range from wholesale domestic and foreign institutional investors to small-scale retail investors. In addition to commercial banks, an important investor segment in many countries is the contractual savings industry (insurance companies and pension funds). Funding of government-backed pension or social security systems through specialized funds has also provided a large, stable demand for fixed-income securities in countries where such funds are active. A diversified investor base for fixed-income securities is important for ensuring high liquidity and stable demand in the market. A heterogeneous investor base with different time horizons, risk preferences, and trading motives ensures active trading, creating high liquidity. On the other hand, even liquid markets can become illiquid in periods where one group of investors leaves or enters the market over a short period and where there are no counterbalancing order flows from other investor groups.

For policymakers, there are a number of important questions to address with regard to the development of the investor base. Should the dominance of banks as investors in government securities be diminished? How can a contractual savings industry be developed? How can mutual funds and other collective savings schemes play a role in government securities market development? How can demand from retail investors for government securities be satisfied most efficiently? Should foreign investors be allowed into the market, and under what conditions (see Chapter 6)?

1.6.1 Banks as Investors of Government Securities

Commercial banks are (in many emerging markets) the dominant investors in government securities. In developed countries, banks still provide a valuable source of demand for government securities.[9] Excessive reliance on the

---

9. Banks use government bonds for stable interest income to balance more volatile investments, such as collateral in repo transactions, for hedging mismatches in other interest rate positions, for short-term liquidity management, for taking views on the future movement of interest rates, and for meeting regulatory reserve requirements.

1

banking system to mobilize savings that fund the purchase of government securities has, however, proved to be costly for many governments and investors. Even in systems where their main assets are government securities, banks have maintained a high margin between deposit rates and the risk-free return on government securities that they hold as assets.[10] An important aspect of developing a broader-based government securities market is, therefore, seeking ways to break this behavior and encourage banks and other financial institutions to promote the sale of government securities to other end investors. A combination of efforts may be used to achieve this goal, including (i) use of an obligation in primary dealer systems to place securities with end investors; (ii) direct access to major savings pools, such as retail and/or foreign investors; (iii) structural reform of pension and retirement funds to encourage their investment in government bonds; and (iv) reform or creation of mutual funds.

1.6.2 Contractual Savings and Government Securities Markets

The contractual savings sector has been especially important for fixed-income securities markets, as it provides a stable source of long-term demand. The sector's demand for fixed-interest, low-credit-risk products also provides an important basis on which to develop standardized, securitized products such as mortgage bonds. Widespread regulatory provisions requiring pension funds and insurance companies to invest a large portion of their assets in so-called gilt-edged assets has helped make this sector prominent in the government securities market.

A variety of countries have embarked on pension, insurance, and health reforms, which are associated with contractual savings reforms. These reforms are technically and politically complex and require the authorities' commitment to a broad and politically difficult set of actions.[11] As these reforms take effect, the contractual savings industry is likely to become

---

10. Part of the spread is maintained to compensate banks for the maturity transformation function they perform by accepting liquid deposits and investing in longer-term assets. With a liquid secondary market for government securities, however, the risks involved are reduced substantially.

11. See Vittas 1998 and 2000.

a more significant factor in capital markets, including the government bond market. In addition to the industry's demand for long-term debt securities, institutional investors will, upon reaching a certain critical mass, increase corporate governance, intensify competition, and spur financial innovation. In contractual savings reform efforts, it is important to keep in mind that their contribution to the development of government securities markets is a useful by-product, but not the primary objective, of contractual savers.

Perhaps more important than the sequencing of securities market development and contractual savings reform is the dynamic interaction between these two areas. The interactive process between government securities markets and the contractual savings industry involves investors acting as a countervailing force to the dominant position of commercial banks in the government securities market. This creates competition and pressure for innovation in securities markets, forcing more transparency and better standards for disclosure of information.[12]

Insurance reforms associated with pension reform have led to the need for annuity markets. In Chile, where such markets are more advanced than in many other emerging countries, insurance companies offering variable rate or index-linked annuities became natural demanders of indexed-linked government bonds. This is yet another channel through which contractual savings reforms help to develop the government securities markets.

In some countries the directional interaction between contractual savings development and capital market development has originated from the capital market end. Some East European countries (the Czech Republic, Hungary, and Poland) that are seeking accession to the European Union (EU) are experiencing capital market development, which, in turn, has facilitated pension reform.

1.6.3 Collective Investment Funds and Government Securities Markets

Collective investment funds, such as mutual funds, can play an important role in the development of the government securities market, especially the

---

12. See Vittas 1998 and 2000.

1

shorter-term segments of the market. They can also serve as an alternative placement for funds other than bank deposits, inducing more competition in this part of the financial sector, and can be a cost-effective way for the government to reach retail investors. Collective investment funds (CIF) that are established domestically or offshore should be allowed into the government securities market. Such entities must be subject to mark-to-market accounting and trading practice regulations. The latter would include disallowing the mingling of funds managed by the CIF and funds managed by related intermediaries, such as banks, or "front running" by the related brokerage entity within the same financial group that sells the CIF. Adequate disclosure to investors and minimum standards for prospectuses are also essential but often lacking.

Allowing entry of foreign institutions into this field has, in many cases, had the benefit of putting pressure on domestic companies to develop their business and lower their costs. The market impact of foreign institutions has been much larger than their share of assets under management would suggest. Restrictions on foreign entry into this financial service area, as well as entry via cross-border provision of these services, should therefore be eliminated or phased out.

1.6.4 Retail Investors and Government Securities Markets

Catering to the needs of retail investors is often an essential part of the overall strategy to develop a more diversified investor base for government securities. Retail investors will contribute to a stable demand for government securities, which, in times of volatility, can cushion the impact of sales from institutional and foreign investors. Retail demand has been developed in many countries through special non-tradable instruments, although this strategy will not contribute to development of the government securities market. For such market development, a better course is to concentrate on developing efficient mechanisms for delivering standard securities to retail clients. In many emerging markets, the administrative and information technology costs of going straight to retail investors have been prohibitive. However, as Internet penetration and wireless communication systems have become more commonplace, this situation is rapidly changing, and possibilities for cost-efficient sale and distribution of government securities are increasing. Utilizing such new technology to access a broader set of potential investors could also have implications for the design and functioning of the primary market, and will put bank dominance in the retail end of the market under pressure.

1.6.5 Foreign Investors and Government Securities Markets

The role, behavior, and importance of foreign investors in national capital markets, including government securities markets, have received much attention in both mature markets and developing countries. Foreign investors are an important source of demand for fixed-income securities. Through the positive pressure they place on the quality and services of intermediaries and their emphasis on sound, safe, and robust market infrastructure, they have contributed to the development of national capital markets in many countries. However, because foreign investors tend to be relatively more sensitive to risk and to manage their portfolios actively, they may make national markets more volatile and vulnerable. A stable macroeconomic environment and prudent capital account liberalization, therefore, are essential to maintain a stable and growing participation of foreign investors in government securities markets.

Foreign investors include funds dedicated to investment in emerging markets, such as some hedge funds and other specialized closed and open-end country or emerging-market funds. They also include crossover investors, such as pension funds and insurance companies not as dedicated to investing in a particular region or even country, as with some types of funds, and other more specialized investors engaged in private capital operations, arbitrage trading across fixed-income securities, and distressed asset investments through specialized distressed asset funds.

Depending on their own liability structure, foreign investment vehicles can place very different emphasis on the liquidity of their prospective investment. For example, hedge funds, which are macro-directional and lacking a long lock-in period on liabilities, will place a very large premium on liquidity. This greatly limits their prospects for investing in many emerging markets and the size of their positions. Crossover investors and more specialized funds will not provide as much liquidity to local markets, but will often be willing to stay in the investment for a longer period, and some policymakers, therefore, see them as especially beneficial.

1

1.7 Secondary Markets for Government Securities

Promoting a vibrant secondary market for government securities has proved to be one of the more difficult aspects of government securities market development. Successful development of the secondary market requires the active participation of many different groups, including investors, providers of trading and settlement infrastructure, and intermediaries. The involvement of these groups can easily be dampened by arbitrary changes in taxation, other government actions affecting the value of government securities, high inflation, economic downturns, and political instability. Without the confidence of these groups in government actions and commitment to market development, countries will, even after extensive reforms in many other areas, most likely end up with low levels of secondary market trading.

Policymakers face some important questions related to secondary market development. Which transactions and market practices should be allowed (short selling, repurchase agreements, futures)? What types of intermediaries should be allowed or encouraged to participate in the market? Should the authorities promote certain systems for trading? What is the appropriate level and form of transparency in the market (see Chapter 7)? In addition, the issues raised in other chapters of the handbook related to the government's issuance strategy, the development of benchmark securities, the settlement structure, and taxation of securities traded on secondary markets will have a bearing on the efficiency and vibrancy of the secondary market.

1.7.1 Transactions and Trading Procedures in Secondary Government Securities Markets

The fundamental form of transaction in the secondary market is a spot trade in which cash is exchanged for the immediate purchase or sale of a security. Authorities should first concentrate on building a safe system for the execution and settlement of spot trades. In fostering secondary markets, the authorities would also wish to develop the use of repurchase agreements (repos), as they serve unique functions for both the private sector and the monetary authority. The concept of bridging the short- and long-term portions of the yield curve is all important. Short selling, swap transactions, futures, and options on interest rates are trading practices that will develop over time.[13] In the nascent stages of market development, however, emphasis should be placed on building the infrastructure to support basic types of transactions, and the development of more advanced instruments should be left to a later stage.

The authorities will need to consider and enforce regulations concerning the trading practices of market participants. Trading practice regulations cover such matters as best execution, self-dealing, insider trading, market manipulation, conflicts of interest, and front running. Without such regulations, market integrity will suffer and investor interest may wane.

1.7.2 Market Intermediaries in Secondary Government Securities Markets

The main function of intermediaries in the government securities market is to place securities with investors and provide liquidity to secondary markets. One of the more important intermediaries in the secondary market is, in many cases, the primary dealer, which often acts as a market maker in government securities. A market-making obligation helps ensure a market for investors who wish to sell a security before its maturity.

Policymakers should recognize both the importance of market-making intermediaries for secondary market liquidity and the need for this activity to be profitable for the intermediaries. Market making entails interest and liquidity risk as the dealer may not always be able to sell at a reasonable price the securities it has purchased from a customer. A dealer must have

---

13. The trading practice of selling securities "short" through the sale of borrowed securities has been prohibited in some emerging markets. Short sales, it is argued, increase market volatility and risks. The ability to sell short, however, can also have a positive effect, by increasing market liquidity and price efficiency through the incentives of market participants with opposing views on the market to trade actively. Approval of short selling will largely depend on the assessment by the authorities of the intermediaries' capacity to handle the extra risk involved. In any case, market participants should be properly measuring and managing the risks associated with their transactions. Short selling (and borrowing and lending securities) can greatly improve the capabilities of market makers to carry out their functions, and in many circumstances should be permitted.

sufficient capital to warehouse open positions and withstand losses. The market maker is rewarded by the private information about investor behavior it derives from trading as well as by the commissions/fees and bid/offer spread it applies to transactions with clients. In the case of primary dealers, there may also be a benefit from privileges or direct remuneration from the authorities. The use of primary dealers is, however, not a necessary condition for market making to develop.

To be effective in undertaking a market-making role, intermediaries must have a means of hedging against interest rate risks, which affect the cost of carrying an inventory of government securities. Without these tools, intermediaries tend to buy and hold securities, diminishing their action as market makers. The existence of forward, futures, swap, and option markets to protect intermediaries against interest rate risk can help improve the functioning of government securities markets.

Fit-and-proper tests and proper certification for those permitted to act as investment advisors or to enter the brokerage business are important for well-functioning secondary markets. These requirements must be objective and should not introduce arbitrary entry barriers. Intermediaries and authorities must jointly reach agreement about such standards, which are being made internationally uniform through work of the International Organization of Securities Commissions (IOSCO) and the Financial Stability Forum (FSF). Uniformity also facilitates action by national authorities to permit foreign entities to offer brokerage and other services and to participate in national government securities markets.

Another form of regulation that can have an important impact on secondary market development is margin requirements that can be applied at four levels—to brokers and clients, broker/dealers, banks, and clearing corporation members, and to self-regulatory organizations (SROs). Margin requirements can apply to securities transactions within and across countries, through cross-margining, and to ex-post collateral-sharing agreements. Margin requirements guard against excessive leverage, require routinely marking overall positions to market, and can change in level in light of market developments. The design of such systems, their relation to securities borrowing and lending, and the consolidation process for determining exposures are essential for market integrity and management of risks. Authorities can set minimum standards for these margin arrangements and for acceptable forms of collateral.

1.7.3 Trading Systems and Conventions in Secondary Markets for Government Securities

Trading and information systems that facilitate an efficient completion of transactions are essential for an effective secondary market infrastructure. Such systems provide information about market prices and an effective venue for traders to meet. Electronic trading has traditionally been developed for equity trading, but it has begun to spread to the government securities market, which has typically been handled through trading by telephone. The scope and possibilities for automated trading of government securities is untested even in mature markets. The continuing development of new technologies in this area might provide possibilities for developing countries to skip some steps in the development of the market and, thus, merits close attention.

Fixed-income securities markets have traditionally been decentralized, with trading in over-the-counter (OTC) markets where the physical trading infrastructure has played a minor role. Trades have been conducted by dealers or large investors who directly contact a number of potential counterparties or by interdealer brokers (IDBs) in the professional dealer market, with trades completed by telephone and confirmed by fax. The relatively informal infrastructure has served the needs of wholesale market participants as well as dealers, brokers, and, to a lesser extent, their institutional clients.

Policymakers are often in a position to influence where trading takes place. The way governments influence trading behavior can be direct—for example, in the form of regulations requiring transactions to take place in a specific place for specific market participants, or indirect, through the provision of trading services or involvement in their development. The degree of government involvement has usually evolved over time, starting out as more interventionist. As the system creates enough liquidity to stand on its own, formal requirements have often been lifted.[14]

---

14. Regulatory requirements to use the exchange for trading have traditionally aimed at concentrating the market in one place to increase overall liquidity and at providing consumer protection and best execution of trades. To accomplish the latter, there may be small order exposure requirements for the exchange, and rules for not allowing dealers to sell directly to clients from their own inventory.

1

In designing the overall regulatory and disclosure framework applicable to secondary market trading systems (extent of entry or exit or whether to allow internalization or force disclosure of order flow, for instance), policymakers will need to consider the rapid advances in technology as well as the size of the country and the extent of its integration in regional and global capital markets. Arrangements to allow access by offshore as well as onshore investors should also ultimately permit participation of foreign investors worldwide, subject to consistency with overall capital account liberalization.[15]

Frequency of trading is also an important consideration in the development of secondary markets for government securities. Newly developed markets are usually thin and illiquid, making execution risk high. For these markets, market efficiency might be improved by short trading sessions (periodic markets). Periodic trading would have the added benefit of equal treatment of orders.[16] As the economy develops, the factors changing the equilibrium price of government securities increase, accompanied by price volatility of securities. For such markets, increased trading frequency would be warranted, and at an appropriate time the market could move to continuous trading.

Automated trading systems are increasingly the preferred venue for most countries, with their costs three to four times lower than those of traditional exchanges using a floor and open-outcry method. These developments increasingly give official issuers the capacity to sell and distribute securities directly to final wholesale and retail investors. Given the rapid pace of technology in this area,[17] freedom of entry to proprietary providers of trading systems that are organized as corporations must be ensured. Electronically based trading systems are characterized by network externalities, since additional users increase liquidity for all users. Under these conditions, questions relating to entry policy, competition, and the so-called first-mover advantage will become important.

---

15. Access by offshore investors to national secondary markets for government securities should include the ability of the issuing country to solicit non-national members to the automated trading system if certain standards are met. The European Union Investment Services Directive permits solicitation within the EU countries without the need for approval by individual country authorities.

16. See Dattels 1997.

17. See Domowitz and Steil 1999.

The design of the regulatory framework also needs to provide adequate transparency in the market. Most fixed-income securities markets have traditionally been opaque, with scant and delayed information on transactions available to the public. Major intermediaries will voluntarily provide pre-trade, or ex ante, indicative prices to the market through information vendors such as Reuters, Telerate, or Bloomberg. In some cases, primary dealers will be required to release prices to the market. Access to consolidated pre-trade information about market prices is, in most cases, very limited. In the United States, however, all completed transactions in the government securities market are reported to an electronic system, GovPX, which makes the information available to subscribers. This centralized reporting and dissemination system has resulted in an extremely transparent government securities market in the United States. In contrast, the general transparency of most government securities markets in the world is low, reflecting the traditional wholesale nature of the market and the perception among some market participants and regulators that there is a trade-off between liquidity and the level of market transparency.[18]

Regulation also needs to guarantee that trading systems have the capability of guaranteeing best execution through either a quote or order-driven market. There must be a clear set of standards developed for OTC and exchange trading of government securities, as well as for alternative trading systems (ATSs). If the overall distribution systems for securities involve dealers and OTC trading of government securities, there may also be a need for systems to support IDB trading, which could even apply over time across countries in a specific region. IDBs are brokers specializing in the wholesale segment of the market who facilitate trade between dealers by providing information and matching orders. They provide a centralized place where other brokers can execute trades, anonymously in most cases. An IDB can be a crucial element in an efficient market-maker system, since it provides

---

18. There is no consensus about the interaction between transparency and liquidity. A trade-off between liquidity and transparency may arise because knowledge of trade prices and quantities may expose market makers to undue risk as they unwind positions. It follows that transparency should be restricted if necessary to ensure adequate liquidity. Some have argued, however, that restricting transparency provides benefits to large traders at the expense of small traders. Still others have questioned whether restricting transparency may also reduce the speed with which market makers adjust prices, thereby reducing market efficiency. A further complication is introduced by the role of quote transparency (see Bloomfield and O'Hara 1999).

a means for market makers to quickly transfer unwanted risk to other market participants.

The ability to use audit trails and other forms of off-market surveillance to detect trading practice violations, such as front running and market manipulation, is also an essential aspect of a trading system. The safeguards, which need to be compatible across trading systems, will be increasingly essential in emerging markets as a defense against systemic risk. Such safeguards could include information sharing on high-risk participants or exchange members and arrangements for consolidation of all cash and derivative positions for the same market participant across financial and nonfinancial contracts.

In addition to outlining the overall trading and regulatory framework of the secondary market, the authorities can directly provide liquidity to the dealer community, give fiscal incentives to banks or broker/dealers, and reduce transaction costs by subsidizing investments needed to set up trading systems. The experience of many countries suggests, however, that indirect intervention by government has been more effective in developing markets. Indirect measures include reducing transaction costs by improving information or, in some instances, defraying the costs of setting up a trading system.

1.7.4 Related Markets and Secondary Markets

Related markets that often operate onshore and offshore can have an important effect on the liquidity of the secondary market for government securities.

The existence of a repurchase agreement (repo) market is essential for permitting the development of an active government securities market. Borrowing and lending among a range of market participants, including banks, financial institutions, and corporates, can be fostered on a safe and secure basis through the use of repurchase agreements that reduce both credit risk and transaction costs. Securities dealers use repos to finance their inventories of government instruments that are needed to make markets and two-way quotes. For this purpose, dealers "lend out" (or repo) securities that are in inventory but are not expected to be immediately sold. Thus dealers are able to leverage their capital and hold a larger inventory. A central bank can temporarily inject liquidity into the system by buying securities under repo. Because of the many uses made of repos, the demand for government securities increases, while the underlying conditions for liquid secondary markets are put in place.

Foreign exchange markets in cash and derivatives provide information to market participants about exchange rate and implicit interest rate risks and allow them to hedge the risk of funding government securities purchases in foreign currency. These markets include the onshore foreign exchange market, which is often OTC and not very liquid, as well as nondeliverable forward contracts traded offshore among large counterparties that have more liquidity. Arbitrage between the domestic and foreign currency markets can, at times, increase volatility in interest rates and exchange rates in emerging markets, forcing authorities to properly integrate such factors into their debt management and monetary policy.

1.8. Securities Settlement Infrastructure for Government Securities Markets

The settlement system, including depository facilities, is a principal component of the infrastructure needed for government securities market development. The design and regulation of this system is a complex and technical matter with implications for the level of risk in the financial system, competition in the market, and ease of access. A number of questions arise for policymakers in this area. How can a sound legal basis for paperless (dematerialized) securities be secured? What is the most efficient way to set up a securities depository (organization, functions, fees, membership)? Should the government be directly involved (as investor or promoter) in setting up the securities settlement infrastructure? How can settlement procedures be designed to minimize risk (see Chapter 8)?

1.8.1 Securities Accounts and Government Securities Markets

An important factor determining the potential efficiency of the bond market is whether bonds are issued as paper or take the form of paperless (dematerialized) securities registered in securities accounts. Improvements in settlement systems have usually been based on replacing paper securities with securities accounts, and priority should be given to achieving this goal early in the process. Dematerialization of securities ensures that transactions take place quickly and cheaply. Dematerialization can therefore play a vital role in reducing the settlement cycle to same-day settlement of trades. Security accounts also protect investors against destruction, loss, theft, or forgery of paper securities, eliminating the problem of tainted script. Most countries have a long legal history based on paper securities, and change will be resisted by some. Change to a system of securities accounts, however, is a prerequisite to further development in the settlement system for government securities. In an automated system, the legal structure must ensure the acceptance of electronic documents with regard to final settlement of transactions, be consistent with bankruptcy legislation, and recognize the beneficiary owner.

1.8.2 Depository Arrangements for Government Securities

Depository arrangements typically involve establishment of a central depository accompanied by subdepositories. Where the system is layered, the subdepositories should be linked to the central depository to prevent problems of multiple pledging of securities. Many countries have, at relatively low cost, developed a securities depository for government securities in the central bank. This is not the only option. Organizing the central depository as a separate agency, even if located within the central bank, allows for a clear delimitation of responsibilities, the possibility of independent oversight, and, at a later stage, full independence of the system. If custody is fully or in part privately provided, the governance arrangements and oversight must be sound. Policymakers should ensure that rules for membership are explicit and transparent, competition is allowed, and the law and external regulations promote proper governance. Those financial institutions that are eligible to use the depository have, in some cases, tried to limit direct access to the depository in order to keep new players out of the market. In other cases where the system is under the central bank, the risk that the central bank restricts members to just the main banks must be avoided, given its tradition of working with them, and its high capital requirements for participation in the payment system. For market development, however, wide access is usually preferable. Because of the centralized nature of a securities depository, policymakers might find regulation of the fee structure necessary to prevent monopoly pricing. In many nascent markets there might not be a sufficient number of transactions to recover the costs of building and running the system without pricing being set at a prohibitively high level. In that case, transitory subsidies to the system may be needed until transaction volume becomes sufficient.

Efforts to link custody arrangements on a cross-border basis should be sought at a later stage to broaden the market base. For markets with a large foreign investor component, an efficient link between the national central securities depository and an international central securities depository, such as EUROCLEAR or Clearstream, has been important for market development. International institutional investors prefer to hold their securities from different markets in one central place, where liquidity from the sale of securities from one country can be used immediately to fund the acquisition of securities from another. The preference for the use of international central depositories, however, also has its background in a more practical back-office argument, as it is administratively easier for the securities manager to deal with only one depository.

1.8.3 Securities Settlement Procedures for Government Securities Markets

A large number of specific actions is usually needed to ensure that settlement of securities trades is secure and can be carried out according to the delivery versus payment (DVP) principle. This infrastructure requires the existence of some form of payment and settlement system for large-value transfers. The reserve accounts of banks are normally debited and credited at the central bank, but other arrangements are possible. A large-value transfer payment or other payment system, such as checks in less-advanced markets, must be seen as secure and provide finality of payment. To ensure DVP, it would be preferable that members of the depository have cash accounts at the central bank, thereby being able to settle both the payment and the securities sides of trades. The depository can, in this way, ensure finality for both securities and cash.

A smooth and efficient securities settlement system, which assures prompt settlement of securities transactions that are not subject to litigation, must have procedures for registration of securities holders and for handling settlement orders and matching of transactions. In addition, the settlement cycle must be determined. Traditionally, countries settled securities transactions on a multilateral net settlement (MNS) basis in which payment obligations are accumulated over some specified period, and at the end of the period the net settlement to be made or received by each participant against the whole set of other participants is calculated and paid to or by the agent running the system. The MNS arrangement is subject to problems of settlement risk, which in the extreme could mushroom into a systemic settlement crisis. Consequently, a different settlement approach is being adopted—the real-time gross settlement system (RTGS). In this arrangement, securities transactions are settled bilaterally through the depository or subdepository on an ongoing basis and as promptly as feasible. The RTGS arrangement considerably reduces settlement risk.

Settlement of government and other forms of securities must be secure. This may require a separate clearing and settlement entity or the handling of clearing and settlement on an exchange. In an OTC market organization, these functions can be worked out bilaterally among counterparties. If such arrangements are not well designed, however, there can be scope for increased counterparty credit risk. Many countries still do not meet minimally acceptable standards in this area. It is important to note, however, that the collection of settlement orders, whether in the central bank or in an independent institution, need not be especially sophisticated. Online electronic communication should clearly be the goal, but even use of telephone, telex, and fax might be appropriate in the early stages, as long as proper validation rules, encryption, and authentication of messages are ensured.

Beyond actions needed to ensure secure trading of government securities, a similar infrastructure is needed to permit secured lending and to facilitate the use of repurchase agreements. An infrastructure that will permit the marking to market of securities borrowing and lending will also be important for these transactions and for recourse in the event of default.

1.9 Legal and Regulatory Framework for Developing Government Securities Markets

One major prerequisite for sound government securities market development is the legal, regulatory, and supervisory framework. The fundamental parts of the legal framework supporting an efficient domestic government securities market usually include an explicit empowerment of the government to borrow, budgetary rules for the issuance of government securities, rules for the organization of the primary market, role of central bank as agent for the government, the debt management framework, rules governing issuance of government securities, and rules pertaining to the secondary market.

There are a number of important legal and regulatory policy issues related to the development of government securities markets that need to be addressed by policymakers. Is there a legal basis (constitution or legislation) for the government's borrowing authority? How can ceilings for government securities issuance be established? What should the legal boundaries for primary markets be? Is there a role for SROs in the government securities market? Should disclosure or rules ensure investor protection in the government securities market (see Chapter 9)?

1.9.1 General Considerations

Legal and regulatory reforms must be in place before a local or offshore government securities market can be developed. A balance must be struck among the needs for proper risk control, market integrity, and market development. The legal framework defines incentives for all market participants—the issuing government, the central bank, regulatory agencies, market intermediaries, end investors, and any SROs.

Some of the more important areas where the legal framework will affect the development of government securities markets include (i) defining the exact parameters under which fiscal budgeting processes will be linked to government securities issuance, (ii) limiting issuance through debt ceilings or other devices such as sinking funds, and (iii) defining the legal properties of government securities and their use as collateral in transactions such as repos. Governance arrangements for appropriate regulatory authorities and proper definition of their enforcement powers also constitute part of this effort.

At another level, the legal framework must define the rights and obligations of parties to debt contracts in the primary and secondary markets for issuers, investors, and intermediaries. This definition should include (i) minimum guidelines for disclosure of material information, (ii) liability for entities involved in distributing securities and for entities handling third-party investment accounts, and (iii) vehicles to allow proper legal recourse against mutual funds, pension funds, and even the government as an issuer. Investment regulations need to permit sufficient flexibility for investors, yet create adequate safeguards for prudent operations and for the safeguarding of fiduciary obligations, as in the case of pensions.

1

1.9.2 Elements of Legal Framework for Government Securities Markets

Authority for the government to borrow in the domestic market needs to be established as the first fundamental aspect of market development. The law in some countries grants the capacity to borrow directly to the legislature; others in government are granted the authority, subject to approval from the legislature. The law may impose prior legislative authorization on the issuance of government securities as a check against abuse of the borrowing authority. As part of its authority, the government should also have the legal ability to delegate borrowing authority and debt management policy to the public agency or department that carries out the debt management work. Some countries have imposed strict limitations on the use of government funding of debt, which in some cases involves an outright ban on domestic borrowing by the government.

Interlinked with the authority to borrow is the need for legislative control of the level of government indebtedness and, therefore, possibly, the need for explicit ceilings for government securities issuance to avoid abuse of the borrowing authority. Limitations on the government's authority to issue debt securities can be established in legislation with a specific ceiling on total debt or minimal net increment limit or by requiring specific approval of the issuance by the legislature. Even without explicit or implicit ceilings for government securities issuance, general oversight by the legislature of the borrowing will be an important element of the legal framework. It is, however, important to strike an appropriate balance between the need for control and the flexibility and discretion of the issuing authority. Loan-by-loan authorization will clearly not facilitate an efficient operation for the government as an issuer and as debt manager. It will constrain, for example, the development of fungible instruments and benchmark issues as instruments for government debt management.

The general rules governing the government's behavior in the primary market are another important aspect of the legal framework. Governments are usually exempt from the disclosure requirements with which private sector securities issuers must comply. This does not mean, however, that governments should be opaque in their operations. An indication of the information market participants seek pertaining to the creditworthiness of an issuer is provided in a general form through the government budgets. The behavior of governments in the primary market, furthermore, should be governed by well-established principles of generality, equality, and publicity. Unlike a private sector company, governments cannot act with contractual freedom and choose, for example, counterparties arbitrarily. Rather, the government should establish a common set of rules to ensure equal access and fair competition. This principle does not exclude the use of primary dealers, but requires the selection to be objective and fair. The principle of publicity requires the government to be open about its future securities transactions. Timely public announcements of the government's auction calendar, including amounts of issues and their maturities, and tender or auction procedures, are also necessary for market awareness and assessment of the government's market activities.

1.9.3   Market Regulation of Government Securities Markets

In most countries, government securities trade in the secondary market along with all other securities and are therefore subject to secondary market regulation. Effective secondary market regulation is necessary to support a viable secondary market. Since government securities are often defined as "exempt securities" (that is, exempt from regular prospectus requirements), it is important to ensure that this status does not undermine the integrity of the secondary market. Effective regulation of the secondary market should include (i) regulation of market intermediaries, (ii) market conduct regulation (including trading rules) and market surveillance, and (iii) transparency requirements, which will vary according to the choice of market structure.

The regulatory framework for securities markets, including government securities markets, is usually seen as having three distinct objectives—assurance of fair, efficient, and transparent markets; minimization of systemic risk; and protection for investors and consumers of financial services.[19] In ensuring fair, efficient, and transparent markets, supervisors aim primarily at preventing improper trading practices such as market manipulation and insider trading. A requirement that information potentially affecting prices be released expeditiously, and to all market participants simultaneously, is also important in ensuring fair and transparent markets. Requiring intermediaries to comply with minimum capital requirements

---

19. See IOSCO 1998.

and internal control procedures reduces systemic risk. Lack of development and standards in this area have led to substantial problems and at times even set back the development of such markets for many years. Also important for systemic risk are reliable systems for settlement of cash and securities transactions. By depending on disclosure for investor protection, supervisors are relying on investors to protect their own interests. Supervision of market intermediaries and the use of "fit and proper" rules for management in securities firms also provide investor protection.[20]

The regulatory structure of securities markets is, in many cases, built around SROs, such as exchanges and securities dealers associations, as a supplement to the government regulatory authorities.[21] SROs typically provide the first layer of regulatory oversight, guiding their members to meet the objectives of regulation. SROs ensure adequate flexibility in the regulation and oversight of securities markets, especially in cases where the introduction of new products and practices has come too rapidly for the traditional supervisory structure. The use of SROs does not imply that a public supervisor is redundant. Public supervision or oversight of SROs is needed to prevent conflicts of interest that might impair the supervisory regime.

Since government securities are traded in only a few cases on organized exchanges, the use of SROs for regulation of the bond market has been limited. It is more common to have market oversight and regulation provided directly by the securities market regulator, the central bank, or, in cases where primary dealers are used, by the minister of finance or the public debt management agency. The authorities also often regulate the relationship between intermediaries and their clients, mainly to ensure best execution of trades. Where there is more than one authority exercising supervision over institutions participating in the market, the actions of these authorities

---

20. In some countries, notably in the EU, investors are ultimately protected within certain limits by an investor compensation scheme. Such a scheme is usually funded by market participants and protects against fraud and negligence by, for example, returning an investor's security that cannot be produced by a bankrupt securities firm. There is normally no protection against market risk.

21. The regulatory responsibilities of government securities markets often are assigned to more than one government agency. Thus in some countries the supervision over a primary dealers' arrangement and the issuance process (auctions, for example) is handled by the Treasury or jointly by the Treasury and the central bank, the regulation of the secondary market by a security regulator (which is often a separate government agency), and the oversight of the settlement arrangements by the central bank.

must be coordinated in order to maintain a fair and competitive environment. In countries where there is cross-border transaction activity in the government securities market, there will be a presence of foreign financial institutions in the domestic market and/or the presence of domestic institutions in foreign markets. This international aspect will require cooperation between domestic authorities and their foreign counterparts.

Capital rules, margin requirements, risk controls, and trading practice regulations applied to intermediaries are likely to grow in importance with technological advances. Nonuniformity of capital requirements within the same class of securities market participants, such as brokers or dealers, can increase both systemic and credit risk for individual market participants. In contrast, nonuniformity of capital requirements across different classes of market participants can be an important factor in creating incentives for self-regulation. If members of securities depository and settlement corporations are required to hold higher levels of capital than nonmembers, the members will have greater incentives to monitor those financial institutions with lower capital requirements. Capital requirements must take into account liquidity, price, and credit risk for assets in the firm's own portfolio, as well as for assets managed on behalf of third parties. Leverage requirements, if imposed, must take account of differing definitions of leverage.

Emerging-market countries may need to permit the operation of private proprietary trading systems, entry of foreign trading systems, or ATSs alongside traditional exchanges that trade government securities. Authorities will need to examine how they would respond to potential demutualization of existing exchanges and the possible implications of this for self-regulatory incentives and the integrity of the market for trading government securities. An increasing issuance and trading of government securities by electronic means will require changes in investor-protection statutes and regulations to control systemic risk in settlement and security account arrangements, in insider dealing, and in the role of SROs. As concentration of positions within and across exchanges or across countries becomes more prevalent, risk analysis will become increasingly important.

Legislation and regulation about the kinds of information that those most intimately involved in government securities markets are required to disclose are also essential to develop and maintain active and sound government securities markets. These rules relate to analysts and their responsibilities, public disclosure by broker firms and by the government as an issuer, credit-rating agencies, and many forms of self-regulatory associations, such as organizations of accountants and auditors. Providing incentives for the preparation and disclosure of high-quality information, and breaking the hold of banks as monopolizers/controllers of information, is important for market development.[22]

1.10 Taxation Policy and Development of Government Securities Markets

Taxation of financial instruments has significant implications for financial market development. Taxation of capital gains and income from securities affects consumption, saving and investment decisions, influencing the general level of savings, the demand for financial assets, and investment. It also strongly affects the allocation of savings. Poor tax policies can be a major impediment to a properly functioning financial market. An inappropriate tax system hampers the emergence of new financial instruments such as mutual funds and asset-backed securities. With regard to the implications of tax policy for the development of government securities markets, policymakers need to focus on some important issues. What is the appropriate balance between fiscal objectives and the development of the capital market? Should tax incentives be used to promote market development (see Chapter 10)?

In developing countries, tax authorities often skew the tax regime to take advantage of a relatively well-institutionalized financial sector from which revenue can be raised easily. Authorities entrusted with the development of a deep and liquid capital market, on the other hand, often favor tax incentives for financial instruments as a way to encourage market development. Considering the importance of financial markets in the development of the national economy, it is important to adopt tax policies that are compatible with financial market development while not seriously compromising principles of good taxation. Good communication between those responsible for tax and financial policies and awareness by officials of how new financial instruments work will assist in developing a balanced tax system.

---

22. See Villar, Diaz de Leon, and Hubert (forthcoming).

Both developed and developing countries have employed various tax incentives for certain financial assets in an attempt to stimulate national savings. Contributions to pension plans and to retirement savings plans through targeted savings promotion plans (such as individual retirement accounts in the United States and the *plan populaire d'épargne* in France) are tax deductible or tax exempt in many countries. Saving through life insurance also receives special tax treatment in many countries. Tax incentives have strong impacts on portfolio composition. Tax incentives used with care can therefore be effective in achieving certain economic goals, such as the promotion of a long-term bond market. This is especially meaningful for developing countries where investors' time horizons are short and short-term securities dominate the fixed-income securities market.

Tax incentives have, however, been criticized.[23] They distort relative prices and lead to inefficient resource allocation. Moreover, they are unfair because nonpreferred sectors must bear heavier tax burdens to compensate for lost government revenue, they undermine administrative simplicity, and they require substantial monitoring costs. If tax incentives are used in order to minimize the associated indirect costs, it is important to manage the incentives in a consistent manner. A sunset clause for tax incentives can be a useful device to prevent the proliferation and perpetuation of such tax benefits, since it forces policymakers to periodically review the efficacy of these incentives.

1.11 Linkages of Government Securities Markets to Subnational and Private Sector Bond Markets

In developing subnational and private sector bond markets, policymakers face a number of questions. What actions should the government take to develop a common infrastructure for a government, subnational, and private sector securities settlement system? What can be done to eliminate or minimize the risk of moral hazard from subnational entities issuing bonds? Should tax incentives be used to promote subnational and private sector bond markets? What should be the role of credit agencies for the private sector securities market? What should be done to strengthen

---

23. Shah (1995) provides an extensive discussion of the pros and cons of tax incentives.

investor protection arrangements in the private sector bond market (see Chapters 11 and 12)?

The government issues bonds and Treasury bills in the domestic capital market to fund budget deficits and manage its short-term liquidity needs. It usually does this in a nonopportunistic way, whether rates are low or high, with the aim of minimizing cost over the long run. In contrast, many subnational (provinces, states, municipalities, and state enterprises) and private sector issuers are opportunistic issuers that often do not have a recurrent financing need. They can, accordingly, look for special opportunities in the market by issuing bonds when interest rates are low or by targeting specific segments with high investor demand. For these issuers, timing and flexibility in the design of bonds are essential.[24]

The subnational and private sector bond markets in many countries have developed a wide range of financial instruments. Major groups of issuers have been mortgage credit institutions, subnational entities, and private sector companies.

The increasing role of subnational entities reflects the trend of decentralization of some governmental functions, particularly for infrastructure investment, from the central government to smaller political jurisdictions. In general, the greater the financial autonomy of subnational units of government, the greater the likelihood that a subnational securities market could develop.

Even with financial autonomy of a subnational unit, however, a number of concerns arise in developing subnational bond markets. The overarching problem of subnational securities issuers is that they often lead to expectations that the central government might assume the liabilities of a distressed subnational borrower, resulting in a moral hazard problem. In addition, to the extent that there is no assurance that the central government will assume the debt obligations of a subnational entity, the creditworthiness status that surrounds such debt obligations has implications for the development of subnational bond markets. The ability of market participants to assess the likelihood of the central government's response to a subnational entity's debt-servicing difficulties for different

---

24. Some governments employ a strategy in which some investor groups are targeted with specific issues designed with this group in mind. For some smaller countries opportunistic issuance is also the primary form of borrowing in foreign markets.

subnational bond issues will determine the prospects of subnational markets to take hold.

In addition, the development of a subnational securities market may fragment the overall government securities market. Moreover, lack of market transparency, weakness of market governance, and weak capacity for financial management of subnational entities impede the development of subnational bond markets. The extent to which a subnational securities market is desirable is ultimately a question of whether the benefits of the greater financial autonomy resulting from decentralization are outweighed by the inefficiencies resulting from moral hazard and market fragmentation.

The financial and nonfinancial corporate bond market has produced a variety of bonds with special characteristics targeted at special investor groups or the specific cash flow needs of the issuer. Most corporate bonds have maturities of less than 10 years. Some are issued with different types of embedded options and/or interest payment schedules.

Mortgage bonds have typically been issued as nominal bonds with less than 10 years maturity or, if longer, as adjustable rate or variable rate bonds. Exceptions are the U.S. and Danish mortgage markets, where 20- to 30-year fixed-interest mortgage bonds are common. These bonds are issued with embedded options giving the borrower the right to repay the loan at par before maturity.[25] One important characteristic of mortgage bonds is their high credit quality. They are secured through special regulation that allows mortgages to be used as indirect or direct collateral. Other types of collateralized bonds have also played an important role in the development of the private sector bond market.

Developing a government securities market supports the development of bond markets for the subnational and corporate sectors. Providing a relatively risk-free asset such as a government bond establishes a reference

---

25. Long-term (10 to 30 years) fixed-interest mortgage bonds are typically issued with embedded options to help protect borrowers against interest rate risk. Embedded options make these mortgage bonds difficult to price. Advanced financial models are used to strip the bonds of their options to arrive at a so-called option-adjusted spread (OAS). Derived yields on the bonds remain model specific, while duration is highly dependent on market yields. These complications make mortgage bonds imperfect substitutes for government bonds as long-term benchmarks even if they are considered to be of high credit quality.

for pricing subnational and corporate bonds, commercial paper, or any kind of private sector fixed-income security. Because of their usually large funding needs, governments seem to be the most suitable providers of a benchmark yield.[26] A benchmark function could also be provided by some private sector–type bonds or by interest rate swaps. Government securities also are used as a hedging tool for interest rate risk, essential for intermediaries, and they serve as underlying assets and collateral for repo, futures, and options markets.

Basic credit information on bond issuers and credit ratings and information provided by the issuing entity are major elements in the information infrastructure needed to develop subnational and private sector bond markets. In addition, the government can help raise standards for many self-regulatory organizations, particularly in auditing and accounting, by requiring auditors to post bonds or by setting minimum standards for accounting, including proper mark-to-market rules. Technology and the Internet may also play a role in the information infrastructure by facilitating the dissemination of pricing information from all potential providers of a financial service and relevant financial information about particular new issues and the issuers.

Rating agency efforts to require ratings of private sector bonds or of the issuers have often been unsuccessful. Establishment of rating agencies in small countries has been difficult and has often favored issuers more than investors. With advances in technology and telecommunications, the lower up-front and operating costs of establishing a rating agency should facilitate rating agency entry into smaller markets. In addition, some of the large international credit agencies have established working relationships with some national credit agencies, allowing the pooling of expertise of the large international agencies with knowledge of the country-specific circumstances.

---

26. The need for a benchmark reference is why some government authorities, such as those in Hong Kong, China, which run government budget surpluses and thus do not need to issue bonds, developed a government bond market as a benchmark for their large mortgage market and the nascent corporate bond market. In some markets, however, other nonopportunistic issuers have at various times provided benchmarks. This is particularly the case in countries with a history of financing mortgage loans through issuance of mortgage bonds.

1.12   Sequencing Development of Securities Markets

Sequencing the different steps in the development of government securities markets is largely dependent on country-specific circumstances. The size of the economy, the level of competition in, and sophistication of, the financial sector, and the different types of investors present in the country and their appetite for fixed-income financial instruments are all important factors determining not only the appropriate sequencing of initiatives to develop a securities market, but also whether the public sector should be actively engaged in the development of different market aspects. However, if the basic prerequisites for developing securities markets are in place (see Section 1.3 above), there are initiatives to which priority should be given at different points in time.

At the nascent stages of market development, priority should be given to strengthen and develop the short end of the market. This requires initiatives related to developing an active money market with market-determined price setting. In most cases progress in this area cannot be achieved without the active participation of the central bank. Supporting the development of an effective repo market is a key priority at this stage. Improving auction procedures; transparency in government securities operations; and, in some cases, the instrument design, especially standardization of issues, are also important priority areas early in the process. Greater competition between intermediaries should also be encouraged; efforts in this area require long-term and multiple initiatives if competition is weak. The key to success at this emerging stage, however, is a clear and unequivocal move away from the use of funding below market rates through captive investor sources. This move might require the use of a legal framework giving the responsible agencies (Ministry of Finance or the central bank) the mandate and the institutional capacity to start the process through a clear borrowing authority. At this stage, where the focus is on fundamental initiatives related to market infrastructure, the more advanced features of a securities market, such as electronic trading mechanisms and advanced securities depositories and settlement procedures, need not be present for the market to develop. The main focus in the area of market infrastructure should initially be on simple, secure solutions capable of handling the limited number of daily transactions expected.

Common pitfalls at this stage in market development are related to the government's commitment to the reform process. Credibility can easily be lost at this point in the process if the government occasionally resorts to below-market-rate financing. Failure by the central bank to implement reforms of the monetary policy regime by, for example, not accepting some sort of interest rate flexibility can also set the developmental process back. Another common pitfall is to focus attention on more technical issues, such as whether to use single versus multiple price auctions, instead of dealing first with such fundamental issues as, for instance, the lack of competition among bidders.

Once a solid basis for a well-functioning, short-term market has been set, the next goal is to move from short- to long-term funding instruments. One option would be to slowly start issuing fixed-rate (nominal) government securities with longer maturities. Alternatively, the government could issue relatively long maturity but indexed (either to prices, currency, or short-term interest rates) securities. Both of these strategies and combinations have been used successfully.

To be sustainable in the long run, however, the move from short- to long-term funding instruments requires initiatives in multiple areas as the market fundamentally changes with this move. The development of an investor base with a long-time horizon—such as for institutional investors—takes on new urgency. Since actions in this area have a long gestation period, other initiatives are needed to bridge the divide. The development of a repo market can help at this stage, as it will allow short-term investors to invest in longer-term instruments without being afraid of not being able to sell the securities when the money is needed. In some cases this has been especially important for the retail investor segment of the market. Mutual funds and investment trust companies (ITCs) can quickly channel retail demand to the short- and medium-term segment of the market and are consequently important entities to develop early on. The main vehicle generating liquidity, however, should be a secondary market, where investors with a short-time horizon are able to sell longer-term securities before expiration. Market regulation and market infrastructure, including development of efficient market intermediaries, become priority areas at this stage, as the integrity of the secondary market and its participants is an important element in creating investor confidence in the market. As volume increases so does the importance of a more sophisticated infrastructure for securities settlement, with dematerialized instruments settled with delivery versus payment.

A frequent problem at this level of market development entails unrealistic expectations as to the pricing of longer-term bonds. Until credibility has been attained, the government may have to pay a premium on its borrowing. At the same time, the higher costs are offset by a reduction in risk, which is a consideration that needs to be taken into account when the developmental approach is evaluated. A strong debt management capacity with a focus on risk management can help in the formulation of the optimal trade-off between cost and risk and thereby help create political consensus for the market development effort. Another issue that needs careful examination is the use of primary dealers. Market participants will often press for this kind of arrangement at this point in the developmental process or even before. The issuer needs, however, to balance the pros of getting a small group of committed players in the government securities market against the cons of reduced market competition. Without fundamental change in the incentives to distribute securities to end investors and adequate (potential) competition from, for example, foreign brokers/banks, the benefits of restricting access to the primary market could be small.

At this point in the developmental process, an active secondary market should provide the basis for a further standardization of the bonds on the market. Issues with the same maturity are now fully fungible, and a further increase in the maturity of the securities becomes feasible. Creating a number of benchmark bonds across the yield curve should then become the goal. As the government increases the maturity of the bonds, it lowers the interest rate risk on its debt portfolio. At the same time, the interest rate risk for investors rises. A priority at this point should be ensuring the existence of a proper risk management framework in the systemically important financial institutions that invest in government bonds. Sound development of more sophisticated auxiliary markets that can allow for better risk management, such as swap, and, ultimately, futures markets, will also be relevant at this level of market development.

Countries looking for a rapid transition through the different stages must not only prioritize between different initiatives that will advance the market to a next stage, but also consider the time horizon of different initiatives. For example, even though pension and life insurance reform should not be seen as fundamental to the early stages of government securities market development, starting the process of pension and insurance reform might be prudent because of the time it takes to feel the positive impact of such reforms on the capital market. Taking concurrent initiatives with short- and long-term effects, therefore, needs to be considered. Initiatives with immediate effect would include standardization of issues, change in

1

auction procedures and schedules, and the reduction and eventual elimination of reliance on captive sources of funding. Medium-term initiatives include upgraded trading facilities, settlement systems, securities depositories, and market regulation. Longer-term initiatives are mostly related to the development of an institutional investor base.

The resources available in both the public and private sectors set limits for this kind of sequenced market development. A needs assessment early in the process will be essential to devise an optimal allocation of the scarce resources among different initiative possibilities.

ANNEX 1.A
Some Elements of a Macroeconomic Framework

Development of a government securities market will be more successful when a consistent macroeconomic policy framework involving fiscal, monetary, exchange rate, and capital account policies is in place. Achieving this goal involves a complex and dynamic process.

Fiscal policy. An institutional and legal framework that can ensure proper *economic governance* and a record of accomplishment of fiscal prudence will influence investor perceptions of default risk and help the government build credibility in its ability to honor long-term obligations. Without such credibility, the development of a longer-term bond market will be more difficult and costly. For example, an enforceable fiscal responsibility law, such as that developed in New Zealand and, more recently, in Argentina and Brazil, is one way to help create incentives for proper economic governance. The government securities markets can become a particularly effective means to exert further fiscal discipline, since the authorities must react credibly by cutting expenditures or raising taxes if debt service rises in response to permanent shocks to the economy.

A reasonably robust *fiscal regime* is another important element of a credible fiscal policy. Such a regime should have the capacity to collect direct and indirect tax revenues, an effective budgeting and expenditure control system, and an ability to take into account large contingent liabilities, including public pensions, health/housing or agriculture-related liabilities, government guarantees, and any central bank deficits covered by the government. A system for tax collection allowing for efficient functioning of financial markets and financial intermediaries is especially important. Lack of such capacity can lead to the use of convenient tax and implicit tax handles offered by the financial system, including those levied on financial transactions such as sales of securities.

Interaction between fiscal policy and *debt management* is very important in building overall credibility. Governments must establish a sound and prudent debt management operation and a policy of broad market access and transparency so that markets can count on substantial predictability in government actions. More broadly, the authorities should establish a sound framework for debt management and asset liability management.[27]

---

27. See IMF and World Bank 2000 and World Bank (forthcoming).

Monetary policy. The existence of an independent, well-managed central bank with a credible nominal anchor, such as an inflation target, can also play an important role in counterbalancing fiscal excesses and improving economic governance. Achieving a sufficient level of consistency in policy formulation and administrative coordination between monetary and fiscal authorities is essential to developing a government securities market. The two authorities have differing policy objectives. The central bank's principal focus is usually on maintaining price stability and financial system soundness, while the Treasury's principal long-term focus is to minimize funding costs of the government, taking into account the risk associated with managing the government debt. The respective objectives of the two authorities must be clearly defined and coordinated in day-to-day operations, particularly since fluctuations in Treasury cash balances at the central bank have a direct impact on reserve or base money that may need to be offset through open market operations. Even the timing and nature of announced monetary and fiscal policies will have to be carefully considered in the context of how they affect expectations of market participants and the credibility of the authorities. The monetary authority cannot, over the long run, contain inflationary expectations if the government is tempted to inflate away a fiscal problem and obtain financing through forced holdings of government securities by captive sources of funding. A noncredible monetary policy will also raise investor perceptions of inflation or devaluation risk, thereby adversely influencing government funding costs and impeding the development of a government securities market. Some countries have relied on a coordination committee with representation from both the Treasury and the central bank to ensure coordination. Others have established the clear-cut independence of the central bank to manage monetary policy, but, at the same time, have promoted coordination at the operating level to ensure that Treasury operations are consistent with central bank objectives.

Exchange rate and capital account policies. A credible exchange rate regime is important, especially for governments seeking foreign investment in the domestic government securities markets. To help ensure this, fiscal, monetary, capital account, and debt management policies will need to be viewed as sustainable and consistent by both local and foreign investors. If exchange rate regimes are perceived to be unsustainable, the exchange rate risk premium will rise rapidly, accompanied by the related costs of government securities issuance and the inability of the government to raise funds beyond very short maturities.

Capital account deregulation and its timing need to be carefully considered regardless of the advantages of having a convertible currency or attracting foreign investors. While unrestricted capital movements can serve as an encouragement for foreign participation in domestic government securities markets, such movements also expose a country to potentially destabilizing capital inflows and outflows that can exert undesirable pressures and shocks on the economy. The vulnerability to capital outflows—particularly through commercial banks' cutting credit lines or reducing exposure by the use of derivatives as well as capital account vulnerabilities more generally— require careful analysis at the time the introduction of a government securities market is contemplated. When levels of short-term government securities are high and significant leverage from the different participants (public or private) is possible, rapid capital account and exchange rate liberalization can lead to financial crises. Better macroeconomic management and more effective monitoring and management of foreign capital flows are often necessary for capital account and exchange rate liberalization to be successful.

1

ANNEX 1.B
Some Elements of Financial Sector Reform

There are four fundamental areas of financial sector reform that usually need particular attention in support of government securities development: (i) transparency and information infrastructure, (ii) banking soundness, (iii) portfolio restrictions and interest rate liberalization, and (iv) entry and exit policies.

Transparency and information infrastructure. Proper *auditing, accounting, and creditor information* are important elements of the basic financial market infrastructure. Without proper disclosure, domestic and foreign investors will be reluctant to deal with domestic financial institutions, and the general ability of investors to provide market discipline will be limited.

Banking soundness: prudential regulations and supervision and safety net. It is essential that a sound banking system be subject to *prudential regulations* (including capital adequacy, lending standards, proper asset classification, income recognition, and reserving policies) that meet or approach international standards and provide for competent supervision and adequate enforcement capacity.[28] A *safety net* that provides (temporary) assistance (usually with collateral) to financial institutions that are solvent but face temporary liquidity problems will prevent the emergence of systemic financial problems. An unsound banking environment will complicate development of a government securities market because important related markets, such as IDB and repo markets, are unlikely to function properly in an unsound and unstable financial environment. An unsound banking environment will also impair investor confidence and hamper secondary market activities and development of new instruments, such as mutual funds administered by banks.

Portfolio restrictions and interest rate liberalization. An area of reform with important implications for the development of local government securities markets is *liberalization of the balance sheet of banks.* Liberalization includes removal of forced investments or credit ceilings, other lending/investment portfolio restrictions, and interest rate controls for liabilities and assets. To lessen the prospect of a credit boom that could lead to

---

28. See Caprio, Atiyas, and Hanson 1993.

excessive leverage of nonfinancial corporations or banks, such liberalization should be accompanied by reforms to improve loan foreclosure, corporate bankruptcy and reorganization processes, and prudential regulations. There is also a need to review the *structure of reserve requirements and taxation* to determine whether such policies impede the growth of important markets essential for the development of government securities markets, including money and repurchase agreement markets. Some countries that have differentiated reserve requirements have imposed new requirements on previously acquired assets. The same is true for taxes on repos. These types of policies can seriously hinder market development.

Competition, entry, and exit. Among the more important areas of reform in emerging markets are policies regarding *entry and exit of financial service providers*. Entry, subject to fit and proper tests and the need to maintain franchise value, should be encouraged. Since domestic banks often play a predominant role in government securities markets in emerging economies, new entrants can stimulate competition and knowledge transfer, especially in the case of foreign-affiliated institutions. Greater competition would limit the ability of banks acting as dealers to exploit their buying, that is, monopsony, power in auctions of government securities. It would also help stimulate a move toward greater disintermediation through development of mutual funds and direct access for nonfinancial corporations to tap the bond market. New entrants can also raise overall liquidity in the markets and information standards. Foreign entrants present an opportunity to import many useful financial services, leading to adopting and adapting standards and procedures for supervision and regulation of banks that are used in other countries. Given new technology, the benefits of liberalizing entry through cross-border provision of services have increased. Such remote access to the market could include access, subject to appropriate licensing provisions for e-trading by virtual brokers, by foreign entities wanting to participate in domestic securities markets via the Internet. New entrants can be important catalysts for bond market development, as illustrated by the experiences of such countries as Argentina, New Zealand, and Panama.

Policies in the area of failure resolution are also important for government securities market development. If the exit of weak or failing institutions is not timely, there can be greater scope for a bidding up of interest rates in the interbank market. The incentive to invest in high-return deposits issued by distressed banks can become pervasive if the safety net is defined or assumed so that investors have confidence they will be, if necessary, paid in full through the safety net provisions on all liabilities. This can have a negative effect on the demand for government securities, which are usually regarded as the only domestic risk-free asset class.

ANNEX 1.C
Key Strategic Steps in Government Securities
Market Development

Link to Money Markets and Monetary Policy Operations
(see Chapter 2, Money Markets and Monetary Policy Operations)

- Establish an adequate forecasting facility in the Treasury (surveillance of receipts, expenditures, and overall forecast).
- Improve management of government cash flows to enable better liquidity management by the central bank.
- Design central bank operations (liquidity management and accommodation policy), keeping in mind the need to stimulate interbank transactions.
- Phase out direct government control over deposits, interest rates, and lending.
- Ensure and make transparent the issuance of securities for both monetary and fiscal policy purposes.

Issuance Strategy and Market Access
(see Chapter 3, A Government Debt Issuance Strategy and Debt
Management Framework; Chapter 4, Developing Benchmark
Issues; and Chapter 5, Developing a Primary Market for
Government Securities)

Issuance Strategy and Debt Management

- Establish a strong commitment to move toward market-based government financing through the use of marketable instruments sold at market price, dismantling of captive sources of funding, and a proactive approach to market development.
- Define and adhere to principles of broad market access and transparency in government funding operations.
- Define clear objectives and a debt management strategy that involves market finance and introduces risk management objectives.
- Develop a sound overall risk management framework.

1

- Build a sound institutional framework for debt management with appropriate governance structures. The responsibilities of the debt managers should be explicitly stated; the organization should be endowed with adequate operational capacity, including the ability to attract and retain professional staff in the debt management functions; and a proper incentive framework ensuring accountability of managers should be put into place.

Primary Market Structure

- Establish efficient distribution channels for securities (auctions, underwriters) in light of the investor base, the state of financial system development, and the structure of intermediaries.
- Identify how technology can be used to create new channels for securities distribution.

Instruments and Yield Curve

- Use standardized simple instruments with conventional maturities.
- Develop the Treasury bill market.
- For large issuers, priority should be given to developing fungible issues that could be turned into liquid benchmarks.
- Establish buy-backs and reopening programs.

Investor Base
(see Chapter 6, Developing the Investor Base for Government Securities)

- Release captive sources of funding government securities from obligations to purchase instruments at below-market prices.
- Reform the contractual savings system and insurance sector to allow participation of private sector nonbank institutions, permit funded pension schemes, and gradually move from a quantitative, restricted investment framework to a "prudent man rule" framework for investment management.
- For mutual funds, ensure that prospectuses provide clear and accurate representations of the performance of their business, assets are marked to market, and fees are properly disclosed.

- Improve information and actuarial disclosure requirements for institutional investors.
- Review laws and regulations applicable to collective investment vehicles in order to maintain proper separation between asset management and investment banking.
- Relate insurance and pension fund reforms to building government securities markets.
- Improve supervision and regulation of financial institutions.
- Examine capital account restrictions and consider liberalization, depending on overall macroeconomic and financial sector conditions.
- Introduce certification standards for investment advisors.
- Evaluate the benefits of encouraging foreign investors, such as eliminating withholding taxes on their investments.
- Promote investment funds specializing in government securities.
- Promote retail investor interests through new distribution channels, including mutual funds and automated trading formats.

Secondary Markets
(see Chapter 7, Developing Secondary Market Structures for Government Securities)

- Promote repo and money markets in order to improve liquidity in the government securities market.
- Promote prudent regulations governing trading practices.
- Promote a system of market makers, where appropriate, through primary dealers.
- Facilitate the emergence of interdealer brokers and organized trading facilities.
- Introduce borrowing and lending of securities and short sales, with proper regulation.
- Eliminate taxes impeding securities transactions.
- Develop automated trading systems to encourage access by onshore and offshore investors (connections to EUROCLEAR, Clearstream).
- Evaluate alternatives for gradually introducing trading in derivative instruments, as well as the preferred venue (exchange or OTC) and overall risk management guidelines. Liberalization in this area must be undertaken cautiously.

- Promote development of a trading culture in the market through professional associations, primary dealers, entry of foreign institutions, and codes of behavior.

Securities Settlement
(see Chapter 8, Developing a Government Securities Settlement Structure)

- Establish payment and settlement procedures for cash and securities, including automated (dematerialized) accounts for securities.
- Develop reliable depository arrangements for recording ownership and settlement of securities.
- Establish a securities settlement system with DVP, allowing for same-day settlement.

Legal and Regulatory Framework
(see Chapter 9, Legal and Regulatory Framework)

- Establish a legal framework and improve enforcement of securities laws and the judicial system.
- Ensure the protection of investors and reduce systemic risk.
- Ensure that markets are fair, efficient, and transparent.
- Set standards for auditing and accounting.
- Strengthen securities supervision and enforcement.
- Strengthen SRO surveillance and risk management processes.

Tax Policy
(see Chapter 10, Development of Government Securities Market and Tax Policy)

- Adopt tax policies that tax earnings on government securities at comparable rates as other taxable income sources.
- Reduce dependence and aim to eliminate securities transaction taxes for government and subnational securities.
- Establish sunset clauses for tax incentives for government, subnational, and private sector securities, and periodically review the efficacy of such incentives.

Linkages to Subnational and Private Sector Bond Markets
(see Chapter 11, Development of Subnational Bond Markets, and Chapter 12, Linkages Between Government and Private Sector Bond Markets)

- Define a proper incentive framework for government securities issuing activities at subnational level and for state-owned enterprises.
- Promote a common infrastructure (settlement system, central securities depository, trading systems).
- Streamline procedures for public issuance of nongovernment securities while ensuring adequate investor protection.
- Abolish restrictions on product design for private sector securities such as caps on coupon rates, use of unsecured bonds, and issuance of floating rate and foreign-exchange-linked bonds.
- Allow underwriter eligibility for new entrants.
- Eliminate transaction taxes, subject to a review of impact on fiscal revenue.
- Develop nongeneral obligation bonds at the subnational level (revenue securitization, project-linked bonds).
- Introduce nonbailout clauses for subnational borrowers through public finance legislation.
- Develop credit information infrastructure, including credit ratings, basic credit information, and related infrastructure.

1

Bibliography

African Development Bank. 2000. "Debt Management in African Countries." Draft. April.

Alexander, William E., et al. 1995. "The Adoption of Indirect Instruments of Monetary Policy." Occasional Paper No. 126, International Monetary Fund, Washington, D.C.

APEC (Asia-Pacific Economic Cooperation). 1999. *Guidelines to Facilitate the Development of Domestic Bond Markets in APEC Member Economies.* Compendium of Sound Practices. APEC Collaborative Initiative on Development of Domestic Bond Markets.

BIS (Bank for International Settlements). 1996. "Changing Financial Systems in Small Open Economies." Policy Paper No. 1, Basel, Switzerland. Available at www.bis.org/publ/index.htm.

———. 1999. *How Should We Design Deep and Liquid Markets? The Case of Government Securities.* Basel, Switzerland.

———. 2000. *Quarterly Review: International Banking and Financial Market Developments.* February. Basel, Switzerland. Available at www.bis.org/publ/index.htm.

Black, Bernard S. 2000. "The Legal and Institutional Preconditions for Strong Stock Markets." Stanford Law School, Social Science Research Network Electronic Library, Working Paper 179.

Blinder, Alan S. 1999. "Central Bank Credibility: Why Do We Care? How Do We Build It?" National Bureau of Economic Research, Working Paper 7161. Available at www.nber.org.

Bloomfield, Robert, and Maureen O'Hara. 1999. "Market Transparency: Who Wins and Who Loses." *Review of Financial Studies* 12 (1): 5–35.

Bossone, Biagio, and Larry Promisel. 1998. "Strengthening Financial Systems in Developing Countries." Background papers for 1998 Annual Meetings, World Bank Group, Washington, D.C. Available at www.worldbank.org.

Bowe, Michael, and James W. Dean. 1997. *Has the Market Solved the Sovereign-Debt Crisis?* Princeton Studies in International Finance, No. 83, Princeton University, Princeton, N.J.

Calvo, Sara. 2000. *Initial Conditions for Debt Market Development.* World Bank, Washington, D.C.

Caprio, Gerard Jr., and Patrick Honohan. 1991. *Monetary Policy Instruments for Developing Countries.* World Bank Symposium, Washington, D.C.

Caprio, Gerard Jr., Izak Atiyas, and James Hanson. 1993. "Financial Reform Lessons and Strategies." WPS 1107, World Bank, Washington, D.C.

Claessens, Stijn, and Daniela Klingebiel. 2000. "Government Contingent Liabilities and Fiscal Vulnerability." Draft. March. World Bank, Washington, D.C.

Claessens, Stijn, Thomas Glaessner, and Daniela Klingebiel. 2000. "Technology and Financial Services: Public Policy Implications." Draft. May. World Bank, Washington, D.C.

Cohen, Daniel. 1991. *Private Lending to Sovereign States*. Cambridge, Mass.: MIT Press.

Cole, David C., and Betty F. Slade. 1999. "Premature Liberalization of Government Debt Markets." World Bank, Washington, D.C.

Dattels, Peter. 1997. "Microstructure of Government Securities Markets." In V. Sundararajan, Peter Dattels, and Hans J. Blommestein, eds., *Coordinating Public Debt and Monetary Management: Institutional and Operational Arrangements*. International Monetary Fund, Washington, D.C.

De Juan, Aristobulo. 1998. *Clearing the Decks: Experiences in Banking Crisis Resolution*. Fourth Annual Bank Conference on Development in Latin America and the Caribbean, San Salvador, El Salvador, June 28–30.

Diwan, Ishac, and Dani Rodrik. 1992. *External Debt, Adjustment, and Burden Sharing: A Unified Framework*. Princeton Studies in International Finance, No. 73, Princeton University, Princeton, N.J.

Domowitz, Ian, and Benn Steil. 1999. "Automation, Trading Costs, and the Structure of the Securities Trading Industry." *Brookings-Wharton Papers on Financial Services*. Washington, D.C.: The Brookings Institution Press.

Domowitz, Ian, Jack Glen, and Ananth Madhavan. 2000a. "International Evidence on Aggregate Corporate Financing Decisions." Draft. March.

———. 2000b. "Liquidity, Volatility, and Equity Trading Costs Across Countries and Over Time." Draft. April.

Dooley, Michael P. 1998a. "A Model of Crises in Emerging Markets." University of California. Draft. September.

———. 1998b. "Origins of the Crisis in Asia." Conference on an Analysis of the Financial Crisis, cosponsored by the Federal Reserve Bank of Chicago and the International Monetary Fund, October 8–10.

Dornbusch, Rudiger, and Mario Henrique Simonsen. 1983. *Inflation, Debt, and Indexation*. Cambridge, Mass.: MIT Press.

IMF and World Bank. 2001. *Guidelines for Public Debt Management.* Available at www.imf.org/external/np/mae/pdebt/2000/eng/index.htm.

IOSCO (International Organization of Securities Commissions). 1998. *Objectives and Principles of Securities Regulation.* Montreal, Canada. Available at www.iosco.org/docs-public/1998-objectives.html.

Litan, Robert E., and Anthony M. Santomero. 1999. *Brookings-Wharton Papers on Financial Services.* Washington, D.C.: The Brookings Institution Press.

Mishkin, Frederic S. 1999a. "International Experiences with Different Monetary Policy Regimes." National Bureau of Economic Research, Working Paper 6965. Available at www.nber.org.

———. 1999b. "Lessons from the Tequila Crisis." *Journal of Banking and Finance,* vol. 23, no. 10.

OECD (Organization for Economic Cooperation and Development). 1998. "The Development of Securities Markets in Transition Economies: Policy Issues and Country Experience." *Financial Market Trends* (June): Paris, France.

Rodrik, Dani, and Andrés Velasco. 1999. "Short-Term Capital Flows." National Bureau of Economic Research Working Paper 7364. Available at www.nber.org.

Shah, Anwar, ed. 1995. *Fiscal Incentives for Investment and Innovation.* New York: Oxford University Press.

Shiu, Barbara, and Stephen Cheung Yan-Leung. 2000. "Development of Government Bond Markets in DMCs–Hong Kong, China." Asian Development Bank Conference on Government Bond Markets and Financial Sector Development in Developing Asian Economies, March 28–30.

Stiglitz, Joseph E. 1993. *The Role of the State in Financial Markets.* Annual Bank Conference on Development Economics, World Bank, Washington, D.C.

U.S. Department of the Treasury. 1992. *Joint Report on the Government Securities Market.* Washington, D.C.: Government Printing Office.

Villar, Rafael del, Alejandro Diaz de Leon, and Johanna Gil Hubert. Forthcoming. "La regulación de protección de datos personales y burós de crédito en América Latina." Proceedings of the International Conference on Credit Reporting Systems.

1

Eaton, Jonathan, and Raquel Fernandez. 1995. *Sovereign Debt*. Institute for Economic Development, IED Discussion Paper Series No. 59, Boston University, Boston, Mass.

Eichengreen, Barry, and Ricardo Hausmann. 1999. *Exchange Rates and Financial Fragility*. National Bureau of Economic Research, Working Paper 7418. Available at www.nber.org.

Federal Reserve Bank of New York. 2000. "Fiscal Policy in an Era of Surpluses: Economic and Financial Implications." Proceedings of a conference sponsored by the Federal Reserve Bank of New York. *Economic Policy Review* 6 (1). Available at www.ny.frb.org/.

Financial Stability Forum. 2000. "Working Group on Capital Flows." Available at www.fsforum.org/Reports/RepCF.pdf.

Fry, Maxwell J. 1997. *Emancipating the Banking System and Developing Markets for Government Debt*. London and New York: Routledge.

Glaessner, Thomas. 1992. *External Regulation vs. Self-Regulation. What Is the Right Mix? An Emerging Markets LAC Perspective*. Regional Studies Program, World Bank, Washington, D.C.

Glaessner, Thomas, and Ignacio Mas. 1991. *Incentive Structure and Resolution of Financial Institution Distress: Latin American Experience*. Regional Studies Program, Report No. 12, World Bank, Washington, D.C.

Goode, Richard. 1984. *Government Finance in Developing Countries*. Studies of Government Finance. Washington, D.C.: The Brookings Institution Press.

Gray, Simon. 1996. *The Management of Government Debt*. Handbooks in Central Banking No. 5, Bank of England, London. Available at www.bankofengland.co.uk.

Greenspan, Alan. 1999. "Lessons from the Global Crises." Remarks before the World Bank Group and the International Monetary Fund Annual Meetings, Board of Governors of the Federal Reserve System, Washington, D.C.

Hausmann, Ricardo, Michael Gavin, Carmen Pages-Serra, and Ernesto Stein. "Financial Turmoil and the Choice of Exchange Rate Regime." Draft. World Bank, Washington, D.C.

Hui, Liu. 2000. "Development of Government Bond Markets in DMCs: People's Republic of China." Asian Development Bank Conference on Government Bond Markets and Financial Sector Development in Developing Asian Economies, March 28–30.

Vittas, Dimitri. 1998. "Institutional Investors and Securities Markets: Which Comes First?" In J. Burki and G. Perry, eds., *Banks and Capital Markets. Annual World Bank Conference on Development in Latin America and the Caribbean.*

———. 2000. "Pension Reform and Capital Market Development: 'Feasibility' and 'Impact' Preconditions." Development Research Group, World Bank, Washington, D.C. Processed.

Working Party on Financial Stability in Emerging Market Economies. 1996. *Financial Stability in Emerging Market Economies.* Bank for International Settlements, Basel, Switzerland. Available at www.bis.org/publ/index.htm.

World Bank. 2000a. *East Asia: Recovery and Beyond.* Report SecM2000 –193. Draft. April.

———. 2000b. *Brazil: Capital Markets Study.* Draft. May.

———. Forthcoming. *Sound Practices in Sovereign Debt Management.*

Money Markets and Monetary Policy Operations

The money market is the cornerstone of a competitive and efficient system of market-based intermediation, and should normally be in good working order before a government bond market is developed. The money market stimulates an active secondary bond market by reducing the liquidity risk attached to bonds and other term financial instruments and assisting financial intermediaries in managing liquidity risk. The money market serves as the medium for government cash management and provides the first link in implementing monetary policy using indirect instruments.

There are three key conditions required to develop a well-functioning money market: (i) banks and other financial institutions must be commercially motivated to respond to incentives to actively manage risk and maximize profit, (ii) the central bank must shift from direct to indirect methods of implementing monetary policy, and (iii) the government must have a good capacity for cash management, thereby giving the central bank greater freedom in setting its operating procedures. The design of the central bank's market operating procedures has a significant impact on banks' incentive to actively manage the risk of running short of reserve money: the greater the incentive, the more

2

banks will transact among themselves and the more liquid the market will become. On the other hand, a weak capacity for cash management by the government limits the extent to which the central bank can tighten incentives to actively manage the risk of running short of reserve money without causing excessive volatility in money market interest rates.

2.1   Introduction

Development of liquidity[29] in the interbank market—the market for short-term lending between banks—provides the basis for growth and increased liquidity in the broader money market, including the secondary market for Treasury bills and private sector money market instruments such as commercial paper and bankers' acceptances. An active, liquid money market greatly assists the development of a well-functioning market in government bonds and private sector bonds. A well-functioning money market supports the bond market by increasing the liquidity of bonds. It makes it easy for financial institutions to cover short-term liquidity needs, and makes it less risky and cheaper to warehouse bonds for on-sale to investors and to fund trading portfolios of bonds. Trading in forwards, swaps, and futures is also supported by a liquid money market, as the certainty of prompt cash settlement is essential for such transactions. The money market's constituent parts and links to other markets are summarized in Figure 2.1.

Development of the money market requires policies that provide incentives for banks to actively manage the risk of running short of excess reserve money (usually by removing disincentives to active management), shift central bank monetary policy implementation from direct to indirect measures, and equip the government with adequate capacity for cash management.

---

29. Liquidity as used in this chapter has two meanings. Market liquidity refers to the level of excess reserves, or liquid funds, available to banks. Transactional liquidity (see Section 2.2.1) refers to the ease of trading in the market.

Lack of a profit maximization motive on the part of banks and other financial institutions hinders money market development by dampening response to changes in the incentives to actively manage risk. State-owned banks are often directed to support the government's budget or policy requirements and do not respond to removal of disincentives to actively manage their liquidity risk,[30] which is particularly important to developing the interbank money market. Deregulating banking, privatizing or incorporating state-owned banks, and establishing effective prudential oversight are major policy initiatives that should precede, or move in step with, initiatives to develop the money market.

Direct methods of implementing monetary policy such as liquid asset requirements, interest rate controls, and directed credit hinder development of a money market. Deregulation and establishing a liquid money market create opportunities for innovation in the way banks manage their balance sheet. A central bank seeking to use indirect methods to implement monetary policy, such as open market operations, will require an effective interest rate transmission mechanism, which also calls for a liquid money market.

Closely related to improved liquidity management is the policy issue of coordinating government debt and cash management with monetary policy implementation. These official actions have a strong impact on bank reserve balances and influence the development of primary and secondary credit markets. In the long run, appropriate monetary policy and good debt and cash management will be complementary, although there may be coordination problems in the short term.

2.2   Developing the Interbank Market

The central bank's operating procedures greatly influence the stability of the money market, as well as banks' incentives to actively use the money market to manage risk. If the central bank's operating procedures are not calibrated to encourage both market stability and active risk management, the money market will be illiquid, volatile, or both. An important

---

30. Liquidity risk is used here to mean the risk of running short of reserves.

Figure 2.1. The Money Market and Links to Other Markets

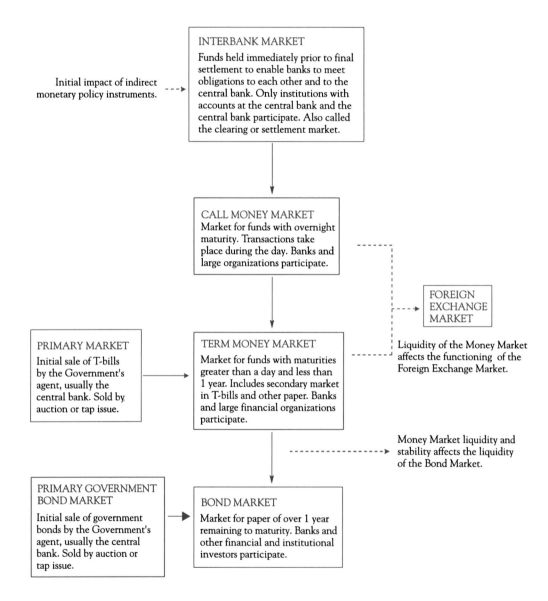

constraint faced by most central banks is the inability to conduct accurate liquidity management due to the poor quality of government cash management.

The trading volume of the money market depends on the incentives banks have to actively manage liquidity and interest rate risk. Central bank operating procedures that particularly influence banks' risk management incentives are the reserve maintenance period, the definition of liabilities on which reserves are levied, accommodation policy,[31] and the accuracy of operations designed to affect market liquidity—that is, the accuracy with which it can control the daily level of excess reserves. The less accurate the central bank's control of excess reserves, the more the central bank must adapt the reserve maintenance period and accommodation policy to compensate in order to avoid excessive volatility in the overnight rate.

Tension exists between the need to provide incentives for active trading and the desire to avoid excessive rate volatility. If the central bank adopts settings for its operating procedures that create incentives for banks to manage liquidity actively, it will increase the sensitivity of the overnight rate to the level of banks' reserve balances. It will also increase the likelihood of excessive volatility in the overnight rate in response to fluctuations in the level of bank reserves.

2.2.1 Creating Incentives that Stimulate Trading in the Money Market

The central bank will encourage more active bank risk management by shortening the reserve compliance period, excluding interbank transactions from the reserve requirements, adopting a costly accommodation policy, and maintaining the daily level of excess reserves very close to that desired by the banks. Excluding interbank transactions from the reserve measure ensures that money market transactions are an efficient way for banks to

---

31. Accommodation policy refers to the central bank's policy on supplying reserve money to the market and accepting deposits of reserve money at the initiative of market participants.

acquire the reserve money they need. The other central bank actions to encourage more active bank risk management increase banks' incentives to transact with each other on a daily basis to secure the reserves they want. (See Box 2.1. for a discussion of why banks are sensitive to the level of excess reserve money.)

Box 2.1. What Are Excess Reserves and Why Do They Matter to the Money Market?

As expressed in the equations below, total reserve money on the books of the central bank comprises required reserves, excess reserves, and currency in circulation. Required and excess reserves are in the form of deposits at the central bank (settlement cash). The quantity of total reserve money is determined by transactions that affect the central bank's net foreign assets, net domestic credit to government, net credit to banks and other financial institutions, and other items net.

$$\Delta RM = \Delta NFA + \Delta NDA$$

$$\Delta(RR + ER + CIC) = \Delta(NFA + NDCG + NCOB + NCOFI + OIN)$$

where: RM is reserve money, NFA is net foreign assets, NDA is net domestic assets, RR is required reserves, ER is excess reserves, CIC is currency in circulation, NDCG is net domestic credit to government, NCOB is net credit to banks, NCOFI is net credit to other financial institutions, and OIN is other items net.

Banks need reserve money to meet both their reserve requirements and their settlement needs. The quantity of excess reserves banks require depends on incentives and technical factors. The incentive is the penalty for failing to have sufficient reserve money to meet the reserve requirement or settlement obligations. The larger the penalty, the greater precautionary demand banks will have for excess reserve money. Banks' demand for excess reserve money will also be larger the less efficient is the payment system, banks' internal management of their liquidity, and the money market, and the more erratic the government's ability to manage its cash flows.

Typically, the central bank does not pay interest on banks' deposits with it, so banks will want to minimize their holdings of excess reserves. Unremunerated excess reserves are a cost to banks, which they must cover through higher loan spreads or other income.

The quantity of excess reserves is under control of the central bank, the monopoly supplier of settlement cash, i.e., funds in the form of balances in banks' accounts at the central bank. There are a number of autonomous transactions not initiated by the central bank that affect the quantity of excess reserves. The central bank must forecast these transactions if it is to accurately control the level of excess reserves. Once it has a forecast of the autonomous transactions, the central bank can initiate its own transactions to maintain excess reserve money at whatever level it desires by altering the supply of settlement cash.

If banks have adequate incentives to actively manage their liquidity, the quantity they will manage is the amount of excess reserves (settlement cash) they hold. The overnight rate will be sensitive to the supply of excess reserves as banks bid up the rate to cover shortages of excess reserves, or bid the rate down to dispose of surplus excess reserves.

2.2.1.1 Reserve Requirements and Incentives to Manage Liquidity

The structure of reserve requirements can make banks' demand for reserve money either inelastic or elastic. Inelastic demand occurs when banks are insensitive to interest rates. In such an environment, regardless of the cost of reserve money, banks will want a fixed quantity, and the overnight rate, depending on the supply of reserve money, will vary over a wide range. Conversely, if the banks' demand for reserve money is elastic, the overnight rate will be stable over a wide range of supply and demand conditions.[32]

Banks' demand for reserve money will be inelastic on any day when banks have to simultaneously meet their settlement and reserve requirement needs. In this case, there will be a fixed demand for reserve money and, given the supply of that money, the quantity of excess reserves will be determined exactly. If there is a shortage of reserve money (negative excess reserves), the banks will bid up the overnight rate in an effort to meet their needs. The limit on how far the banks will bid up that rate is determined by the cost of acquiring funds from the central bank (accommodation policy). If there is a surplus of reserve money (excess reserves), banks will seek to dispose of the excess, driving the overnight rate down. The limit on how far down the overnight rate is driven is determined by the return on excess reserves left on deposit at the central bank.

Having to meet both the settlement and reserve requirement needs for reserve money on a daily basis represents the maximum tightness for the design of reserve requirements, in the sense that it provides banks with the maximum incentive to actively manage their liquidity. Banks will also need to meet the settlement requirement needs on a daily basis when there are no reserve requirements or a zero requirement.

The length of the compliance period for required reserves has an important effect on bank liquidity management. If banks must meet their required reserve requirement every day, they have little flexibility.

Longer compliance periods for required reserves allow banks to average their reserve money needs over time. A surplus in reserve holdings over that required on one day can be used to meet a preceding or subsequent shortage. While the settlement need for reserve money must be met every day, the reserve requirement must only be met on average over the compliance period, as the banks have no need on any one day to acquire or dispose of a

---

32. For a detailed discussion, see Borio 1997.

given amount of excess reserves. They thus have less incentive to drive the overnight rate to either of the limits implied by the central bank's accommodation policy.

Under a reserve averaging system, banks will on some occasions need to simultaneously meet both the settlement and reserve requirement need for reserve money. This can happen toward the end of the reserve maintenance period, when the ability to make further reserve account changes gradually declines to zero and the exact amount required to achieve compliance becomes clear. At this point, banks seeking compliance may drive the overnight rate toward the bounds set by accommodation policy. The ability to arbitrage reserve balances is also reduced when reserve accounts are held separately from settlement accounts since funds in the reserve account cannot be used to meet settlement needs.

2.2.1.2 *Interbank Transactions in the Calculation of Reserve Requirements*

If interbank transactions are excluded in the liability base upon which the reserve requirement is calculated, the amount a bank borrows from another bank will result in a lower reserve requirement for the borrowing bank. Including interbank transactions in the reserve calculation can lead to perverse results. This is illustrated by the case of India in 1995, where money market activity came to a halt every second Friday (reserve calculation day), when banks tried to reduce their reserve requirement by eliminating interbank borrowing. As there was little or no demand for interbank funds on the second Friday, the overnight rate fell to 0 percent. (See Figure 2.2) The collapse of money market liquidity and the overnight rate every second Friday inhibited the development of a liquid money market yield curve beyond 13 days.

2.2.1.3 *Accommodation Policy and Incentives to Manage Risk*

Whereas the central bank's liquidity management policy covers the way the central bank supplies or withdraws reserve money at its own initiative, the central bank's accommodation policy covers its supplying reserve money to the market and accepting deposits of reserve money at the initiative of market participants.

If accommodation policy makes it easy and cheap for banks to obtain funds from the central bank, or if the central bank remunerates over-

Figure 2.2. Daily Average Call Rate in India—July-September 1995

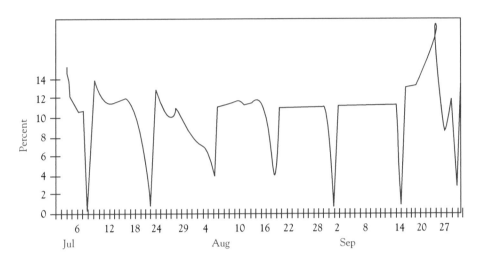

2

generously excess reserves deposited with it, banks will find it more convenient to transact with the central bank. Consequently, banks will transact less with each other and will not invest in the staff and information systems required to actively manage their liquidity. A money market will not readily develop under these conditions.

The central bank can use accommodation policy to encourage the development of a money market by making banks' use of central bank lending and deposit facilities expensive and limited. The more expensive and difficult the central bank makes use of its accommodation facilities, the higher the overnight rate can be driven when there is a shortage of excess reserves. The lower the rate the central bank pays on excess reserves deposited with it, the lower the overnight rate can drop when there is a surplus of excess reserves. The central bank's accommodation policy thus can establish a ceiling and floor on the interbank rate if it meets all bank liquidity needs.

2.2.1.4 Market Liquidity Management and Incentives to Manage Risk

Market liquidity management refers to actions the central bank takes to manage the overall level of reserve money and, through this, to regulate general conditions in the money market. Much of this management is focused on offsetting the impact on excess reserves of transactions between accounts held at the central bank and accounts held at commercial banks in order to avoid volatility in excess reserves causing unnecessary volatility in short-term interest rates. Managing the level of excess reserve money promotes trading volume in the money market and enhances the clarity of monetary policy signals by preventing unnecessary interest rate volatility. The tools for this management are similar whether the central bank has an interest rate or a quantitative target.

Successful market liquidity management requires that the daily level of excess reserves in the banking system be close to the level demanded by banks as a group. Not every bank will have the same reserve position. Some banks will have excess reserves, while others will have reserve deficiencies, creating an incentive for banks to borrow from or lend to one another. The key to successful liquidity management by the authorities is that they understand the banks' demand for excess reserves and are able to anticipate changes in this demand. For this, authorities need to forecast with reasonable accuracy the autonomous transactions affecting excess reserves that the central bank may need to offset through open market operations. (See Box 2.2.) Of these autonomous transactions, government receipts and payments are often the most unpredictable. The central bank must also have the tools for flexible and prompt intervention.

Poor liquidity management is often the major factor that prevents a central bank from maximizing the incentives for commercial banks to actively manage their liquidity risk. It is thus often the major barrier to developing market liquidity and achieving moderate volatility in interest rates in the money market. Poor liquidity management can result from both poor knowledge of banks' demand for excess reserves and from poor ability to forecast the autonomous transactions that affect excess reserves.

If the central bank systematically over- or under-estimates banks' aggregate demand for excess reserves, the amount of excess reserves it leaves in the banking system will be biased toward either surplus or shortage, resulting in either volatility in interest rates or an undesired trend in rates. Both these cases inhibit the development of transactional liquidity in the money market by creating one-way markets in which all participants are on either the bid or offer side. A sizeable surplus removes any incentive to transact, as there is no need to manage liquidity to meet reserve and settlement

Box 2.2. Managing the Level of Excess Reserves: Importance of Government Cash Management

Good government cash management is critical for good liquidity management, important for debt management, and necessary for effective collaboration between the sovereign debt manager and the central bank. Good cash management is the most important contribution that the debt manager can make to developing the money market.

Controlling the level of excess reserves is an important part of avoiding excessive volatility in money market interest rates, irrespective of whether the central bank has an interest rate or quantitative target. A shortage of excess reserves will cause banks to compete to acquire more, driving the overnight rate up. A surplus will cause banks to try to sell their surplus, driving the overnight rate down. The figure in the box shows the daily smoothing of excess reserves by the Reserve Bank of New Zealand in 1990. The RBNZ's operations (daily open market operations, weekly bill auctions, etc.) are based on sufficiently accurate information that they offset the autonomous flows (dotted line) almost exactly each day. This results in very stable levels of excess reserves (solid line).

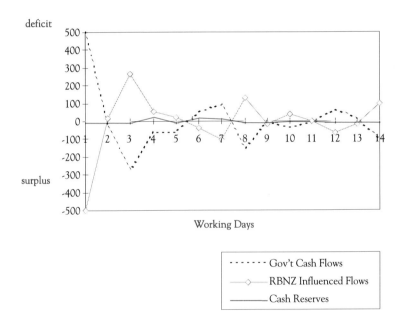

Notes: "Deficit" and "surplus" refer to government deficit or surplus on a given day. When there is a deficit on a day, the government is having a net expenditure and the government cash flows line (dotted) is above zero. In consequence, the RBNZ has to withdraw funds to offset the government actions and RBNZ's influenced flows (diamond line) is below zero. When there is a "surplus," the government is receiving net revenue and the dotted line is below zero.

Continued

2

Box 2.2. (Continued) Managing the Level of Excess Reserves: Importance of Government Cash Management

Examples of transactions that affect the quantity of excess reserves, and the initiating party, are:

- Government:
  - Revenue deposited to, and expenditure from, accounts at the central bank.
  - Maturing debt.

- Banks:
  - Purchase and return of notes and coin.
  - Use of central bank on-demand accommodation facilities.

- Central bank:
  - Open market operations.
  - Foreign exchange transactions with banks.

  - Change in reserve requirements.

Often the central bank's major problem in accurately managing the level of excess reserves is a poor ability to forecast the autonomous transactions affecting excess reserves, particularly government revenue and expenditure. Without good forecasts of the autonomous factors, the central bank's market operations (e.g., Treasury bill sales, repurchase operations) will not maintain excess reserves in the target area. The central bank's poor forecasting is, in turn, usually the result of poor government cash management; i.e., the central bank is unable to obtain good information on future government revenue and expenditure from the Ministry of Finance.

---

needs, while a sizeable shortage removes the ability to transact, as no one is willing to trade.[33]

Lacking adequate tools with which to manage the level of excess reserves can cause similar problems to those caused by poor forecasting. Central banks typically have a range of methods available to supply and withdraw funds from the market. These methods include sales of government securities and foreign exchange, repurchase and reverse repurchase transactions (repos), and accommodation windows. When central banks do not have means available to them, market volatility results. Figure 2.3 shows, in the case of Zambia in 1998, the undesirable patterns of reserve

---

33. The relationship between the size of the surplus and shortage of excess reserves and conditions for a two-way market (surpluses and shortages of excess reserves are reasonably evenly spread between participants) may be seen in the case of Malawi in 2000. On the 65 percent of occasions when the opportunities for trading were minimal, the average *absolute* level of excess reserves was 450 million kwacha. This contrasts with the average *absolute* excess reserve level of 48 million kwacha on the 15 percent of occasions when conditions for two-way trading were met, and the 150 million kwacha of average *absolute* excess reserves on those occasions when trading was possible but some participants would be left significantly long or short.

Figure 2.3. Settlement Cash and the Overnight Rate: Zambia 1998

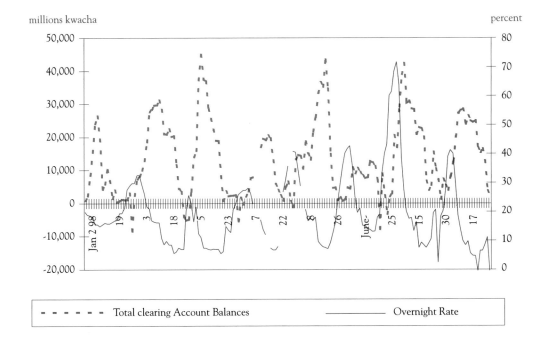

accounts and overnight rates that can result when reserve accounts fluctuate. Such patterns suggest the absence of central bank repurchase operations (see below) to manage the level of liquidity within the month. This
led to a repeating pattern of surplus excess reserves in the middle of the
month due to net government expenditure (all on the offer side) and shortages at month-end due to net government revenue (all on the bid side).

2.2.2 Avoiding Excessive Volatility in Excess Reserves and Money Market Rates

Creating the incentives for banks to actively use the money market to manage their liquidity risk should be combined with steps to avoid excessive
interest rate volatility. Excessive interest rate volatility reduces the volume
of trading in the market, adds an uncertainty premium to interest rates,
inhibits the development of a money market yield curve, and diminishes
the transparency of monetary policy signals.

The money market yield curve out to 90 days or so typically slopes upward, even though at times expectations may invert the yield curve, bending the longer-term bond market segment down. The overnight rate is determined by the central bank's policy objectives and operating procedures. Longer money market rates are sensitive to current and expected liquidity conditions, monetary policy expectations, and the degree of risk perceived in extending the term of funding.

In developing-country markets, the illiquidity or volatility of the money market may be severe enough to limit the ability of investors to undertake maturity transformation along the yield curve. If the market for overnight funds is liquid and the overnight rate is relatively stable, a bank may feel it is worth the risk to take on a funding mismatch by borrowing overnight, adding a margin, and lending for 14 days. The lower the risk of term extension and the more competition, the lower the margin will be. If the 14-day market is liquid and stable, the bank may fund at 14 days and lend at 30 days, and so on. In this way, liquidity is established across the yield curve. (See Figure 2.4.) Banks will only accept the maturity mismatch required to create a liquid yield curve if the availability of funds (liquidity) and the variability of interest rates (interest rate risk) is manageable at each maturity. Lack of liquidity, erratic liquidity, and excessive interest rate volatility will make the risk of undertaking the mismatch too high, and development of the yield curve will be inhibited.

2.2.3 Central Bank Interaction with Market and Interest Rate Volatility

The ability to manage the quantity of reserve money accurately will give the central bank freedom to provide incentives to market liquidity and to restrain volatility of interest rates. Unfortunately, the single greatest problem most central banks face is poor ability to manage the quantity of excess reserves. They are not able to forecast well the autonomous transactions that affect the level of excess reserves, often because of poor government cash management. (See Box 2.2. and Box 2.3.)

In the absence of accurate liquidity management, the central bank needs to adopt offsetting operating tactics. The central bank's choice of settings for the target level of excess reserves, the reserve compliance period, and accommodation policy will be constrained by the need to compensate for the possible effects of poor liquidity management on market volatility.

Box 2.3. Why Do Differences Occur Between the Treasury's Funding Needs and the Central Bank's Liquidity Management Needs?

The transactions that affect the level of excess reserves are grouped below to illustrate the reasons for divergences between the public sector borrowing requirement, which are the concern of the Treasury, and fluctuations in the level of excess reserves, which are the concern of the central bank. In the list below, (+) indicates that the transaction increases excess reserves and (–) indicates a decrease.

Government transactions

a. Revenue (–)
b. Expenditure (+)
c. Debt maturing and interest paid (+)
d. Debt sold (–)

Central bank transactions

e. Purchase of foreign exchange in the market (+)
f. Sale of foreign exchange to the market (–)
g. Purchase of note and coin from banks (+)
h. Sale of note and coin to banks (–)
i. Decrease in reserve requirements (+)
j. Increase in reserve requirements (–)
k. Open market operations (+) or (–)
l. Maturity of open market operations (+) or (–)
m. Banks obtaining funds from accommodation facility (+)

The Treasury is concerned with transactions (a) through (d). The central bank is concerned with transactions (e) through (m).

In practice, the major differences between the Treasury's demand for funding and the central bank's desire to manage liquidity have two sources: (i) central bank foreign exchange transactions and (ii) note and coin transactions. Foreign exchange transactions are usually a problem when the government is funding domestic expenditure through foreign borrowing or grants and, at the same time, the central bank needs to build up foreign exchange reserves. The domestic expenditure's impact on excess reserves needs to be sterilized, and this can be achieved either by selling the foreign exchange received from the foreign borrowing or by selling domestic debt. The ministry does not want to sell debt, as it has already financed the expenditure offshore. The central bank does not want to sell the foreign exchange, as it wants to build up foreign exchange reserves. The problem is lack of coordination between debt management and reserves management.

Banks' purchases of bank notes can be very seasonal, especially in developing countries with seasonal agricultural production of major commodities. The seasonal impact of banks buying bank notes to meet client demand during the harvest and returning bank notes as the harvest passes will cause the central bank to want to sell, respectively, less and more debt than the government.

One tactical remedy is open market operations after final clearing has occurred, when the exact quantity of excess reserves is known. This tactic permits only daily control. However, greater market stability would result if the central bank were to use flow forecasts to select maturities for repurchase operations that smooth the profile of excess reserves some distance into the future.

Another procedure for managing liquidity is to adapt the target level of excess reserves to allow for forecasting errors. The target can be set a suitable margin away from the aggregate demand for excess reserves to reduce

Figure 2.4. Short-Term Yield Curve Development

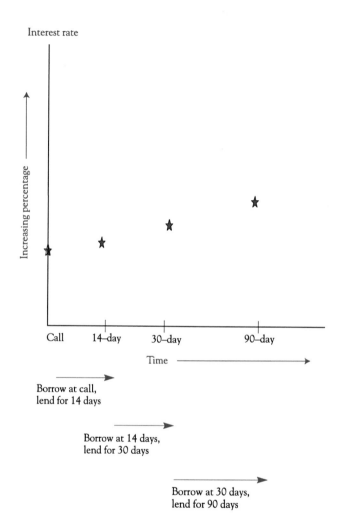

the frequency of large shortages or surpluses caused by poor forecasting. This procedure will, of course, induce less interbank activity.

The central bank can also moderate interest rate volatility through the design of its accommodation policy. An accommodation window with a preannounced secured lending rate and no limits on its use places a ceiling on the overnight rate. Similarly, paying interest on deposits left with the

2

central bank places a floor on the overnight rate. The narrower the differential between the rate on advances and the rate on deposits, the smaller the range within which the overnight rate will fluctuate. The advantage that this arrangement has for the central bank is that the overnight rate will clearly reflect its policy stance. The disadvantage of a narrow differential is a greater likelihood that banks will transact with the central bank rather than with each other. This will be a problem especially in less-developed markets, where banks are less sensitive to the marginal cost of funds. In a less-developed market, where banks may not have strong treasury systems, the differential may have to be several hundred basis points or more before banks will be drawn into trading with other banks.

In developing markets, a two-tier accommodation window can create appropriate disincentives for borrowing from the central bank by limiting the amount or frequency of such borrowing, while reducing interest rate volatility caused by central bank liquidity management errors. In this case, borrowing up to the limit occurs at the standard rate, which typically has a role in signaling monetary policy. Borrowing in excess of the limit occurs at the second-tier rate, a penalty rate, which is set at a large enough margin above the standard rate to encourage banks to use the money market. In this way, the first tier accommodates the central bank's liquidity management errors without causing unnecessary interest rate volatility and provides an incentive for the more efficient banks to trade with each other. The second tier encourages such interbank trading without imposing this cost on the entire system each time the central bank makes a liquidity management error.

Accommodation policy is sometimes structured as a discount window. Banks can discount short-dated government instruments with the central bank or borrow from the central bank by pledging government securities as collateral, either at a predetermined rate or at a margin above the current market rate. A discount window facility that charges at a margin linked to the current market rate does not provide a stabilizing mechanism in the event of a spike in interest rates.

Paying interest on deposits by banks at the central bank may be difficult for some central banks that do not have the resources to meet the cost of interest payments, and where the Ministry of Finance is reluctant to budget for such payments. If these difficulties result in a zero or very low deposit rate, the central bank will not be able to set the spread between its deposit and lending rates to control volatility.

2

Accuracy in managing the level of excess reserves is more precisely described as accuracy relative to the reserve compliance period. As noted above (Section 2.2.1.1), a daily reserve compliance period (or no reserve requirement) requires daily accuracy in managing the level of excess reserves to avoid unnecessary volatility. A monthly reserve compliance period requires a lower degree of accuracy in liquidity management, as the averaging provision means that the quantity of excess reserves is not determined until late in the compliance period. This makes bank demand for reserve money flexible over much of the period.

2.2.4 Resources for Central Bank Open Market Operations

If the central bank has a sufficient portfolio of outstanding government securities to absorb liquidity, it can sell these outright to the market or use them in reverse repurchase agreements to the same end. Such open market operations may be done by the central bank as needed.

The repurchase agreement, whereby the central bank lends securities against cash, or the reverse repurchase agreement, whereby the central bank borrows securities against cash, has become the main instrument for market operations in many countries. In such agreements, government (and sometimes other) securities of any maturity can serve as collateral. The rate on these agreements is independent of the rate on the underlying collateral, and can be aimed at or close to prevailing secured interbank lending rates. The central bank can thus stabilize the interbank rate, while leaving room for change for rates on Treasury bills and other government securities.

The choice of reserve management methods to absorb excess reserves, however, will have little effect on liquidity if the central bank has insufficient access to securities needed for market intervention. If the central bank does not itself have sufficient resources, it may employ add-ons to Treasury bill auctions, issue its own bills, or accept deposits from banks for intervention purposes.

In many emerging countries, where a range of market intervention instruments has not yet been developed, add-ons to the Treasury bill auction are the main instrument for liquidity management. The central bank adds, for monetary policy implementation purposes, Treasury bills additional to those tendered to meet the government's cash needs. Issues surrounding the use of add-ons include market development, budget costs and sterilization of proceeds, and coordination between the government and the central bank.

Where government securities are already in circulation and financial markets are thin, using the same instrument by both the Treasury and the central bank avoids market fragmentation and supports the role of government securities as a tool for general market development. At the same time, add-ons may confuse the market, since participants may not be made aware of what portion of the tender will be used for implementing monetary policy and what portion for financing the government. Transparency to the market can, however, be achieved by announcing the amount of central bank add-ons.

Monetary tightening through add-ons raises budget costs, since add-ons increase the amount of government debt on which the Treasury must pay interest, and the resulting market tightening may drive up interest rates for government securities.[34] Furthermore, the proceeds from central bank auction add-ons should not be available to the Treasury, but rather held in sterilized accounts, if liquidity is to be taken from the market. The cost to the government would also be higher, but less transparent, if the central bank conducted its own intervention and passed the cost on to the Treasury at the end of the year through lower profits or a loss the Treasury must cover.

Central bank/Treasury coordination of add-ons has proved to be a problem in some countries. In Mauritius, where large capital inflows forced the authorities to conduct massive absorption operations, the Treasury in 1991 discontinued its support for the use of government securities in monetary operations. In the Philippines in the early 1980s, an arrangement between the Treasury and the central bank initially permitted add-ons and froze the proceeds, but the Treasury later resisted allowing the full amount of add-ons desired by the central bank and insisted on modifying the arrangement to freeze the proceeds. The central bank then resorted to issuing its own securities to supplement the add-ons permitted by the Treasury. In 1987, the Treasury allowed for the possibility of overfunding the fiscal deficit for monetary reasons and to placing the proceeds in fixed-term deposits with the central bank.[35]

---

34. The effect on interest rates will be greater the more closed and the less integrated with global markets the economy is.

35. See Quintyn 1994.

2

Alternatives to add-ons that are more under central bank control are central bank bills which are issued like add-ons as a market intervention instrument, or deposits by banks at the central bank. These obligations can substitute for Treasury bills where there is not yet a working Treasury bill auction. They also can be useful in post-chaos situations where the central bank is the only official institution with credibility. In addition, they can be a convenience in regional monetary arrangements where the multinational central bank finds it more appropriate to sell its own securities rather than those of individual national governments.[36] Where central bank issues are under its control, they can be used flexibly, and market participants can distinguish monetary policy operations from Treasury operations. By changing the amounts auctioned, a central bank can alter the funds available to the market as needed for monetary purposes, without being confined to auction schedules for government securities. Central bank-issued securities have proved to be a useful early step for central banks that are developing instruments for market intervention.

Central bank–issued securities can be traded in the market, and thus can help facilitate development of a secondary market in countries without a Treasury bill market. However, central bank–issued securities have disadvantages. Where there is a Treasury bill market, central bank–issued bills may fragment demand, especially if Treasury bills and central bank bills carry similar maturities. Central bank–issued bills may be preferred because they are a transparent instrument, with their use clear to market participants. To avoid immediate competition with Treasury bills, some central banks have auctioned interest-bearing deposits instead of central bank–issued securities. Such deposits can serve the same purposes as central bank–issued securities, but are not (unless issued as certificates of deposit) marketable instruments that may be used in secondary market trading. (Interest-bearing deposits by banks at the central bank may also be used as part of accommodation policy.) The issuance of either central bank securities or deposits requires coordination between the Treasury and the central bank about timing, amounts, and, possibly, payment of interest that can prove to be difficult. A disadvantage of both central bank–issued securities and interest-bearing deposits is that they may impose a financing burden on the central bank. A further limitation of both central bank–issued securities

---

36. See Quintyn 1997.

and central bank deposits is that they are normally limited in size because of the financing burden they place on the central bank and in order to keep Treasury securities as the centerpiece of official offerings.

Experience with central bank–issued securities has been varied. Some central banks find them useful, while others, after an initial experience, have ceased issuing or reduced reliance on them. Brazil found central bank–issued securities useful in absorbing liquidity in the stabilization programs that began in the mid-1990s. By 1998, nearly one-third of securities in the market were liabilities of the Central Bank of Brazil.[37] The Central Bank of Brazil auctions central bank–issued securities weekly, while national Treasury securities are auctioned monthly.[38] The Bank of Korea, which previously relied on central bank–issued securities for its open market operations, since 1999 has been using repurchase type agreements.[39] The Bank of Mauritius, which has been issuing five-year Bank of Mauritius bonds, in late 1999 shifted its monetary control operations to emphasize repurchase-type agreements.[40] The Central Bank of Chile's monetary policy implementation relies essentially on regular auctions of its own promissory notes.[41]

Once financial markets have reached a certain size and degree of liquidity, problems associated with central bank–issued securities become less significant. The central banks of Denmark and Sweden conduct transactions in central bank securities to influence market liquidity and often conduct repos on the basis of these securities. The Reserve Bank of New Zealand (RBNZ) employs a combination of primary issues of central bank securities, outright transactions in government and central bank securities, and repos on the basis of both securities. The RBNZ clearly separates its own securities from those of the government and defines their uses. Thus, there is no confusion in the market. The New Zealand government issues special securities for the central bank's monetary purposes and pays the cost of both government and central bank securities used for open market operations.

---

37. See Banco Central do Brasil 2000a.

38. See Banco Central do Brasil 2000b.

39. See Bank of Korea 1999.

40. See Bank of Mauritius 2000.

41. See Central Bank of Chile 2000.

2

There are two additional ways a central bank can obtain resources if it has an insufficient stock of government securities for use in open market operations. First, existing central bank loans to the government can be converted to government securities, preferably Treasury bills, which would be most useful for outright operations. As the existing loans may carry below-market rates and the Treasury bills would carry higher market rates, the government may, however, be unwilling to do this. Similarly, the central bank can convert holdings of low-yielding, long-term government securities to Treasury bills. The government may have a similar objection to this approach and require that the long-term securities first be marked to market. This might so reduce their value that the resulting Treasury bills would be insufficient for central bank purposes.

Another way for the central bank to obtain a sufficient stock of government securities would be to recapitalize the central bank, a step which may encounter political resistance. This was effected in the Philippines with the passage of the Central Bank Act of 1993. It was also carried out in Uganda in 1999.

The problem of obtaining sufficient central bank resources for open market operations pertains to operations absorbing market liquidity. Open market operations supplying liquidity to the market rely on the central bank's ability to create money by crediting accounts held with it and do not require central bank resources in the form of short-term securities.

2.2.5 Infrastructure and Capacity

Three issues that particularly affect the development of money markets in developing countries are lack of treasury capacity in banks, lack of multilateral trading, and weak banks.

The money market will not develop if banks have inadequate incentives to develop treasury capacity, which is the ability to actively manage liquidity and interest rate risk. (See Box 2.2.) Accommodation policy, as discussed above, determines these incentives.

In less-developed markets, price discovery occurs between pairs of banks at discrete time intervals, and knowledge of these transactions is not available to the market. There is thus a lack of multilateral trading where price discovery is between all institutions in the market. This results in large differences in pricing within the market over relatively short intervals and reduces the information content of market price signals. It is not possible to know, without discussion with the parties to the transaction, whether a higher rate represents an assessment of credit risk, liquidity pressure, or merely ill-informed transacting. Where trading information is more readily available, prices can embed all information available in the market and pricing is more multilaterally unified. The central bank can assist the development of better trading systems by encouraging the formation of a trading mechanism and of standard market trading practices. (See Chapter 7, Developing Secondary Market Structures for Government Securities.)

Weak banks cause segmentation in the interbank market, which leads to volatility in the overnight rate and a lack of unified pricing. Given the lack of widely available price information, this can cause confusion as to the cause of interest rate differentials. Interbank transactions are typically based on unsecured lines of credit up to a limit, beyond which security is required. In situations where there are weak banks and reported information is not readily available or not trusted because of weak accounting conventions, security will be required. The requirement for security on all transactions constrains the flow of funds to meet settlement needs. It shrinks the effective size of the market, as often one or more banks will run out of eligible securities to offer.

When securities are in short supply, the banks needing cash will bid up the rate they are willing to pay. This can result in an interest rate spike or in a continuing two-tier market with weaker banks paying a higher rate than stronger banks. Interest rate spikes and lack of price unity are particularly troublesome in a market that is not transparent, so that the cause of the spikes and rate differentials is not clear to all market participants.

A central bank penalty-lending rate puts pressure on banks to turn to the market for their liquidity needs. As the penalty rate is based in part on market rates, the presence of weak banks with poor treasury management will greatly increase the effective penalty cost. This will add to market volatility and cause some confusion among the stronger banks, which may not see a consistent relationship between their own cost of funds and the cost of funds at the central bank. The problems caused by weak banks are solved only by their recapitalization, sale, merger, or closure.

2.3 Coordination Between Government Debt/Cash Management and Central Bank Open Market Operations

2

Government debt/cash management and central bank open market operations interface with market participants. Cash management is the short-term aspect of debt management and is sometimes placed in an organization separate from, but reporting to, the debt manager. Coordination is required to avoid conflicts between debt/cash management and open market operations.

The timing and amounts of government securities issuance will not always coincide with the needs of the central bank's open market policy. The government may need to issue securities when the market is already short of liquidity. The central bank must then choose whether or to what extent it will provide additional liquidity to the market to meet the government's needs. At a minimum, coordination requires that the issuer inform the central bank of its intentions in advance of taking action. At a maximum, the issuer may be able to adjust the timing and amount of borrowing to better conform to market conditions. Coordination may be simplified if the central bank acts both as agent for the government in securities issuance and in its own capacity for open market operations. In this case, the respective roles of the central bank and the issuer need to be made clear if the central bank is to retain sufficient independence for monetary policy and the market is not to be confused. Other organizational forms separating the issuance function from the central bank will more easily clarify the organizational roles but may require more explicit mechanisms for coordination. (See Chapter 3, A Government Debt Issuance Strategy and Debt Management Framework, for discussion of issues related to coordination in issuance of government securities.) Whatever the organizational form, there will be a need for accurate forecasting of government operations, and for coordination between the issuer and the central bank.

The choice of primary market participants can also cause coordination problems. (See Chapter 5, Developing a Primary Market for Government Securities, and Chapter 8, Developing a Government Securities Settlement Structure.) With regard to the choice of market participants, the optimum choice is probably wide participation. In contrast, the optimum choice for open market policy operations, as detailed above, may be limited to banks.

A single set of primary market participants would be preferable, but in some emerging-market countries this must wait development of automated accounts and communication to permit delivery versus payment for securities transactions and prompt final settlement of both cash and securities transactions. As the purposes of government financing transactions and central bank open market operations differ, different groups of participants in these two operations need not be confusing as long as their distinct purposes are made clear.

Government debt and cash management can coordinate with monetary policy by moderating the effect of government expenditures and receipts on the banks' cash balances and by keeping the central bank informed of government cash flows. (See Box 2.4.) The only way to achieve accurate forecasting is to develop day-by-day forecasts for revenues and expenditures for items being received or paid by the government. The transactions that need to be forecast as part of improved coordination with monetary policy are those that cause a shift of funds between an account at the central bank and an account at a commercial bank, since those are the only ones that affect the government's net position at the central bank. However, full cash forecasting can be important for the government's own purpose, as good cash management can result in cost savings for the government through lower transaction balances and fewer mistakes in payments. Achieving an understanding of the importance of this project in each responsible government department is a major challenge, which requires good communication among government departments and between the finance ministry and the central bank.

A government debt/cash manager might not only forecast government payments and receipts, but also conduct cash management operations that would tend to neutralize the effect of these receipts and payments on banking reserves. In doing so, the cash manager would remove an important task of the open market manager at the central bank, though the open market manager would still have the task of offsetting other autonomous transactions. (See Box 2.3.) While good government cash/debt management lessens the task of the open market manager and the coordination problem, complications might arise in execution because the government's cash manager might also be conducting simultaneous operations with the same market participants and with comparable instruments. Careful coordination would thus be required, which might limit the central bank's use of its own bills because the maturities of issues by both managers might conflict. The

---

Box 2.4. Elements of Sovereign Cash Management

Quality cash management requires accurate forecasting of the cash flows between the government sector and the banking system, to ensure that there is neither an undue surplus nor a squeeze in excess reserves. It is important that key banks, money market dealers, and investors have a high level of confidence in how the Treasury, debt office, and central bank manage this aspect of the financial system. The only way to achieve accurate forecasting is to develop a day-by-day worksheet or spreadsheet that shows revenues and expenditures for all items being received or paid by the government. This spreadsheet must contain all sources of tax receipts and other receipts such as dividends, government borrowing, and international aid flows. It must also contain all expenditures by each government department, which is best achieved by ensuring that each department is responsible for monitoring its own expenditures. Each day's gross expenditure needs to be known across departments. Because actual cash flows will differ from the initial forecast, a process of review and updating is a basic requirement for improving the quality of the forecasts.

The spreadsheet should be extended out at least 3 months, and preferably be a 12-month rolling forecast, to allow the earliest possible identification of the days with unusually large cash flows. These are most likely to be the result of tax payments, debt repayments, proceeds from new borrowing, and pay days.

The staff who prepare the forecasts must be able to obtain reliable information from all government departments. This means that the job of knowing the expenditure of each department must also be reliably known by each department's chief accountant or chief finance officer. Achieving an understanding of the importance of this project in each department is a major challenge and a key requirement for success. Individual departments need to be brought into the process, be informed of the project's objective, and motivated to provide high- quality forecasts. Forecasting also requires good communication among government departments and between the finance ministry and the central bank.

The Treasury or debt office staff who coordinate all the individual forecasts must update them daily as the departments revise their own forecasts. The staff must also have good lines of communication with the key individuals in each department and be able to contact them directly to follow up on late or incomplete forecasts or other items of doubt. Attention to detail and strict time-reporting deadlines are also important for accuracy and success.

Source: Maloney 2000

---

cash manager might also shift balances between government accounts at the central bank and accounts held at banks. Therefore, care must be taken to ensure that banks do not become overly dependent on government deposits and that moral hazard is not created—a problem that can be avoided with the help of prudential oversight. Coordination would be further complicated by a need, as markets and official intervention become more sophisticated, to distance the government cash manager from inside information about monetary policy available to the open market operations manager. Another possible complication is the practice, still existing in many countries, of allowing government overdrafts from its accounts at the central bank. Such overdrafts create new money which, if spent by the government, adds to reserve balances and the probable need for offset by open market operations.

2.4   Conclusion

Money markets are essential for conducting indirect, market-based monetary policy operations and for providing the liquidity necessary for a market in government bonds and in private sector securities. The way market policy is implemented will largely determine the incentives that market participants have to buy and sell securities. A proper accommodation policy by the central bank will set the reserves held by banks with the central bank at a level sufficient to allow trading, but not so high that there is no need for banks to alter their holdings by borrowing or lending or by buying and selling securities. By careful management, the central bank can carry out its monetary objectives and encourage money market transactions without fostering excessive interest rate volatility.

A vital element in conducting effective monetary policy is knowledge of government cash flows, which, like central bank open market operations, also affect banks' reserve balances. Government debt and cash management can coordinate with monetary policy by moderating the effect of government expenditures and receipts on the banks' cash balances and by keeping the central bank informed of government cash flows. Money markets will not operate effectively if they are constrained by direct government controls over deposits, interest rates, and lending.

Bibliography

Baliño, J. T. Tomàs, and Lorena M. Zamalloa, eds. 1997. *Instruments of Monetary Management: Issues and Country Experiences*. International Monetary Fund, Washington, D.C.

Banco Central do Brasil. 2000a. *Annual Report 1998*. Brasilia, Brazil. Available at www.bcb.gov.br/ingles/banual98/banual.shtm.

———. 2000b. *Central Bank of Brazil: Structure and Functions*. Brasilia, Brazil. Available at www.bcb.gov.br/ingles/html1900.shtm.

Bank of Korea. 1999. *Annual Report 1999*. Seoul, Republic of Korea. Available at www.bok.or.kr/index_e.html.

Bank of Mauritius. 2000. *Monetary Bulletin*. December 1999, Port Louis, Mauritius. Available at www.bom.intnet.mu/publicat.htm#monthly.

Borio, Claudio E. V. 1997. "Monetary Policy Operating Procedures in Industrial Countries." In *Implementation and Tactics of Monetary Policy*. Conference Papers, No. 3, Bank for International Settlements, Basel, Switzerland. Available at www.bis.org/publ/work40.htm.

Central Bank of Chile. 2000. *Monetary Policy of the Central Bank of Chile: Objectives and Transmission*. Santiago, Chile. Available at www.bcentral.cl/publicaciones/politicamonetaria_obje/monetary.

European Central Bank. 2000. *Treasury Activities Affecting Liquidity in the Euro Area*. Frankfurt, Germany. Available at http://www.ecb.int/head.htm.

Hanke, Steve H. 2000. "Indonesia's Central Bank Goes Bust." *Wall Street Journal*, February 16, 2000.

Hellmann, Thomas F., Kevin C. Murdock, and Joseph E. Stiglitz. 2000. "Liberalization, Moral Hazard in Banking, and Prudential Regulation: Are Capital Requirements Enough?" *American Economic Review* 90 (1): 147–65.

Her Majesty's Treasury. 1999. *Debt Management Report for 1999–2000*. London, U.K. Available at http://hm-treasury.gov.uk/pub/htm/docs/dmr9900.pdf.

Maloney, Paddy. 2000. "The Value of Cash Management: Its Relevance to Debt Management." In *Proceedings of the Regional Debt and Liquidity Management Workshop, Centurion, South Africa*. World Bank, Washington, D.C.

Quintyn, Marc. 1994. "Government Versus Central Bank Securities in Developing Open Market Operations." In J. T. Tomás Baliño and Carlo

Cottarelli, eds., *Frameworks for Monetary Stability: Policy Issues and Country Experiences.* International Monetary Fund, Washington, D.C.

———. 1997. "Government Versus Central Bank Securities." In V. Sundararajan, Peter Dattels, and Hans J. Blommestein, eds., *Coordinating Public Debt and Monetary Management.* International Monetary Fund, Washington, D.C.

Schaechter, Andrea. 2000. "Liquidity Forecasting." MAE Operational Paper 00/7. November. International Monetary Fund, Washington, D.C.

Schaechter, Andrea, Mark Stone, and Mark Zelmer. 2000. "Inflation Targeting: Experience Yields Practical Suggestions for Emerging Market Countries." *IMF Survey* 29 (20): 348–49.

Sundararajan, V., Peter Dattels, and Hans J. Blommestein, eds. 1997. *Coordinating Public Debt and Monetary Management.* International Monetary Fund, Washington, D.C.

Wilton, David. 2000. "Reducing the Cost of Government Finance in a Deregulated Market." In *Proceedings of the Regional Debt and Liquidity Management Workshop, Centurion, South Africa.* World Bank, Washington, D.C.

2

3

A Government Debt Issuance Strategy and Debt Management Framework

To be a successful issuer of government securities, the government must earn the confidence of financial market participants. In addition to pursuing sound and sustainable fiscal and monetary policies and establishing an appropriate legal and regulatory infrastructure, the government needs a credible government bond issuing strategy, based on a strong commitment to market financing and a well-structured management framework. The strategy must provide a clear mapping of the portfolio structure and the instruments to obtain that structure. It must also devise procedures for marketing government securities issues and managing the government's cash position in ways that establish efficient distribution channels and encourage the development of secondary markets.

3.1 Introduction

Increased reliance by governments on market sources for finance and the greater exposure to financial risks resulting from financial liberalization and larger international capital flows have created new opportunities and challenges for government debt management. This new financing environment can provide governments with a large and more diversified investor base, which can reduce its refinancing risk and lead to lower debt-service cost over time. In order to attract new investors and manage the risks associated with new market-based financial instruments, many governments have improved the quality of their macroeconomics and regulatory policies, as well as their debt management policies and operations.

This chapter discusses some of the key measures that the government as an issuer, and in particular as a debt manager, can consider in order to support the development of the government bond market. The focus is on the more strategic considerations, such as the market orientation of the funding strategy and the need for a sound debt management framework, rather than on more technical issues, such as developing a primary market and building the yield curve. These technical issues are addressed in subsequent chapters. This chapter draws heavily on the *Guidelines for Public Debt Management*, which was produced by the IMF and the World Bank, working in cooperation with national debt management experts.[42]

3.2   Market-Oriented Funding Strategy

A market-oriented government funding strategy is an essential pillar for developing a domestic securities market. Such a strategy includes the government's adherence to basic market principles in its funding operations, the need to design a sustainable issuance strategy, and the government's proactive approach in developing the necessary regulatory framework to support market development.

3.2.1   Adherence to Basic Market Principles

To embrace market financing, the government needs to adopt market discipline, ensure broad market access and fairness, and take steps to make government debt issuance and operations transparent and credible to the investor. This requires a change of outlook and the political commitment to

---

42. See IMF and World Bank 2001.

sustain the reformation in the face of adverse market conditions. The specific steps needed are outlined below.

3.2.1.1 *Commitment to Market Discipline*

A commitment by the government to finance its borrowing needs through the market requires it to introduce market-based financial instruments and to follow market discipline. An early step is for the government to accept the principle that debt instruments should be priced at market rates. Irrespective of whether the buyer is the central bank, a commercial bank, or another entity, or whether the sale is conducted though auctions or underwriting, the price of government securities should reflect market conditions. For countries with a large or rapidly growing government debt, moving to full market pricing of debt instruments can lead to a major increase in the government's debt-servicing costs.[43]

Converting to market financing of government borrowing means that the government should phase out or immediately cease borrowing from the central bank and also remove requirements that force commercial banks and other captive institutions to lend to the government at below-market interest rates. Governments should also give careful consideration to the liquidity of the market, the volume of securities issued in nonmarketable form, and the rate of interest that the government pays on such debt. The debt manager may need to accelerate the conversion of this debt or part of it to support market development.

Committing to be a price taker and maintaining the commitment to market pricing over time is essential. The likely increase in the government's debt-servicing costs associated with market-based funding constitutes the major challenge to adopt a commitment to market pricing of government bond issues. This may lead to political pressure to continue relying on subsidized funding through compulsory investment regulation

---

43. When governments borrow at below-market rates, they are introducing distortions in terms of reducing the income of financial intermediaries, causing them to change their portfolio allocation decisions in other areas and, in many cases, forcing them to increase interest rate spreads for commercial banks. Borrowing from the central bank at below-market rates may appear less costly to the government, but such borrowing can result in inflation.

or borrowing from the central bank at below-market rates. Although the long-term benefits of market-based government funding have been confirmed in academic literature and the experience of countries practicing market-based pricing for government securities, political pressure to continue what seem to be low-cost and assured sources of financing is often considerable.

If the government's funding needs are very large relative to domestic savings, the government may try to preserve some captive sources of funding or phase them out gradually. There is, however, a danger in doing so, as the government debt market may not fully develop because investors perceive a lack of government commitment to market financing. Continued reliance on captive sources for government funding and the resulting limited development of the market may set a vicious circle in motion, perpetuating the manager's reliance on captive funding sources.

3.2.1.2 Broad Market Access and Fairness

Measures that establish broad access to the government securities market, and treat investors fairly and equitably, can be important in earning investor confidence and helping to lower the government's borrowing costs. Providing broad access requires that the government understand the sources of demand for its instruments and review the nature of the barriers that inhibit participation by different types of investors.

Fairness considerations in issuing government securities mean that the government should provide a level playing field for all market participants and not seek to profit by taking advantage of privileged information, such as budgetary information that is not in the public domain.

If the government wants to build trust and credibility in its commitment to market forces, investors will need to be confident that the government's debt managers are not opportunistically transacting on the basis of privileged or inside information. To reduce investors' uncertainty, many governments ensure that the timing of auctions and other issuance activities are predictable by publishing auction timetables for a 12-month period, deviating from these timetables in exceptional circumstances only if, for instance, the budget situation changes significantly. Governments also need to ensure that regulatory measures do not result in captive investors for their securities, which would distort pricing. Establishing a level playing field requires the government to provide clear, transparent, and equitable rules and regulations that apply to all market participants. This is essential in order to build trust among investors and intermediaries and attract the greatest number of market participants.

3.2.1.3 *Transparency of Government Securities Issuance and Debt Management Operations*

A government can strengthen its credibility by providing timely and relevant information on the government's finances; its debt portfolio, including its redemption profile; its borrowing strategy; and data on primary and secondary market activity.[44] Producing and disseminating relevant debt and budgetary information that is generated by different government agencies and departments requires considerable coordination. It also needs modern information systems that link various data producers with the debt office and the debt office with the market.

Several emerging market governments have recently started to disclose more comprehensive information about their debt exposure. Others, with less-developed markets, still do not regularly disclose the maturity profile or the structure of their debt. Regular disclosure of the nature of the government's indebtedness is essential in order to reduce uncertainty for investors. One of the factors that catalyzed the Mexico financial crisis of the mid-1990s was a drastic loss of market confidence, abetted by the government's failure to disclose adequate information about the issuance of U.S. dollar–linked government securities (tesobonos).

An important feature of a market-oriented strategy is the two-way nature of the information process between the issuer and the market. Debt managers need to listen to investors' and market makers' views on ways of improving the efficiency and openness of financial markets and, in turn, provide information on a range of topics such as the government's debt management objectives, debt strategy, current and projected borrowing needs, and arrangements surrounding the sale of government securities.

---

44. This discussion of transparency is consistent with IMF and World Bank work on transparency practices in the conduct of public policy (see IMF 1998, 1999, 2000; IMF and World Bank 2000) as they relate to debt management operations.

The information provided needs to be of high quality if investors are to maintain confidence in the government's debt management. Providing this information requires management information systems and processes that control inconsistencies and hold the source agencies accountable for their data. The quality of information depends on a set of generally accepted accounting rules that meet, as much as possible, international standards. For many emerging markets, this will require training staff in the debt office to disclose information in a systematic way. For governments with some experience in international markets, this will be a matter of transferring that discipline to a domestic market context.

Governments need to exercise judgment in deciding what information to release. For example, governments may not want to release in advance information on their intentions to buy back or exchange large amounts of foreign currency debt. In many instances, however, the need to be concerned about releasing market-sensitive information is driven more by the timing of when the information should be released rather than a determination to permanently withhold the information from the public.

3.2.2 A Sustainable Issuance Strategy

A transparent, flexible, and effective medium-term issuance strategy is the backbone for any sustainable public debt management program. This strategy should be consistent with the macroeconomic framework and published as a measurable goalpost in order to establish clear accountability. The strategy should build on a comprehensive assessment of current debt management practices and should address the main shortcomings, if possible, with a proposed sequencing of key measures with targeted implementation dates. The strategy needs to be discussed with market participants and reflect the specific needs of market development. A consensus should be reached that helps reduce political pressure for a short-term-focused financing stance.

Three principles should be considered absolutely essential: First, the macroeconomic policy framework should be consistent with denomination of new issues. For example, if a country is moving toward dollarization, it makes little sense to pay a premium for new issuance in domestic currency. Conversely, if a country is aiming to reverse a dollarization trend and to reduce an existing currency mismatch, it becomes necessary to develop short-term benchmarks in domestic currency. Moreover, in case foreign portfolio investors are part of the targeted investor base, capital account issues (such as convertibility) as well as taxation issues (such as double-taxation treaties) should be clarified prior to new issuance.

Second, the principle of sharing risks at market rates should be established, which allows the issuance of government bonds with progressively higher risks. For example, if a country is issuing fully indexed short-term bonds that are securitized by foreign collateral, the market is assuming minimum risk at the expense of the government. In this case, the issuance strategy should aim to move away from collateral-backed issuance, to progressively extend maturities, and to phase out indexation by establishing a fixed-rate benchmark. Although the move away from indexation (that is, floating rate bonds) normally requires several years, in some cases in which a derivate market exists, it may be facilitated by a transitional step where an instrument is stripped into the equivalent of an underlying fixed-rate instrument (new benchmark) plus an additional derivative instrument (interest-rate future), where the latter component is phased out over time.

Third, a strong link between bond market development and growth of institutional investors should be recognized, which suggests that needs of institutional investors should be taken into account when the government designs new instruments. Otherwise, markets become fragmented and segments become captive, which often leads to lower domestic savings and/or capital outflows. For example, pension funds and insurance companies take long-term liabilities on their balance sheet, which need to be balanced by long-term assets, ideally linked to long-term prices. In this case, by offering long-term inflation-linked bonds, the government could meet market needs while simultaneously achieving lower yields in addition to higher confidence in its policies that target price stability. At the same time, debt dynamics require that long-term real interest rates remain below long-term real growth rates in order to remain on a sustainable path.

While following these principles, the government should maintain some flexibility to respond to adverse market conditions. For example, the debt manager may confront situations in which it is considered very important to extend the average maturity in order to reduce the refinancing risk, at the price of reducing duration or increasing exchange rate exposure. Moreover, it may become too costly to keep extending the yield curve during adverse market conditions, when the debt manager may have to consolidate the shorter segment of the yield curve by issuing shorter maturity debt. It is important that the debt manager develop a proper analytical framework that allows for the quantification of costs and risks as well as the evaluation of these trade-offs over time.

Strategic portfolio benchmarks can be effective tools to help governments choose their issuance strategies and carry out debt management. They represent the portfolio structure that the government would prefer to have, given its cost/risk preferences, debt management horizon, borrowing needs, constraints imposed by market conditions, choice of instruments and market development considerations. The benchmark portfolio may be adjusted periodically, to incorporate changing market conditions and government policies. It sets the direction for debt management and provides a framework within which alternate issuance strategies are evaluated, guiding the debt manager to move closer to the strategic benchmark portfolio.[45]

3.2.3   A Proactive Government Approach

The final component of a market-oriented funding strategy is for the government to be proactive in accelerating the development of the government bond market. As highlighted in a recent APEC publication, "the government can play a catalytic role" in developing a government bond market, and "it should develop a comprehensive strategy in consultation with the central bank, the relevant regulatory agencies, and market participants."[46]

Such an approach can be particularly important when there is a need to develop the secondary market in order to intermediate transactions among investors, such as institutional investors, who require considerable market liquidity in order to transact efficiently. This was the case in many OECD countries during the 1970s and 1980s, when financial market deregulation and the development of efficient public debt markets was also stimulated by strong government interest in attracting foreign institutional investors.

A proactive approach could include elements such as supporting the active engagement of market makers and interdealer brokers (IDBs) that could facilitate large transactions among intermediaries and between intermediaries and institutional investors; promoting an efficient and safe infrastructure with prompt and reliable delivery versus payment; seeking a

45. See IMF and World Bank 2001.

46. See APEC 1999.

primary market organization that provides the proper concentration of paper (regularity and fungibility) and an efficient distribution of securities (by primary dealers, for example); actively supporting a competitive environment among intermediaries; and facilitating the proper flow of information and transaction links among different market segments. In each of these areas, the debt manager can promote and support the development of efficient market practices. These types of government involvement are described in detail in subsequent chapters of the handbook.

However, given the involvement of different government agencies and private sector institutions, the challenge is how best to articulate and coordinate a proactive approach among the different participants. One way of doing so is to create a high-level committee led by the Ministry of Finance with representation from the central bank, the different supervisory agencies involved in the markets (banking, insurance, pensions, and securities), and principal market participants.[47] The committee's main function would be to establish and manage the agenda for developing the government bond market, maintain consensus within and outside the government regarding this process, and ensure a coordinated effort by the government agencies involved. Such a committee would also ensure that the bond market development agenda is consistent with debt management mandates and the objectives of fiscal and monetary policy.

3.3 Sound Debt Management Framework and Operations

Sound debt management will improve the credibility of the issuer and enable the debt manager to develop an issuing and debt management strategy that is sustainable over time. It may also contribute to improving the country's credit rating and facilitate access to domestic and foreign markets in a cost-effective way. Moreover, it should help to make the debt manager more accountable and less subject to political pressure while assuring the markets of the government's policy framework.

The principal components of sound debt management in many countries are based on the importance of having clear debt management objectives,

---

47. APEC (1999) recommends a high-level coordination committee.

proper coordination between debt management and monetary and fiscal policy, a prudent risk management framework, an effective institutional framework, and a strong operational capacity enabling efficient funding and sound risk management practices. This capacity is essential to implement the market-oriented funding strategy described above.

3.3.1 Clear Objectives of Debt Management

Several countries express their government debt management objectives in terms of expected cost and risk. A typical objective might be "to ensure that the government's financing needs and its payment obligations are met at the lowest possible cost over the medium to long run, consistent with a prudent degree of risk." Development of the domestic debt market is also often included as a prominent government objective. This objective is particularly relevant for countries where short-term debt, floating rate debt, and foreign currency debt are, at least in the short run, the only viable alternatives to extensive borrowing from the central bank

Clear and transparent objectives make the debt manager more accountable and less subject to external political pressures that could result in poor debt management decisions, including undesirable trade-offs between cost and risk. With prudent macroeconomic policies and a sound regulatory framework with respect to the capital market, clarity of debt management goals and adoption of policies and practices that ensure they are being met are important for reducing uncertainty among investors and attracting their support. In many emerging market economies, the objectives for debt management have often not been clearly defined, and the governance framework and the legal authority are vague. This can lead to substantial uncertainty among government debt managers, investors, and intermediaries.

3.3.2 Coordination with Monetary and Fiscal Policies

An important component of a sound debt management operation is proper coordination of debt management with monetary and fiscal policy decisions. The *Guidelines for Public Debt Management* suggest the following:

> Debt managers, fiscal policy advisors, and central bankers should share an understanding of the objectives of debt management, fiscal, and monetary policies given the interdependencies between their

different policy instruments. Debt managers should convey to fiscal authorities their views on the costs and risks associated with government financing requirements and debt levels. Policymakers should understand the ways in which the different policy instruments operate, their potential to reinforce one another, and how policy tensions can arise. Prudent debt management, fiscal and monetary policies can reinforce one another in helping to lower the risk premia in the structure of long-term interest rates. In this context, the monetary authorities should inform the fiscal authorities of the effects of government debt levels on the achievement of their monetary objectives. Borrowing limits and sound risk management practices can help to protect the government's balance sheet from debt servicing shocks. In some cases, conflicts between debt management and monetary policies can arise owing to the different purposes—debt management focuses on the cost/risk trade-off, while monetary policy is normally directed towards achieving price stability. For example, some central banks may prefer that the government issue inflation-indexed debt or borrow in foreign currency to bolster the credibility of monetary policy. Debt managers may believe that the market for such inflation-indexed debt has not been fully developed and that foreign currency debt introduces greater risk onto the government's balance sheet. Conflicts can also arise between debt managers and fiscal authorities, for example, on the cash flows inherent in a given debt structure (e.g., issuing zero-coupon debt to transfer the debt burden to future generations). For this reason, it is important that coordination take place in the context of a clear macroeconomic framework.

Where the level of financial development allows, there should be a separation of debt management and monetary policy objectives and accountabilities. Clarity in the roles and objectives for debt management and monetary policy minimizes potential conflicts. In countries with well-developed financial markets, borrowing programs are based on the economic and fiscal projections contained in the government budget, and monetary policy is carried out independently from debt management. This helps ensure that debt management decisions are not perceived to be influenced by inside information on interest rate decisions, and avoids perceptions of conflicts of interest in market operations. A goal of cost minimization over time for the government's debt, subject to a prudent level of risk, should not be viewed as a mandate to reduce interest rates, or to influence domestic monetary conditions. Neither should the cost/risk objective be seen as a justification for the extension of low-cost central bank credit to the government, nor should monetary policy decisions be driven by debt management considerations.

Debt management, fiscal, and monetary authorities should share information on the government's current and future liquidity needs. Since monetary operations are often conducted using government debt instruments and markets, the choice of monetary instruments and operating procedures can have an impact on the functioning of government debt markets, and potentially on the financial condition of dealers in these markets. By the same token, the efficient conduct of monetary policy requires a solid understanding of the government's short- and longer-term financial flows. As a result, debt management and fiscal and monetary officials often meet to discuss a wide range of policy issues. At the operational level, debt management, fiscal, and monetary authorities generally share information on the government's current and future liquidity needs. They often coordinate their market operations so as to ensure that they are not both operating in the same market segment at the same time. Nevertheless, achieving separation between debt management and monetary policy might be more difficult in countries with less-developed financial markets, since debt management operations may have correspondingly larger effects on the level of interest rates and the functioning of the local capital market. Consideration needs to be given to the sequencing of reforms to achieve this separation.

3.3.2.1 Role of Central Bank in Debt Management Operations

In many countries, the central bank provides services for the government debt managers, including operating Treasury bill and bond tenders, undertaking cash management operations, and providing registry services. In many emerging markets, the central bank also undertakes the foreign currency borrowing and, in some countries, the domestic borrowing. This is usually because the central bank has a larger number of staff with capital market expertise, and some of this information is needed to monitor levels of market liquidity as part of assessing monetary conditions.

In providing these services, it is desirable that clear quality standards be agreed upon between the debt manager and the central bank and there be discussions on how these functions can be undertaken without conflicting with the central bank's monetary policy functions. Wherever possible, there should be a clear separation between the central bank's debt management objectives and its accountability for monetary policy.

Over the last two decades, a consensus has emerged on the need to ensure that responsibility for debt management policy is managed within the Ministry of Finance and that, where the central bank has an operational role for debt management, the nature of these outputs and their timing and quality be specified. In most cases, the operational responsibility for debt management is assumed by the Ministry of Finance or an autonomous debt management organization (DMO) established outside the ministry. In emerging-market countries, where there is often a shortage of staff with financial skills in the Ministry of Finance, the central bank may need to transfer or second employees to the ministry in order to provide the needed capability. This has been the practice in some OECD countries, which have recently established an independent DMO, such as Hungary, Portugal, and the United Kingdom.

Even in cases in which this shift of responsibility has occurred, the central bank has often continued to run auctions on behalf of the government. If such activities are properly supported by clear procedures, there should not be any conflict with the central bank's monetary policy responsibilities.

3.3.3 Prudent Risk Management Framework

When developing debt management strategies and deciding between different funding strategies, debt managers in emerging-market countries are often required to manage different types of risks (see Box 3.1), given the constraints they face in the local and international markets. Some of these decisions require assessing different trade-offs of cost against risk with respect to alternative debt management and funding strategies. In order to help evaluate and manage these risks, many government debt managers have developed analytical frameworks grounded in risk analysis.

The *Guidelines for Public Debt Management* suggests the following:

Box 3.1. Risks Encountered in Sovereign Debt Management

Risk	Description
Market Risk	Refers to the risks associated with changes in market prices, such as interest rates, exchange rates, and commodity prices, on the cost of the government's debt servicing. For both domestic and foreign currency debt, changes in interest rates affect debt servicing costs on new issues when fixed-rate debt is refinanced and on floating rate debt at the rate reset dates. Hence short-duration debt (short-term or floating rate) is usually considered to be more risky than long-term, fixed-rate debt. (Excessive concentration in very long-term, fixed-rate debt can also be risky, since future financing requirements are uncertain.) Debt denominated in or indexed to foreign currencies also adds volatility to debt servicing costs as measured in domestic currency owing to exchange rate movements. Bonds with embedded put options can exacerbate market and rollover risks.
Rollover Risk	The risk that debt will have to be rolled over at an unusually high cost or, in extreme cases, cannot be rolled over at all. To the extent that rollover risk is limited to the risk that debt might have to be rolled over at higher interest rates, including changes in credit spreads, it may be considered a type of market risk. However, because the inability to roll over debt and/or exceptionally large increases in government funding costs can lead to, or exacerbate, a debt crisis, thereby causing real economic losses in addition to the purely financial effects of higher interest rates, it is often treated separately. Managing this risk is particularly important for emerging-market countries.
Liquidity Risk	There are two types of liquidity risk. One refers to the cost or penalty investors face in trying to exit a position when the number of transactors has markedly decreased or because of the lack of depth of a particular market. This risk is particularly relevant in cases in which debt management includes the management of liquid assets or the use of derivatives contracts. The other form of liquidity risk, for a borrower, refers to a situation in which the volume of liquid assets can diminish quickly in the face of unanticipated cash flow obligations or a possible difficulty in raising cash through borrowing in a short period of time.
Credit Risk	The risk of nonperformance by borrowers on loans or other financial assets or by a counterparty on financial contracts. This risk is particularly relevant in cases where debt management includes the management of liquid assets. It may also be relevant in the acceptance of bids in auctions of securities issued by the government as well as in relation to contingent liabilities and derivative contracts entered into by the debt manager.
Settlement Risk	Refers to the potential loss that the government could suffer as a result of failure to settle, for whatever reason other than default, by the counterparty.
Operational Risk	This includes a range of different types of risks, including transaction errors in the various stages of executing and recording transactions; inadequacies or failures in internal controls, or in systems and services; reputation risk; legal risk; security breaches; or natural disasters that affect business activity.

Source: IMF and World Bank 2000.

A framework should be developed to enable debt managers to identify and manage the trade-offs between expected cost and risk in the government debt portfolio. . . . An important role of the debt manager is to identify these risks, assess to the extent possible their magnitude, and develop a preferred strategy for managing the trade-off between expected cost and risk. Following government approval, the debt manager also is normally responsible for the implementation of the portfolio management and risk management policies. To carry out these responsibilities, debt managers should have access to a range of financial and macroeconomic projections. Where available, debt managers should also have access to an accounting of official assets and liabilities, on a cash or accrual basis. They also require complete information on the schedule of future coupon and principal payments and other characteristics of the government's debt obligations, together with budget projections of future borrowing requirements.

To assess risk, debt managers should regularly conduct stress tests of the debt portfolio on the basis of the economic and financial shocks to which the government—and the country more generally—are potentially exposed. This assessment is often conducted using financial models ranging from simple scenario-based models to more complex models involving highly sophisticated statistical and simulation techniques.[48] When constructing such assessments, debt managers need to factor in the risk that the government will not be able to roll over its debt and be forced to default, which has costs that are broader than just to the government's budget. Moreover, debt managers should consider the interactions between the government's financial situation and those of the financial and non-financial sectors in times of stress in order to ensure that the government's debt management activities do not exacerbate risks in the private sector.[49]

---

48. Complex simulation models should be used with caution. Data constraints may significantly impair the usefulness of these models, and the results obtained may be strongly model dependent and sensitive to the parameters used. For example, some parameters may behave differently in extreme situations or be influenced by policy responses.

49. Of course, governments should also take corrective measures, such as eliminating policy biases that may encourage excessive risk taking by the private sector.

The extent to which governments need to develop this capacity for risk analysis and evaluation depends on the overall risk of the government debt portfolio and the nature of those risks. For a country like the United States, with a strong sovereign credit rating and where all the central government debt is fixed-rate domestic currency debt distributed along a 30-year government yield curve, the portfolio risks are relatively small. Where governments have substantial amounts of foreign currency debt, foreign-currency-linked debt, or floating rate debt in their debt portfolio, or have considerable rollover risk, the government should develop techniques for assessing and managing those risks.

3.3.4   Building a Strong Institutional Framework

A sound institutional framework for government debt management embodying good governance practices, prudent procedures, and strong capacity for managing operational risks, is essential given the size of government debt portfolios and the close linkages between debt management policies and government macroeconomic and regulatory policies.

3.3.4.1 Governance

As outlined in the *Guidelines for Public Debt Management*, a clear legal framework, well-specified organizational arrangements, and public disclosure and auditing procedures are key elements of an effective governance structure for public debt management:[50]

> The legal framework should clarify the authority to borrow and to issue new debt, invest, and undertake transactions on the government's behalf. The authority to borrow should be clearly defined in legislation.[51] Sound governance practices are an important component of sovereign debt management, given the size of government debt portfolios.
>
> The soundness and credibility of the financial system can be supported by assurances that the government debt portfolio is being

---

50. For more details on the legal framework, see Chapter 9, Legal and Regulatory Framework.

51. See Section 11.2 in IMF 1998.

managed prudently and efficiently. Moreover, counterparties need assurances that the sovereign debt managers have the legal authority to represent the government, and that the government stands behind any transactions its sovereign debt managers enter into. An important feature of the legal framework is the authority to issue new debt, which is normally stipulated in the form of either borrowing authority legislation with a preset limit or a debt ceiling.

The organizational framework for debt management should be well specified, and ensure that mandates and roles are well articulated.[52] Legal arrangements should be supported by delegation of appropriate authority to debt managers. Experience suggests that there is a range of institutional alternatives for locating the sovereign debt management functions across one or more agencies, including in one or more of the following: the ministry of finance, central bank, autonomous debt management agency, and central depository.[53] Regardless of which approach is chosen, the key requirement is to ensure that the organizational framework surrounding debt management is clearly specified, there is coordination and sharing of information, and that the mandates of the respective players are clear.[54]

Many debt managers file an annual debt management report, which reviews the previous year's activities, and provides a broad overview of borrowing plans for the current year based on the annual budget projections. These reports increase the accountability of the government debt managers. They also assist financial markets by disclosing the criteria used to guide the debt program, the assumptions and trade-off underlying these criteria, and the managers' performance in meeting them.

In order to support the governance structure and provide quality assurance in respect to the operations of the debt managers, many governments have introduced an advisory board (or a similar structure) between the minister of finance and the head of the DMO.

---

52. See also Section 2.1 of the *Guidelines* and Section 1.3 in IMF 1999.

53. A few countries have privatized elements of debt management within clearly defined limits, including, for example, back-office functions and the management of the foreign currency desk stock.

54. See Section 3.3.2.1. above.

3

The advisory board's mandate could be to provide advice on a range of management issues or extend into more technical issues relating to debt management strategy. Interdepartmental or interagency committees are also frequently established to discuss and exchange information that is important for liquidity management. These committees often include representatives from the Ministry of Finance and the central bank.

Debt management activities should be audited annually by external auditors.[55] The accountability framework for debt management can be strengthened by public disclosure of audit reviews of debt management operations. Audits of government financial statements should be conducted regularly and publicly disclosed on a preannounced schedule, including information on the operating expenses and revenues.[56] A national audit body, like the agency responsible for auditing government operations, should provide timely reports on the financial integrity of the central government accounts. In addition, there should be regular audits of debt managers' performance and of systems and control procedures.

3.3.4.2 Operational Capacity

For many governments that have only recently moved to market-based financing, debt management has traditionally involved very basic operations. In these countries, debt management has usually been focused on back-office practices (debt registry, disbursements, and debt-service payments), with limited strategic and financial analysis carried out by the debt management team. Important financing and strategic decisions have often been taken by the minister of finance or in the central bank (sometimes in the context of a fiscal or balance of payments crisis), with the debt office playing a limited role.[57]

---

55. See Section 3.3.2.1. above.

56. The audit process may differ depending on the institutional structure of debt management operations.

57. During the 1980s and early 1990s, Latin America, among other regions, became involved in major debt restructuring (Paris Club, Brady bonds) that demanded high-quality debt management skills. In most cases, the process was carried out by consultants reporting directly to the minister of finance or by senior officials of the central bank.

The most attractive issuers in the different regions have been active in the international markets for several years. They have strengthened the analytical capacity within the debt office and, in many instances, established portfolio management teams with responsibility for negotiating and executing borrowing and hedging transactions in the market.[58]

In many emerging market countries, however, inadequate levels of skilled debt management staff and a lack of management information systems (or expertise on their most effective adaptation) has been a major constraint in building debt management capacity. Building this capacity should be an important priority, especially when the portfolio is large and contains risky debt structures.

The *Guidelines for Public Debt Management* offer the following measures for managing operational risks:

> Risks of government losses from inadequate operational controls should be managed according to sound business practices, including well-articulated responsibilities for staff, and clear monitoring and control policies and reporting arrangements. . . . Sound risk monitoring and control practices are essential to reduce operational risk.
>
> Operational responsibility for debt management is generally separated into front and back offices with distinct functions and accountabilities, and separate reporting lines. The front office is typically responsible for executing transactions in financial markets, including the management of auctions and other forms of borrowing, and all other funding operations. It is important to ensure that the individual executing a market transaction and the one responsible for entering the transaction into the accounting system are different people. The back office handles the settlement of transactions and the maintenance of the financial records. In a number of cases, a separate middle or risk management office has also been established to undertake risk analysis and monitor and report on portfolio-related risks, and to assess the performance of debt managers against any strategic benchmarks. This separation

---

58. In Latin America, for example, it was only in the early 1990s that Argentina, Colombia, and Mexico started to upgrade the front office for external debt, while countries such as Brazil decided to build this capacity within the central bank.

helps to promote the independence of those setting and monitoring the risk management framework and assessing performance from those responsible for executing market transactions. Where debt management services are provided by the central bank (e.g., registry and auction services) on behalf of the government's debt managers, the responsibilities and accountabilities of each party and agreement on service standards can be formalized through an agency agreement between the central bank and the government debt managers.

Government debt management requires staff with a combination of financial market skills (such as portfolio management and risk analysis) and public policy skills. Regardless of the institutional structure, the ability to attract and retain skilled debt management staff is crucial for mitigating operational risk. This can be a major challenge for many countries, especially where there is a high demand for such staff in the private sector, or an overall shortage of such skills generally. Investment in training can help alleviate these problems, but where large salary differentials persist between the public and private sector for such staff, government debt managers often find it difficult to retain these skills.

Debt management activities should be supported by an accurate and comprehensive management information system with proper safeguards. Countries who are beginning the process of building capacity in government debt management need to give a high priority to developing accurate debt recording and reporting systems. This is required not only for producing debt data and ensuring timely payment of debt service, but also for improving the quality of budgetary reporting and the transparency of government financial accounts. The management information system should capture all relevant cash flows, and should be fully integrated into the government's accounting system. While such systems are essential for debt management and risk analysis, their introduction often poses major challenges for debt managers in terms of expense and management time. However, the costs and complexities of the system should be appropriate to the organization's needs.

Staff involved in debt management should be subject to a code-of-conduct and conflict-of-interest guidelines regarding the management of their personal financial affairs. This will help to allay concerns that staff's personal financial interests may undermine sound debt management practices.

3.4   Conclusion

Building the government's credibility as an issuer of government securities and developing a broad investor base for such issues requires commitment by the government to an overall market orientation supported by a suitable funding strategy and a strong institutional framework for debt management.

The government must fully endorse the principles of broad market access, fairness, and transparency in its interaction with market participants. To implement these principles, a durable funding strategy must be developed, whose important elements must include issuing marketable instruments at market prices, dismantling captive sources of borrowing, and supporting the development of efficient market infrastructure and sound regulatory practices. Coordination between the government debt managers, the fiscal authorities, and the central bank is also critical and will result in smoother liquidity management by the government. This will lead to an issuance strategy that will build liquidity in a range of benchmark securities and will also help to improve investor confidence and strengthen the development of the local government bond market.

Governments can support the development of the government bond market and enhance their credibility as an issuer of debt by building a strong institutional framework for debt management. Such a framework must ensure that debt management objectives are clear and are able to guide debt management decisions. Investor uncertainty is reduced by prudent fiscal management and by a legal framework that controls the volume of government debt and the number of issuers in addition to assuring investors that the government stands behind the transactions entered into on its behalf by the government debt managers.

Experience in many countries suggests that building credibility as an issuer of government debt and developing an efficient government bond market can be a difficult and lengthy process and require coordination across many policy fronts. Changing political sentiment and financial market crises can occasionally check or reverse these processes. However, the benefits from pursuing these reforms and developing an efficient market in government securities as well as a strong reputation as an issuer of government securities usually substantially outweigh the adjustment costs.

3

Bibliography

APEC (Asia-Pacific Economic Cooperation). 1999. *Compendium of Sound Practices: Guidelines to Facilitate the Development of Domestic Bond Markets in APEC Member Economies.*

Deutsche Bundesbank. 2000. *Protokoll der Pressekonferenz in Anschluss an die auswärtige Zentralbankssitzung der Deutschen Bundesbank am 15. Juni 2000 in Trier.* Frankfurt, Germany. Available at www.bundesbank.de.

Eichel, Hans. Press Conference, Berlin, February 16, 2000. Bundesministerium der Finanzen, Berlin, Germany. Available at www.bundesfinanzministerium.de.

IMF (International Monetary Fund). 1998. *Code of Good Practices on Fiscal Transparency: Declaration of Principles.* International Monetary Fund, Washington, D.C. Available at www.imf.org/external/np/fad/trans/code.htm#code.

————. 1999. *Code of Good Practices on Transparency in Monetary and Financial Policies: Declaration of Principles.* International Monetary Fund, Washington, D.C. Available at www.imf.org/external/np/mae/mft/code/index.htm.

————. 2000. *Supporting Document to the Code of Good Practices on Transparency in Monetary and Financial Policies.* International Monetary Fund, Washington, D.C. Available at www.imf.org/external/np/mae/sup/index.htm.

IMF and World Bank. 2001. *Guidelines for Public Debt Management.* International Monetary Fund and World Bank, Washington, D.C. Available at www.worldbank.org/fps/guidelines/www.imf.org/external/np/mae/pdebt/2000/eng/index.htm.

OECD (Organization for Economic Cooperation and Development). 1993. *Government Securities and Debt Management in the 1990s.* Paris, France.

Sundararajan, V., Peter Dattels, and Hans J. Blommestein, eds. 1997. *Coordinating Public Debt and Monetary Management.* International Monetary Fund, Washington, D.C.

World Bank. Forthcoming. *Sound Practices in Sovereign Debt Management.* World Bank, Washington, D.C.

3

Chapter 4

Developing Benchmark Issues

By concentrating government bond issues in a relatively limited number of popular, standard maturities, governments can assist the development of liquidity in those securities and thereby lower their debt-issuance costs. Markets, in turn, can also use such liquid issues as convenient benchmarks for the pricing of a range of other financial instruments. In addition, spreading the relatively few benchmark issues across a fairly wide range of maturities—building a "benchmark yield curve"— can facilitate more accurate market pricing of financial instruments across a similar maturity range and more generally facilitate better risk management in financial markets. Most industrial countries and some emerging economies have succeeded or made significant progress in developing a benchmark government bond yield curve that spans short-term bills to long-term bonds. Many other countries are in the early stages of developing a yield curve, and often do not have much freedom to issue securities in the full range of maturities needed for a complete yield curve. These countries may seek to develop a more limited number of benchmark securities in those maturities for which there is a market.

4.1   Introduction

Governments can often reduce their debt-service costs through measures that promote the development of deeper, more liquid government securities markets by concentrating their government bond issues in a relatively limited number of maturities. Market participants are typically prepared to pay a premium for a security that can be subsequently traded in a more liquid market—i.e., where sellers or buyers can more readily and cheaply conduct transactions without moving the price of the security against themselves—compared to an otherwise similar security for which the market is less liquid. Debt managers can capture this liquidity premium by standardizing debt instruments in as simple a form as possible and by issuing relatively more of this standardized debt at key maturities. Goldstein and Folkerts-Landau (1994) cite the views of several developed-country debt managers to the effect that such savings for their countries (the difference in rates that had to be paid on benchmark bonds, as opposed to less liquid, non-benchmark issues) were on the order of 5 to 15 basis points.

As long as the maturity and other underlying features of the issues are in reasonable accord with market preferences, larger issues tend to be more liquid because market participants' typical transactions (including those of the government) are smaller relative to the total supply. Therefore, they can buy or sell desired amounts with less chance of moving the market against them. The market recognition of this liquidity tends to be reinforcing: once some part of the market recognizes an issue as being very liquid, other participants also tend to concentrate their activities in these issues, which makes the security even more liquid. Indeed, since liquid benchmark securities can be readily bought or sold as a vehicle for hedging other financial transactions, many market participants use them as a hedging vehicle in corporate asset and liability management.

Beyond the cost savings to governments, there are also beneficial side effects of building benchmark government bonds in terms of developing a broader financial market. In particular, markets tend to use yields on benchmark government securities to price a range of other financial instruments.[59] In pricing a corporate bond, for instance, a spread reflecting

---

59. Benchmark bonds are typically securities of the highest credit quality—i.e., in many cases they are government securities (although this need not always be the case), owing to their sovereign backing, assuming the government in question is a credible issuer

default risk, liquidity risk, and other specific risks can be added to the yield curve of the benchmark security with the same maturity as the corporate bond.[60] Likewise, by spreading its benchmark issues across a relatively wide maturity spectrum to construct a benchmark yield curve, governments can indirectly facilitate more accurate market pricing across a similarly wide range of maturities for other instruments. Indeed, in many countries the benchmark yield curve underpins the pricing of repo, interest rate futures, and other derivatives markets, such as the interest rate swap market. The existence of these derivatives markets provides additional interest rate hedging options for domestic securities market participants, thereby further enhancing the demand for government securities. In short, building benchmark issues and a benchmark yield curve can contribute importantly to broader securities market development.

These broader benefits may be particularly relevant in emerging and less-developed markets where the development of institutional investors and improved market transparency has further to go. Many transparency problems in the market and difficulties in implementing market-oriented regulation are a direct result of securities-pricing inefficiencies. Accurate pricing of less-liquid debt instruments, such as corporate bonds, is needed for fairness among different groups and generations of investors, and this would be difficult without the reference points provided by benchmarks. Benchmarks can be helpful pricing guides in the case of private pension funds of the unitized type, which are popular in many Latin American countries and increasingly elsewhere. In unitized pension funds, monthly contributions are invested at a net asset value–based price,

---

(see Chapter 3, A Government Debt Issuance Strategy and Debt Management Framework). Benchmark securities are also typically the largest and most liquid issues. This is because the prices of liquid and actively traded securities are generally more stable than those of other securities, other things being equal, so that such securities are more reliable as benchmarks for the pricing of other securities.

60. A yield curve is the relationship between the yield on securities and their maturities at a particular point of time. In graphical terms, it can be represented as the plot of yield to maturity on the y-axis against the time to maturity, shown as the maturity date, along the x-axis. It can serve as an important analytic device for markets and policymakers, as well as a guide for more efficient pricing and risk management. The most useful form of yield curve would reflect the yields and maturities of market-based securities of similar nature, credit quality, and liquidity. A "benchmark yield curve" refers to a yield curve constructed from the yields on benchmark securities.

and accumulated contributions are transferred at the same price. Benchmarks offer similar price guidance for mutual funds, shares of which can be bought and redeemed at frequent intervals. A number of countries are developing matrices for the valuation of less-liquid debt instruments based on net present value, where the rate of discount is calculated by reference to the relationship between the rating of a particular bond and the rating of a risk-free benchmark government bond.

Governments, however, need to be conscious of the trade-offs that, at least in principle, underlie any chosen debt management strategy. In smaller or less-advanced markets such trade-offs may often be more marked. In such markets, even though some of the benefits of the strategy might actually be higher than in other countries, there may nevertheless be important constraints on the extent to which, or the speed with which, a strategy that seeks to develop benchmark issues and a benchmark yield curve can be implemented.

In particular, if the total government debt stock that is tradable is small relative to the size of issue that the market would need before it considers that issue to be liquid,[61] the number of benchmark maturities that the debt manager can potentially build up is obviously more limited than otherwise. The fewer the benchmarks that can be built up—implying the debt stock is concentrated in a limited number of maturities—the more likely that rollover risk becomes a concern for the debt manager. Concerns about rollover risk may cause the debt manager to question the desirability of striving to build benchmark government securities issues.

In normal conditions, the trade-off between building liquidity and minimizing rollover risk can be minimized, to some extent at least, by reducing the number of large issues, concentrating issues on maturities that the market considers key, and, if possible, spreading them across a relatively wide range of maturities. However, the ability to issue longer-term securities can often also be constrained where uncertainty about future macroeconomic

---

61. The debt stock available for market trading may be relatively small because the volume of domestic debt issuance is itself small (e.g., the government may have had a long history of strict fiscal discipline or may have funded itself through foreign borrowings), or because an important proportion of the total amount of the issue is held by institutions that are either required holders of government securities or buy-and-hold investors.

stability is substantial, since this may significantly raise the term premium that the government will be required to pay when selling longer maturity securities. In less extreme cases, the government will need to weigh how much more it is willing to pay (as a form of investment) to begin developing a longer-term instrument. In a highly unstable macroeconomic environment, there may be no demand for long-term instruments, even at very high rates of interest.

Authorities in many industrial countries and some emerging economies have worked to create a government securities benchmark yield curve that spans short-term bills to long-term bonds. Authorities in less-developed countries, where there may be an unstable macroeconomic environment or a limited domestic government securities market, have been unable to do so. In countries facing such constraints, the current focus is to develop a small number of benchmark securities rather than trying to issue securities across the yield curve.

4.2   Country Experiences with Benchmark Issues

Some insights into how to weigh and reconcile, in practice, the benefits and trade-offs of developing benchmark government securities issues can be gained by examining country experiences in this area. Box 4.1 illustrates some of the essential differences between more liquid and less liquid issues, even in the deepest government securities market in the world, and explains some of the common terminology associated with benchmark issues.

Most industrial countries have successfully developed a benchmark yield curve in their domestic government securities markets.[62] (See Figure 4.1 for the benchmark yield curve for Germany and the United States.) Nevertheless, within the overall benchmark yield curve in these countries, the number of benchmark issues varies quite widely, as shown in Table 4.1, while the relative size of benchmark issues compared to nonbenchmark issues—i.e., the extent to which the debt structure is concentrated in benchmark issues—also varies considerably. (see Table 4.3.)

---

62. See Fleming (2000) and commentary thereon for recent U.S. experience with benchmark issues.

Box 4.1. Benchmark Bonds, Benchmark Issues, On-the-Run and Off-the-Run Issues

An *on-the-run issue* is the most recently issued bond (for a certain term-to-maturity), and is usually treated by the market as a **benchmark bond** because it tends to be the most liquid or actively traded issue around that term-to-maturity. The new issue will be considered the on-the-run issue until it is replaced by a new bond of the same original term-to-maturity. Once an issue ceases to be on-the-run, it becomes a seasoned issue or an *off-the-run issue*. A well-seasoned issue is called an *off-off-the-run issue*. A *when-issued security* is an on-the-run security that has yet to be auctioned but trades on a when-issued basis in the brief period between the official announcement of a forthcoming auction and the date at which it is actually delivered to the market.

A good illustration of the difference between the various types of securities described above can be found by perusing the various U.S. Treasury note securities with original terms-to-maturity of approximately 10 years that were trading on October 6, 2000. On that date, the **on-the-run** security was the 5.75 percent August 2010 security, yielding 5.82 percent because this was the security that had been most recently issued by the U.S. Treasury in that part of the yield curve. Meanwhile, several other Treasury notes with similar terms-to-maturity, which had been on-the-run when they were first issued—such as the 6.5 percent February 2010 and the 6 percent August 2009—are no longer being issued by the U.S. Treasury. These latter two securities are thus considered to be **off-the-run**; they yielded 5.91 and 5.93 percent, respectively, on that date.

The liquidity of off-the-run issues is normally poor compared with on-the-run issues. For off-the-run issues, spreads may be higher and transaction sizes difficult to predict. The table below summarizes key measures of liquidity in U.S. 10-year Treasury note issues (using data between December 1992 and August 1993). Most striking are liquidity differences across different issues. The on-the-run segment has, on average, a transaction every 6.4 minutes, the average volume of transactions is nearly 1,100 million, and the average number of transactions per day is 215. The most recently auctioned securities (on-the-run) and the to-be-auctioned securities (when-issued) have considerably more depth than seasoned issues (off-the-run and off-off-the run) along all dimensions of liquidity.

Liquidity of U.S. 10-Year Treasury Note

| | | | Statistics for Daily Transactions | | | | | |
| | | | Number | | Volume (in millions) | | Time Between Trades (in minutes) | |
Maturity	Number of Transactions	Number of Days	Mean	SD	Mean	SD	Mean	SD
When-issued	8,501	42	202.4	170.5	1,091	924	5.8	11.5
On-the-runs	40,459	186	215.5	96.3	1,099	536	6.4	5.6
Off-the-runs	1,589	71	22.4	12.0	98	70	26.9	30.2
Off-off-the-runs	458	59	5.8	5.9	28	28	49.4	62.2

Source: Sundaresan (1997)

Figure 4.1. Yield-to-Maturity Curves in German and U.S. Government Bond Markets (March 29, 2001)

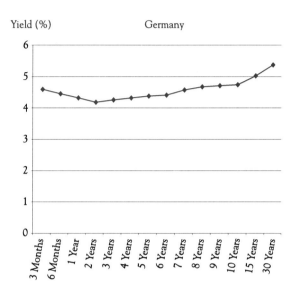

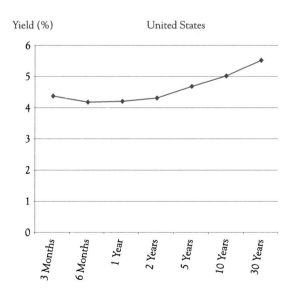

4

Table 4.1. Benchmarks and Their Selections in G–10 Government Bond Markets

	Canada	*Italy*	*Japan*	*United Kingdom*	*United States*
Number of benchmarks	Seven (3- and 6-month, 1-, 2-, 5-, 10- and 30-year)	Five (2-, 3-, 5-, 7-, and 10-year)	One (10-year)	Four (5-, 10-, 20-, and 30-year)	Seven (3-, 6-month, 1-, 2-, 5-, 10-, and 30-year) for fixed-coupon securities Two (10- and 30-year) for index-linked bonds
How is benchmark selected?	No official rules On-the-run issues for each maturity are usually regarded as benchmarks	No official rules On-the-run issues (with the highest trading volume) for each maturity are usually regarded as benchmarks	No official rules The 10-year bond issue, with large issue amount, long remaining maturity, and being traded near par value, is regarded as the benchmark	No official rules On-the-run issues for each maturity are usually regarded as benchmarks The government targets to create benchmarks for 5-, 10-, 20-, and 30-years	No official rules On-the-run issues for each maturity are usually regarded as benchmarks

	Belgium	France	Germany	Netherlands	Sweden	Switzerland
Number of benchmarks	Two (5- and 10-year)	Seven (3- and 6-month, 1-, 2-, 5-, 10-, and 30-year) Two (10- and 30-year) for index-linked bonds	Four (2-, 5-, 10- and 30-year)	Two (10- and 30-year)	Twelve (2-, 3-, 4-, 5-, 6-, 7-, 8-, 9-, 10-, 11-, 12- and 16-year)	Seven (7-, 9-, 10, 11, 12, and 13-year)
How is benchmark selected?	No official rules On-the-run issues for each maturity are usually regarded as benchmarks	No official rules On-the-run issues for each maturity are usually regarded as benchmarks	No official rules On-the-run issues for each maturity are usually regarded as benchmarks	No official rules On-the-run issues with a size of at least Dfl 10 billion for each maturity are usually regarded as benchmarks	All bonds that can be reopened are called benchmarks A new benchmark is created from the first auction of about SKr 4 billion There is also a repo facility of SKr 11 billion so that total available volume outstanding is SKr 15 billion	No official rules Government favors building up liquid benchmarks with maturities of around 10 years

Source: BIS (1999)

125

A number of industrial countries have begun facing a new challenge in maintaining a well-functioning yield curve—a declining debt stock resulting from a number of years of fiscal surpluses.[63] To date at least, this has not brought seriously into question the approach of concentrating on benchmark issues, though it could do so in the future.[64] At this stage, the situation is being dealt with by gradually reducing the size of benchmark issues, buying back older off-the-run issues to maintain new issuance volumes for benchmark issues, and/or reducing the number of benchmark issues. In the United States and Canada, for example, debt managers have taken steps to reduce the number of benchmark maturities. They have stopped issuing securities at the three-year term, and are considering whether to eliminate or substantially reduce issuance volume for other benchmark maturities. They have also been buying back older off-the-run issues in order to maintain new-issuance volumes in the remaining benchmark terms.

The government of Singapore apparently has considered the benefits of benchmark government securities for broader securities market development to be so important that it has established a government securities issuance program at least in part to meet that need, even when it has no pressing need to borrow for its own account (because of a long history of fiscal prudence). Hong Kong, China, likewise, has not had a large need to finance government deficits, but it has issued a range of new governmental bonds to allow for more effective monetary management operations, while also recognizing the usefulness of such securities as benchmarks for financial markets. (See Box 4.2.)

In many less-advanced countries, interest rate benchmark development has not been a policy priority, either because they faced only limited and sporadic financing needs or because monetary policies are conducted

---

63. See Bennett, Garbade, and Kambhu (2000) and commentary thereon.

64. If the stock of government securities were to become too small in some countries to provide a benchmark yield curve, there may be some other instruments in those countries that can, at least to some degree, approximate the benchmark function of government securities. These might include government agency debt, mortgage-backed securities, good-quality corporate debt, and the swap market. Similarly, foreign investors in some emerging-market countries without well-developed domestic markets sometimes use interest rate and currency swap transactions to construct an approximate local currency yield curve. See Fleming (2000) and commentary thereon.

Box 4.2. Development of Hong Kong Bond Market

In Hong Kong, 1990 is an important dividing line in local bond market development. Prior to 1990, secondary market liquidity in Hong Kong's local bond market was very low and market infrastructure was underdeveloped. The need for a bond market was very limited, because Hong Kong had a well-developed banking sector, the stock market provided the corporate/private sector with necessary funding, and the government rarely had any deficit financing needs. The Hong Kong Monetary Authority, gradually realizing the importance of a healthy local bond market, initiated the Exchange Fund Bills and Notes program in 1990. Under this program, bills of 91-, 182-, and 364-day maturity were launched in 1990 and 1991. Two-year and three-year Exchange Fund Notes were introduced in May 1993 and October 1993, respectively. The inaugural issue of 5-year, 7-year, and 10-year Exchange Fund Notes followed in September 1994, November 1995, and October 1996, respectively. Twenty-eight-day bills were introduced in November 1996. While debt instruments with different maturities were being developed, the government also worked hard to improve market infrastructure and enhance market demand for government securities. As a result of these efforts, the government was able to establish a market-based, liquid, and reliable benchmark yield curve for Hong Kong dollar debt. This benchmark curve covers a maturity spanning from 28, 91, 182, and 364 days to 2, 5, 7, and 10 years.

---

through direct credit control. In China, for instance, until 1998 both deposit rates and loan rates of banks were fixed by the People's Bank of China (the central bank) and monetary policy was implemented through credit plans. Recently, as China has started to liberalize interest rates, the need to develop benchmark securities for indirect monetary policy has been recognized.

In Asia before the 1997 financial crisis, most East Asian emerging-market country governments, except for China and the Philippines, had not been active issuers of government securities because they were running fiscal surpluses. When government securities were issued, most of the securities were held to maturity by financial institutions and contractual saving sectors, resulting in an illiquid secondary market. The yields of such issues were, therefore, not market based and not reliable enough to serve as benchmarks.

4.3 Building a Benchmark Yield Curve: Strategy and Implementation

Although it is ultimately the market that judges whether a security is to be treated as a benchmark, governments typically attempt to develop certain securities into benchmarks through a variety of measures that take into account the features that markets desire. The market often takes on-the-run issues of certain maturities as benchmarks. However, on-the-run issues are occasionally not large and liquid enough to become benchmarks when they are first issued, so they may need to be reopened several times.

While all governments need to understand what market preferences are likely to be, in countries at the early stage of market development, governments may need to be more proactive in influencing what the underlying market preferences are. Governments need to examine market circumstances carefully and consult with the market closely when choosing to target particular issues such as benchmark bond issues.

4.3.1 Standardizing Debt Instruments

A broad variety of debt instruments may allow the debt manager to address the preferences of diverse investors. Too many products, however, can "fragment" the market, to the extent that for any given level of bond market trading volume, the debt stock would be divided into too many instruments to support active trading of any one instrument. Experiences in more mature markets suggest that the cost of market fragmentation far outweighs the benefit of product diversification. Consequently, governments should generally narrow the variety of debt instruments by consolidating and standardizing government securities issues, with an emphasis on issuing marketable Treasury bills and bonds.

An important basic step in building benchmark issues is standardizing a large part of the government securities issue. There are many forms of fragmentation that can arise from the existence of different types of bonds, coupon rates, maturities, issue sizes and frequencies, and whether an issue is an on-the-run or off-the-run issue. Also contributing to fragmentation are different investor profiles. From the policymaker's perspective, fragmentation presents a serious impediment for creating liquidity and developing benchmark bonds. A fragmented debt structure hinders substitutability between bonds (fungibility), reduces the size and trading volume of benchmark issues, and disperses market liquidity over many issues rather than over a more limited number of benchmark instruments. Fragmentation also limits dealers' market-making capacity by forcing them to hold a larger number of securities in their inventories or to engage in extra, and possibly costly, risk management activities. Fragmentation still

---

Box 4.3. Reducing Fragmentation in the Canadian Government Bond Market

In most developed markets, government debt is now issued on a regular basis, in a limited set of maturities (i.e., benchmark maturities) and in relatively large sizes. Market fragmentation is minimized by these practices. However, this was not always the case. For example, in Canada before 1992, the size, maturity, and frequency of domestic marketable bonds were based on market preferences. Consequently, the stock of domestic bonds had irregular original maturities. As of end 1991, 112 fixed-rate C$-denominated marketable bonds were outstanding for a stock of C$157 billion, suggesting a highly fragmented debt stock, with negative implications for the liquidity of the bonds outstanding. However, in 1992, Canada began regularizing its issuance around benchmark securities, with positive results. As a result, in July 2000 there were 68 issues outstanding for a stock of debt of C$286 billion; the number of issues outstanding will eventually decline to less than 50 as the previously issued irregular maturities are gradually retired.

4

exists in many developed government securities markets, although it is declining over time as governments consolidate their securities issues in Treasury instruments. Box 4.3 illustrates the decline in fragmentation that has taken place in Canada.

Many emerging economies face severe market fragmentation. In addition to Treasury securities, these countries have many other types of government securities issues outstanding. In some countries (e.g., China, Israel, and the Republic of Korea), special purpose government bonds have been issued to finance specific projects. These special bonds typically are not traded in the secondary market; or, if traded, their size and liquidity are limited by the scope and refinancing needs of the project. These bonds are not in the Treasury-bond class and reduce the size and liquidity of Treasury bonds. As a result, many of these economies are addressing fragmentation on two fronts, since they need to standardize both the Treasury bond market and the government bond market as a whole.

Box 4.4 summarizes the Republic of Korea's experience in dealing with these challenges. Recognizing the problem brought on by fragmentation of too many government debt instruments, the Korean government in 2000 decided to merge the Grain Security Bond into Treasury bonds. In Brazil, as another example, more than 250 different types of federal securities are currently issued, of which 30 are reported to be "relatively actively" traded and only 10 are somewhat liquid.

Conventional Treasury bonds should serve as the main government funding instrument, and issues of special purpose bonds should be discouraged.

The special character of the latter fragments the market and complicates budget management by earmarking certain receipts for specific expenditures.

In many emerging economies, development of the government securities market is also hampered by the existence of both Treasury and central bank securities. (See Chapter 2, Money Markets and Monetary Policy Operations.) Brazil, among others, has started to merge central bank–issued securities into Treasury issues.

Reliance on nonmarketable government securities should also be discouraged. Since the mid-1980s, Israel has taken steps to streamline its government debt instruments by gradually reducing the issuance of nonmarketable government securities in order to develop liquidity for marketable government bonds.[65]

4.3.2 Developing Appropriate Maturity Distribution for Benchmark Issues

In most developed domestic government securities markets, benchmark yield curves have been established with a view toward spreading the government's maturities over time to alleviate rollover risk. Table 4.2 provides information on maturities of benchmark and other issues in the domestic bond markets of G–10 countries. The number of original maturities existing in a market can differ significantly from that of benchmark maturities. Most countries tend to have between 5 (in the United Kingdom) and 12 (in Switzerland) original maturities in their issues. However, the number that is deemed by the market to be benchmarks tends to be much less. In many countries the main benchmark maturities are 3 and 6 months, and 1, 2, 5, 10, and 30 years.

In Belgium, Japan, and the Netherlands, benchmark issues are concentrated at the long end of the yield curve, 5- and 10-year maturities for

---

65. Before 1990, government-financing instruments in Israel were dominated by nonmarketable government bonds, most of which paid a fixed, higher than market, yield. The process of developing a tradable bond market began in 1986, and the nonmarketable component has steadily declined, thereby significantly improving the tradability/liquidity of the bond market. As a result, the proportion of tradable government bonds has increased from 16 percent of the domestic debt in 1986 to 52 percent by December 1999. The market value of tradable government bonds stood at US$36 billion equivalent in December 1999.

Box 4.4. Fragmentation in the Korean Government Bond Market

In the Republic of Korea, six types of domestic government securities are issued: Treasury Bonds (one, three, and five years), Foreign Exchange Stabilization Fund Bond (FESF Bond), Grain Security Bond, National Housing Bond (I) and (II), and Public Land Compensation Bond. The outstanding debt of each bond is depicted in the figure below. Treasury Bonds are relatively liquid. However, because of the wide fragmentation of these instruments, the size of the government bonds, including Treasury bonds, is still very limited. Within the class of Treasury bonds, those issued on different dates were all treated as separate issues,

fragmenting the market. Consequently, the trading volume for each issue of Treasury bonds tended to be too small to support the amount of trading needed to create liquidity.

In order to establish Treasury bonds as benchmark securities, the government now concentrates debt issues on Treasury bonds, which account for about 70 percent of annual government debt issuance, and to gradually phase out other types of government securities through buyback programs. The government launched its first fungible issue on May 16, 2000, for a five-year government bond, and now most issuance is fungible, reducing market fragmentation.

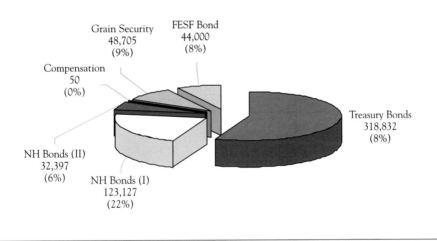

Belgium, 10-year for Japan, and 10- and 30-year for the Netherlands. In contrast, in Canada, France, the United States, and many other countries, benchmark issues cover the whole yield curve as described above. The reason for the diverse maturity mix of benchmark issues has much to do with market preference. Most governments like to create benchmarks covering the whole yield curve, but whether an issue can become the benchmark for a particular maturity is ultimately determined by market practice.

Table 4.2. Maturity Distribution of Debt Instruments and Benchmarks in G–10 Countries

	Canada	Italy	Japan	United Kingdom	United States
Number of original maturities	7	10	8	5	7[1]
Original maturities (M – month, Y – year)	3, 6M, 1, 2, 5, 10, 30Y	3, 6M, 1, 1.5, 2, 3, 5, 7, 10, 30Y	3, 6M, 2, 4, 5, 6, 10, 20Y	3M, 5, 10, 20, 30Y	3, 6M, 1, 2, 5, 10, 30Y
Distribution by original maturity[2]					
1 yr and under	32%	17%	5%	7%[3]	21%
1–5 years	29%	32%	8%	29%[3]	62%
5–10 years	27%	48%	78%	34%[3]	
Over 10 years	12%	3%	9%	30%[3]	17%
Number of benchmarks	7	5	1	4	7

	Belgium	France	Germany	Netherlands	Switzerland
Number of original maturities	7	8	6	6	12
Original maturities (M – month, Y – year)	3, 6M, 1, 5, 10, 15, 30Y	3, 6M, 1, 2, 5, 10, 15, 30Y	6M, 2, 4, 5, 10, 30Y	3, 6M, 1, 5, 10, 30Y	3, 6M, 5, 7, 9, 10, 11, 12, 13, 14, 15, 20Y
Distribution by original maturity[2]					
1 yr and under	19%	10%	2%	4%	27%
1–5 years	6%	27%	32%	10%	23%
5–10 years	43%	53%	61%	74%	13%
Over 10 years	32%	10%	5%	12%	37%
Number of benchmarks	2	7	4	2	7

[1]The number of original maturities in the United States dropped to 7, after it stopped issuing 3-year securities in 1995.
[2]Distribution is based on the volume outstanding.
[3]Figures are for the remaining maturity, not for the original maturity.
Note: Indexed bonds are not included in table. Data for Sweden are not available.
Sources: BIS 1999a, 1999b; Inoue 1999

While long-term, fixed-interest debt instruments are essential for developing a benchmark yield curve, most developing countries do not have the leeway to issue such instruments given the limited size of their public debt or a history of macroeconomic and financial instability. As a result, some of these countries have opted to issue floating-rate notes and bonds with variable rates. While these instruments have contributed to market fragmentation, they have played an important role in extending the maturity of government securities.

4.3.3 Determining Appropriate Size and Frequency of Benchmark Issues

Once the maturity distribution is decided, the next question facing the debt manager is to set the appropriate size and frequency for benchmark issues. The size of new government securities issues varies across countries, and, as indicated in Figure 4.2, for many countries appears to be closely related to the size of the government bond market.[66]

In some countries, as shown in Table 4.3, the size of benchmark issues is considerably larger than that of other issues.[67] This reflects the government's efforts to have large benchmark issues to enhance market liquidity. The relative size of these issues also indicates the degree of market fragmentation and the difficulty governments face to consolidate their issues and focus on benchmark issues.

Issuance size also depends on market conditions. With the launch of the Euro in 1999—and hence the elimination of intra-Euro-zone currency speculation as a trading motivation—market participants began to pay more attention to the liquidity of the zone's various government debt instruments. Since issuance size and liquidity tend to move hand-in-hand, the size of new government securities issues in the Euro-zone countries is converging despite differences in the amount of government debt outstanding. In general, as the global economy becomes increasingly open and integrated, market influence on debt issuance decisions should strengthen.

While governments should not prejudge what size issues can ensure market acceptance of government securities as benchmarks, they do need

---

66. See BIS 1999a and BIS 1999b.

67. If all issues are benchmarks, the average issue size and benchmark size are identical.

Figure 4.2. Volume of Government Bonds Outstanding Versus Benchmark Issue Size (US$ billion)

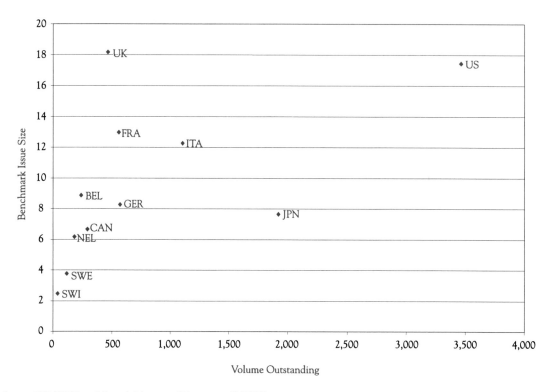

Source: BIS (1999) and French Ministry of Finance staff (2000)

some basic projections, based in good part on consultation with the market, to determine the appropriate size. The size question can be partly solved by reducing auction frequency and increasing the total amount offered at each auction. The downside to this approach is that a large auction amount per issue may not have enough bidders. Given the total size of a government's annual borrowing program and the desirability of having auctions on a regular basis over the course of a year, governments may need to explore the possibility of reopening previously issued securities to make new bonds fungible and to achieve the volume needs of the market.

Table 4.3. Size Differences Between Average Issues and Benchmark Issues
(US$ billions)

	Average Issue Size	*Benchmark Size*
Belgium	1.7	5.9*
Canada	2.3	6.7
France	11.5	13.0
Germany	4.8	5.3
Italy	5.5	12.3
Japan	5.2	5.7
Netherlands	3.5	6.2*
Sweden	4.0	3.8*
Switzerland	0.8	2.5*
United Kingdom	5.6	15.2*
United States	13.9	15.5

Note: Benchmark sizes are given for a typical (recent set of) 10-year benchmark issues.

*The following issues were used: Belgium, 6.25% due 3/2007; Netherlands, 5.27% due 2/2007; Sweden, 6.5% due 5/2008; Switzerland, 4.25% due 1/2005; United Kingdom, 5.25% due 12/2007.

Sources: BIS 1999a, 1999b; French Ministry of Finance staff 2000

4.4 Reopening and Buyback Operations to Build Benchmark Issues

Reopening and buyback operations (see Box 4.5 for definitions) are used to increase the fungibility of benchmark issues by reducing the number of issues outstanding and concentrating remaining issues on a few benchmark bonds. Such operations help debt managers achieve the desirable size and life cycle for benchmark issues.[68] Reopening the same bond with the same maturity and coupon for several consecutive auctions reduces the need to open another issue, keeps the bond in its life cycle, and gradually builds outstanding volume to the desired benchmark level. Buybacks can be used in

---

68. The "life cycle" of a benchmark issue refers to the period between the issue date of a bond and the date it becomes on-the-run.

combination with reopenings to build the size and lengthen the life cycle of those issues targeted to serve as benchmark issues by eliminating non-actively traded bonds, standardizing current outstanding bonds, and maintaining or increasing the volume of bonds targeted for benchmark issues. Details on the use of reopening and buyback operations in various countries are provided in Annex 4.A and Annex 4.B.

Policymakers need to pay attention to the proper timing of reopening and buyback operations. An on-the-run issue may not always be the most liquid of the benchmarks. Even if the life cycle of a government security is long enough to maintain its on-the-run status, it may lose its benchmark status. If the time between issues is too long, the security may reach the point where its maturity no longer corresponds to the needs of the investment community and it may no longer be the most actively traded of the benchmark instruments even though it may still technically be an

---

Box 4.5. Reopening and Buyback Operations

Reopenings

A reopening operation helps overcome limited dealer bidding/subscription capacity at a single auction. A reopening operation means that the same bond (with the same maturity and coupon) is issued on more than one occasion to gradually build its outstanding volume to the desired level. Reopening operations improve debt fungibility and provide a tool for the government to concentrate its issuance on a few benchmark issues. Reopenings also have other benefits. In many OECD countries, they have been used to prevent a market squeeze by issuing additional amounts of the same security when it appears that one or more market participants have cornered the existing supply and are able to use their position to command excessive prices from those who would need to acquire the security. In some countries, they are used to create new benchmarks. In the United States, for example, one-fourth of the benchmark six-month Treasury bills are actually reopened one-year T-bills because the T-bills roll down the yield curve, and as off-the-run issues eventually become a benchmark for original maturity six-month bills.

Buybacks

A buyback operation is the repurchase of government bonds prior to maturity. These operations are conducted in the form of reverse auctions, outright purchases in the secondary market, or through bond conversions. Buyback operations have been used to assist the development of a benchmark yield curve by eliminating unwanted bonds, standardizing current outstanding bonds, and maintaining or increasing new issuance volumes. A common problem faced by the government in its efforts to improve the liquidity of targeted benchmark bonds is the limited stock of such bonds. By buying back less liquid and often off-the-run issues ahead of maturity, the government can increase the amount of benchmark securities being issued, in essence using the proceeds from the new debt issues to finance buyback operations.

In addition to assisting benchmark yield curve development, buybacks are widely used for other related purposes. France uses buybacks to smooth debt maturities and manage rollover risk; Austria and Italy use them to reduce government debt; and Belgium and Finland use them to accelerate the redemption schedule of illiquid government bonds.

on-the-run issue.[69] Understanding the limits of continuing on-the-run issues helps the government to decide the timing of reopenings and buy-backs. A government should not continue to reopen an issue that has aged and lost its benchmark status—perhaps an old, large, off-the-run benchmark issue that has rolled down the yield curve. In this situation, buying back the instrument may end the circulation of such illiquid securities, thus allowing the government to concentrate on building new benchmark issues.

4.5   Conclusion

Promoting the development of benchmark issues can offer many benefits. It may reduce government borrowing costs for a given maturity, as governments are able to capture the liquidity premium. It reveals price information in the form of a yield curve that facilitates the issuing and refinancing of government securities and the actions of private investors and borrowers, and it helps underpin the development of associated derivatives markets. By fostering more active and informed markets, benchmark issues help to strengthen the transmission mechanism for monetary policy.

Development of benchmark issues, however, can aggravate rollover risk if the government debt outstanding is concentrated in a small number of maturities. In the short run at least, attempts to build benchmark issues along the yield curve may raise debt-service costs, since term premiums tend to be larger for longer-term maturities. The cost of longer-term government securities obviously will be higher in countries with unstable economic conditions. In the long run, however, by providing a better maturity structure to the market, the presence of benchmark securities may help reduce or limit risk premiums on government securities.

Building benchmark issues requires government commitment to a borrowing schedule that may not always coincide with its current funding needs. It will also lead governments that have relied on direct monetary

---

69. For example, a large seven-year original maturity off-the-run old benchmark issue rolling down the yield curve becomes a bond with five years of remaining life. Its five-year benchmark status might compete with a five-year original maturity on-the-run issue that now has only a four-year maturity, but still maintains its on-the-run status because of reopenings that lengthen its life cycle.

policy control measures to shift to indirect methods that allow markets to function more efficiently.

The balance between the benefits and costs to be derived from promoting benchmark issues will vary from country to country. Authorities thus must determine the appropriate course of development actions. In some countries, political uncertainties and unstable macroeconomic and financial policies will be too pervasive, thereby preventing the emergence of markets for longer-term securities regardless of steps the authorities might take to encourage the development of these markets. In others, the environment may permit development of only a limited number of benchmark issues.

Proper sequencing of measures in developing a benchmark yield curve is important. First, the government needs to assess the benefits and costs of developing such a yield curve and how far out in the future such a curve should extend. Next, the government should take steps to develop the desired yield curve. In addition to achieving macroeconomic stability and improving market regulation and infrastructure, the government, as the most creditworthy domestic issuer, should take the lead in developing benchmark issues through its issuing activities. Ultimately, however, the market will determine which maturities and issues become benchmarks.

The government's credibility as a government security issuer is established by developing a credible market-oriented funding strategy that emphasizes enhancing market liquidity by issuing mainly tradable instruments, reducing market fragmentation, and improving issue fungibility. Under such a strategy, the government or debt manager can use a variety of issuing activities to develop the benchmark yield curve. The first step is to improve issuing policy choices, such as standardizing government securities instruments, forming a proper maturity mix of benchmark securities, and determining the appropriate size and frequency of the issues. As development progresses, the government may find that operations beyond issuance, including more technical market operations, can be used to help implement policy choices. Such operations can include reopening on-the-run government bonds and/or repurchasing or buying back government bonds from the market.

Annex 4.A
Reopening Operations and Their Role in Developing Benchmark Issues

4.A.1   Reopening Operations

Reopening operations have become a standard practice in many countries. As shown in Table 4.4, only Japan, among industrial countries, does not reopen previously issued securities. In France, there is a basic rule that every bond, from a few months to 30 years' maturity, can be reopened. The practice is also well accepted in other markets, and strongly supported by local and international dealers and investors. In New Zealand, it is common to offer the same maturity bond for 12 consecutive auctions over a period of up to 12 months.

Many emerging economies have started using reopenings to reduce the number of government bond series and to enhance the liquidity of bonds targeted to serve as benchmarks. In 1990, Israel had 261 series of marketable government bond series and a new series was issued each month in that year. This resulted in a large number of small thinly traded bonds. Realizing the size and the liquidity problem, the government has been trying to reduce the number of bonds issued by reopening the same series over a period of a year or longer. By December 1999, only 135 series were outstanding. (See Figure 4.3.) Because of the reduction in the number of bond series, the average size rose from $250 million equivalent in 1990 to $1.25 billion equivalent in 1999. While reopenings enhance liquidity of the benchmark and other issues, the tax treatment of the discount or premium on a bond at the time of issuance could be an impediment to employing the reopening practice. Box 4.6 summarizes the tax considerations for the use of reopenings in the case of the Republic of Korea.

Table 4.4. Bond Reopening Systems in G–10 Countries

When and how are securities reopened?

Canada	There are 2 types of reopening: 1) to build up new issues via regular reopenings, and 2) to keep the integrity of the market.
	• Regarding 1), a new issue is built up by several reopenings, following a regular pattern since 1992 for each maturity, e.g., 2-year bonds are reopened once, 5- and 10-year bonds are reopened 3 times, and, since 1998, 30-year bonds are reopened 3 times.
	• Regarding 2), when market integrity is challenged by market manipulation, the Treasury reserves the right to reopen. However, the Treasury considers this a drastic measure and has never reopened an issue outside its regular schedule.
	The reasons the government does so, instead of holding a large initial auction are: 1) a consensus has been reached between bond market participants and the authorities on the maximum size for an auction that dealers can bear, 2) the financing requirements of the government during any period tend not to exceed the size of the reopening, and 3) one is able to "freshen up" issues by adding some bonds to actively trading market participants, who are contrary to the buy-and-hold market participants who tend to take the bond out of circulation.
Italy	There are 3 types of reopening: 1) to build up new issues via regular reopenings, 2) to provide specialists with an additional supply of bonds in "reserved reopenings," and 3) to maintain market integrity.
	• Regarding 1), a new issue is built up by several reopenings, following a regular pattern for each maturity, e.g. 10-year bonds are reopened around 8 times.
	• Regarding 2), "reserved reopening" takes place in the afternoon of the auction day, where 10% of the principal auction's amount is offered to the specialists at the price determined in the principal auction. The submission deadline for "reserved auction" is 17:00.
	• Regarding 3), when market integrity is challenged by, for example, an attempt to manipulate the market, such as a short squeeze, the Treasury is prepared to provide the market with an additional supply of any security by reopening the issue.
United Kingdom	There are 2 types of reopening: 1) to build up new issues at 5, 10, 20, and 30 years, and 2) to maintain market integrity.
	• Regarding 1), a new issue is built up by several reopenings, following a normal timetable.
	• Regarding 2), when market integrity is challenged by, for example, an attempt to manipulate the market, such as a short squeeze, the government is prepared to provide the market with an additional supply of any security by reopening the issue.

Continued

Table 4.4. (Continued) Bond Reopening Systems in G–10 Countries

When and how are securities reopened?

United States	There are 2 types of reopenings: 1) to create benchmarks in the 3- to 6-month range, and 2) to keep market integrity.
	• Regarding 1), benchmarks for 3- and 6-month range are created by reopening existing 1-year T-bills. One-year bills are issued every 4 weeks and both 3- and 6-month bills are issued weekly; therefore, 1 in 4 6-month bills is a reopened 1-year bill, and all 3-month bills are reopened 6-month bills.
	• Regarding 2), when market integrity is challenged by, for example, an attempt to manipulate the market, such as a short squeeze, the Treasury is prepared to provide the market with an additional supply of any security by reopening the issue.
Belgium	There are 2 types of reopening: 1) to build up new issues via regular reopenings, and 2) to maintain market integrity.
	• Regarding 1), a new issue is built up by several reopenings, not by a single auction. A reopening is conducted at the market's request during regular meetings with primary dealers. However, no special rules for reopenings exist. The decision to issue new tranches on existing lines or to reopen a line is published on information vendor screens 1 week before the auction takes place.
	• Regarding 2), when market integrity is challenged by attempt to manipulate the market, the Treasury reserves the right to reopen.
France	There is 1 type of reopening: to build up new issues via regular reopenings.
	The reopening is almost systematically used as the Treasury favors successive securities sales that are parts of a single issue in order to build up sufficiently large securities reserves.
	Rules for reopening are:
	• There are Obligations assimilables du Trésor (OATs, or fungible Treasury bond) issues every month. Each year, the Treasury issues only 1 or 2 new 10-year bonds perceived as benchmark issues. Hence, reopening occurs between 6 and 12 times per year.
	• Bons du Trésor à taux fixe et à intérêts annuels (BTANs notes) are issued every month. Every 6 months, the Treasury normally creates 1 line of 2-year BTANs and one line of 5-year BTANs. Therefore, subsequent monthly issues are attached to these lines.
	• The rule for Bons du Trésor Bons du Trésor à taux fixe, et à intérêts precomptes (BTFs) is a bit more complex. Like OATs and BTANs, BTFs are fungible securities, but with an initial maturity of up to 1 year. At its weekly auction, the Treasury systematically issues 1 13-week BTF and, alternately, 1 6-month BTF and 1 12-month BTF. The original maturities may be adjusted to attach BTFs to existing lines (i.e., reopening the lines). There can be short-dated BTFs with maturities of 4 to 6 weeks, half-yearly BTF issues with maturities of 24 to 29 weeks, and annual BTF issues with maturities of 42 to 52 weeks.
	Reopenings are not conducted to prevent market manipulation.

Continued

Table 4.4. (Continued) Bond Reopening Systems in G–10 Countries

When and how are securities reopened?

Germany	There are 2 types of reopening: 1) to build up new issues via regular reopenings, and 2) to increase the amount set aside for market management operations.
	• Regarding 1), a new issue is built up by several reopenings, not by a single auction. The major aim of reopening an issue is to enhance its volume and liquidity (e.g., DM 30 billion).
	• Regarding 2), reopenings are conducted to increase the amount set aside for market management operations and not to prevent squeezes.
Netherlands	There is 1 type of reopening: to build up new issues via regular reopenings.
	• Issues are reopened several times to become benchmarks (approximately Dfl 10–15 billion)
	Reopenings are not conducted to prevent market manipulation.
Sweden	There is 1 type of reopening: to build up new issues via regular reopenings.
	• Reopening 1 of the 12 benchmark bonds is the normal issue procedure. However, new benchmark bonds can be added.
	Reopenings are not conducted to prevent market manipulation.
Switzerland	There is 1 type of reopening: to build up bonds of sufficient liquidity, especially benchmarks (Sfr 2–4 billion) via regular reopenings.
	Reopenings are not conducted to prevent manipulation.

Note: Japan is the only G–10 country that has no reopening system.
Source: BIS 1999a, 1999b

Figure 4.3. Number of Tradable Government Bond Series and Average Size of Series in Israel

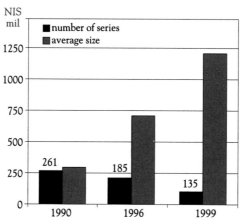

ce: Ministry of Finance, State of Israel (2000)

Box 4.6. Tax Impediments for Reopening Practices—The Case of the Republic of Korea

In the Republic of Korea, while there was consensus among practitioners and policymakers that reopenings should be employed to enhance the liquidity of the benchmark and other issues, tax treatment of the discount or premium on a bond at the time of issuance was an impediment. The fiscal authority taxed the coupon amount and the income, amortizing the amount of any discount at the time of issue over the life of the bond to obtain the total income from it each year. This was a reasonably simple way to determine the tax liability, but it prevented the establishment of a series of fungible bonds with which to achieve the objective of a liquid benchmark issue.

In building a fungible series of bonds, it is necessary to allow multiple auctions of the same bond maturity, so that individual bonds become indistinguishable in the secondary market. In sequential offerings of the same bond maturity, bonds will be sold at different prices and yields in each auction. Because current tax treatment of the amount of discount on a bond when it is sold into the primary market is different for each auction, bonds from sequential auctions cannot be combined in investor and dealer portfolios to make them fungible. Thus, the tax treatment of the discount or premium on a bond needed to be addressed before the government could achieve liquid benchmark bond issues through sequential selling of the same bond.

This problem could be resolved in two ways. The definition of taxable income could be changed to one based on the market valuation of the bonds, so that the amount of discount at the time of issue was no longer an element in the calculation. This method would, however, effectively create a capital gains tax on bonds, as any increase in their market value would become taxable income. Given the complexity of introducing a capital gains tax, and the likely need to extend its application to other types of investment such as equities, this may not have been an attractive solution for the problem for Korea.

An alternative was to tax only the coupon interest for reopened issues of government bonds and ignore the discount or premium at issuance. This would be revenue neutral in three ways.

First, the increase or decrease in taxes caused by this alternative treatment would be reflected in the price of the bonds, and this would offset the change in tax revenues. For example, suppose interest rates rose following the first issuance of a new bond, so that it is reopened at a lower price. Under this alternative, the tax revenue would be lower than under the current regime. However, the favorable tax treatment of a discount government bond would raise the price of the bond, offsetting the decline in tax revenue. So far as the government was concerned, the change in tax treatment could be considered revenue neutral. In fact, considering the potential decrease in interest cost due to an increase in liquidity, the proposed change in tax treatment may even be revenue enhancing.

Second, the decline in tax revenues in the case of a discount would also be offset by the increase in revenue in the case of a premium issuance. If an increase in the interest rate was as likely as a decrease, then the change in tax treatments should not change the expected tax revenue.

Finally, the proposed change in tax treatment would not affect the tax revenue, because interest income and capital gains of a financial institution were taxed as a part of corporate income tax. Since the majority of government bonds were held by financial institutions, they were subject to corporate income tax, and thus the proposed tax change would have little overall effect on tax revenue.

Following this line of argument, the government abolished taxation of discount or premium of a bond, and introduced fungible issues on May 16, 2000.

Source: World Bank, Financial and Corporate Restructuring Assistance Project by Capital Market Department 2000

ANNEX 4.B
Buyback Operations and Their Role in Developing Benchmark Securities

A buyback is the repurchase of government bonds prior to their maturity. Using the proceeds of new issues to acquire less-liquid instruments typically uses buybacks to pay down debt in an environment of fiscal surpluses, to disperse redemption concentration and manage rollover risk, and to maintain new issuance volume in benchmark issues.

Box 4.7. highlights the basic principles in conducting buyback operations.

4.B.1   Buyback Operations

Three variants of buyback operations are a reverse auction, outright repurchases in the market, and bond conversions. These operations may be conducted by the government debt manager or by the central bank in its open market operations.

4.B.1.1   Reverse Auction

A reverse auction is often used for large-scale repurchase of government bonds. A reverse auction is conducted in a manner similar to a regular auction, except that it is for purchase instead of sale of bonds. Table 4.5 illustrates how a reverse auction works and how it compares with a regular auction, using Canada as an example.

Box 4.7. Basic Principles in Selecting Buyback Candidates

The following are basic principles in selecting bonds to be repurchased that are observed by many countries:

Choose only less-liquid and off-the-run issues for buyback programs. Do not buy back current or targeted benchmark issues.

Consider the maturity and coupon structure when selecting bonds to be repurchased. Buybacks should be based on an evaluation of the current debt portfolio, including currency composition, duration, and maturity distribution.

Be aware of other bond market operations. One should not choose a bond to be repurchased if a great proportion of the bond has been stripped.

Consider the impact of buyback programs on the pricing of secondary market issues and weigh the effectiveness and cost of each potential buyback operation.

**Table 4.5. How a Reverse Auction Works:
The Case of Canada**

Reverse Auction	*Regular Auction*
• A quarterly announcement is made indicating when the reverse auctions will take place and the maturity ranges of the bond(s) of interest.	• A quarterly announcement is made indicating when the bond auctions will take place and which bond maturities will be issued.
• Roughly one week before each reverse auction, a call for tender notice is issued giving the maximum amount the government wishes to repurchase.	• A week before each auction, there is a call for tender notice that gives the amount to be issued and maturity date of the issue.
• Upon release of notice, the issue trades, as it did before the notice, in the secondary market. The secondary market serves as the forward or when-issued market for the security to be repurchased.	• Upon release of the notice, the bonds to be issued begin to trade on the forward or when-issued market.
• Tenders by primary distributors are submitted on auction day (same day as regular auctions of bonds with similar terms to maturities). Tenders must be received no later than 1:30 p.m.	• Tenders by primary distributors are submitted on auction day. Tenders must be received no later than 12:30 p.m.
• Dealers can submit several tender offers in terms of yield that total up to the announced maximum repurchase amount.	• Government securities dealers and primary dealers can submit several tenders in terms of yield (each must be of minimum size equal to C$250,000) up to their individual bidding limits (maximum 25 percent of bonds being issued).
• Competitive offers are accepted in descending order until the fair-value price (as determined by the government) is reached, subject to the maximum amount being repurchased.	

Source: Gravelle (1998)

The most significant difference between a reverse auction and a regular auction is the uncertain size of a reverse auction. In a reverse auction, only the maximum amount the government plans to repurchase is announced. This stands in contrast to a regular auction, where the amount to be issued is known in advance, but the government reserves the right to reject individual bids. This feature allows the government to reject offers that are below the internally set cut-off yield and to reduce the auction amount. It protects the government from locking itself into purchasing bonds at a significantly higher than fair-market price.

4.B.1.2 Outright Purchase

In an outright purchase, the government contacts market makers to solicit directly their offers to sell government bonds. Outright purchases are often used for much smaller-scale repurchase operations than in a reverse auction.

Two types of outright purchases are the "coupon purchase" and the "reverse tap purchase." A coupon purchase is the purchase of an unspecified amount of bond issues within a specific maturity range. It is frequently used in the Federal Reserve's open market operations. In a typical coupon purchase, the Fed requests offers to sell government bonds from its primary dealers. The mechanism of the coupon purchase is similar to that of a reverse auction, but there are also some subtle differences. A coupon purchase does not go through a formal auction process. Unlike a reverse auction, the maximum amount to be repurchased in a coupon purchase is not specified before the operation is finished. In this manner, a coupon purchase is more open ended than a reverse auction. A coupon purchase only announces the government's interest to purchase bonds within a specified maturity range, while a reverse auction tends to focus on a much more restricted range of bond issues, e.g., one or two bond issues. Another important difference is the very short period between the announcement of a coupon purchase and the completion of the operation. The whole process often takes only 10 to 20 minutes.

Box 4.8 describes how the Federal Reserve Bank of New York conducts a coupon purchase repurchase in an open market operation and offers additional operational details on coupon purchases.

In addition to the coupon purchase, the reverse tap purchase is also used to conduct outright (re)purchases. As its name implies, a reverse tap purchase is the inverse of the tap sales of government bonds. In a reverse tap purchase, the government directly contacts primary dealers or brokers in the secondary market and purchases government bonds from them. The reverse tap purchase is good for a relatively small buyback program.

4.B.1.3 Bond Conversion

Another way to conduct a buyback program is a "conversion" or bond exchange. In a conversion program, the government buys back from bondholders some particular series of government bonds, and the payment for the repurchase is made in terms of another series of government bonds,

---

Box 4.8. Coupon Purchase Operation in the United States

Staff at the Federal Reserve Bank of New York and at the Board of Governors of Federal Reserve System provide the open market operation desk with estimates of the average supply of and demand for reserves to project open market operation needs. If staff projections indicate a large and persistent imbalance between reserve demand and supply, say for a month or more, the desk may conduct an outright purchase or sale of securities. Such transactions permanently increase or decrease the size of the Federal Reserve's portfolio. The desk conducts far more outright purchases than outright sales, primarily because it must offset the reserve drain resulting from the public's increasing demand for currency.

Before 1995, the desk entered the market to conduct outright operations only a few times each year. It would wait until reserve needs were large enough to warrant a sizable transaction, on the order of $3–4 billion, in part because such operations, especially coupon purchases, were time consuming. For a coupon purchase, the desk must review numerous offers on about 200 securities. Automation of the bidding process in 1994 decreased the time needed to evaluate offers, but dealers still had to wait a significant amount of time between submitting offers and learning whether their offers had been accepted. For that reason, dealers, in pricing their offers, took into account the risk that market prices might move adversely while they were waiting.

In November 1995, the desk changed its approach to outright coupon purchases. It now divides a purchase of coupon securities, focusing on only a portion of the maturity spectrum rather than on all maturities at once. This approach has further decreased the turnaround time for such operations and has likely resulted in better prices to the desk. The desk still purchases all maturities of Treasury coupon issues, but it generally spreads its purchases over several weeks in keeping with the size of estimated reserve needs. With this new procedure, the desk is better able to tailor its purchases to reserve needs. In addition, the operations, which had been conducted only in the early afternoon, can now be conducted in the morning as well.

When purchasing securities in the secondary market, the desk entertains bids from primary dealers on all securities of a particular type (Treasury bills or Treasury coupon securities) and, for coupon securities, in a particular portion of the maturity spectrum. In determining which bids to accept, the desk considers the bids that represent the highest yield (for purchases) or the lowest yield (for sales) relative to the prevailing yield curve. To avoid holding too large a share of any one issue, the desk also considers the size of its holdings of the particular issue relative to the total amount outstanding.

Source: Edwards 1997

---

which are often newly issued, more liquid bonds. A conversion can also be used in combination with reopening operations, i.e., the newly issued bonds that are used to pay for the conversion can be a reopened issue. By replacing a less-liquid issue with a more liquid benchmark issue, a bond exchange may be used as an active market management tool to develop benchmark bonds and maintain market liquidity.

A bond conversion can be carried out in either of two methods, representing two distinct means to determine the price ratio (or conversion ratio) of the converted bonds to new bonds. The first is a competitive-offer format, where the conversion ratio is determined by the bids submitted by market participants. The participants also submit bids on the amount of the conversion. A competitive-offer format can be implemented by either a reverse auction or a coupon purchase operation. They are the same as a conventional auction and a conventional coupon purchase, respectively, except that their offers are in terms of a price ratio and in essence they are paying for the new bonds by another, old bond.

The second manner of conducting a bond conversion is a fixed-rate format, where the conversion ratio is predetermined by the government according to the prices prevailing in the secondary market at the time of announcement. After the government's announcement of a conversion program, holders of the targeted bonds have a limited amount of time to decide whether to accept the government's offer before it closes. The actual volume of conversions is determined by the market; the conversion amount will be open ended and there is no guarantee that the government will be able to buy back all the targeted bonds.

4.B.2   Choice of Buyback Program(s)

Effectiveness and cost of the operation are the two basic criteria for choosing a buyback program.

Effectiveness is determined by the government's ability to repurchase government securities in large volume, to consolidate government bonds outstanding, and to establish liquid benchmarks. The reverse auction and bond conversions can handle larger-scale repurchases of government bonds, the coupon purchase is good for medium-scale repurchases, and the reverse tap works best for small repurchases.

The government suffers a cost when repurchasing the bonds at a price above the fair value. This could happen because the government repurchase announcement has an impact on the price of related bonds in the secondary market. The degree of impact has much to do with the mechanism of the operation. It is negatively correlated to the time between the announcement and the closing of the transaction. Gravelle (1998) examined the secondary market pricing implication of buyback operations and concluded that the reverse auction and bond conversions are most likely to put the government in an unfavorable position when pricing buybacks. The reverse tap tends to give market participants the least opportunity to charge the government a price above the fair price. Table 4.6 summarizes the effectiveness and cost of different types of buyback programs. Reverse auction

Table 4.6. Effectiveness and Cost of Buyback Programs

Buyback Program	Effectiveness	Cost
Reverse Auction	Best	Highest
Outright Purchase		
Coupon Purchase	Average	Average
Reverse Tap Purchase	Worst	Lowest
Conversion	Best	Highest

Note: Effectiveness is measured by the ability to conduct a large amount of buybacks, and cost is measured by the potential adverse price movements that the government might face after announcement of the buyback program.

4

and bond conversion allow the government to conduct a large amount of buybacks, but also most likely subject the government to unfair prices; the opposite is true for the reverse tap. The coupon purchase results in average effectiveness and cost.

Bibliography

APEC (Asia-Pacific Economic Cooperation). 1999. *Proceedings of APEC Workshop on Development of Domestic Bond Markets.* Hong Kong.

BIS (Bank for International Settlements). 1999a. *How Should We Design Deep and Liquid Markets? The Case of Government Securities.* Basel, Switzerland.

————. 1999b. *Market Liquidity: Research Findings and Selected Policy Implications.* CGFS Publications No. 11. May. Basel, Switzerland.

Bennett, Paul, Kenneth Garbade, and John Kambhu. 2000. "Enhancing the Liquidity of U.S. Treasury Securities in an Era of Surpluses." Federal Reserve Bank of New York, *Economic Policy Review* 6 (1): 89–119. Available at www.ny.frb.org/.

Campbell, John Y., and Robert Shiller. 1996. *A Scorecard for Indexed Government Debt.* Yale University Discussion Paper No. 1125, Yale University, New Haven, Conn.

Edwards, Cheryl. 1997. "Open Market Operations in the 1990s." *Federal Reserve Bulletin.* 83 (11): 859–74.

Fabozzi, Frank. 1996. *Bond Markets, Analysis and Strategies.* Englewood Cliffs, N.J.: Prentice Hall.

Fleming, Michael J. 2000. "The Benchmark U.S. Treasury Market: Recent Performance and Possible Alternatives." Federal Reserve Bank of New York, *Economic Policy Review* 6 (1): 129–45. Available at www.ny.frb.org/.

Goldstein, Morris et al. 1994. *International Capital Markets: Developments, Prospects, and Policy Issues.* International Monetary Fund, Washington, D.C.

Gravelle, Toni. 1998. "Buying Back Government Bonds: Mechanics and Other Considerations." Bank of Canada Working Paper. Ottawa, Canada.

————. 1999. "Liquidity of the Government of Canada Securities Market: Stylized Facts and Some Market Microstructure Comparisons to the United States Treasury Market." Bank of Canada Working Paper 99–11. Ottawa, Canada.

Hong Kong and Shanghai Banking Corporation (HSBC). 1999. *A Guide to the Philippine Domestic Debt Capital Market.*

Hui, Liu. 2000. *Development of Government Bond Markets in DMCs: People's Republic of China.* Asian Development Bank Conference on

4

Government Bond Markets and Financial Sector Development in Developing Asian Economies.

Inoue, Hirotaka. 1999. *The Structure of Government Securities Market in G–10 Countries*. Bank for International Settlements, Basel, Switzerland.

IMF (International Monetary Fund) and World Bank. 2000. *Draft Guidelines for Public Debt Management*. Washington, D.C. Available at www.imf.org/external/np/mae/pdebt/2000/eng/index.htm.

Kahn, Michael. 2000. "Promoting Liquid Government Securities Benchmark: The Case of Israel." Second OECD/World Bank Workshop on Development of Fixed-Income Securities Markets in Emerging Market Economies. Washington, D.C.

Price, Robert. 1997. "The Rationale and Design of Inflation-Indexed Bonds." Working Paper 97/12, International Monetary Fund, Washington, D.C. Available at www.imf.org.

Sundaresan, Suresh. 1997. *Fixed Income Markets and Their Derivatives*. Cincinnati, Ohio: International Thomson Publishing.

World Bank. 1999. Financial and Corporate Restructuring Assistance Project (FCRA). World Bank, Washington, D.C.

4

Chapter 5

Developing a Primary Market for Government Securities

A well-functioning primary market for government securities is essential for the orderly funding of government financing requirements, the foundation for a secondary market, and a source of price (interest rate) signals in many less-developed markets. The government has the responsibility for establishing a primary market. Its choice of procedures will depend on country circumstances.

5.1 Introduction

The selection of selling procedures or distribution channels for government securities encompasses a number of policy decisions. The selection should, to the extent possible (i) ensure cost-effectiveness; (ii) encourage participation from a relatively wide range of investors, including foreign institutions; (iii) maximize competition; (iv) minimize placement risk; and (v) foster transparency. For most advanced economies, the main sales technique is typically auctions. For countries in the early stage of debt-market development, selling may take the form of syndication, tap sales, underwriting, or private placement. Whether to use primary dealers and, if so, how the dealers are to be chosen and organized, are important related questions.

By making government securities straightforward in design, tailoring their maturities to meet market demand, and announcing borrowing plans in advance, the government can make its securities more attractive. There is also the question of the choice of auction administrator, which may be the Treasury or an agent of the Treasury, such as the central bank, a debt management office, or other organization. (See Chapter 3, A Government Debt Issuance Strategy and Debt Management Framework, and Chapter 4, Developing Benchmark Issues.)

By providing securities accounts (i.e., book-entry custodial services), the government can facilitate the issuance of government securities and make their trading and lending more feasible than if they were kept in paper form. (See Chapter 8, Developing a Government Securities Settlement Structure.) Primary market participants must be sufficiently creditworthy to fulfill their responsibility to purchase government securities. Supervision is needed for this purpose as well as for general oversight of government securities market operations. (See Chapter 9, Legal and Regulatory Framework.)

5.2   Techniques for Marketing Government Securities

Auctions have become the predominant distribution technique for government securities in industrial countries because they have proved to be more cost effective and transparent than other methods. For the same reasons, when financial systems in developing countries have reached a certain level, auctions have also become the main distribution procedure for issuing government securities in these countries. Other selling arrangements (syndication, underwriting, and tap sales) may prove more appropriate than auctions in the early stages of market development.

5.2.1   Auctions[70]

Governments in both developed and developing countries are increasingly using auctions as their main distribution channel for selling government securities. (See Table 5.1.) There are two main types of auctions, multiple price and uniform price, each with advantages and drawbacks. Governments need to be aware of the features of each type, such as their revenue potential and vulnerability to noncompetitive behavior

---

70. For a review of auction theory, see Sundaresan 1996 and Sundaran 1997.

(manipulation) by bidders, when selecting an auction procedure. Other types of auctions are largely a combination of these two.[71]

In multiple-price auctions, the issuer orders bids by price in descending order and accepts the higher bids until the issue is exhausted. Each winning bidder pays the price it bid. In uniform-price auctions, the issuer, as in multiple-price auctions, orders bids in descending order and accepts those that allow full absorption of the amount up for issue. In uniform-price auctions, however, all successful bidders pay the price of the lowest successful bid. In both techniques, the lowest accepted price is the cut-off price.

Multiple-price auctions have advantages for the issuer. They maximize revenue for a given demand curve, as the issuer obtains the maximum price each participant is willing to pay, and the issuer thereby obtains the consumers' surplus.[72] In a uniform-price auction, by contrast, since successful bidders pay only the lowest (marginal) price regardless of what they were initially prepared to pay, the consumers' surplus is shared between the issuer and the bidders.

There are studies, however, that suggest that the selection of auction procedure can influence the demand curve for securities.[73] Multiple-price auctions tend to shift the demand curve down and to the left for a given quantity. Bidders bid more cautiously (i.e., offer lower prices) in these auctions, because bidders who paid higher prices could face larger capital losses if the trading in these securities starts below the marginal price set at the auction. This is known as the "winner's curse." The "winner's curse" can be an important problem in emerging markets where price volatility may be high. The "winner's curse" does not arise in uniform-price auctions. Uniform-price auctions tend to minimize uncertainty, encourage broader participation, and, everything else being equal, make bidders more willing to pay higher prices than they would pay in multiple-price auctions.[74]

---

71. A combination of the multiple-price and uniform-price auction involves, for example, an auction where bids at the marginal price are allocated at the marginal rate and the rest of the successful bids are allocated at an average between the marginal rate and the highest bid.

72. The consumers' surplus in this case refers to the forgone proceeds that a government incurs when it offers securities at a price that is lower than the marginal price of each bid.

73. See Bartolini and Cottarelli 1997.

74. Uniform-price auctions may produce greater revenue on average, but they present greater uncertainty about revenue at any given auction (see Malvey et al. 1995).

Table 5.1. Methods of Issuance of Government Securities in Selected Developed and Developing Countries

Country	Issuance Mechanism	Frequency Bonds	Bills
Developed Markets			
Canada	Multiple-price auction in general and uniform price for inflation-linked bonds	Monthly	Weekly
France	Multiple-price auction	Monthly (1st Thursday OATs, 3rd Thursday BTANs)	Weekly
Germany	Multiple-price auction	Quarterly (2-, 5-year bonds)	Weekly
Italy	Multiple-price auction (bills), uniform-price auction (bonds)	Every 15 days	Every 15 days
Japan	Multiple-price auction	Monthly	
Sweden	Multiple-price auction	Every 15 days (nominal bonds), on tap (index-linked bonds)	Every 15 days
United Kingdom	Multiple-price auction (gilts and bills, Euro notes and bills), uniform-price auction (index-linked)	Quarterly (conventional gilts, index-linked gilts, Euro notes)	Weekly (national currency bills), monthly (Euro bills)
United States	Uniform-price auction	Monthly (2-year notes), quarterly (5-, 10-year fixed principal notes), semiannually (10-, 30-year indexed notes and bonds, 30-year fixed-principal bonds)	Weekly (13-, 26-week bills), quarterly (52-week bills)
Emerging Markets			
Brazil	Multiple-price auction	Monthly	Weekly
Hungary	Multiple-price auction	Every 15 days	Weekly
Rep. of Korea	Multiple-price auction	Quarterly (3-, 5-year fungible bonds)	
Malaysia	Multiple-price auction	Irregular (2- to 21-year bonds, 3- to 7-year floating rate)	Irregular
Mexico	Multiple-price auction	Weekly (3-year floating rate bonds); biweekly (3-, 5-year inflation-indexed bonds)	Weekly
Poland	Multiple-price auction	Every 1–4 months (fixed-rate 2-, 5-year bonds), quarterly (1-, 3-year floating-rate notes), irregular (10-year floating-rate bonds)	Weekly

Table 5.2. Auction Techniques for Selling Government Securities

	Bidding Method			
	Uniform Price	Multiple Price	Other	Total
Discount	—	8	—	8
Price	2	21	1	24
Yield	—	10	—	10
Total	2	39	1	42

Source: Bartolini and Cottarelli 1997.

The susceptibility to noncompetitive behavior is another factor that needs to be considered in the selection of an auction technique. On the one hand, multiple-price auctions can encourage competitive bidding, because each bidder is aware that it will have to pay the price it bid, not just the minimum accepted price. This circumstance can minimize the risk of manipulation at the auction. On the other hand, it is possible that uniform-price auctions, being simpler, could reduce the need to prepare for the auction and encourage more participation, thus reducing incentives to collude.

The study by Bartolini and Cottarelli (1997) confirms that multiple-price auctions are more widely used in practice than other auction techniques. (See Table 5.2.) In a survey of auction techniques in 42 countries using auctions, multiple-price auctions were the most common, accounting for 90 percent of the countries in the survey. In recent years (post 1997), some countries, including the United States, have adopted the uniform-price auction method as a result of their assessment of the net benefits of this technique over multiple-price auctions.

Experience in developing countries suggests, however, that the choice of auction technique is less important for the functioning of the government securities market than other factors, such as the way the market is liberalized and how competition is developed, including entry of foreign institutions.

5.2.1.1 Participants in Government Securities Auctions

Auctions are an open issuing channel that allows broad participation, which generally means more competition, and is, therefore, desirable from the point of view of the issuer. Nonetheless, trade-offs exist when determining the degree of participation, and governments need to be aware of policy options and their implications.

In general, auctions tend to become more open in terms of participation as the bond market develops. However, some governments want to promote broad participation, including retail bidding, from the start, in order to broaden the investor base as much as possible, stimulate competition in the financial sector, and develop financial products and markets. This approach usually works well in countries with low levels of competition in the financial sector. By opening the auction to a wider range of participants such as pension funds, mutual funds, and securities houses, governments can foster increased competition among the banking sector and improve the auction's results.

At the other extreme, some countries have opted to establish narrow participation in auctions by appointing a group of intermediaries that will on-sell securities to other financial institutions or final clients. Narrow participation usually implies granting benefits to a select group of professional market participants, e.g., primary dealers, in exchange for their distribution capabilities. (See Section 5.3.) This group may be selected because they hold accounts at the central bank, they are most willing to promote the sale of government securities to their clients, or they are most likely to make a secondary market in government securities. Narrow participation makes auction processing simpler and less costly. However, these advantages are becoming less significant as auctions become increasingly automated.

There are also intermediate arrangements for participation in auctions. Some countries allow financial institutions and institutional investors to participate in auctions but explicitly exclude retail investors. Others have set up a system allowing indirect participation through third-party bids, wherein retail investors, or final investors in general, participate in the auction through a financial institution, usually paying the average price of the auctioned securities. Even in those countries that allow open participation in auctions, not all potential bidders will wish to bid at the auction. Nonparticipants will have alternatives of buying from a primary dealer.

Participation in government securities auctions may also vary depending on the maturity of the auctioned securities. Typically, banks are more interested in short-term securities to match their short-term liabilities, while pension funds and insurance companies prefer longer-term securities.

Wider participation in auctions results in more competition, yielding better price and allocation outcomes for the issuer. However, if the auction is open to participants other than banks, the regulation and supervision of those participants and the security of payment systems become important issues.

5.2.1.2 *Competitive Auction Bids*

For an auction to be meaningful, it is essential that auctions be run on a competitive bidding basis. In many emerging countries, where state-owned commercial banks, pension funds, and insurance companies are prevalent, if these institutions are major investors and auction participants, the government must make clear the need for competitive bidding on the basis of the institution's own commercial requirements. If these institutions either are required to accept the government's issuing price or are able to set a unique offering price, the auction becomes a fiction.

One important consideration in auction design is whether to establish ceilings on competitive bids. Ceilings on maximum possible allocation per bidder are considered anti-cornering instruments, useful to prevent manipulation of the auction by one large participant. However, not many countries use bidding limits.[75] On the other hand, typically governments impose minimum bid amounts primarily for operational reasons. If a government decides to establish a minimum bid amount, the amount should strike a balance between a high figure that might discourage participation and a low figure that would increase the administrative costs of the auction. This decision will ultimately depend on the government's vision of a desirable market structure. If the government intends to develop a market with heavy retail participation, the minimum size of bids will naturally be lower than if the intention is to develop a wholesale, professional market.

As a rule, ceilings per bid are helpful to ensure competition among bidders and to protect the integrity of the auction. However, they appear to be easier to apply in mature markets than in frequently cash-strapped emerging countries. The application of minimum limits is an operational issue and will depend largely on each market's operational capacity.

---

75. Canada and the United States have increasingly used such limits. In the case of Canada, the limits also apply to dealers' customers.

5.2.1.3 Noncompetitive Auction Bids

Noncompetitive auction bids are a more efficient way to encourage retail participation than having a large number of retail investors bidding competitively on their own. The total of all noncompetitive bids is usually capped by an upper limit in order to allow the price at the auction to be determined by a sufficiently large number of competitive bids. Noncompetitive bids may also be subject to individual caps to ensure their retail nature. (A sample of noncompetitive bid limits is shown in Table 5.3.) Where central banks are permitted to participate in government securities auctions, the central bank may be a noncompetitive bidder. For transparency, central bank participation should be made clear to the market before the auction.

Securities are normally allocated to noncompetitive bidders at a weighted average price of the successful competitive bids in the case of a multiple-price auction or at the cut-off, or marginal price, in a uniform-price auction. Sometimes access to noncompetitive bids is granted as a benefit for being a primary dealer. (See Section 5.3.) Such access can be useful for bidding on behalf of retail clients.

5.2.1.4 Frequency of Auctions

The timetable for auctions is a function of debt management decisions and a desire to promote a secondary market. Too frequent auctions may lead to small auction volumes, less meaningful price information results, or even too many issues in the market for liquid secondary market trading.

A typical issuing pattern for government securities is a weekly or biweekly Treasury bill auction.[76] Longer-term instruments such as Treasury notes or Treasury bonds can be issued at longer intervals (monthly or quarterly). A quite common practice is to set a fixed day of the week for bond auctions, thereby leaving secondary market trading on the other days unobstructed by the auction. Such auction scheduling may also be helpful in providing more comparable measurement of yield curve points when the secondary market is not very active.

---

76. Weekly auctions are quite common for Treasury bills in some countries, and it is not clear whether this impairs trading in the secondary market. Other factors such as who buys at the auction—dealer versus end-buyer—also determine how actively T-bills will be traded.

5.2.1.5 *Announcement of Government Borrowing Requirements and Borrowing calendar*

For transparency purposes and to build credibility, governments should regularly disclose their forecast for public sector borrowing requirements, as well as an overall estimated issuance figure for the year and a borrowing

Table 5.3. Noncompetitive Auction Bids and Limits on Bid Amounts, in Selected Developed and Developing Countries

Country	Noncompetitive Bids	Limits on Bid Amounts
Developed Markets		
France		Small quotas allowed, after competitive tenders
Germany		No limits
Japan	For 10-year bonds, only financial institutions whose share in syndicate is less than 3 percent can bid	40% of total issue times the bidder's share in the syndicate
	2-, 4-, 6-year bonds; share reserved varies	Each participant can bid up to 500 million yen
United Kingdom	Primary dealers and others eligible to participate	Limit: 0.5 percent of auctioned amount for primary dealers, $824,000 equivalent for others
	Index-linked auctions	10% of amount offered is reserved for primary dealers, allocated according to participation in previous auctions
United States		Maximum: $5 million
Emerging Markets		
Hungary		10% of competitive bids
Korea	20 percent of newly issued Treasury securities	An individual or corporation can subscribe up to 1 billion won
Mexico		Noncompetitive bids are only allocated if there are leftovers from the competitive process

Sources: France, Germany, Japan, United Kingdom, and United States data are from Bank of International Settlements (BIS 1999); Hungary and Mexico data are from J. P. Morgan (1997); and Korea data are from Ministry of Finance and Economy, Seoul, South Korea.

calendar. (See Chapter 3, A Government Debt Issuance Strategy and Debt Management Framework.) There is a trade-off that should be recognized between the flexibility of tapping the market when conditions are favorable and the benefits of transparency attained by announcing the borrowing calendar. This problem can be minimized by disclosing broad information about borrowing requirements yearly or quarterly, but making known information on the amount to be auctioned only days before the auction.

The government has a number of options regarding what information to disclose immediately before the auction. The issuer can, for instance, announce the exact amount of the issue, and then accept bids at any price until the issue is covered. Alternatively, it can announce a tentative amount to be issued, but retain some flexibility in terms of final allocation. Alternatively, it can decide not to announce what amount will be issued and test market demand. In the latter case, when there is a high level of market uncertainty, the authorities may decide on a minimum price below which bids will not be allocated (an undisclosed cut-off price). At other times, the authorities may need to consider whether to announce this cut-off price publicly. This will sometimes be a useful guide for the market, but it risks encouraging all bids at that minimum price. Some countries (e.g. Italy) have made use of automatic formulas to eliminate discretion from the decision to accept or reject certain outlying bids.

The best long-run procedure to build market confidence, in most cases, is to announce the exact amount tendered and accept bids at any price until the issue is covered. While this may result in unexpectedly low prices at some auctions, the resultant greater market confidence should reduce the risk premium on government securities and, therefore, result in lower rates.

5.2.1.6 Announcement of Auction Results

As much aggregate information as possible should be disclosed after the auction. No information should be disseminated that might identify individual bidders.

Aggregate data of special interest for the market are the amount of bids, the allocated amount, and the weighted and marginal prices (yields). Typically, as markets develop, the announcement of details becomes more transparent, and this in turn improves confidence in the market.

5.2.2 Syndication of Government Securities Issuance and Underwriting of Government Securities

In small economies, market participants may sometimes be only two or three institutions, too limited a number for the government to run an auction since these institutions can easily collude and force the price against the issuer, or simply agree not to participate in the auction. Under such circumstances, the government can try to achieve cost-effectiveness by appointing a group of institutions which, for a negotiated fee, will subscribe to its bond issues and then sell them on to other retail or institutional investors. This is usually known as syndication.

Syndication is most useful when the demand for government securities is very uncertain, which is frequently the case in many developing countries, since it helps minimize placement risk. Syndication can also play an important role when the government is trying to launch new debt instruments and needs a supporting arrangement to introduce them in the market. However, syndication can also have disadvantages in terms of transparency, which is the reason why, even in emerging markets, auctions are often preferred. The main disadvantage of syndication is that it involves a negotiation regarding price and fees between the government and the banks and other financial institutions that will subscribe to the issue. In contrast, auctions do not involve negotiation and are more transparent.

An alternative government securities issuance method that governments can use under conditions of uncertain demand is underwriting. In an underwriting arrangement, the government establishes a minimum price at which the underwriter, for a commission, subscribes to the entire issue. Since commission is charged, the government has to consider whether underwriting is worth the price, as is the case of syndication.

At early stages of market development, syndication and underwriting can be suitable ways to ensure success in the issuance of government securities. However, these forms of issuance are normally phased out as the market develops and demand for bonds becomes more stable.[77] The use of primary dealers is usually considered a more competitive arrangement for the issuance of government securities than the use of syndication or underwriting. Primary dealers tend to shrink commissions when markets become

---

77. Germany used a government bond syndication as a natural complement to federal government securities auctions until the end of 1997.

more competitive in order to maintain market share, while the fees negotiated in a syndication remain fixed for the agreed-upon period (typically one year).

Specific situations in developed countries have also favored, for practical reasons, the use of syndication instead of auctions. This is the case in some smaller European countries after the introduction of the Euro. Since their government securities no longer have benchmark status and governments are no longer certain about investors' demand, they have had to employ syndications to minimize placement risk.

5.2.3   Tap Sales of Government Securities

Tap sales can meet many of the Treasury's government securities issuance objectives in a flexible way. With tap issues, the government announces the availability of a certain amount of securities to be sold, and bids are received during a specified period. Tap sales can be set at a fixed price or at a minimum price that can be changed depending on demand conditions. Their main advantage is flexibility, as the government can decide to tap the market when conditions are most favorable.

The use of tap sales is sometimes also closely linked to the government's cash management capabilities. If these capabilities are limited, tap sales can help provide timely access to funds. When demand for government securities is unpredictable, as is the case in many developing countries, tap sales can adapt to demand more readily than auctions. Tap sales also have the advantage of attracting retail investors and broadening the investor base.[77]

Tap sales are often found in combination with auctions, but governments should be aware of potential conflicts in doing so. The expectation that tap sales will follow the auction could undermine the amount of bids received or the quality of price information obtained from the auction. As the market will be unsure of what amount will in the end be issued, but certain that securities will be available at a later date, participants may have an incentive to bid lower prices.[78] If the rate on the tap issue is fixed,

---

77. At other times, tap sales may be reserved for primary dealers as an incentive for them to develop the bond market.

78. Another issue is what to do when not all the bonds have been sold in the auction. The issuer needs to consider how to make available the remaining amount with minimum market impact.

this can inhibit the potential for price increases in the secondary market, and may cause the issuer to pay a higher yield than would otherwise be necessary.

Auctions can make the market more dynamic than passive tap sales. In addition, provided there is an announced schedule, auctions tend to be more transparent and superior to tap sales in terms of pricing, thereby minimizing borrowing costs.

5.2.4 Private Placement of Government Securities with Banks and Other Market Participants

Governments face a trade-off between adapting their government securities issuance techniques to a possibly wide range of investor preferences and standardizing products as much as possible to promote liquidity. In their attempt to meet market needs, governments sometimes design securities targeted to a specific investor or group of investors, such as pension funds or insurance companies. If conducted with banks, private placements are very similar to a syndication. Issues placed directly with investors can at times be convenient for the issuer as a safeguard in difficult market conditions.

On the negative side, private placements do not contribute to market liquidity as much as other issuance techniques, since bonds placed privately are usually held to maturity by buyers and rarely traded. For this reason, private placements can be less cost effective and contribute less to secondary market development than auctions or tap sales.

5.2.5 Combination of Government Securities Issuance Techniques

Most countries prefer to use a combination of the techniques described above. This is probably the most practical approach, provided it is organized consistently so that it does not lead to market segmentation. In combining different issuance methods, it is essential to maintain consistency and to recognize that issuance techniques should support the efficient functioning of the government securities market structure. Countries that rely on primary dealers will probably want to issue government securities on a regular basis, with an announced calendar and relatively low frequency, in order to encourage the primary dealers' role. Countries with limited cash management capabilities may adopt tap sales to issue securities when market conditions are favorable. In the very early stages of market development, countries may find it useful initially to rely on syndication or underwriting to facilitate the development of their government securities markets. Subsequently, they may find it more cost effective to shift to auctions and primary dealers.

5.3   Role of Primary Dealers in the Issuance of Government Securities

Many governments have designated a primary dealer group of specialized intermediaries with a series of obligations and privileges to assist in developing the government bond markets. (See Table 5.4 for a sample listing of primary dealers and their obligations.) The main role of primary dealers is to participate in the primary (issuing) market of government securities, ensure the absorption of newly issued securities, and distribute securities to final investors, particularly to wholesale markets dominated by institutional investors where liquidity is especially valued. Primary dealers are also frequently required to be market makers, i.e., to provide two-way prices for some or all securities, in order to enhance liquidity in the market. Depending on how they are set up, primary dealers can bring more competition and more capital to the market. Setting up a primary dealer system can also facilitate the changeover from the usage of captive sources of government funding, common in many developing economies, to a system of government finance that is market based.

The main risk involved in designating a group of privileged financial institutions to serve as primary dealers is the possibility of collusion. This risk is especially relevant when the few firms willing to be primary dealers form a bidding cartel to force down prices. They may also keep intermediation margins too wide and thereby depress demand from final investors. Setting up a primary dealer system in a country with a small financial sector could also be detrimental for market development because of the greater likelihood of collusion when fewer institutions are participating. In addressing this problem and as ways to introduce more competition, governments could authorize foreign financial institutions to be primary dealers and open up auctions to institutions—both domestic and foreign—with different investment preferences.

Table 5.4. Primary Dealers in Selected Developed and Developing Countries

Country	Number	Obligations/Comments
Developed Markets		
Canada	12 for T-bonds 10 for T-bills 20 distributors	• Participation in auctions above a threshold • Participation in auctions above a threshold • Participation in auctions
France	20	• Act as market makers on secondary markets • Need to minimize bid/ask spreads based on preset limits
Italy	32; among which, 15 market makers	• Primary dealers are required to take up stock in the auctions • Market makers are, in addition, required to provide 2-way quotes.
Sweden	10	• None since 1998; dealers not required to quote 2-way prices
United Kingdom	16	• Provide tight bid/ask quotes • Have 1% average market share on 6-month rolling basis
United States	37	• Not obligated to make markets for each other or customers • Required to make reasonably good markets with Federal Reserve's trading desk
Emerging Markets		
Brazil (under consideration)		• Starting to provide 2-way prices
Rep. of Korea	24	• Provide bid/ask quotes with minimum volume and maximum spread • Minimum trading requirement — 2% of total secondary market interdealer trading every 6 months • 2% minimum underwriting requirement every 6 months
Malaysia	12	• Make secondary markets
Mexico	6	• Quote 2-way prices on a continuous basis
Poland (under consideration)		• Considering more formal arrangements, and market making through electronic systems

Sources: Data for Canada are from the Bank of Canada; for France, Italy, Sweden, United Kingdom, and United States, data are from Bank of International Settlements (BIS 1999); for Brazil, Hungary, Malaysia, Mexico, and Poland, data are from J. P. Morgan (1997); for Malaysia data are from Arab-Malaysian Merchant Bank (2000); for Korea data are from Ministry of Finance and Economy; and for Poland data are from OECD 2000.

5

Primary dealers are only one way to distribute government securities. In fact, although most developed countries have set up a system of primary dealers at some point in the development of their domestic securities markets, several countries have succeeded without them.[80] The development of electronic trading systems and the Internet can play a useful role in the issuance and absorption of government securities, and, over time, could reduce the role of primary dealers in the government securities market.

5.3.1 Obligations of Primary Dealers

The obligations of primary dealers, beyond auction participation, can vary considerably. Dealers may be required to comply with auction quotas, act as market makers in government securities, or provide the government with information about market conditions.

The principal obligation of a primary dealer is to support the government in the sale of government securities. The government designates a group of primary dealers mainly to take advantage of their distribution capacity. Most countries require primary dealers to take a certain amount of securities at government auctions. Many of them also set a requirement for a quarter, a year, or a minimum per auction, which normally is a function of the primary dealer's size or its share in the secondary market. Others do not specify a quantitative amount and expect a commitment from primary dealers to bid at auctions. The strictness of the arrangements depends on market conditions and could change over time. Applying strict requirements to bid at auctions when the market is thin can become burdensome for primary dealers, and often needs to be offset by granting some privilege or incentive. Some countries have progressively tightened requirements as the market has developed. The more mature a market becomes, the less the need for strict requirements to bid at auctions, as those markets typically enjoy larger demand and more diversified participants.

Primary dealers are usually required to act as market makers. Market-maker arrangements can be either strict—an obligation to quote firm prices and to observe specific bid/ask spreads along the entire yield curve—or

---

80. Australia, Germany, Japan, New Zealand, and Switzerland, for example, are countries that do not have primary dealers. But even some of those countries have relied on a group of intermediaries to support the development of their government securities markets, e.g., with the syndication in Germany.

flexible—an obligation to quote tentative prices for certain, usually benchmark, securities. Alternatively, in some countries, the government requires primary dealers to quote (at least) one-way prices on a continuous basis. Especially when markets are developing and price volatility is high, market-making requirements should not be too strict, as primary dealers can face significant losses and disengage from market-making activity.

One of the more difficult issues to resolve in a primary dealer arrangement is the width of any required bid/ask spread and trade size. If spreads are too wide, the obligation will become meaningless and liquidity will not be improved. If spreads are too tight and volatility is high, there is a risk that the market will not attract buyers because of potential losses. The size of the spread will also be related to the volume of business. Primary dealers must cover certain fixed costs before making a profit. The larger the number of transactions, the smaller the spread needed to cover costs.

In emerging markets, an obligation for primary dealers to quote firm prices under all trading conditions can be unrealistic. Governments thus need to be in close communication with primary dealers and possibly allow spreads to widen or trade sizes to narrow at times when the market becomes unsettled. In some cases, different types of institutions can be allowed to specialize in different market segments or bond maturities depending on their expertise or customer base. The requirement to quote firm prices could also be limited in the early stages of market development to the bigger and more liquid benchmarks. As the market matures, the obligation of quoting firm prices may require that each primary dealer be assigned a mix of benchmark and off-the-run securities, with periodic rotation of the mix. These considerations need to be made in the context of specific market conditions.

As the market develops and volatility decreases, the market-making obligation can be tightened. The spread may be reduced and the number of securities for which the dealer is required to quote two-way prices may be enlarged. Even in emerging countries, some governments (e.g., Czech Republic and Turkey) are of the view that primary dealers should not be given any special privileges in exchange for their market-making function, as the bid/ask spread already provides them a sufficient award. Other countries (e.g., Australia and New Zealand) maintain that, given the development of their markets, variety of participants, and trading volume, market making should develop naturally and the government should not provide any special incentives.

The third major obligation of a primary dealer is to provide the issuer with information about market conditions and market preferences, particularly for when-issued[11] trading—i.e., trading of a security before it is actually issued. Information can be communicated during periodic meetings between the primary dealers and government officials. In the early stages of market development, primary dealers can be required to report on market conditions to the government on a weekly basis. As the market matures, less frequent reporting could suffice. Primary dealers can also be required to post quotes on electronic information systems.

Finally, some countries also require primary dealers to help develop a retail market by maintaining a network for marketing securities to final investors.

5.3.2   Incentives/Privileges for Primary Dealers

In return for obligations assumed, primary dealers may receive a number of privileges. These privileges are probably justified in nascent, possibly volatile markets. As markets mature, the case for privileges becomes weaker and the issuer should be prepared to phase them out. In a mature market, governments should avoid giving primary dealers privileges other than the recognition of their special designation or status or, at most, some informational advantages from meetings with the Treasury or the central bank. Other incentives, such as those discussed below, should be restricted to the early stages of market development.

Primary dealers can be granted the exclusive right to bid at auctions of government securities, bid on a noncompetitive basis, or purchase securities on tap. Sometimes they are given exclusive access to second rounds in auctions or the right also to be a primary dealer for central bank monetary policy operations. Some governments have granted primary dealers exclusive access to auctions to reward them for their role in distributing government securities and providing liquidity to the market. This exclusivity gives them a commercial advantage and helps them earn a mark-up from selling government securities to final investors. These kinds of privileges are justified in nascent markets and under volatile market conditions, but should be understood as temporary, and therefore periodically revised. The government should consider phasing them out and broadening access to auctions as soon as market conditions allow.

In the secondary market, primary dealers are sometimes given exclusive access to blind interdealer broker screens. This access allows them to take or unwind positions without disclosure (thus the term "blind"). Anonymity in an environment of dealing with financial institutions with similar credit rating as their own allows primary dealers to manage their positions more actively with confidence that the trade will be honored than if the counterparty were known.

Primary dealers at times are permitted to perform a wider range of activities than other traders, including central bank repos, short selling, or coupon washing trades.[81] At times, primary dealers have privileged access to credit lines from the central bank or have the facility to obtain securities on repo from the central bank. Tax rebates have also been given, although generally only in the initial stages of market development, with the disadvantage of requiring government outlays, and counting as unequal treatment to market competitors who have not been granted this privilege.

In sum, although primary dealers may seek a variety of privileges, it is questionable whether authorities should grant them or grant them all. By giving privileges to a specific group of institutions, governments discourage market participation by others, thereby impairing longer-run market development. Central bank credit lines to primary dealers in effect are equivalent to an easing of monetary policy. While they may facilitate bidding at the auction, their extension could undermine monetary policy objectives.

Repurchase agreements and borrowing/lending of government securities are important instruments to support any dealer operation, primary or not. Borrowing securities is used by market participants to cover short positions (a sale when the seller does not own the security) and is a practice recommended by the Group of Thirty as a way to minimize settlement risk (the risk that a seller does not deliver the security at the settlement date).[82] Standards for these types of operations must be in place in the very early stages of securities market development. (See Chapter 7, Developing Secondary Market Structures for Government Securities.) Lending of securities can be especially useful when transactions are settled same day (T). A primary dealer asked at the end of the day to sell a security which is not in

---

81. Coupon washing trades refer to the possibility of exploiting different tax treatments, for instance, between domestic and foreign investors.

82. Group of Thirty 1988.

the inventory may have difficulty finding the security in the market for reasons of timing. If settlement were T+1 or over, the dealer would have more time to find the security but this would have other risk implications. (See Chapter 8, Developing a Government Securities Settlement Structure.) Treasuries sometimes commit to assist primary dealers in managing their securities through the possibility of tap sales or bilateral trades if there is a supply/demand mismatch or a corner.

5.3.3   Eligibility Criteria for Primary Dealer Designation

Eligibility criteria for being designated a primary dealer usually include a sound financial capacity, measured in terms of capital requirements; adequate management skills; technical capacity; active market presence, measured by trading activity; and willingness to provide information to the authorities. Financial capacity requirements are crucial, as the obligation to quote two-way prices exposes primary dealers to major market (interest rate) risks. To maintain market efficiency, the selection criteria need to reviewed and adjusted as appropriate.

Most of these criteria can be quantified in terms of auction participation, trading volume, and capacity to quote two-way prices. Participation in auctions should be measured in terms of volume taken rather than in terms of volume of bids. More weight is usually given to participation in long-term than short-term auctions. Trading volume criteria focus on a number of benchmark issues, both in the OTC market and, if available, in the electronic market. Trading in nonbenchmark issues should also be also taken into consideration, although with a lower weight. The capacity to quote two-way prices takes into account both the number of days the institution is quoting and the volume per trade. The final evaluation is based on a performance index of this series of quantitative indicators.

No primary dealer should be admitted who is not supervised adequately or does not meet supervisory requirements, especially the requirement for adequate capital. Selection criteria should be as transparent as possible so that candidates are aware of their potential obligations as primary dealers and to allow other market participants who meet these criteria to be considered to be designated primary dealers.

Recognizing the benefits of having a diversified base of primary dealers with different businesses and customer bases, some countries have introduced quotas to ensure that different types of institutions are represented. For instance, a percentage of primary dealers' licenses is sometimes distributed according to the proportion of certain types of institutions (commercial banks, security houses, investment banks) in the applicants' pool. Within each type of institution, primary dealers are selected based on the performance index of criteria noted above. Outside this group, the other primary dealers could be selected purely on performance regardless of type of institution.

In evaluating the performance of primary dealers, especially in the early stages, the government needs to find a balance between evaluating too early and too often (with the risk that primary dealers will not have time to learn the business) and too infrequently (with the risk of hampering competition). Evaluating how good a job a primary dealer has done is not always easy, especially if there are no electronic information systems to compile trading volume data.[83, 84] Sometimes even book-entry systems cannot provide information on trading by institution. Also, the performance of some obligations (bids, bid/ask spreads) cannot be measured through a book-entry system, which usually provides information on ex-post trades but not on ex-ante quotes.

It is essential to maintain a competitive primary dealer market structure in which new entrants can challenge current participants, particularly if the latter try to exploit an oligopoly advantage. Some countries have used a trial period during which interested institutions provisionally act as primary dealers. After this period, those that have been active according to agreed-upon criteria are formally designated as primary dealers for a specific time, ranging from one to two years. The remaining institutions can continue to apply to become a primary dealer. After every year or two, the list of designated primary dealers would then be reviewed, allowing the most active outsiders who meet the eligibility criteria to replace the relatively inactive primary dealers.

---

83. When evaluating a primary dealer, the Treasury also needs to distinguish real trades from those taking place only to inflate performance figures.

84. Interdealer broker screens and MTSs (electronic market for government securities in Europe—see Box 7.2 in Chapter 7) have been actively supported by governments not only for their important benefits for market development, but also because such technology facilitates the proper evaluation of the performance of primary dealers, especially the obligation of quoting firm prices.

Some countries (e.g., the United States) use the same financial institutions for primary dealers that the central bank uses for monetary policy operations, but two sets of primary dealers are possible, one for the issuing government and one for central bank market operations, with each having distinct privileges and obligations. One set of primary dealers with dual purposes of issuance and support to central bank operations would require increased coordination between the issuer and the central bank. (See Chapter 2, Money Markets and Monetary Policy Operations.) In addition, using the same group of primary dealers for central bank open market operations and for the issuance of government securities discriminates against security firms and investment banks since the requirements of the open market operations bias these operations to heavily capitalized banking institutions with accounts in the central bank.

Active secondary market trading could develop among those financial institutions enjoying primary dealer status. (See Chapter 7, Developing Secondary Market Structures for Government Securities.) While banks may be large holders of long-term government securities, they typically have more interest in the short end of the maturity spectrum. Other participants, such as investment banks and securities houses, are likely to be more active in developing the government securities market, and these institutions might be attracted by primary dealer status. Authorities will also have to weigh the participation of foreign institutions as primary dealers, with its obvious advantages (more competition/more capital) and disadvantages (political sensitivities/more difficult supervision/taking advantage of an incipient market).

While extending the designation of primary dealers beyond banks is desirable, doing so can raise settlement problems. (See Chapter 8, Developing a Government Securities Settlement Structure.) In addition, if there is a broader group of institutions serving as primary dealers, supervisory authorities will need to ensure the creditworthiness of each type of institution in a way that maintains competition for securities trading among the different types of institutions.

Market size will usually be a determining factor in deciding the appropriate number of primary dealers. Too few primary dealers can be detrimental to competition, while too many could eliminate the incentive to take on that role.

Finally, the legal or formal status of a primary dealer can take different forms in different countries. At one extreme, some countries (e.g., Turkey) designate primary dealers under a contract stating the rights and obligations of the parties, while others expect primary dealers to maintain reasonable cooperation in their operations with the Treasury and the central bank.

5.4   Conclusion

By tailoring the maturities of government securities to meet market demand and announcing borrowing plans in advance, the government can make its securities more attractive for trading. (See Chapter 3, A Government Debt Issuance Strategy and Debt Management Framework; Chapter 4, Developing Benchmark Issues; and Chapter 6, Developing the Investor Base for Government Securities.)

The principal objectives in designing a well-functioning primary market for government securities is to ensure that the government's borrowing requirements are met in an orderly, reliable, and cost-effective manner; that the issuance of government securities allows broad participation; and that the issuance techniques are administered in a transparent mode.

Developing a primary market is a dynamic process that depends on a country's initial conditions and on the sequencing of reforms. As always, countries have followed different approaches and no size fits all. However, general considerations such as choice of issuance of government securities technique, participation, competition, and transparency are important considerations for developing a well-functioning primary market.

The most common technique of issuing government securities is auctions. Many developing countries are already running auctions as their main mechanism for the issuance of government securities. However, results are often far from satisfactory because of insufficient demand or because the small number of participants have the ability through collusion to set a low price. Governments, therefore, should try to encourage broader participation as a first step to bringing more competition to auctions. Broader participation can be achieved in many ways, including allowing nonbanking financial institutions (pension funds, mutual funds, other institutional investors, retail and foreign investors) to participate directly in auctions. The simplicity of uniform-price auctions over multiple-price auctions could encourage more participants to bid. Lowering minimum bid limits or launching a marketing campaign to retail segments can bring in more interest from retail investors. Applying ceilings to

5

individual bids will help maintain competition among the different participants and protect smaller investors.

Another important consideration to improve auction results is the credibility of the government as an issuer. Credibility can be enhanced by such basic actions as providing accurate information about the government's projections for borrowing requirements for the year and net and gross issuance projections, by providing frequent updates as the year progresses, and by announcing the auction calendar on a timely basis. Information on auction results at an aggregate level, which enables participants to learn about the minimum accepted price, the amount issued, and the average price at the auction, tend to reduce uncertainty and encourage participation. Establishing clear and transparent rules about auction procedures and adhering to them is also essential to gain confidence in the markets.

The government can also facilitate participation at government securities auctions by promoting the development of a secondary market through ensuring availability of needed infrastructure. Improving money market development, and establishing a repo and a when-issued market in which participants can obtain some information about price levels at the auction, should improve the prospects of achieving successful auctions.

Operational considerations, such as allowing sufficient time between auctions to create an appetite for a security, or fundamental improvements in the government securities market structure, such as issuing securities at market prices or reducing reliance of the government on captive sources of funding, can also improve auction results.

Some developing countries, typically at earlier stages of government securities market development, do not use auctions, or use them in combination with other distribution techniques such as tap sales or syndications. In such cases, the advantages in terms of transparency and pricing that an auction can bring make it worthwhile to move to auctions to issue government securities as soon as government cash management capabilities improve.

In the case of countries using syndication to sell government securities, governments might want to explore the possibility of distributing through primary dealers. Use of these dealers is considered a more competitive arrangement, as they tend to reduce their commissions in order to maintain market share, while the fees negotiated in a syndication remain fixed for the agreed-upon period. As the market develops, the government should reduce primary dealers' privileges and open up auctions to broader participation.

Bibliography

Arab-Malaysian Merchant Bank. 2000. *Development of Government Bond Markets in DMCs: Malaysia.*

Bartolini, L., and Carlo Cottarelli. 1997. "Designing Effective Auctions for Treasury Securities." Federal Reserve Bank of New York, *Current Issues in Economics and Finance* 3 (9). Available at www.ny.frb.org/.

BIS (Bank of International Settlements). 1999. *Market Liquidity: Research Findings and Selected Policy Implications.* Basle, Switzerland.

Castellanos, J. 1996. *Developing Government Bond Markets.* Inter-American Development Bank, Washington, D.C. Available at www.iadb.org.

Committee on the Global Financial System. 1999. *Issues for the Design of Liquid Markets.* Bank for International Settlements, Basel, Switzerland. Available at www.bis.org/publ/index.htm.

Dattels, Peter. 1997. "Microstructure of Government Securities Markets." In V. Sundararajan, Peter Dattels, and Hans J. Blommestein, eds., *Coordinating Public Debt and Monetary Management: Institutional and Operational Arrangements.* International Monetary Fund, Washington, D.C.

Gray, Simon. 1997. *Government Securities: Primary Issuance.* Handbooks in Central Banking No. 11. Bank of England, London, U.K. Available at www.bankofengland.co.uk.

Group of Thirty. 1988. *Clearance and Settlement Systems in the World's Securities Markets.* Washington, D.C. Available at www.group30.org.

Gulde, Anne-Marie, Jean-Claude Nascimento, and Lorena M. Zamalloa. 1997. "Liquid Asset Requirements: Role and Reform." In J. T. Tomás Baliño and Lorena M. Zamalloa, eds., *Instruments of Monetary Management: Issues and Country Experiences.* International Monetary Fund, Washington, D.C.

IOSCO (International Organization of Securities Commissions). 1999. *The Influence of Market Makers in the Creation of Liquidity.* Emerging Markets Committee. Montreal, Canada. Available at www.iosco.org.

J. P. Morgan, 1997. *The J.P. Morgan Guide to Emerging Local Markets.* November. J. P. Morgan.

Malvey, P., et al. 1995. *Uniform-Price Auctions: Evaluation of the Treasury Experience.* Office of Market Finance, United States Department of the Treasury, Washington, D.C.

5

McConnachie, R. 1996. *Primary Dealers in Government Securities Markets.* Handbooks in Central Banking No. 6. Bank of England, London, U.K. Available at www.bankofengland.co.uk.

————. 1997. *The Retail Market for Government Debt.* Handbooks in Central Banking No. 13. Bank of England, London, U.K. Available at www.bankofengland.co.uk.

OECD (Organization for Economic Cooperation and Development). 1999. *Electronic Trading in Government Debt.* Committee on Financial Markets. Paris, France. Available at www.oecd.org.

————. 2000. *Tenth OECD Workshop on Government Securities Markets and Public Debt Management in Emerging Markets.* Warsaw, Poland.

Oh, Chang Seok. 1999. *Setting Up a Primary Dealer System for Treasury Bonds in the Republic of Korea.* World Bank Financial and Corporate Restructuring Assistance Project (FCRA). World Bank, Washington, D.C.

Quintyn, Marc. 1994. "Government Versus Central Bank Securities in Developing Open Market Operations." In J. T. Tomás Baliño and Carlo Cottarelli, eds., *Frameworks for Monetary Stability: Policy Issues and Country Experiences.* International Monetary Fund, Washington, D.C.

Rhee, S. Ghon. 2000. *Further Reforms after the "Big Bang": The Japanese Government Bond Market.* University of Hawaii.

Sundaran, R. 1997. "Auction Theory: A Summary with Applications to Treasury Markets." National Bureau of Economic Research, Working Paper 5873. Available at www.nber.org.

Sundaresan, S. 1996. "Discriminatory Versus Uniform Treasury Auctions: Evidence from When-Issued Transactions." *Journal of Financial Economics,* vol. 42 (September): 63–104.

5

Chapter 6

Developing the Investor Base for Government Securities

Government securities issuers need buyers. Policymakers can do much to develop voluntary demand by financial institutions, nonfinancial institutions, and retail investors. Historically, governments have relied on their taxation and coercion powers to ensure adequate demand for their securities issues, resulting in captive sources of government funding. They did not always achieve their aim of lowering the cost of finance, but a certain outcome of this forced funding was economic inefficiency from misallocated resources. Although most developed countries have shifted from captive sources of government funding toward reliance on a diverse base of voluntary investors, captive sources of government funding are still a major feature of government finance in some developing countries. Governments can, through appropriate reform programs, licensing, regulation, and supervision, encourage the development of wholesale investor institutions that invest in government securities for income, hedging, trading, and repo transactions. Governments can also develop a retail investor base for government securities, and can further broaden and diversify the investor base by opening the market to foreign investors.

6

6.1   Introduction

Governments issuing securities need to understand the factors that motivate demand for their product, identify investor segments of the market, develop instruments with characteristics that match the features sought by different types of investors, and mount focused marketing campaigns. Stimulating demand for government securities is as important as developing the market infrastructure for more efficient trading. (See Chapter 3, A Government Debt Issuance Strategy and Debt Management Framework; Chapter 8, Developing a Government Securities Settlement Structure; and Chapter 9, Legal and Regulatory Framework.)

Policy issues concerning development of the investor base begin with conversion from captive to voluntary investors and include promotion of financial institutions and their active trading. These objectives can be accomplished by incorporating organizational, regulatory, and supervisory measures favorable to investment and markets into financial reforms, taking steps to attract nonfinancial investors, including retail, to trade government securities, and allowing entry of foreign investors into the domestic government securities market.

6.2   Captive Sources of Government Funding and a Diverse Investor Base

Historically, government issuers have paid inadequate attention to voluntary demand for short- and long-term government securities, relying instead on their powers of taxation and coercion to raise funding. Not only in developing countries, but also in most advanced countries, regulations compelled commercial banks to meet reserve and liquid asset ratios by holding Treasury bills and bonds. In addition, insurance companies and pension funds, as well as social security funds, were required to invest in government bonds, often specially issued nonmarketable instruments with substantially below-market yields. Many countries also imposed quantitative restrictions on holdings of nongovernment securities by insurance companies and pension funds. Such restrictions were often motivated by prudential considerations, but their net effect was a form of indirect coercion to hold government securities, and insurance companies and pension funds were thereby induced to heavily invest in them.

6.2.1 Pitfalls of Reliance on Captive Sources of Government Funding

Extensive reliance on captive sources of funding characterized government financing patterns in most of Western Europe and in some English-speaking countries (for example, Australia, Canada, Ireland, New Zealand, and South Africa) until the 1980s. Various deregulation initiatives since the early 1980s, which substantially lowered or eliminated reserve requirements on banks and eliminated prescribed investment ratios on insurance companies and pension funds, have dramatically reduced government reliance on this form of funding in most high-income countries. A notable exception among high-income countries to this trend is Singapore, where the Central Provident Fund is still required to heavily invest in nonmarketable government securities, although affiliated workers have been allowed to direct balances in excess of a specified level to a broad list of approved investments.

In contrast to most high-income countries, reliance on captive sources of government funding is still a major feature of government financing in developing countries. The minimum reserve and liquid asset requirements on banks continue to be quite high in many of these countries, providing the principal source of government funding. Several countries require their national provident funds or social security funds to invest heavily in nonmarketable securities. In addition to Singapore, Egypt, India, Jordan, Malaysia, and Sri Lanka are among the better-known cases—although the affected institutions in all these countries have been given some latitude in recent years to invest in equities and other marketable securities.

Prescribed investment restrictions on pension funds and insurance companies in many countries result in an indirect form of pressure for these institutions to hold government securities. Such investment restrictions are prevalent in most countries of continental Europe and Asia, as well as in developing and transition countries that reformed their pension systems in the 1980s and 1990s. The new private pension funds in Latin American and Eastern European countries either are not allowed to invest in equities and overseas assets (for example, Bolivia, Mexico, and Uruguay), or such investments are subject to low limits (for example, Argentina, Hungary, and

Poland). Insurance companies are subject to broadly similar investment restrictions. Although these funds and companies are free to place their investable funds in bank deposits and corporate bonds, pension funds in practice invest heavily in government securities out of yield and safety considerations.

Reliance on captive sources of government funding is not necessarily synonymous with low cost for the government and low yields for investors. Cyprus, Jordan, and Malaysia are countries where the real returns offered on this form of government funding have been high. Most Latin American and Eastern European countries offer market rates of return that, at the margin, are determined by the level of international demand for their government bonds. Captive sources of government funding may even occasionally receive generous remuneration, especially if governments miscalculate or adjust their rates slowly in response to market changes. In general, however, captive sources of government funding have received low returns, in some instances much below market levels and in some cases much below the rate of inflation. Worst-case examples in this respect have been Egypt, Peru, and Zambia, where, during most of the 1980s, real returns on the reserves of pension and provident funds were between 10 and 20 percent below the rate of inflation and lower than interest rates paid on short-term bank deposits.[85]

A negative effect of reliance on captive sources of government funding is that such arrangements stifle the development of government securities markets, especially when nonmarketable securities are issued to these sources of financing. Such securities are segmented from the rest of the market, not listed on any exchange, and not available for trading. Minimum reserve and liquid asset requirements on banks cause an artificial lowering of yields for those instruments that meet the legally imposed requirements and a concomitant drying up of liquidity for such instruments. Even when captive sources of funding involves traded securities, they tend to have an adverse impact on market development, since financial institutions are forced to buy and hold eligible government securities and are discouraged from engaging in active trading. This was the case in South Africa until the late 1980s, when the prescribed investment ratio imposed on pension funds and insurance companies was abolished. Policymakers should recognize that

---

85. See World Bank 1994.

underdevelopment of government securities markets and low levels of trading deprive countries of the main benefits of active markets—more efficient price discovery and a dynamic process of financial innovation, both of which lower the cost of capital and promote a more efficient mobilization of savings and allocation of resources.

To develop sound and vibrant demand for government securities, policymakers need to move away from reliance on captive sources of government funding and draw on voluntary sources of funds that provide a better indication of the true cost of finance and thus help avoid a persistent misallocation of scarce economic resources.

6.2.2 Advantages of a Diverse Investor Base

To lower the cost of government debt and the volatility of market yields, policymakers need to stimulate a diverse investor base and develop instruments, trading facilities, and distribution networks that best suit the needs of those investors.

A diverse investor base that includes both domestic and foreign investors is essential for promoting market stability and enhancing market efficiency. A diverse investor base removes the threat to an issuer of being held hostage by a particular group of investors. A strong base of domestic and foreign investors provides the government assurance that it will be able to meet its funding requirements in an orderly manner. A strong foreign investor presence, in addition to broadening the diversity of the investor base for trading and holding government securities, will contribute to the introduction of financial technology and innovation, thereby leading to higher market efficiency.

A diverse investor base provides greater opportunities for financial innovation. A number of market innovations over the past 30 years, from floating-rate and zero-coupon bonds to inflation- and foreign-currency-linked instruments, have been developed to meet the requirements of different types of investors.

There are four general categories of potential investors in government securities instruments: domestic and foreign and, for each of these categories, financial (banks, the contractual savings sector, and collective investment funds) and nonfinancial (nonfinancial corporations and individual investors). The contractual savings sector and collective investment funds comprise the legal entities that invest in government securities in a principal

6

capacity. They include insurance companies and pension funds, which invest their accumulated reserves, and mutual funds, which invest pooled funds.

There has been a remarkable expansion of the activities of a wide range of financial institutions in recent years, including their participation in government securities markets. Institutional investors, comprising pension funds, insurance companies, and mutual funds, have grown at an explosive rate over the past two decades. The total assets of institutional investors in OECD countries rose from $3.2 trillion in 1981, equivalent to 38 percent of total GDP, to $26 trillion in 1996, corresponding to 105 percent of total OECD-area GDP. The average annual growth rate amounted to 15 percent. The assets of institutional investors grew nearly three times faster than the annual income in OECD countries. Outside the OECD region, several countries also experienced dramatic growth in institutional investors, including Brazil, Chile, Cyprus, Egypt, and South Africa.

The growth of institutional investors is summarized in Annex 6.A.

6.3   Financial Investors of Government Securities

6.3.1   Commercial Banks

Commercial banks invest in government bills, bonds, and other debt instruments in order to meet liquid asset requirements, obtain a stable interest income to offset other more volatile investments, manage their short-term liquidity, and take positions on the future movement of interest rates. They also use their government securities holdings to hedge their interest rate positions and to provide collateral for repo transactions with customers and for discount window borrowing from the central bank. The growing role of repo facilities provides a strong reason for commercial bank investment in longer-term bonds.

Commercial banks have been in many countries the largest captive source of government funding. By setting high minimum reserve and liquid asset ratio requirements and ensuring that government securities are the only eligible assets that satisfy these requirements, governments have been able to borrow substantial amounts at below-market rates of interest. Commercial banks should not, however, be forced to hold government securities, but should be allowed to invest and trade in them as part of their overall balance sheet management and provision of financial services. In modern financial settings and as a result of the role of repo facilities, commercial banks can be major investors in government securities on a gross basis, with active trading of government securities, while being small holders on a net basis.

While commercial banks are a major investor source for government securities, their strong presence in the government securities market at times may reflect some fundamental shortcomings in their commercial banking operations. Heavy investments in government securities by commercial banks may reflect weaknesses in their primary function, which is lending. Such operating weaknesses as ineffective screening and monitoring capabilities of loans, a dearth of reliable information on creditworthy borrowers and projects, and weak legal systems induce a flight to safety by banks to government securities. Once these operating deficiencies are corrected, banks will become less significant holders of government securities.

6.3.2 Contractual Savings Sector—Pension Funds and Insurance Companies

Pension funds and life insurance companies have traditionally been important investors in government securities, especially for longer-term issues. Pension funds and life insurance companies used to concentrate their activities in direct loans to corporations and households. Over time, their investment focus has shifted to marketable securities, which are traded on organized exchanges or over-the-counter markets and are valued on the basis of publicly available information.

Pension funds and insurance companies have a symbiotic and dynamically interactive relationship with securities markets. (See Chapter 7, Developing Secondary Market Structures for Government Securities.) Under certain conditions, they stimulate the development of securities markets. At the same time, well-functioning securities markets enhance the operating efficiency of the institutions, lowering the saving rate needed to attain a capital accumulation target for pensions or the cost of insurance.

Pension funds generate long-term financial resources and are ideally suited for investing in long-term instruments such as equities and bonds, including government, corporate, and mortgage bonds. During the accumulation phase, the liabilities of pension funds are linked to the growth of earnings of policyholders. This is particularly the case with defined benefit plans, but also holds for defined contribution plans with targeted replacement rates that are related to the evolution of incomes. During the decumulation (pay out) phase, the liabilities of pension funds depend on the terms and conditions of the pension plan, and particularly on whether nominal or inflation-protected pensions are offered. To avoid exposure to reinvestment risk, pension funds need to match the maturity of their assets with that of their liabilities, which reflects the age structure of policyholders. In countries where equity markets are well developed, pension funds have tended to invest extensively in equities, especially if they are allowed some flexibility in their investment options. If they are subject to stricter investment requirements, they have tended to hold more balanced portfolios consisting of bonds and equities. In countries with less well-developed equity markets, pension funds have tended to invest in bonds.

The nature and composition of their liabilities also determine the investment policies of life insurance companies. To the extent that their life and annuity policies are set in nominal terms, they have an inclination to invest in bonds, aiming to match the maturity of their assets and liabilities in order to avoid reinvestment risk. Because some of their liabilities, such as annuity products, carry very long maturities that exceed those of available assets, life insurance companies cannot completely hedge their reinvestment risk. So long as annuity business represents a small fraction of their total business, such reinvestment risk can be covered by their own equity funds. Life insurance companies typically invest the reserves that originate from equity-linked policies in equities.

Depending on the state of development of bond markets, both pension funds and life insurance companies show a preference for investing in corporate and mortgage bonds and in asset-backed securities. By maintaining a well-diversified portfolio of nongovernment bonds, they obtain a high return without assuming a high default risk. In the United States, life insurance companies invest only 3 percent of their assets in government securities, while they place 41 percent in corporate bonds, 9 percent in agency securities, and 21 percent in equities, with the remainder in other assets (real estate, loans, and bank deposits). In countries where nongovernment bond markets are underdeveloped, pension funds and life insurance companies invest more heavily in government bonds.

The concentration by pension funds and insurance companies of their investments and reserves in government bonds on a voluntary basis at times reflects weak and poorly developed equity and corporate bond markets. As the deficiencies of the latter markets are addressed, pension funds and insurance companies, if given investment-choice options, will become less significant holders of government securities.

6.3.3 Collective Investment Funds—Mutual Funds

Governments that have substantial borrowing requirements may also look to collective investment funds, such as mutual funds, as a funding source.

Mutual funds offer professional management and asset diversification with high liquidity and low cost. Some mutual funds serve other institutional investors, but the vast majority focus on retail investors. The primary purpose of mutual funds is to invest in marketable securities—equities and bonds—on behalf of the public. Mutual funds are dependent on efficient and well-functioning securities markets.

Unlike pension funds and life insurance companies, which ideally maintain well-diversified portfolios, mutual funds are often created with specialized investment objectives. They, therefore, consciously carry unbalanced portfolios, with heavy concentration in bonds (either corporate or government) or equities (either diversified or sector specific). Bond mutual funds and money market mutual funds play active roles in government markets and provide a good source of government funding.

An interesting feature of mutual funds for developing countries is that their development does not depend on complex social security and insurance sector reforms. They can, therefore, grow fast, if they operate in a robust regulatory framework that promotes market integrity and protects the interests of small investors. Their rate of growth will depend on the conditions supporting desintermediation from traditional bank products (bank deposits) to capital market instruments.

6.3.4 Impact of Institutional Investors on Capital Market Development

6.3.4.1 Institutional Investors and Capital Market Development

Institutional investors can have a potentially large impact on the way financial institutions compete and on how markets operate.[86] In addition to

---

86. Vittas 1998.

making financial markets more competitive, institutional investors often are at the forefront in promoting efficient market practices and financial innovation. They typically favor greater transparency and market integrity, in both primary and secondary markets, seek lower transaction costs and encourage efficient trading and settlement facilities, and stimulate innovation in both products and trading practices that are tailored to more efficient management and hedging of their liabilities.

Pension funds and other institutional investors can act as a countervailing force to commercial and investment banks as well as other market intermediaries, forcing them to be more competitive and efficient and to lower their spreads on loans and their fees for issuing and trading securities. They stimulate financial innovation, especially the development of financial instruments such as zero-coupon bonds and asset-backed securities that meet the specific needs of the investing community. In developing countries, institutional investors have been instrumental in promoting the transfer of financial technology and the use of instruments and markets that have thrived in high-income countries. (See Box 6.1.)

6.3.4.2 *Contractual Savings Sector and Capital Market Development*

In addition to serving as a stimulus to financial innovation, the contractual savings sector provides a market for price-indexed securities and assets with long-term maturities. The minimum funding requirements of defined pension plans in the United Kingdom and the United States and elsewhere led to the development of immunization techniques and the demand for new financial instruments such as zero-coupon bonds, inflation-indexed bonds, collateralized mortgage obligations, as well as index options and futures.[87] In addition, because of their long-term liability position, the contractual savings sector represents a strong and stable demand for long-term marketable financial assets. Figure 6.1 shows how the development of contractual savings (measured as the share of financial assets over GDP) and the maturity of government debt (long-term over total debt) are positively correlated.

The contractual savings sector contributes to the development of government securities markets through advance funding of future contingent

---

87. See Davis 1995.

Box 6.1. Financial Innovation

The past three decades have witnessed major financial innovations in, as well as a large expansion of, the financial services industry. Most innovations in the 1970s were prompted by an increase in the level and volatility of interest rates. Institutional investors, especially pension funds, and regulatory changes were also major forces stimulating this innovative process.

The response of most lenders and borrowers to the high and unpredictable interest rates of the early 1970s was to move to floating rate debt, including adjustable rate mortgages—a process that had already taken place in Britain during the 1960s. However, pension legislation enacted in 1974 codified the liabilities of private pension funds in the United States and imposed minimum funding requirements. This created a strong demand for long-duration fixed-income securities by pension funds, and contributed to the emergence and growth of both zero-coupon bonds and mortgage-backed securities.

The immunization strategies of pension funds also promoted the use of derivative products, such as index options and futures contracts, while pension funds spurred innovations in equity markets. The first indexed (or index-tracking) mutual fund was created for pension funds in 1971, in response to the growing realization that active investment management generally failed to achieve higher net returns than a fund passively invested in a market index. Since then, there have been several additional innovations, including index-tracking funds for bonds, midcap and small cap equities, value and growth equities, and international equities.

More recently, in response to the growing popularity of defined contribution retirement plans and the demand for more effective management of investment risk, new synthetic investment products have been developed. These minimize the downside risk of equity investments by providing a floor on the value of the investments over some period of time, while allowing some participation in the upside potential of the equity market.

Examples of Financial Innovation in Developing Countries

In Chile, the *bonos de reconocimiento* are zero-coupon indexed bonds that originated in 1987 in recognition of the state's liability to contributors in the old pension system. These bonds are in great demand by insurance companies because of asset-liability matching requirements, and are also eligible assets for pension funds. A later innovation was to make these bonds transferable, to allow affiliates to opt for early retirement. Since 1990, they have been traded on the local exchanges. The *mutuos hipotecarios*, another innovation, were created especially for life insurance companies. They are a kind of illiquid mortgage bond whose only guarantee is the specific real estate property behind the debt. However, other innovations have not been successful. For instance, real estate corporations were especially created for pension funds, but only two were established and they disappeared by mid-1995, after four years in business, because of their relative tax disadvantages with respect to real estate investment funds, from the perspective of pension funds.

In Argentina, the common investment funds (*fondos comunes de inversión*) were created especially for pension funds in 1992. They represented 6.9 percent of the pension fund assets in 1998. Negotiable obligations, mortgage securitization, and leasing contracts are other new financial instruments gaining popularity in Argentina. Negotiable obligations must be held until their maturity, since they do not have a secondary market. Nonetheless, the size of this market has grown fivefold since 1992. Of the total amount invested in this security, banks issued about 51 percent in 1994 and only 9 percent in 1998. This reflects a significant increase in the relative importance of the corporate bond market for pension funds.

Sources: Bodie and Crane (1998), Vittas (1998), and Walker and Lefort (2000).

Figure 6.1. Long-Term Government Securities and Contractual Savings Development

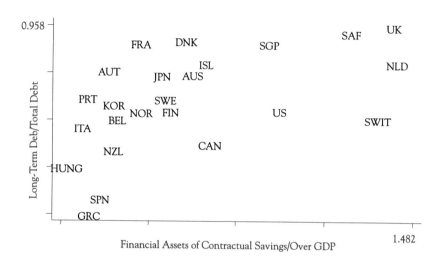

Source: Elias, Impavido, and Musalem 2001.

Note: Data are for 1996.

liabilities. In particular, private sector-funded pension plans reduce the size of the government debt and moral hazard that would otherwise result from explicit or implicit guarantees to alternative pension arrangements. Thus, such pension plan funding should improve the financial position of governments, thereby reducing the credit risk (and interest rate) on government debt instruments.[88]

By promoting the lengthening of the maturity of fixed-income securities, the contractual savings sector lowers borrowers' refinancing risks. A government debt profile with short maturities, requiring frequent rollover of the entire stock of debt, exposes governments to the risk of periodic refinancing crises. On the other hand, a well-structured debt profile with maturities across a range of longer-term maturities shields governments

---

88. See Impavido and Musalem 2000.

from refinancing crises and hence reduces the need for governments to tighten fiscal policy dramatically (by sharply lowering expenditures and/or raising taxes) in order to meet its debt-service obligations when market conditions are not conducive for refinancing government debt.[89] The short-term average maturity of Mexico's public debt, for example, exacerbated the 1994–95 peso crisis.

The potential contribution from the contractual savings sector to the development of government securities markets is not guaranteed. This sector can have a strong impact on the development of government securities markets if governments pursue sound monetary and fiscal policies. An environment of high inflation and large and growing fiscal deficits will discourage the contractual savings sector from investing in government securities with long maturities, and the development of the long end of the government securities market will thus be thwarted. Similarly, the use of the contractual savings sector as a captive source of government funding with below-market yields will act as a deterrent for the contractual savings sector to invest voluntarily in government securities.

6.3.4.3 *Money Market Mutual Funds and Capital Market Development*

Money market mutual funds, which invest predominantly in short-term money market instruments, including Treasury bills, have grown mainly in countries that have restricted the payment of interest on short-term bank deposits. Money market mutual funds in the United States received a major boost in the 1970s, when they first appeared, from the then-tight regulation of interest that commercial banks and other deposit-taking institutions were allowed to pay on retail deposits (Regulation Q). Although deposit institutions were gradually given more latitude to set their retail interest rates in the face of high inflation, they were forced to pay rates that were far below the rate of inflation. This gave a strong impetus to the emergence and growth of money market mutual funds. These funds invested in short-term money market instruments, comprising Treasury bills, large certificates of deposit, and commercial paper, and were able to pass on to their retail customers the considerably higher returns obtainable on wholesale funds.

---

89. See Alesina, Prati, and Tabellini 1990.

Money market mutual funds also offered attractive services, including a limited range of payment facilities. They grew rapidly and established a strong foothold in the U.S. financial system that survived the subsequent deregulation of deposit rates. France has also for many years applied tight limits on interest rates on retail deposits with banks and, in the 1980s and 1990s, promoted the creation of money market mutual funds that invested in Treasury bills and other short-term money market instruments.

Once established, money market mutual funds have continued to thrive even after the removal of interest rate regulations, probably because investors use them to park funds for subsequent investment in marketable securities. Australia, France, Greece, Japan, Spain, and the United States have relatively large-sized money market mutual funds.

The use of money market mutual funds for transaction purposes may also explain their emergence in countries such as the United Kingdom, where interest rates on short-term deposits have not been regulated. Given the competitiveness of bank deposits, however, money market mutual funds in these countries are unlikely to acquire the relative importance they enjoy in countries that have imposed strict regulations on the remuneration of short-term instruments and markets that have thrived in high-income countries.

6.3.4.4 Market Environment for Institutional Investors and Capital Market Development

Institutional investors are managed by trained professionals who are usually more aware than ordinary investors of the potential conflicts of interest and agency problems facing corporate management. They are thus better able to insist on legislation that protects the rights of minority shareholders and ensures market integrity. They also have an interest in promoting more effective corporate governance structures and in developing a more robust regulatory framework. Institutional investors can also exert effective pressure for more modern and efficient trading, clearing, and settlement facilities, including the creation of central securities depositories and book-entry systems.[90]

---

90. For an empirical analysis of the relationship between the development of contractual savings and capital markets, see Catalan, Impavido, and Musalem 2000.

Realization of these potential benefits is not automatic, but depends on the environment for institutional investors.[91] A favorable environment includes a critical mass of investors, regulations that provide institutional investors scope for investment options, and a diversified financial structure. In addition, factors such as new technology, globalization, and regional integration also play important roles in capital market development.

When they first emerge, institutional investors control few resources and have little control over the evolution of market practices. When they reach some critical mass, they can begin influencing market development. When institutional investors are small but growing quickly, as in most countries that have recently reformed their pension systems, they tend to engage in buy-and-hold strategies and to use new inflows of funds for rebalancing their portfolios. Their impact on trading volumes is, therefore, smaller than in the case of larger and more mature institutional investors.

Regulations that provide institutional investors scope for investment options are also important. In countries where pension funds and insurance companies are required to invest in nontraded government securities, the direct impact on capital market development is negligible. Even quantitative asset-holding requirements expressed as upper limits on holdings of various asset classes are inhibiting, especially if they are binding. Among other reasons, overprotective regulations, such as minimum yield requirements (as is the case in Colombia, for example), has forced institutional investors to become holders of short-term securities.

Even in those countries where quantitative asset-holding requirements are not binding (i.e., the institutions hold, for example, fewer equities than what they are allowed according to the regulations), insurance companies in some of these countries do not adopt profit-maximizing behavior. They tend to follow conservative investment policies by investing predominantly in government securities. This practice has long prevailed in continental Europe and has inhibited the potential beneficial impact that institutional investors can have on capital market development. While their preference for bonds may help the development of bond markets, their nonmaximizing behavior has led them to adopt conservative valuation policies and to hold various debt instruments to maturity. In light of such investment conduct,

6

---

91. Vittas 2000.

pension funds and insurance companies in these countries have made little contribution to the development of more efficient trading practices and have provided little stimulus to financial innovation.

The presence of a large number of different financial institutions stimulates competition and innovation and allows changes in investment policies to be effected more smoothly than where the financial structure consists of a few undiversified financial institutions. In Egypt, Jordan, and Sri Lanka, for example, where national provident funds or social security corporations dominate the institutional investor sector, their impact on capital market development has been constrained by the absence of a pluralistic financial structure. Such dominant institutions have been constrained to change their investment portfolio from bonds to equities for fear of causing a major adverse price impact and market instability, as well as concern about the corporate governance implications of a public sector agency holding controlling stakes in corporate entities. In contrast, large private pension funds in countries with large numbers of different types of financial institutions (for example, the United States and the United Kingdom) have been able to shift from bonds into equities without facing major obstacles.

6.3.5 Policies to Promote Institutional Investors

While the primary objective of pension funds is to provide affordable and sustainable pension benefits and of insurance companies to offer efficient insurance facilities, these financial institutions can be helpful in securities market development. In order to derive such market-development benefits from these institutions, governments need to adopt policies that promote their growth.

The specific needs of institutional investors go beyond demands for adequate return and security. These investors seek greater transparency and market integrity in both primary and secondary markets. They seek lower transaction costs and encourage efficient trading and settlement facilities. They stimulate innovation in both financial products and trading practices that are tailored to more efficient management and hedging of their liabilities. Institutional investors also give support to the adoption of accounting and regulatory policies that emphasize optimizing behavior, such as reliance on the prudent expert approach and permission to engage in securities lending and derivatives trading.

6.3.5.1 Promotion of Pension Funds and Insurance Companies

In promoting pension funds, policymakers need to pay attention to the overall organization of the social security system and the respective roles of public and private, as well as funded and unfunded, components. Where a government has decided to transform its government-sponsored pension fund system to a privately funded and privately managed system, care needs to be taken to assess the costs of transition and to ensure that the public system is not burdened with unsustainable financial obligations.

The promotion of private pension funds requires introduction of a robust and effective regulatory framework that resembles in its main elements the regulatory framework imposed on other types of financial institutions, including banks, insurance companies, and mutual funds. However, since pension plans involve very long-term contracts, spanning 60 years or more, their regulatory and supervisory framework needs to be particularly strong and effective. Pension fund regulations should stipulate clear licensing criteria to prevent the participation of unqualified institutions. They also need to stress the segregation and safe external custody of assets, prudent diversification and market valuation of assets, frequent actuarial reviews and audits, and extensive information disclosure and transparency. Effective supervision to ensure enforcement of the various rules and regulations is equally essential.[92]

Similar considerations apply to the development of more efficient insurance sectors. In most developing and transition countries, insurance sectors have suffered from repressive regulation, extensive fragmentation, and poor regulation and supervision. In many cases, a restructuring and consolidation of the insurance sector is necessary in order to provide more efficient insurance services and to support the success of pension reform programs. As in the case of pension funds, insurance regulation requires a robust framework for licensing and supervising insurance companies. Life insurance companies are institutions with long-term liabilities, and they can be insolvent but not illiquid for long periods. The restructuring and consolidation of the sector often requires mergers of small but viable companies and liquidation of insolvent companies. Their liquidation is often a lengthy process. Insurance

---

92. For a detailed study of pension funds, and justifications and strategies to promote their development, see World Bank 1994.

reform, like pension reform, is complex and requires a long period for the realization of promised benefits.

In both pensions and insurance, opening local markets to foreign participation and integrating them into global markets facilitate the transfer of financial technology, ensure that individual institutions operate prudently, and lead to well-capitalized institutions. A common feature in most countries that have reformed their pension and insurance sectors in the past two decades is the extensive involvement of large foreign groups, often through joint ventures with large local groups.

6.3.5.2 *Promotion of Mutual Funds*

The promotion of mutual funds often requires enactment of enabling legislation or regulation and introduction of a robust regulatory framework with effective supervision. Because mutual funds are relatively new institutions in most developing and transition countries, there is less need to restructure existing institutions. Mutual fund legislation or regulation is usually based on prototype models developed in North America and the EU that may need relatively little adaptation to local conditions. If there is a major challenge, it lies in ensuring that regulatory agencies have adequate numbers of well-qualified staff and sufficient authority to implement effective supervision.

Problems may arise, however, if mutual fund regulation and supervision deviate from sound practice, as suggested by the recent experiences of India and the Republic of Korea.[93] Mutual funds should not offer guaranteed rates of return, unless they are expressed as guaranteed spreads over some benchmark. Mutual funds should also be required to mark their assets to market. Failure to use market valuations and to reflect these in published reports

---

93. In 1999, investor concerns in India about the financial health of a mutual fund, Unit Scheme 64 (US–64), which is managed by the state-run Unit Trust of India (UIT) and had carried a guaranteed 20 percent annual dividend, triggered a wave of equity selling, causing the Bombay share index, which represents the country's leading equity market, to lose 7 percent of its capital value on October 5, 1999. In the Republic of Korea, the Asian banking crisis of 1997, followed by insolvency of Daewoo, one of Korea's largest financial/industrial groups, in 1999—whose bonds were extensively held by mutual funds in Korea—triggered a virtual collapse of the industry. It had to seek substantial government assistance, mainly because Korea's mutual fund industry has, until recently, offered predominantly fixed-interest investments to its customers.

and advertised returns may give investors the false impression that they can redeem their mutual fund shares at the posted prices. If mutual fund assets include long-term bonds, they will be exposed to substantial falls in market prices in case of big rises in interest rates. The combination of long-term, fixed-interest assets and redemptions on demand at posted prices creates a heavy mismatch that is bound to cause large losses either for the mutual funds or for their investors.

One way to overcome the mismatch between illiquid bond markets and redeemable mutual fund shares is to operate closed funds. The shares of closed funds are not redeemable by their managers, but can be traded freely on the stock exchange. The problem with closed funds is that they often trade at a hefty discount to the net asset value of the fund and thus are not popular with investors. Another option is to offer funds with a fixed life, a fixed portfolio, and a guaranteed return. Provided there are no defaults among the bonds held in the portfolio, such funds can operate without a mismatch of assets and liabilities. On maturity, they could be rolled over into a new fixed portfolio. A third alternative is to authorize hybrid funds, known as "clopen" funds. Shares in such funds are not redeemable on demand but rather at specified monthly, quarterly, or annual intervals. Limits could be set on the proportion of shares that could be redeemed, and sufficient advance notice could be required.

Another obstacle to the development of mutual funds relates to the existence of an efficient distribution network. In the United States and the United Kingdom, for example, mutual funds have been promoted by independent financial groups and have been distributed through stock-brokers and financial planners or by direct marketing. In continental European countries and most developing countries, distribution networks have been controlled by commercial banks, which are the major sponsors of mutual funds.

Banks may face conflicting motivations in their mutual fund operations. At one level, their mutual funds may compete with their own deposit base, especially in the case of money market and bond mutual funds. In most countries, with the United States and the United Kingdom being exceptions, banks are the predominant managers and distributors of mutual funds. By offering their customers the opportunity to invest in mutual funds, particularly money market funds, they are disintermediating against themselves. Their cheap deposit base may be eroded, with adverse consequences for lending spreads and profits.

At another level, banks may fail to maintain a firewall between the allocation of assets for their own investment account and for the accounts of mutual funds under their management. To ensure that such malpractice does not occur, regulatory agencies need to be rigorous in their supervision and impose heavy sanctions when they detect deviations. Despite potential conflicts of interest, banks have successfully promoted mutual funds in most countries where they have been authorized to do so.

6.3.5.3 *Taxation and Promotion of Institutional Investors*

In many countries, institutional investors are promoted through tax incentives. In the case of pension funds, tax incentives often involve tax exemption of annual contributions and investment income, with retirement benefits taxed when they are received. This approach avoids the double taxation of long-term savings and provides incentives for retirement saving. In the case of life insurance, similar incentives are sometimes offered for premiums paid on long-term life policies. Some incentives are often offered, as well, on investment in equity mutual funds, as part of a set of policies to encourage savers to diversify their investments. Most exemptions are subject to stipulated ceilings. In most countries, when the assets of institutional investors become too large, the tax benefits are either withdrawn or substantially reduced. The case of Spain offers a good example of the use of tax incentives, legislative and regulatory changes, and the creation of new markets to develop mutual funds. (See Box 6.2.)

6.4   Nonfinancial Investors of Government Securities

6.4.1   Nonfinancial Corporations

The first group of nonfinancial investors is nonfinancial corporations, such as commercial and industrial companies. These companies are not long-term investors in government and other securities, but use these markets for efficient management of their liquid assets. Nonfinancial corporations can have a positive impact on the development of money markets if given direct or indirect access to its products. A particularly efficient means is through

Box 6.2. Development of Mutual Funds in Spain

Spain in the 1990s followed a course of dramatic expansion of the investment fund industry (see figures below), promoted within the framework of legislative and regulatory changes designed to facilitate (i) the creation of an investment fund industry, (ii) the establishment of repo and derivative markets, and (iii) accounting and taxation reforms aimed at making investment through funds more attractive.

In the initial phase of development, between 1985 and 1988, growth was slow due to the aversion of traditional banks to disintermediate. The liberalization of the financial system, increased competition, and the increasing loss of interest in fixed-term deposits gave rise to interest-paying checking accounts in 1987. At the same time, the deposit margin of investment funds was replaced by fees that rarely exceeded 2 percent overall. It is thus not surprising that financial conglomerates would devote few resources to promoting their funds. However, the government established a positive relationship with the banks that controlled the distribution networks by convincing them that lost earnings from lending spreads on deposits would be more than compensated by the fee income they could earn from managing investment funds. The government, in association with the banks, mounted a major campaign of publicity and public education.

The growth of investment funds during the late 1980s received a significant additional push from the very favorable tax treatment in effect since 1992. Mutual funds had been for years accumulating assets, to avoid a withholding tax on dividends. Yet, capital gains were subject to general income tax, after some partial adjustment for past inflation. Since 1992, the inflation adjustment was replaced by a fixed reduction of 7 percent per year elapsed, in excess of the first two years. This strong discrimination relative to ordinary capital income encouraged mutual funds, particularly those investing in bonds, to invest in shares, as capital gains from direct investment in shares received even more favorable tax treatment. Since 1996 (Law 7/1996), a new tax regime for capital gains has reduced, but not eliminated, the tax discrimination favoring mutual funds. (Capital gains are taxed after two years, but without further adjustment, at a flat 20 percent rate, well below marginal income tax rates.) This has made mutual funds attractive as longer-term savings vehicles, in contrast to deposit accounts, on which interest would be taxed at the full personal rate. In addition, there is an exemption on the first 200,000 pesetas of gains.

In 1990, the commercialization of *FondTesoros* added the element of security to mutual funds. The *FondTesoros* are privately managed investment funds that, under an agreement with the Treasury, invested exclusively in government debt instruments and are subject to lower maximum fees than ordinary funds, but profit from the Treasury's publicity. *FondTesoros* gave liquidity to the market and introduced government guarantees, which further contributed to development of the industry.

Spain has been no exception to the typical development of the mutual fund industry through money market funds, which tend to be the leaders at an early stage of fund development, as investors make their first moves out of bank deposits and into securities. Money market funds decline in relative importance as investors become more confident and move into longer-term bonds and equities.

The boom in the investment fund industry has promoted liquidity and efficiency in Spain's capital markets. The government debt market was the first and the main beneficiary, as liquidity and depth were added to the money market industry and the repo market, and subsequently to longer-term instruments (see figure below). In fact, bond and money market funds still dominate the Spanish market for investment funds, although equity investment and investment in international securities are now gaining in popularity.

Continued

Box 6.2 (Continued). Development of Mutual Funds in Spain

The rapid growth of a supplementary (third-pillar) funded pension regime (Law 8/1987) has also favored the growth of mutual funds, as well as the market for government bonds. There is no restriction on the percentage of a fund that can be invested in bonds issued by the Spanish government or international organizations of which Spain is a member.

Sources: Garcia-Vaquero (1999), and Analistas Financieros Internacionales 1997.

Investment Fund Growth in Spain—Market Value

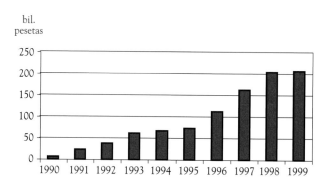

Investment Funds in Spain: Long Term Versus Market Markets

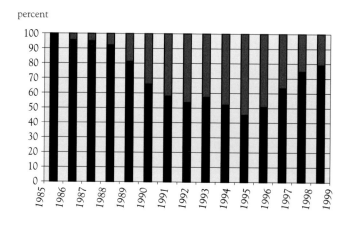

---

repo facilities, which allow investment in long-term bonds to be converted into short-term instruments. (See Chapter 7, Developing Secondary Market Structures for Government Securities.)

6.4.2   Retail Investors of Government Securities

In funding its borrowing requirements, governments often devote particular attention to individual investors in the retail market. Catering to the needs of retail investors is an essential part of an overall strategy to develop a diverse investor base. Retail investors add to overall demand for government securities and are relatively stable holders of such financial instruments.

Governments and other issuers, however, need to consider the processing and distribution costs of reaching and dealing with the retail market directly. Attracting retail investors indirectly through mutual funds may lower costs. Mutual funds appear to be particularly suitable for diversification of retail investor risk, as they can be vehicles for investment in a variety of securities such as corporate and mortgage bonds and corporate equities. Governments also can reduce the cost of directly accessing retail investors through automation.

The banking sector in the past has typically been reluctant to act as an intermediary for the government to handle security trading for the retail market because banks are wary of losing depositors who would withdraw deposits from a commercial bank in order to invest in retail government securities. However, given that mutual funds are offering government securities for the retail market and earning fees for this service has led some banks to enter this retail trade and thereby obtain similar income from this service.

The development of electronic trading systems of government securities has potential significance for broadening the investor base to the retail sector. Although it is still early, the Internet could open the door to a more efficient and cost-effective distribution of government securities in terms of price and administrative aspects.

Governments in many countries, both developed and developing, have historically catered to the needs of retail customers by issuing special, non-marketable financial instruments, often called national saving certificates. The basic objective of these certificates is to encourage the saving habit, especially among people who have limited access to formal financial institutions, and to assist in financing the government. The saving certificates are sold through post offices or banks, with maturities not exceeding five years and with interest income exempt from tax. To encourage long-term investment, the interest rate rises with the length of the deposit-holding

6

period. In addition, various penalties are assessed on premature redemption. To limit the tax benefits that wealthy individuals could obtain by investing in such certificates, ceilings are often imposed on individual holdings.

The use of national saving certificates has been criticized for their expense, ineffectiveness, and distorting effects on banking competition. These certificates are processed manually, often at considerable cost, and they incur high distribution costs. They are offered at higher rates than those available, or permitted, on bank deposits and are thus criticized as representing unfair competition against banks. They also are segmented from other debt securities, and often are more expensive than debt instruments sold through organized markets. Although premature redemptions are subject to penalties, these are typically not large enough to change the perception of certificates as liquid instruments.

A more integrated approach to developing the retail market started to take root in the 1970s. It was developed by countries that faced large borrowing requirements, a lack of domestic institutional investors, and a strong need to obtain noninflationary finance outside the banking sector that did not put undue upward pressure on domestic interest rates. Greece and Italy, for example, have followed this approach by issuing instruments with characteristics that appeal to retail investors. These include high security, high yield, a lower minimum amount than usually required for investment in government securities, and protection against depreciation of local currency by linkage to an international currency. Commercial banks and post offices are used to distribute these instruments. To lower transaction costs, building an automated registration system that can evolve over time into a book-entry system is proving useful.

The initial success of this approach with short-term instruments, reinforced by lower inflation, may lead to the issuance of longer-term instruments, including notes and bonds denominated in local currency without an exchange rate link, as well as bonds linked to domestic inflation. In countries with high inflation and unstable economic conditions, however, investors may have little trust in the domestic inflation index and may require instruments linked to a foreign currency. Policymakers should, however, be aware of the trade-off between cost and risk when linking domestic currency securities to a foreign currency or to inflation, and as part of a prudential debt management strategy, they should keep the total risk exposure of the debt portfolio under control. (See Chapter 3, A Government Debt Issuance Strategy and Debt Management Framework.)

In developing the retail market, governments need to take account of the characteristics sought by individual investors. These include security, high yield, and ease of access, but not active trading and hedging facilities. It is also important to maintain effective control over issuing and distribution costs and to develop an efficient and automated registration system.

The decision of what instruments to offer in the retail market should ultimately follow the government's overall issuing strategy. A deep and liquid secondary market for government securities can reduce the funding cost. However, such a market can best be promoted by concentrating government issuance in a few standard marketable instruments. If the total size of government securities is limited, the temptation to tap into the retail market through nonmarketable instruments may hinder the liquidity of the secondary market, and, therefore, undermine the cost-effectiveness of government funding.

6.5   Foreign Investors in Government Securities

Foreign investors can enlarge the investor base for government securities. In the process, foreign financial institutions often contribute to financial innovation in domestic markets, thereby yielding efficiency gains through increased competition and the introduction of good practices in the provision of financial services. Foreign investors can also contribute to liquidity and maturity extension of government securities when the government securities market is initially centered on short-term maturities.

Despite these potential benefits, there are also risks associated with foreign investors participating in government securities markets. Their involvement can make host economies more susceptible to market volatility. Such concern may be all the more warranted if the economy in which foreign investors hold securities deteriorates and has weak fiscal policies, unsound banking systems, and distorted domestic markets. Under such circumstances, foreign investors are likely to withdraw abruptly from such a market, thereby aggravating the financial weakness of the country. The entry of foreign financial institutions can also erode margins already narrowed by competition stemming from domestic financial liberalization.

6.5.1 Growth of Foreign Investors in Government Securities Markets

Foreign investors of government securities hold an increasing share of the government securities market for some countries. While broader markets supported by a growing presence of foreign investors can facilitate governments in meeting their borrowing requirements at reduced costs, at the same time they make it more difficult for countries with a strong foreign investor presence to pursue domestic goals because of an increasing interdependence of financial markets.

Countries that have received the largest portfolio inflows have experienced the largest increase in market capitalization, and there seems to be considerable scope for increasing the share of emerging-country securities market assets in the portfolios of OECD-area institutional investors. From both the demand and supply sides, there would thus appear to be a great potential role for foreign investors in the development of developing-country domestic government securities markets.

In developing a domestic government securities market, developing countries face the challenge of reaping the potential benefits that foreign investors can offer while minimizing the associated risks. A country seeking to draw on foreign investors to widen the investor base for government securities should thus create an environment that will appeal to foreign investors.

The growth of the involvement of foreign investors in other countries' financial markets, including in government securities markets, is summarized in Annex 6.B.

6.5.2 Impact of Foreign Investors on Capital Market Development

The increased investor base when foreign investors are present is particularly important for capital market development, including government securities market development, as it helps deepen liquidity and extend maturities. Through sophisticated trading and investment strategies, foreign institutional investors can create additional liquidity in the form of arbitrage activities and diversification of investor portfolios.[94] Foreign investors

---

94. Institutional investors themselves are very much interested in market liquidity—the ability to transact in large size without moving the price against them and at low

can also contribute to maturity extension of government securities when the government securities market is initially centered on short-term maturities. In the development of the Spanish government securities market, for example, foreign investment banks played a key role in maturity extension of government securities by holding, in 1993, more than 50 percent of outstanding balances of medium- and long-term bonds.

The import of financial services also results in efficiency gains. Capital flows tend to cause specialization in the production of financial services, thereby creating global efficiency gains. For some countries, importing financial services will be more efficient than producing them locally.[95] Financial services can be imported primarily through domestic establishment of branches of foreign companies, and through cross-border delivery.

The import of financial services can also bring dynamic efficiency to the domestic financial sector. The increased competition from abroad can make domestic producers of financial services more efficient, promoting innovation and enhancing productivity.[96]

The process of financial innovation has been strongly driven by the growth of institutional investors and has been relatively slow in markets where the domestic institutional sector is less developed. Foreign investors can speed up the financial innovation process. They may, for example, introduce sophisticated trading arrangements and investment techniques, which may be quickly adopted and further developed by domestic financial institutions. At an early stage of Spanish government securities market development, domestic institutional investors were a rather unimportant group, but grew as the debt market developed. At the

---

transaction cost. They demand a market infrastructure characterized by specialized wholesale markets that can process large transactions speedily and contribute to liquidity (see Blommestein 1997).

95. "The fact that the production of many financial services, wholesale financial services in particular, is characterized by economies of scale and scope implies that their production will be concentrated in certain countries on efficiency grounds." (Eichengreen et al. 1998a, p. 12.)

96. When the domestic banking system is weak, opening it up to competition to foreign banks (through either acquisition of domestic banks or startups of new institutions) is a delicate matter. Placing too much sudden pressure on a weak banking system can incur great risk to the domestic banking sector. For example, increased international competition may cause decreases in franchise value, giving domestic banks incentives to assume excessive risks.

same time, foreign investors played an important role in introducing financial innovations into the Spanish market, and their innovations were quickly copied and extended by domestic banks and asset managers. One example of such an innovation is the introduction of guaranteed-return mutual funds.

6.5.3   Risks Associated with Foreign Investors in Domestic Financial Markets

The presence of foreign investors can amplify the effects of policy distortions and agency problems associated with domestic financial liberalization. Domestic financial liberalization, by intensifying competition and squeezing margins in the financial sector, can bring risks to an economy. Without adequate prudential supervision and regulation, domestic financial liberalization can allow financial institutions to take on risks which are beyond their capacity to handle. Opening the domestic market to foreign financial institutions can expose the economy to additional risks. The entry of foreign financial institutions can erode margins further. If a culture of implicit guarantees exists (for example, a situation in which both lenders and borrowers perceive an exchange rate peg as a link in a chain of implicit guarantees), the high nominal interest rates characteristic of emerging markets can induce foreign investors to pour substantial short-term capital flows into such markets.

Countries with substantial short-term external debts are vulnerable to a self-fulfilling crisis. If foreign investors suddenly lose confidence in the creditworthiness of a country, they may refuse to roll over its stock of short-term debt, and the country will be forced to finance its debt service from its foreign currency reserves. If the reserves prove inadequate, a sharp reversal of capital flows follows. Mexico in December 1994, with extensive short-term dollar-denominated government debts and limited dollar reserves, found itself in a crisis when, simultaneously, previous lenders demanded repayment and no new lenders of dollars could be found.

It has been suggested that in the 1992 ERM crisis, the bond market turbulence of 1994, and the recent Asian crisis, hedge funds precipitated major movements in asset prices. The popular view is that hedge funds take large, highly leveraged positions against unsustainable currency pegs and other misaligned asset prices and can quickly reverse these positions so that major market moves result.

Some analysts,[97] however, suggest that hedge fund capital is small relative to the resources at the command of other institutional investors.[98] News of changes in hedge fund positions, however, may induce other investors to follow. Hedge funds would thus play an important role in herd behavior.[99] Nonetheless, according to the limited econometric evidence, there is some indication that hedge funds herd together, but no indication that other investors regularly follow the lead of hedge funds.[100] While some of the case study evidence points to the role of hedge funds as a leader (with the 1992 ERM crisis most frequently cited), it is equally possible to cite episodes where hedge funds were followers of the market rather than leaders.

It would be possible to limit the ability of hedge funds and other foreign investors to take positions in domestic financial markets by (i) taxing short-term capital inflows (as is done by Chile), (ii) requiring banks and brokers to raise margin and collateral requirements, and (iii) limiting the ability of financial institutions to provide the domestic credit needed to short the currency and to loan the securities needed to short equity and fixed-income markets. With a country's proven ability to provide a sustainable macroeconomic balance, these measures should be taken on an exceptional basis, as the benefits of the entry of foreign investors generally outweigh its risks.

6

6.6   Conclusion

A diversified investor base is an essential element of well-functioning government securities markets, with carryover benefits to capital market development in general. Such an investor base will allow governments to

---

97. See Eichengreen et al., 1998b.

98. One conservative estimate of hedge fund capital is US$90 billion (excluding funds of funds), of which US$30 billion belongs to macro funds that take large directional positions in currency markets. These figures pale beside those for other institutional investors. The assets of institutional investors in mature markets exceed US$20 trillion. Although hedge fund capital can be substantial relative to smaller emerging markets, macro funds concentrate a substantial share of their resources in particular emerging markets only under exceptional circumstances (see Eichengreen et al., 1998b).

99. The notion that other investors regard hedge fund managers as relatively well informed and hence follow their lead can be interpreted as an information cascade effect.

100.   See Eichengreen et al. 1998b.

lengthen the maturity structure of their debt portfolio and lower the cost on their outstanding fixed-income debt. Moreover, a diversified and competitive investor base, by deepening secondary markets and market liquidity, will result in lower market volatility. In addition, the participation in government securities markets of investors with different institutional perspectives and investment motives will stimulate financial innovation in the government securities market, including the development of instruments with features that meet the demands of various types of investors, as well as the adoption of better transparency and regulatory practices and standards in government securities markets.

With the rapid expansion of the contractual savings sectors and collective investment funds, the potential sources of demand for government securities have widened considerably in recent years. In addition, retail and foreign investors have become important sources of demand for fixed-income securities. As governments move away from reliance on captive sources of government funding by financial institutions, they need to create an environment and promote policies that attract investors with different time horizons, risk preferences, and trading objectives. While a diversified investor base is a necessary condition for ensuring broad-based demand for government securities, a stable macroeconomic environment and prudent capital account liberalization are essential to maintain a stable and growing participation of the full range of investors in government fixed-income securities.

Annex 6.A
Growth of Institutional Investors

Institutional investors, comprising pension funds, insurance companies, and mutual funds, have grown at an explosive rate over the past two decades. The total assets of institutional investors in OECD countries rose from $3.2 trillion in 1981, equivalent to 38 percent of total GDP, to $26 trillion in 1996, corresponding to 105 percent of total OECD-area GDP. The average annual growth rate amounted to 15 percent. The assets of institutional investors grew nearly three times faster than the annual income in OECD countries.

Within the OECD region, institutional investors grew fastest in the G-7 countries, where they now represent more than 110 percent of GDP. Among the G-7 countries, the rate of growth was higher in France and Germany, two countries that had lagged in the development of institutional investors. Outside the G-7, the Netherlands and Switzerland, and to a lesser extent Sweden, have very large institutional investor sectors.

Outside the OECD region, several countries experienced dramatic growth in institutional investors, including Brazil, Chile, Cyprus, Egypt, and South Africa. Although they have large institutional investors, Malaysia and Singapore did not register very high growth, mainly because their national provident funds were already large in the early 1980s, the beginning of the period under review. Several other countries, especially in Latin America and Eastern Europe, implemented systemic pension and insurance reforms in the 1980s and 1990s that laid the foundation for rapid future growth of institutional investor assets. Starting from a very low base, insurance companies and pension funds in these countries are already experiencing growth rates of over 50 percent per year. They are, however, still relatively small and continue to play a secondary part in their national financial systems.

In 1980, there were probably no more than 10 countries in which institutional investors controlled resources exceeding 50 percent of GDP. These countries included the United States, the United Kingdom, Switzerland, the Netherlands, Singapore, and South Africa, and a few more English-speaking and Scandinavian countries. Seventeen years later, nearly all OECD-area countries had institutional investors with resources exceeding 50 percent of GDP. Among developing countries, Chile and Malaysia joined this group. In Chile, the total assets of institutional investors grew from less than 1 percent of GDP in 1980 to more than 60 percent in 1997. In the United Kingdom, the Netherlands, Switzerland, the United States, and South Africa, total assets of institutional investors now exceed 150 percent of GDP.

The structure of institutional investors varies considerably across countries. Pension funds tend to be very large in countries where government-sponsored social security systems offer modest benefits. These countries include the Netherlands and Switzerland among continental European countries, and the United Kingdom and the United States outside continental Europe. Pension funds are weak or nonexistent in France, Germany, Italy, and other continental European countries where government-sponsored social security systems continue to offer generous benefits.

Several developing countries have large national provident funds (e.g., Malaysia and Sri Lanka) or partially funded social security corporations (e.g., Egypt, Gambia, Ghana, and Jordan). Their role in the securities markets is largely confined to investing in government securities. In addition, a growing number of developing and transition countries, especially in Latin America and Eastern Europe, have reformed their pension systems and created private pension funds. Except for Chile, which reformed its pension system in 1981, private pension funds in these countries are still relatively small and have had limited impact on securities markets. In reforming pension systems and pension funds, policymakers should recognize the important role that these intermediaries can play in furthering an efficient securities market.

Life insurance companies are large in many countries that also have large pension funds because of the role they play in managing pension plans and insuring pension plan benefits. This is the case in Australia, Canada, the Netherlands, South Africa, Switzerland, the United Kingdom, and the United States. However, life insurance companies have experienced high growth rates even in countries with dominant government-sponsored social security systems. In France, total assets of life insurers exceeded 45 percent of GDP in 1997, up from only 8 percent in 1980. In Austria, Belgium, and Germany, life insurance companies have amassed assets equivalent to nearly 25 percent of GDP in 1997.

In Latin America and Eastern Europe, pension reform programs provide a strong stimulus for the development of life insurance business. These programs often require the provision of term life and disability insurance for the protection of workers and their families, and they also involve the purchase of annuity policies when workers retire. In Chile, the assets of life insurance companies exceed 10 percent of GDP.

Policymakers should also bear in mind the potential importance of mutual funds for government securities market development. Recent years have witnessed an explosion in the growth of mutual funds, fuelled by the spectacular performance of equity markets in most developed countries. In the United States, mutual fund assets rose from 5 percent of GDP in 1980 to 50 percent in 1997 and 65 percent in 1998. In the United Kingdom, they increased over the same period from 7 to 25 percent. Mutual funds have a strong presence in Canada; France; Hong Kong, China; Italy; and Spain, where they range between 35 and 50 percent of GDP. In several other countries, including Belgium, Germany, Greece, the Netherlands, Portugal, Sweden, and Switzerland, mutual fund assets exceed 20 percent of GDP. In Luxembourg and Ireland, mutual fund assets are very large relative to GDP, but most are offshore funds that attract foreign investors for tax reasons. Mutual funds have also been growing rapidly in many developing countries, but, except in a few countries such as Brazil, India, Republic of Korea, Malaysia, and South Africa, their assets generally amount to less than 5 percent of GDP.

There is considerable variety in the structure of mutual funds among countries. Mutual funds follow the relative development of equity and bond markets, although various features of the regulatory framework also seem to affect the demand for different types of funds. Equity funds account for the vast majority of mutual fund assets in countries where equity markets are large or have grown rapidly in recent years (for example, Hong Kong, China; Sweden; Switzerland; and the United Kingdom). The share of equity funds in total mutual funds has also increased sharply in the United States because of the very strong performance of U.S. equity markets. There has been a substantial change in favor of equity funds over the past few years in most European countries because of the lowering of real interest rates and the strong performance of equity markets.

In contrast, bond mutual funds have been predominant in most continental European countries, especially in the countries of Southern Europe, and in most developing countries. This probably reflects the lower efficiency and weaker attractiveness of equity markets in these countries and the high level of real interest rates.

Annex 6.B
International Diversification of Securities Portfolios

6.B.1 Growth of Foreign Institutional Investors in Emerging Markets

Investment in securities of emerging markets by foreign institutional investors is a relatively recent phenomenon. Only since the mid-1980s have closed-end investment funds (including country funds) begun to invest in emerging-country bond and stock markets. Pension fund investment in emerging markets is an even more recent phenomenon. Expansion of the pension sector in OECD-area countries has become a main source of continued capital flows into emerging markets. Investment of pension funds has been through mutual funds or directly on the pension funds' own account.[101]

Countries that have received the largest portfolio inflows have experienced the largest increase in market capitalization,[102] and there seems to be considerable scope for increasing the share of emerging-country securities market assets in the portfolios of OECD-area institutional investors.[103] From both the demand and supply sides, there would thus appear to be a great potential role for foreign investors in the development of developing-country domestic government securities markets.

The 1990s have seen an explosive growth of cross-border flows of portfolio capital. A number of developing countries has attracted an increasing share of such capital, but still far less than industrial countries.[104]

An increasing interest in emerging markets has corresponded with "push" factors, such as a drop in U.S. interest rates and a slowdown in U.S. industrial production. This implies temporary and unstable capital flows to emerging markets. "Pull" factors include increasingly stabilized macroeconomic environments (at least before the Asian crisis) and continuing efforts toward economic and financial liberalization on the part of

---

101. See Blommestein 1997.

102. See World Bank 1997.

103. See Blommestein 1997.

104. Whereas gross inflows of portfolio investment to industrial countries during 1989–96 amounted to US$892.9 billion, such inflows to developing countries were US$23.4 billion (see Eichengreen et al. 1998a).

developing countries. Empirical evidence seems to point to the importance of push factors in explaining portfolio capital flows to developing countries, but country-specific developments could be at least as important for some regions, and seem to be more important for bond flows than for equity flows.[105]

6.B.2   Importance of Foreign Investors in Domestic Government Securities Markets

Institutional investors can diversify their portfolios globally by investing in foreign securities. By diversifying with emerging-market securities, many investors believe (or believed before the Asian crisis) that they could reduce portfolio risk and increase return. There is a gradual trend toward internationally diversified portfolios of pension funds. Portfolios of life insurance companies, however, are less diversified than those of pension funds. The portfolios of mutual funds in larger OECD countries have become significantly more diversified than those of insurance companies and pension funds.[106]

Institutional investors as a group are much less internationally diversified than would be true if they held a world market portfolio. Reasons for this home bias have been identified in the literature and include, for emerging countries, exchange rate risk, interest rate risk, transfer risk, settlement risk, and liquidity risk.[107] The use of hedging instruments, such as forwards, futures, and options, can reduce exchange rate risk,[108] but these instruments are not always available for emerging-market currencies. Furthermore, the price of hedging instruments will offset part of the gain from foreign investment, they may only be available for short periods, and trust deeds for pension funds may limit their use. In addition, transfer risk (exchange controls and nationalization of foreign assets) may affect the ability to repatriate returns. Settlement risk in less-developed securities markets may be large, with a high proportion of delayed or failing transactions, and liquidity risk may be significant in narrow overseas markets.

---

105. For example, see Chuhan, Claessens, and Mamingi 1998.

106. See Blommestein 1997.

107. See Blommestein 1998.

108. See BIS 1986.

Other impediments to international diversification include the nature of institutional investor liabilities. Many pension schemes and life insurance contracts have very precisely defined nominal liabilities. In these cases, the preferred investment strategy may be to match domestic liabilities with domestic assets. Regulatory constraints on foreign investments, the benchmark orientation of fund managers, and treatment by institutional investors of more diversified portfolios market securities as a separate asset class constitute yet other impediments.[109] Limitations on the proportion of fund assets that can be invested in developing-country securities by the portfolio allocation guidelines outlined in the prospectuses of broad-based mutual funds (in contrast to dedicated developing-country mutual funds) also restricts the scope of international portfolio diversification.

---

109. See IMF (1995a) for statistical evidence on the hypothesis of investors treating developing-country equities as a separate asset class.

Bibliography

Alesina, A., A. Prati, and G. Tabellini. 1990. "Public Confidence and Debt Management: A Model and a Case Study of Italy." In Rudiger Dornbusch and Mario Draghi, eds., *Public Debt Management: Theory and History*. Cambridge, U.K.: Cambridge University Press.

Analistas Financieros Internacionales. 1997. *Spanish Financial Sector: 1987–1997: A Decade of Transformations*. Emilio Ontiveros and Francisco J. Valero, eds. Department of Applied Finance, Grupo Analistas, Madrid, Spain.

BIS (Bank for International Settlements). 1986. *Recent Innovations in International Banking*. The Cross Report. Basel, Switzerland.

Blommestein, Hans J. 1997. "Institutional Investors, Pension Reform and Emerging Securities Market." Working Paper 359. Office of the Chief Economist, Inter-American Development Bank, Washington, D.C. Available at www.iadb.org.

———. 1998. "Impact of Institutional Investors on Financial Markets." In *Institutional Investors in the New Financial Landscape*. Organization for Economic Cooperation and Development, Paris, France.

Bodie, Zvi, and Dwight B. Crane. 1998. "The Design and Production of New Retirement Savings Products." Working Paper 98070. Harvard Business School, Harvard University, Cambridge, Mass.

Catalan, M., G. Impavido, and A. R. Musalem. 2000. "Contractual Savings or Stock Market Development: Which Leads?" World Bank Policy Research Paper 2421. World Bank, Washington, D.C.

Chuhan, P., S. Claessens, and N. Mamingi. 1998. "Equity and Bond Flows to Latin America and Asia: The Role of Global and Country Factors." *Journal of Development Economics* 55 (2): 439–63.

Davis, E. P. 1995. *Pension Funds: Retirement Income Security and Capital Markets*. Oxford and New York: Oxford University Press.

Eichengreen, Barry et al. 1998a. *Capital Account Liberalization: Theoretical and Practical Aspects*. Occasional Paper No. 172. International Monetary Fund, Washington, D.C.

———. 1998b. *Hedge Funds and Financial Market Dynamics*. Occasional Paper No. 155. International Monetary Fund, Washington, D.C.

Elias, J. J., G. Impavido, and A. R. Musalem. 2001. *Contractual Savings and Governments' Financing Choices*. World Bank, Washington, D.C. Processed.

6

Garcia-Vaquero, Victor. 1999. "The Boom of the Investment Fund Industry: Causes, Implications and Future Prospects." Bank of Spain. *Economic Bulletin*. July–August. Madrid, Spain.

IMF (International Monetary Fund). 1995a. *International Capital Markets: Development Prospects and Key Policy Issues*. Washington, D.C.

———. 1995b. *Private Market Financing for Developing Countries*. Washington, D.C.

Impavido, Gregorio, and A. R. Musalem. 2000. "Contractual Savings, Stock and Asset Markets." World Bank Policy Research Paper 2490, World Bank, Washington, D.C.

INVERCO (Asociación de Instituciones de Inversión Colectiva y Fondos de Pensiones). Available at www.inverco.es.

Kaminsky, Graciela, Richard Lyons, and Sergio Schmukler. 2000. "Managers, Investors, and Crisis: Mutual Fund Strategies in Emerging Markets." Working Paper No. 7855. National Bureau of Economic Research. Available at www.nber.org.

Vittas, Dimitri. 1998. "Institutional Investors and Securities Markets: Which Comes First?" In J. Burki and G. Perry, eds., *Banks and Capital Markets: Annual World Bank Conference on Development in Latin America and the Caribbean*. (World Bank Policy Research Paper 1892, World Bank, Washington, D.C.)

———. 2000. *Pension Reform and Capital Market Development: "Feasibility" and "Impact" Preconditions*. World Bank Development Research Group, World Bank, Washington, D.C. Processed.

Walker, Eduardo, and Fernando Lefort. 2000. "Pension Reform and Capital Markets: Are There Any Hard Links?" World Bank, Washington, D.C. Processed.

World Bank. 1994. *Averting the Old Age Crisis*. Policy Research Report. World Bank, Washington, D.C.

———. 1997. *Private Capital Flows to Developing Countries: The Road to Financial Integration*. World Bank, Washington, D.C.

6

Developing Secondary Market Structures for Government Securities

A strong primary market in government securities is supported by a liquid and efficient secondary market. Authorities may consider, within the context of the country's own stage of development and institutional context, the development of a market structure—instruments, transaction types, trading mechanisms, and market intermediaries—that will support a liquid and efficient market.

7.1   Introduction

This chapter focuses on the microstructure of secondary markets and the government's role in the development of market structures—including transaction types, the role of intermediaries, trading mechanisms, and market transparency—that promote efficient price discovery and liquid secondary markets. A principal objective of policymakers is to have well-functioning and liquid secondary markets for government securities. The central bank is interested in efficient interest rate determination; the government debt manager needs low intermediation costs; and the securities market regulator is interested in an infrastructure that promotes efficient, sound, and fair trading, in addition to providing opportunities for market surveillance and an adequate level of consumer protection.

7.2 Types of Transactions in Secondary Markets

The development of secondary markets adds new attributes to government securities and broadens the role and importance of government securities in the financial system. Government securities can have near-money like properties when secondary markets facilitate rapid and low-cost conversion into cash. Bonds can become a medium of exchange for the borrowing and lending of funds. Secondary markets also open avenues for risk management through various types of transactions whose pricing can be derived from government securities markets. These unique features of government securities markets help deepen the number and type of transactors in government securities which, in turn, help achieve the aim of establishing liquid and efficient secondary markets. The design of secondary market transactions and structures—discussed in more detail below—should seek to maximize such attributes and incentives to trade, thereby encouraging the development of secondary markets.

7.2.1 Spot Transactions

Scope for fast liquidation of securities and deployment of cash makes government securities attractive as cash-like investments.[110] To effectively compete with money, secondary government securities markets must provide for the immediate purchase and sale of government securities. Such on-the-spot transactions should have the following features: (i) low transaction costs, (ii) widely available and continuous pricing, (iii) wide access to trading systems and intermediaries that provide immediate execution, (iv) safe and rapid settlement of transactions, and (v) efficient custodial and safekeeping services.

A starting point and foundation for the organization of secondary markets—which is necessary to attain the above features—is the standardization of arrangements for "spot transactions." This usually involves establishing conventions governing when pricing and trade execution services are made available, and the times from execution of trades to their final settlement.

---

110. Government securities pay interest and principal and are deposit-like, but are backed by the government rather than a bank. Like deposits or currency, government securities are easily divisible into small units of value when in book-entry form.

An important design and organizational feature is the time frame from trade execution to settlement. The shorter the gap in time from trade execution to settlement, the more cash-like government securities become. This decision on convention needs to be taken in conjunction with the design and infrastructure of the clearing and settlement systems, which establish limits to what is possible. For instance, a system of automated trade execution that is linked to a system for clearing and settlement and provides settlement against delivery of securities on a real-time basis will allow for almost instantaneous settlement after trade. On the other hand, in cases where bond trades are executed on more traditional stock exchanges, time needed to clear and settle may take up to several days.

In the context of market development, the standard for the time from trade to settlement for government securities will normally need to be higher than that for equity markets. In many countries, for at least a class of government securities, in particular Treasury bills, a T+0 or same-day settlement will be very desirable. So as to be able to process all trades efficiently on a same-day basis, a cut-off time for same-day settlement of trades is sometimes established. For instance, trades that occur during the morning will be settled the same day, while trades executed in the afternoon may be settled the next day (T+1). The capability to work with the technology of such systems and establish a reasonably narrow time gap between trade execution and settlement are important design considerations.[111] The immobilization or dematerialization of government securities constitutes a key step in the movement toward shorter settlement cycles.

7.2.2 Repurchase Agreements

In fostering secondary markets, the authorities may wish to develop the use of repurchase agreements (repos), as they serve unique functions for both the private sector and the monetary authority. Borrowing and lending among a range of market participants, including banks, financial institutions, and corporates, can be fostered on a safe and secure basis through

---

111. The Committee on Payment and Settlement Systems (CPSS) and the Technical Committee of the International Organization of Securities Commissions (IOSCO) issued a consultative report in January 2001, "Recommendations for Securities Settlement Systems," that covers the design, operation, and oversight of securities settlement systems.

the use of repos that reduce both credit risk and transaction costs. Securities dealers use repos to finance their inventories of government instruments that are needed to make markets and provide two-way quotes. For this purpose, dealers lend out (or repo) securities that are in their inventory but are not expected to be immediately sold. Thus, dealers are able to leverage their capital and hold a larger inventory. A central bank can temporarily inject liquidity into the system by buying securities under repo. Because of the many uses of repos, the demand for government securities increases, while the underlying conditions for liquid secondary markets are put in place.

A repurchase agreement is effectively a collateralized loan that is realized through the sale and subsequent repurchase of a security at a specified date and price. More specifically, it is the combination of an immediate sale of a security with the agreement to reverse the transaction at a specified future date. The first leg of the repo begins when one party (the seller) sells a security to the second (the buyer) for cash. In the agreement, the seller is required to buy back the security after a passage of time, typically ranging from overnight to two weeks. This second leg gives the arrangement its name, since the initiating party repurchases the security. In contrast with genuine collateralized loans, however, ownership of the underlying security is transferred to the lender, which, with certain legal differences, makes a repo transaction more secure for the lender. Repos are arranged for short periods, typically up to two weeks, and carry interest rates close to the interbank rate. They can be implemented in a variety of ways, depending on market infrastructure, practice, and country law.

While from an economic perspective a repo is similar to a collateralized loan, from a legal perspective the two types of transactions differ significantly.[112] By design, repo transactions may offer more protection to a cash lender than a collateralized loan in the case of insolvency of the borrower. In a repo transaction, the buyer acquires full ownership of the underlying security and, thus, may sell it if the original seller defaults on his or her repurchase obligation. Depending on the market value of the security at

---

112. Since a repo incorporates a future transaction, it raises legal complexities that will differ depending on the country's legal system. Whether or not more protection is afforded depends on the applicable law. Laws in G–10 jurisdictions generally recognize the intention of the parties to the Master Repurchase Agreements, including netting of outstanding obligations.

that time, the buyer may recover most of the principal amount of the loan, or if the security was purchased at a sufficient discount from the market value, the buyer may be fully compensated for the principal and interest. If there is insufficient value in the security to pay principal and interest in full, the shortfall can be pursued in bankruptcy proceedings, where the buyer will have an unsecured claim against the seller. This mechanism is known as netting.

In developing repo markets, the authorities will want to ensure that a framework is established that governs the following elements of the transaction and addresses the risks that arise (Box 7.1):

Payment and transfer: The seller is required to deliver against payment the security to the buyer on the purchase date, and the buyer is required to deliver the security to the seller on the repurchase date. Payment must be in immediately available funds, and the securities must be transferred on the official book-entry system.[113]

Default and netting: In settling a default, the net value, or closeout balance, is defined as the difference between the current market value of the collateral security plus margin amounts and the cash borrowed plus interest. This is the amount owed to the lender (or borrower if less than zero). The key advantage in repos is that only net amounts and not the full value of the cash loan will need to be claimed under bankruptcy.[114] Netting provisions (as with margins discussed below) depend on the availability of a transparent market value of the repo security on a daily basis. In the absence of a well-functioning secondary market and transparent prices, other arrangements must be made.

Margins: Margin payments are transfers of cash or securities made during the repo contract to reflect changes in the market price of the underlying security, which can reduce potential losses associated with credit risk in the face of a drop in prices. However, margin provisions can only be

7

---

113. As specified in the standard contract, transfer need not take place on the official book-entry system. The parties can agree to another method, including transfer on a subdepository account or through segregation on the seller's books. This last method is not recommended for new markets.

114. In some countries, the principle of netting may require a change in bankruptcy law. For netting purposes, the repo contract must be treated as a single transaction rather than separate buy and sell trades. This would elevate the nondefaulting party's claim above those of other creditors, if the law supports repos.

Box. 7.1. Risks in Repurchase Transactions

Interest Risk

Interest rate risk results from changes in the market value of underlying securities. This risk increases with (i) the time to maturity of the underlying security and (ii) the length of the repo contract. From the cash borrower's perspective, a drop in market interest rates would raise the value of the underlying security. If the lender defaults—that is, he is unable to return the security for repurchase—the borrowed funds could be less than the (new) market value of the security, resulting in a loss for the cash borrower. A rise in market interest rates would correspondingly reduce the value of the underlying security. Thus a default by the cash borrower would leave the lender facing a possible shortfall, since the proceeds from the sale of the collateral might not cover the loan principal and interest. Margin payments offer some degree of protection against interest rate risk. While interest rate risk can affect both lender and borrower, the cash lender often protects him- or herself against rising interest rates and a decline in the value of the underlying security by lending less than the full market value of the collateral security.

Credit Risk

Both parties in a repo transaction face risk since the agreement incorporates a future action. *Credit (or counterparty) risks* stem from the possibility that either party may fail to honor the future transaction, but the nature of repos reduces the potential costs of these events. When the seller (cash borrower) fails to repurchase the security, the buyer (cash lender) has the collateral, which, with netting provisions, greatly reduces his or her cost of the seller's default. When the buyer (cash lender) fails to resell the security—if, for example, he had earlier sold it to another party and cannot repurchase it for resale—the original seller can keep the cash loan. In both cases, any outstanding balances will need to be settled.

Operational Risk

The consequences of a default are increased if ownership of the repoed security is not transferred on the official registry or subdepository. There are several variations on repo transactions that trade off the protection gained from transfer against transaction costs. For example, in a *letter repo,* the parties can agree to have the security seller (often a dealer) hold the security on his or her books, but in a segregated account. *Triparty repos* fall in between traditional repos and letter repos. In this case, a third party, for example, a commercial bank, transfers cash and securities for both parties; it holds the security in trust for the duration of the repo contract; this offers some protection in the case of default but introduces the possibility that the third party may not perform. Because of their added complexity, these options are not recommended for a developing market.

---

enforced when secondary markets are sufficiently developed to provide market prices. This hampers their use in new markets.

Substitution: The parties in a repo transaction may agree to allow the borrower to substitute replacement securities for a repoed security during the life of a repo contract. There is little disadvantage to the cash lender because he receives another security of equal or higher value as replacement collateral. However, significant benefits accrue to a securities dealer (the cash borrower) because substitution allows him in effect to recall and then sell a security that has been temporarily sold under repo. Particular securities may be in demand and thus command a premium price (or become "special")—for example, as the security's maturity date nears and other market participants need to cover short positions. Thus it may be in the dealer's interest to sell a particular security outright. If the security had previously been repoed, the dealer may then substitute it with a security less in demand. Substitution entails some transaction costs and requires the agreement of both parties.

Interest payments: If interest (or coupon) payments are made on a collateral security during the repo, the buyer is required to transfer the payment to the seller. This provision simplifies the pricing of collateral securities and reduces the incentive for arbitrage transactions as the security nears the coupon payment date. A key consideration is the tax treatment of the repurchase. To promote the use of the instrument and avoid distortions, a repurchase agreement should be treated as a loan that generates interest income or expense.

To standardize these practices, the terms and conditions noted above are provided for in a Master Repurchase Agreement (MRA), which is set up and signed in advance by the parties to the trade in order to enable rapid processing of the transaction.

7.2.3　Derivatives and Risk Management Instruments

Secondary markets can be further developed to provide opportunities for risk management through the development of various instruments whose pricing can be derived from government securities markets. In turn, the use of these instruments by participants further adds to the liquidity in secondary government securities markets. Derivatives and risk management instruments described below can be used to protect the value of an investment or transform income flows from assets (or liabilities) into alternative forms. Futures and forward contracts provide the ability to hedge risks, a strategy that involves choosing assets such that the prices of the assets systematically offset each other. Accordingly, the greater the correlation between the price movements of the underlying investment instrument and the hedge instrument, the larger is the scope for reduction of risk. For example, yields on government securities serve as benchmarks for pricing yields on private securities, and there is usually a complete pass-through of changes in the general level of interest rates on government securities to other fixed-income securities of the same maturity. The generally strong correlation between government and yields on private debt securities means that government securities can be used to hedge general interest rate risks. A brief description of such instruments and transactions is provided below. Annex 7.A to this chapter discusses the management of risks in the development of such instruments.

7.3.3.1 Short Selling

Short selling, the sale of borrowed securities, can promote market liquidity and price efficiency. Short selling allows for sophisticated trading strategies, including arbitrage and hedging, which contribute to efficient price discovery. In addition, dealers can better provide asset and maturity transformation services, which help promote liquidity (see below) where short selling is allowed. However, short selling should not be permitted without the existence of conditions for appropriate risk management of participants. A graduated approach may first permit short selling by dealers that are adequately capitalized and properly supervised before opening up short selling to general participants.

7.3.3.2 Strips

The depth of secondary markets can be enhanced with the development of zero-coupon Treasury derivative securities known as strips. This practice involves separating future coupon payments and principal payment at maturity from a Treasury bond. Investors can then purchase series of coupon payments or principal separately. This can create more demand for government securities because institutions can purchase a stream of future cash flows that match liabilities. Investors who desire only a single future payment can buy at a discount the promise to repay principal at maturity without the risk of reinvesting the coupon payments at some unknown interest rate while avoiding the associated administrative burden. This unbundling of payment streams also allows for the development of secondary markets for zero coupons. In designing the features of securities instruments and securities registration systems, authorities should consider the features necessary for the introduction of strips.

7.3.3.3 Forward Transactions

Forward transactions are commitments made today to make or take delivery of an asset at a future date. Usually such transactions are tailor-made to the needs of the parties involved in the trade. Nonetheless, in markets where forward transactions are permitted, conventions are usually established as to the forward periods for which market intermediaries provide quotations, as, for example, in the case of Spain. Since forward trades involve a future action, there may be a question of the ability of contracting parties to meet such obligations, opening the way for liquidity or credit risk.

A special type of forward transaction is the *when-issued market*. This involves the sale of government securities before and immediately following the auctions but before settlement. When-issued trading allows dealers to distribute primary issues before participation in the auction. Such trading can deepen the primary market and promote secondary market trading by opening avenues for pre-auction distribution and encouraging price discovery leading into auctions. Preconditions for when-issued trading include a regular pattern of issuance that establishes the trading period, sufficiently deep primary markets so that the likelihood of an auction failure is very small (constant sufficient bid cover), a sufficiently well-developed clearing and settlement system, and adequate regulatory oversight to prevent misuse or uncompetitive practices from emerging.

7.3.3.4 Swap Transactions

Swap transactions provide risk management opportunities by altering cash flows and allow flexible risk strategies tailored to the type of flow. The most basic swap transaction is a fixed-for-floating interest rate swap, involving a net exchange of a fixed-rate stream of income, usually expressed as a spread over the Treasury security corresponding to the swap maturity, for a floating interest rate. The floating rate is usually tied to a short-term interest rate, such as London Interbank overnight rate (LIBOR), or a Treasury bill rate.

7.3.3.5 Futures and Options

Futures and options have become indispensable risk management tools in developed markets. In emerging markets, they can contribute to broadening risk management opportunities and promoting more liquid markets. Futures are standardized contracts involving a commitment to take or make future delivery of a specified financial asset for which the price at delivery is set at the time the contract is entered into. An options contract provides the additional flexibility of allowing an action *contingent* on some price and may take many forms. For example, a call option allows, but does not require, the option holder to buy a Treasury security at a preset price during the period the option remains valid. A put option allows, but does not require, the option holder to sell a Treasury security at a preset price during the period the option remains valid.

7.3 Features of Market Structures[115]

There are a number of choices to be considered in developing a government securities market structure. The features of different market structures, including trading mechanism, information systems, and scope for competition, can influence the outcome of price discovery and liquidity. This section discusses the salient features of different market structures at a broad level by examining in particular: (i) periodic versus continuous markets, (ii) dealer markets versus auction-agency markets, and (iii) electronic versus floor-based markets.

7.3.1 Periodic Versus Continuous Markets

As the name suggests, periodic markets involve trading at periodic (or discrete) intervals. A periodic market may also feature execution at a single price—that is, at a price determined by all orders coming to the market at the trading interval.[116] Between trading intervals, buying and selling interest is allowed to build, increasing the number of traders present during each trading session (intertemporal consolidation of order flow), thereby improving liquidity and adding to market depth. The execution of trades (multilateral) at a uniform price reduces transaction costs, that is, the bid/ask

---

115. This section draws upon Dattels 1997.

116. This type of periodic market is referred to as a "call market" and is the most common form of periodic market.

spread associated with continuous markets (discussed below) is eliminated, which is another important benefit of periodic markets. By centralizing trading, periodic markets provide economies of scale in order handling. The single (uniform) price outcome gives the same execution to all traders (fair treatment) and simplifies the clearing and settling of transactions, reducing costs and the possibility of errors.

In continuous markets, trading goes on without interruptions and trades are executed continuously, permitting more flexible trading strategies than periodic markets. The continuous price discovery process provides contemporaneous information on prices, transactions, and market conditions. There are two basic types of continuous markets: dealer markets and auction-agency markets.

7.3.2   Dealer Versus Auction-Agency Markets

In dealer markets, the random arrival of orders to the market is bridged by intermediaries—dealers—that maintain continuous market conditions. Dealers provide two-way (bid and offer) quotations, supplying a high degree of immediacy to traders that may either buy or sell against those quotations. Dealer markets are often described as "quote-driven" markets, underscoring the dealer's function in maintaining continuous markets.

Interdealer brokers (IDBs) are a specialized type of market intermediary that provide trade execution services to other market intermediaries in a dealer market. The IDB provides information on the prices and quantities at which other dealers are willing to transact. In so doing, they consolidate information about competing quotations for government securities, thereby encouraging efficient price discovery. In many cases, IDBs keep the identity of the dealer anonymous, which tends to protect intermediaries against execution risk that may arise if other participants are aware of the full extent of the trading interest or inventory position. The IDB earns a fee on each transaction and, therefore, is reliant on large volumes of trading. Accordingly, in developing markets, IDBs can play an important role in educating participants and encouraging trading activity.

Auction-agency markets facilitate the interaction of buying and selling interest of public traders through a centralized auction and agency process. Reflecting this characteristic, these markets are often referred to as order-matching or order-driven markets. Public traders can compete as

7

suppliers of liquidity by submitting limit orders, while those demanders of liquidity can execute immediately by submitting market orders.[117]

On the other hand, auction-agency markets rely on natural order flow to maintain continuous market trading: liquidity and market depth depend on the random arrival of orders from traders and speculators. If order flow is uneven, the market may become one-sided or imbalanced, and spurious price volatility (deviations of the market price from the underlying equilibrium value) may result. It follows that individual orders will be subject to execution risk as the size of that order increases relative to the depth of the market. Therefore, the average price at which a large order is executed depends on the depth or elasticity of the order book at the time of trade execution. In contrast, dealers insure traders against execution risk by setting quotes in advance.[118]

7.3.3   Automation and Electronic Market Structures

Electronic technology (computers, telecommunications, and so forth) is rapidly changing all market structures. In general, it has improved the efficiency of markets by (i) replacing the mechanical aspects of trading functions—order routing, order ticket writing, processing, and so on—thereby increasing the operational efficiency of markets; (ii) providing instantaneous information dissemination (real-time information) on market prices and transactions, thereby improving the transparency of markets and increasing competition; and (iii) creating new market structures offering automated trade execution, thereby replacing some traditional functions of intermediaries.

Electronic call and auction-agency market structures potentially enhance market deepening and liquidity. In floor-based auction-agency or call auction markets, very short-run trading in response to order flow (interactive price discovery) is generally confined to the traders on the floor of the exchange (typically called the crowd). By removing the spatial limitations of physical trading floor arrangements, electronic trading

---

117. A limit order is an order to buy or sell contingent on price. A market order is an order to execute a trade of a certain size at the best price available in the market.

118. This does not mean that in a dealer market there is no price volatility, only that the execution price is known in advance.

expands the potential size of the crowd, promoting deeper and more liquid markets with more efficient price discovery. Consequently, there is a distinct trend away from floor-based call auction and auction-agency markets and toward electronic markets for these types of market structures.

In electronic dealer markets, dealer quotations are centralized onto a screen-based network. Market orders are entered onto the network and executed automatically against the quotations. Compared to decentralized over-the-counter market structures, they offer the following advantages: (i) increased transparency of price and transaction information; (ii) price and time priorities to public traders—trades are executed on a first-in basis, against the best dealer price; (iii) information and intermediary functions that are performed by traditional IDBs are replaced by the centralized quotation system,[119] and (iv) the facilitation of real-time auditing of transactions for market surveillance.

An electronic dealer market also changes the nature of traditional OTC dealer markets in a number of subtle ways. Centralized trading with transparent trade reporting reduces opportunities for dealers to compete for internalized (dealer-client) order flow and profit from that information (by transacting with other less-informed dealers). This may lower incentives for dealers to participate in the market, reducing the supply of dealer services. In addition, dealers are unable to differentiate between uninformed and informed traders, as trading is anonymous. As a result dealer quotations may be for smaller size, and bid/ask spreads may be wider in an electronic market, so as to guard against being adversely selected by informed traders. Box 7.2 describes the MTS SpA (Mercato dei Titoli di Stato, or Government Bond Market) in Italy, the country with the most experience with this particular market system.

In summary, each market structure contributes to price discovery and liquidity in different ways. A variety of market structures are present across the range of countries. It follows that the suitability of market structures for a particular country is partly a function of the institutional characteristics of the national market, as discussed in detail below.

---

119. It is important to note that in such markets, IDBs themselves might transform to provide some of the infrastructure development, and many continue to perform other roles including trade origination and education.

7.4   Efficiency and Liquidity Issues in Market Structures

In assessing the choice of market structure with the goals of liquidity and efficiency in mind, authorities should consider frequency of trading, transparency, and competition, all of which have an impact on liquidity and efficiency.

7.4.1   Trading Frequency

Frequency of trading means the choice between a periodic market and a continuous market. The concentration of orders in a periodic market develops liquidity and market depth at the trading interval and reduces price volatility.

In nascent markets, the number of participants may be small, and the trading interest may initially be low. This can occur in secondary markets that are characterized as thinly traded, illiquid, and with a high degree of execution risk. In such circumstances, market efficiency might be improved by a low-trading frequency. The call auction trading feature has the added benefit of equal treatment of orders. The transparency and integrity of the market are high because orders of all participants receive the same treatment, creating confidence in a developing market place. In such situations, trading fixed-income securities on an organized exchange at specific times during the week or even the month could help create a more efficient market.

As the economy develops, the number of factors changing the equilibrium price of bonds will start to increase, accompanied by bond price volatility. Market risk associated with periodic markets therefore rises. The clearing frequency should then be allowed to increase and, at an appropriate stage, become continuous.[120] Since in continuous markets trades take place throughout the trading day, price discovery is also continuous and uninterrupted, creating additional confidence in the price. The use of sophisticated trading or hedging strategies needs continuous markets because such strategies require continuous pricing. The continuous pricing mechanism is also capable of absorbing a large amount of information or a large number

---

120. In situations in which government needs are sizable and the issuance volumes are large and growing, it may be difficult to keep the frequency of trading low even in the early stages.

Box 7.2. Development of the Electronic Dealer Market: The Case of Italy

MTS SpA is the wholesale interdealer electronic trading market for government bonds in Italy. The Bank of Italy and the Italian Treasury, in collaboration with the primary dealers, launched MTS in 1988. It was created to provide a supportive environment for major policy changes toward more market-oriented debt management, that is, from firm sales of government securities to a conventional auction-based system, among others. In creating MTS, the Italian Treasury played a major role by setting the general framework in which the new market was to operate through a legislative measure. The Treasury held a stake in the management of MTS, which was sold to the major market makers in 1997.

MTS has been extremely successful, currently trading about 90 percent of turnover in Italian government bonds. The success of MTS has led to cloning of the platform elsewhere, especially in Europe. EuroMTS was launched in April 1999 as an international trading system for European benchmark government bonds. In addition, newly established local electronic trading platforms along the lines of MTS include MTS Amsterdam, MTS Belgium, MTS France, and MTS Portugal. Brazil and Korea have also adopted electronic bond-trading systems along the lines of MTS.

MTS is an example of a dealer market with hybrid features. On the one hand, it is a quote-driven, multidealer system in which major market makers are obliged to display bid/offer prices continuously during operating hours. On the other hand, it can be characterized as a centralized cross-matching system as market makers' quotes are aggregated in a single order book to match best anonymous bids and offers automatically subject to nondiscretionary priority rules. This unique market architecture enables MTS markets to simultaneously benefit from the strengths of two distinct systems: transparency and cost-efficiency of a central electronic cross-matching system as well as liquidity and immediacy of the quote-driven system.

MTS Italy consists of three different dealer groups. The *primary dealers* are committed to display bid/offer quotes on a continuous basis on selected bonds. They must meet stringent capital adequacy ratios. The *specialists in government bonds* are selected among the primary dealers and are obliged to display bid/offer quotes on the screens of MTS on a continuous basis. In addition, the Treasury closely monitors their market-making activities in terms of the quality of the two-way price quotes. In the primary market, specialists are committed to subscribe to specified shares of auctions. In return, they are the only dealers entitled to participate in supplementary auctions and are usually the only counterparties selected by the Treasury for buy-back auctions. *Dealers* cannot enter quotes into the system, and they must trade bonds on the basis of bid/offer quotes placed by the primary dealers and specialists.

---

of variables, whereas the periodic market will have more difficulty producing smooth pricing in such circumstances.

7.4.2 Consolidated Versus Multiple Markets

In developing markets, consideration might be given to the benefits and possible costs of competing marketplaces. When order flow is low, it may be beneficial to consolidate trading interest in a single marketplace. Such an approach would prevent the fragmentation of orders that may result in less-efficient price discovery and lower liquidity. On the other hand, competition among marketplaces can encourage competition for order flow that leads to the development of more efficient marketplaces. In addition, different market structures may be tailored to different types of investors. For example, in some countries, auction-agency markets tend to serve retail investors that transact in small amounts, while institutional investors transact in larger block sizes through dealer markets. Accordingly, this issue depends on a number of factors specific to the country context, including the types of investors and transactors, the stage of development, and the incentives for the creation of efficient trading systems. As discussed in Section 7.4.8, efforts to provide consolidated price information can enhance transparency and efficiency when transactions occur across different markets or different intermediaries.

7.4.3 Degree of Security Fragmentation

The degree of security fragmentation may also influence the suitability of market structure for the type of government security. A unique feature of "cash" government securities in comparison with futures or equities is the fragmentation into different issues, each with a different maturity date or coupon rate. In particular, Treasury bills tend to be highly fragmented as they are normally issued with high frequency (weekly auctions) and across the maturity spectrum (for example, with original maturities of 3, 6, and 12 months). Such security fragmentation increases the need for dealers to provide asset transformation services. Dealers, as part of their market-making business, accommodate switches by public traders into and out of maturities of the same security, maintaining a so-called book of long and short positions of outstanding maturities. Accordingly, in countries where the development of auction-agency market structures is promoted, the authorities would wish to reduce the degree of fragmentation to support the liquidity function of those market structures.

7.4.4 Wholesale Versus Retail

In countries where typical investors are small or "retail," the authorities may wish to promote auction-agency markets because trading is typically in large volume but low value. In this environment, auction-agency markets provide lower-cost transaction services and provide greater transparency and equitable execution owing to the consolidation of order flow and rules governing priorities for the execution of orders. On the other hand, in countries where investors are more typically large institutions, dealer markets may more naturally result. These institutions tend to trade in block sizes (low volume but high value) and prefer dealer markets, which provide insurance against execution risk.

7.4.5 Competition Among Market Intermediaries

Competition in the government securities market between market intermediaries improves liquidity and efficiency. Dealer markets work best when there are sufficient numbers of dealers that can compete for order flow, lowering transactions costs. As a general principle, however, the authorities should not increase the number of dealers if this would result in the entry of unqualified and poorly capitalized participants or perpetuation of lax standards. Accordingly, in countries that lack sufficient numbers of well-capitalized dealers, call auction or auction-agency market structures are likely to be more efficient than dealer markets.

As a transitional arrangement, when trading volumes are insufficient to attract or support competing dealers, or possibly when conditions of adequate capitalization and competition are not met, some countries have in the past assisted in the development of a dealer market structure by beginning with a single (monopoly) dealer or a limited number of dealers.[121] Once established, the discount house, operating in the government securities market, attracts order flow in sufficient volumes that warrant the capital investment. Later, as the market develops, the discount house would form part of a broader arrangement—such as the formation of a primary dealer group—encouraging the emergence of competing dealers. Box 7.3 describes the experience of India and Malaysia in assisting market intermediary development.

---

121. It is important to stress that the so-called monopoly does not involve an exclusive legal right preventing other dealers from competing. In the context of a nascent market, with insufficient order flow and scarce capital resources, one or a few discount houses—whose role it is to provide liquidity to the secondary market through buying and selling of outstanding securities—are formed (sometimes by the pooling of capital of financial institutions, possibly including some capital ownership by the authorities, and generally supported by a line of credit from the central bank permitting them to function effectively as a market maker and inventory securities).

There are risks to the above strategy. Particularly important factors are the extent and nature of competition and the potential conflicts with policy goals of the central bank. Licensing one or a limited number of discount houses may stifle competition. Thus the establishment of discount houses should form part of an articulated strategy to develop efficient market structures. Even if only one discount house exists, other financial institutions should be permitted to trade in securities and be allowed to emerge as dealers over time, adding to competition. As the market develops and the demand for trading services increases, licensing should be expanded while privileges are reduced, encouraging the development of a market of competing dealers.

Moral hazards for the central bank may arise when it contributes capital to the discount house and provides arrangements supporting the discount house's operations. The profitable operations of the discount house become a direct responsibility of the central bank, a fact that may distract it from conducting monetary operations to achieve its primary goal of price stability. Thus the participation of the central bank in the formation and operation of the discount house should be carefully considered.

7.4.6 Execution Risk and Secondary Market Liquidity

In nascent markets, there is a high liquidity risk to dealers accommodating customer trades to and from securities inventories, since two-way markets are not yet fully developed. In these circumstances, and to foster the development of nascent, competing dealer markets, the central bank might consider opening a secondary market window to support market making. Typically, under certain conditions, the central bank is prepared to buy or sell securities from those dealers that are supporting secondary market trading. This window tends to reduce liquidity risk, which encourages dealers to supply quotations to the public and maintain continuous market conditions. As markets become more developed and liquidity risk falls, the central bank may withdraw from market-making activity, either by closing the secondary market window altogether or transforming the window for the sole purpose of conducting open market operations or for active debt management policies.

Attention needs to be given to the design and implementation of the window to ensure that operations do not conflict with monetary objectives (by absorbing amounts of securities that result in aggregate liquidity changes) or act to reduce incentives for market making (by setting spreads too narrowly). Box 7.3 lists countries that have utilized a secondary market window.

In the context of auction-agency markets, which may be subject to a higher degree of execution risk, the authorities can play a role as price stabilizer by participating directly in the auction-agency market as an active auctioneer. This role should not be so great as to discourage the emergence of "speculative stabilization" by private sector intermediaries. Nor should it influence price trends. Arrangements, therefore, must be carefully designed so as not to conflict with market development or monetary or debt management objectives. As the market develops and deepens, the price stabilization role of the authorities should likewise diminish and, ideally, be eliminated. Box 7.3 discusses the experiences of countries that have performed this role in auction-agency markets.

7.4.7 Liquidity Risk

To foster a competing dealer market structure in the absence of well-developed funding markets (repo or call money markets), central banks often establish lines of credit with primary dealers. In less-developed markets, this encourages dealers to provide secondary market liquidity and cost-effective execution services. Such lines reduce financing risk that may arise if, after undertaking an inventory position during the course of trading, funding is unavailable (or available only at exorbitant costs) to the dealer. Many countries have collateralized established lines of credit to support primary dealers—for example, India, Italy, Canada, and the United Kingdom. Later, as efficient funding markets developed, the central bank provided only indirect support through the conduct of open market operations (as in the United States and France) or reduced the size of such lines, diminishing their importance (as in Canada) relative to the size of the market.

7.4.8 Transparency

Transparency promotes an efficient and fair markets. Information made available about trading interest and the prices at which market participants are willing to transact is central to efficient price discovery. Such information

---

Box 7.3. Transitional Arrangements: Country Experiences

Discount House

In India, the Discount Finance House of India (DFHI) was formed to develop the money market by pooling capital from several financial institutions, including the Reserve Bank of India. In 1994, the Government Securities Trading Corporation (GSTC) was similarly established to develop the bond market. As trading volumes increased, the Reserve Bank of India established criteria (1995) for the development of a group of competing primary dealers. In this arrangement, the GSTC and the DFHI are two in a larger group of dealers under the same obligations and sharing equal access to the same facilities as other members of a primary dealer group.

In Malaysia, the authorities licensed a limited number of discount houses without central bank capital, but with special privileges in order for them to operate efficiently in the money and government securities market. Later, as the market developed, special privileges were removed, and discount houses became part of a larger group of government securities dealers.

Secondary Market Window

Examples of countries that have instituted a secondary market window as a transitional arrangement include Jamaica, Iceland, Thailand, Malaysia, and Nepal. A developed market example is provided by the Bank of England, which had operated a secondary market window for gilt-edged, index-linked instruments to encourage the market to develop for that instrument.

Examples of countries that have participated as price stabilizers in an agency-auction market include Germany, Ireland, and Malta. In Germany, the Bundesbank, on behalf of the government, participates in the market on eight regional exchanges, buying and selling occasionally, as appropriate, to reduce price volatility and provide continuity and stability in secondary market trading. The Bundesbank also participates in the fixing session (call auction). In Ireland, the National Treasury Management Agency (NTMA) acts as a "market maker of last resort," quoting prices on benchmark bonds listed on the exchange in order to help market confidence and stability (see Horgan 1995). Malta is another example of the central bank performing this function.

Brokerage System

In Poland, the National Bank of Poland (NBP) provided a screen-based IDB system—called Telegazette—for central bank and Treasury bills, with supporting facilities to clear and settle government securities transactions. Dealers appointed by the NBP can communicate their buying and selling interest to the bank via telephone. Bank personnel would display bids and offers to the other dealers in possession of the screen display system. After establishing a functioning market, the NBP has all but closed its facility.

---

may include post-trade price and volume, pretrade price and volume, and identity of the market intermediary or client. Depending on the choice of market structure, policymakers may take steps to strengthen or promote transparency.

In traditional agency-auction exchanges, for example, there is a level of pretrade transparency (usually to a certain number of incoming orders) and full post-trade transparency, including the identity of the parties to the trade. However, many dealer markets do not require either or pre- or

---

Box 7.4. Transparency Development: Country Experience

The U.S. authorities have chosen to promote transparency through the development by participating intermediaries of an automated reporting system called GovPX. Through GovPX, market intermediaries are required to report pre- and post-trade price and volume information. Pretrade information is available in real time to the public on a consolidated basis (best bid or ask price and total volume), and no identity is attached to the information. Post-trade price and volume information is also available in real time on a trade-by-

trade basis without the identity of the trader attached. The GovPX system provides a very high level of transparency.

The Indian authorities have introduced transparency through the depository system and settlement facilities. Price information is recorded through the settlement process and provided to the public at the end of the trading day on a consolidated basis for each issue. This information can instill confidence in investors and encourage efficient pricing.

---

post-trade reporting to a central mechanism nor public reporting of any information. Rather, these systems rely on a strongly connected market intermediary community to organize price discovery informally (through telephone conversation or screen-based systems). Box 7.4 provides the experience of the United States and India.

In the absence of real-time price information and poorly developed counterparty relationships between potential dealers, as well as a lack of available brokerage expertise and clearing arrangements, the authorities may institute a brokerage/trading system, patterned after the market structure of monopoly IDBs. Lending the authority's name and infrastructure to such facilities can promote confidence among major market participants and develop trading expertise. Moreover, these systems enhance the price discovery process and provide transparency to developing markets. As the market develops, scope for private sector entrants increases, and the need for such a facility may well diminish. Box 7.3 includes the experience of Poland in supporting such facilities.

7.4.9 Development Strategies

As discussed above, caution should be exercised in undertaking direct involvement in market structure that would shift undue risk to the central bank or debt management office. Such practices may interfere with the development of natural liquidity if the authorities are not able to transition to natural liquidity providers. Practice is, therefore, gradually moving away from the authorities providing direct market-making services to the market (thereby absorbing market risk) toward strengthening natural liquidity by design of benchmarks, reducing liquidity risks by providing some form of collateralized borrowing/lending and securities borrowing and lending, and promoting transparency by encouraging market participants to promote price transparency.

7.5   Conclusion: Suitability and Selection of Market Structure

Considering the role of the secondary government securities market as well as its moving parts (different types of transactions, settlement, payment, risks, market intermediaries, investors) and the effects of these choices on efficiency and liquidity, depending on the stage of development, a number of microstructure arrangements are possible:

1. Countries in the nascent stage of development with thin markets are good candidates for periodic markets with low trading frequency, which leads to market deepening and efficient price discovery.
2. In small countries that lack sufficient numbers of well-capitalized dealers, call auction or auction-agency market structures are likely to be more efficient than dealer markets.
3. Countries where government securities are held and actively traded by the retail sector are good candidates for auction-agency markets or call auction markets that provide low transaction costs and a high level of transparency.
4. Countries where holdings of government securities are concentrated in institutions that have large-sized portfolios and a high demand for immediacy are good candidates for dealer markets.
5. Countries where the monetary authorities are instituting indirect (market-based) monetary control may foster dealer market structures because dealers are natural counterparties for the conduct of monetary operations and promote, over time, continuous markets with immediacy of execution to ensure the effective implementation of monetary policy.
6. Countries with sophisticated traders and sufficient trade volume should adopt electronic market structures for auction-agency or call

markets, deriving the full benefits of technology for operational efficiency and market liquidity.

7. Countries with limited supervisory capabilities and institutions that lack a track record of integrity are strong candidates for electronic market structures that promote transparency and self-regulation.

8. Countries with quote-driven OTC markets where authorities prefer centralized trading structures for transparency and ease of surveillance may encourage the development of electronic dealer markets.

7

Annex 7.A
Risk Management Issues in Derivatives Market Structures[122]

The risks associated with the use of derivative instruments require the development of practices and institutions that will help to manage the various types of risks present. In the context of market development, authorities should bear in mind that risk management is carried out differently depending on the type of market structure. In OTC markets, trading, clearing and settlement, risk management, and contingency management are generally dealt with on an informal and bilateral basis. The management of counterparty risk is decentralized and located within individual institutions; there are no formal centralized limits on individual positions, leverage, or margining, nor are there any formal rules for risk and burden sharing or mechanisms for ensuring market stability and integrity. Because of these aspects, intermediaries are responsible for dealing with much of the credit and operational risks that are present. In OTC markets, contracts need to be developed that clearly outline the rights and responsibilities of the trading parties, in order to best ensure the creditworthiness of the parties. Clearance and settlement procedures must be well defined to ensure that trades are completed in a timely and orderly manner. The legal documentation must ensure ownership status of the securities, and the accounting framework must guarantee the proper recording of transactions. Box 7.5 outlines some of the risk elements in OTC derivatives markets and the manner in which they are addressed.

In contrast to OTC markets, organized exchanges are more regulated and centralized, with more clearly defined frameworks for the organization of trading and promotion of market stability. Consequently, practices regarding trading, clearing and settlement, and risk and contingency management are more institutionalized. Exchange trading has four main elements: membership requirements; rules governing conduct (including risk management); centralized trading, clearing, and settlement; and rules that mutualize risk, including loss-sharing arrangements. These rules are designed to ensure market integrity, promote efficient price discovery, and

---

122. This section draws on IMF 2000.

Box 7.5. Managing Risks in OTC Derivatives Markets

Market Risks

Market risks in OTC derivatives are managed using such tools as value-at-risk (VaR) models, which measure how much of the firm's capital could be lost owing to swings in the value of its portfolio, under various assumptions. However, recent developments have revealed limitations in these simplifying assumptions because standard VaR models ignore the confluence of credit and market risk, which can be particularly complicated for options, as option credit exposure varies nonlinearly with the price of the underlying security.

Credit Risk

Counterparty credit risk is frequently managed like other credit risks, namely, "one at a time," evaluating techniques such as internal ratings, models of rating migration, estimates of default probabilities, and expected loss from spreads on other senior unsecured claims and scenario analysis. Some dealers explicitly mark to market the credit risk in their swap books. A more fundamental approach would be to model the credit risk of counterparties. However, such an approach for credit risk is more difficult than market risk.

Operational Risk

OTC derivatives contracts give rise to operational risks, including the clearing and settlement risks, legal risks, and others. For example, models of derivatives prices may be misspecified, miscoded in management information systems, or may break down unexpectedly, resulting in model risk. Legal risks are an additional element of operational risk, especially risk associated with the use of collateral. While swap transactions may be less prone to difficulties, the enforceability of collateral arrangements can be problematic, particularly in cross-border transactions. Because operational risks are difficult to quantify, market participants have taken several steps to address operational risks, including formalizing and standardizing OTC derivatives transactions, especially with respect to the Master Repurchase Agreement (MRA), limiting exposures to countries where legal risks are pronounced, limiting and reserving against exposures that seem vulnerable to operation risks, and strengthening back-office systems and automating the trade-capture process.

---

safeguard resources. To maintain market stability and financial integrity, exchanges impose requirements on members that govern soundness, disclosure, transparency, and prudential requirements. Box 7.6 discusses the practices developed in exchange markets to minimize market, credit, and operational risks.

The development of secondary markets requires a framework supported by sound institutions, well-established procedures and operating systems, and intermediaries that can provide the expertise and risk management functions to facilitate efficient and liquid markets. In developing countries, the advantages that auction-agency market structures provide for the design of risk containment systems suggest that risk management instruments (options and futures) should be best placed in an auction-agency market structure.

Box 7.6. Managing Risks in Organized Exchange Markets

Market Risk

Market risk is broadly addressed through various arrangements designed to ensure the overall stability and soundness of the exchange and its members. For example, exchanges should impose minimum capital requirements and arrangements for protection of customers' funds as well as reporting and compliance regulations. Trading activity should be monitored to identify large customer positions or concentrated exposures. Transparency should be achieved by reporting positions, turnover, and price data and by determining daily settlement prices. Some clearinghouses share information and assess members' net exposure across markets.

Credit Risk

Exchanges that deal with derivatives should have a central counterparty to trades. The clearinghouse, which may or may not be part of the exchange, manages credit risk by serving as the legal counterparty to every transaction. Members' positions are marked to market daily, and in the case of default, the clearinghouse normally has the right to liquidate the member's positions; take the member's security deposit, margin, and performance bonds; attach other assets; and invoke any guarantee needed from the member's parent company. In the case of insufficient funds, the clearinghouse should be able to invoke loss-sharing rules of the exchange. Regulated trade comparison, clearance and settlement periods, delivery versus payment, and book-entry accounting should be in place to reduce timing delays that may increase potential credit risk.

Operational Risk

Operational risks are reduced through many of the practices that formalize risk management. Trading procedures should be institutionalized and computerized (usually with backup systems), and geographical diversity of counterparties, collateral instruments, and custodial entities should be monitored. In addition, rules may be developed to protect the exchange from activities of nonmembers who operate through members. Legal risks stemming from the enforceability of collateral arrangements should be addressed through a party's obligations as a member of the exchange, including margins, security deposits, surveys of their financial position, and, ultimately, the ability to access resources available through loss-sharing rules.

Bibliography

BIS (Bank for International Settlements). 1999. *Market Liquidity: Research Findings and Selected Policy Implications.* Basel, Switzerland.

Bloomfield, Robert, and Maureen O'Hara. 1999. "Market Transparency: Who Wins and Who Loses." *Review of Financial Studies* 12 (1): 5–35.

————. 2000. "Can Transparent Markets Survive?" *Journal of Financial Economics* 55 (3): 425–59.

Chakravarty, Sugato, and Asani Sarkar. 1997. *Traders' Broker Choice, Market Liquidity and Market Structure.* Staff Reports No. 24. August. Federal Reserve Bank of New York. Available at www.ny.frb.org/.

Committee on the Global Financial System. 1999. *Implications of Repo Markets for Central Banks.* Report of a Working Group, Bank for International Settlements. Basel, Switzerland. Available at www.bis.org/publ/index.htm.

Dattels, Peter. 1997. "Microstructure of Government Securities Markets." In V. Sundararajan, Peter Dattels, and Hans J. Blommestein, eds., *Coordinating Public Debt and Monetary Management: Institutional and Operational Arrangements.* International Monetary Fund, Washington, D.C.

Domowitz, Ian, and Benn Steil. 1999. "Automation, Trading Costs, and the Structure of the Securities Trading Industry." *Brookings-Wharton Papers on Financial Services.* Washington, D.C.: The Brookings Institution Press.

FESCO (Forum of European Securities Commissions). "The Regulation of Alternative Trading Systems in Europe." Paper for the EU Commission, Ref: Fesco/00–064c. Paris, France. Available at www.europefesco.org.

Fleming, Michael J., and Eli M. Remolona. 1997. "What Moves the Bond Market?" *Economic Policy Review.* Federal Reserve Bank of New York. Available at www.ny.frb.org/.

Flood, Mark D., Ronald Huisman, Kees G. Koedijk, and Ronald J. Mahieu. 1999. "Quote Disclosure and Price Discovery in Multiple-Dealer Financial Markets." *Review of Financial Studies* 12 (1): 37–59.

Fry, Maxwell J. 1997. *Emancipating the Banking System and Developing Markets for Government Debt.* London and New York: Routledge.

Gwangheon, Hong, and Arthur Warga. 2000. "An Empirical Study of Bond Market Transactions." *Financial Analysts Journal.* March/April.

7

IMF. 2000. *Modern Banking and OTC Derivatives Markets*. Occasional Paper 203.

Lee, Ruben. 1998. *What Is an Exchange? The Automation, Management, and Regulation of Financial Market*. Oxford and New York: Oxford University Press.

Meulendyke, Ann-Marie. 1998. *U.S. Monetary Policy and Financial Markets*. Federal Reserve Bank of New York.

Naik, Narayan Y., Anthony Neuberger, and S. Viswanathan. 1999. "Trade Disclosure Regulation in Markets with Negotiated Trades." *Review of Financial Studies, Special*. 12 (4): 873–900.

O'Hara, Maureen. 1995. *Market Microstructure Theory*. Cambridge, Mass.: Blackwell Publishers, Inc.

Plexus Group. 1999. *Study of Transaction Costs on the London Stock Exchange*. London, U.K. Available at www.plexusgroup.com/.

President's Working Group on Financial Markets. 1999. *Hedge Funds, Leverage, and the Lessons of Long-Term Capital Management*. Commodity Futures Trading Commission, Washington, D.C.

Saporta, Victoria. 1997. "Which Inter-Dealer Market Prevails? An Analysis of Inter-Dealer Trading in Opaque Markets." Working Paper No. 59. Bank of England, London, U.K. Available at www.bankofengland.co.uk.

SEC (U.S. Securities and Exchange Commission). 1997. *The Impact of Recent Technological Advances on the Securities Markets. Report to the Congress*. Securities and Exchange Commission, Washington, D.C.

———. 2000. *Market 2000: An Examination of Current Equity Market Developments*. Division of Market Regulation, Securities and Exchange Commission, Washington, D.C.

Shah, Ajay. 1999. "Institutional Change in India's Debt Market." *Economic and Political Weekly*. Vol. 34, Nos. 3 and 4, January 16–23.

Sundararajan, V., Peter Dattels, and Hans Blommestein, eds. 1997. *Co-ordinating Public Debt and Monetary Management: Institutional and Operational Arrangements*. International Monetary Fund, Washington, D.C.

Thomas, S. 2000. "Derivative Markets for Debt Market Development." Background paper *for Developing Debt Markets: A Manual for Policy Makers*. International Finance Corporation, Washington, D.C. Processed.

7

Developing a Government Securities Settlement Structure

A modern, efficient securities settlement system is a principal component of the infrastructure necessary for development of securities markets in general and the government securities market in particular. The settlement system (including depository facilities) affects the degree of confidence investors have in the market infrastructure, determines whether trading in the primary and secondary markets flows smoothly, and influences the capacity a market has to expand. The condition of the securities settlement and depository arrangements is a major direct determinant of systemic risk. The structure of the settlement system will vary with country circumstances. In developing markets for government securities, authorities should place a high priority on establishing a securities settlement infrastructure suited to country and market circumstances.

8.1 Introduction

Adequate depository and settlement procedures for cash and securities are basic policy initiatives supporting government securities market development. A well-functioning securities settlement infrastructure will include automated (dematerialized) accounts for securities, reliable custody arrangements for the recording of securities ownership, and a settlement system with delivery versus payment allowing for same-day settlement.

Without an adequate securities settlement infrastructure, there can be considerable systemic risks. Failure of one party to a large securities transaction can lead to a series of subsequent failures. International organizations, study groups, and others have directed considerable attention on the potential dangers for financial markets in general of inadequate securities settlement arrangements. Studies by these bodies include recommendations for strengthening and harmonizing settlement arrangements and procedures to minimize risk.[123] The International Organization of Securities Commissions (IOSCO) and the Committee on Payment and Settlement Systems (CPSS) have published several studies, including in 1997, *Disclosure Framework for Securities Settlement Systems*,[124] as a tool for risk management, and are currently preparing for comment a set of core principles for securities settlement.

These studies draw heavily on the needs, operational and policy issues, and experiences of highly developed markets in the securities settlement area. While this chapter draws on the experience in more advanced markets, it also focuses on the needs of emerging national markets, noting recent successful and unsuccessful country experiences.

Policymakers will need to address the development of a government securities infrastructure from a variety of perspectives. The economic perspective will be on efficient and low-risk settlement facilities. From a market supervision perspective, the focus will be on information, since any trading development, and notably anomalous ones, will be known by the depository system before any other authority. The market information perspective will be on comprehensive, timely, and reliable information on holders of government securities and on trading developments (volume, participants, conditions,) in OTC markets. The legal perspective will be mainly registration of ownership and changes thereto, while the regulatory perspective will be on the framework for trading in government securities.

Improvements in settlement systems have been based, without exception, on replacing paper certificates with paperless securities, variously known as dematerialized securities, book-entry securities, or securities accounts. The technically more accurate term of securities accounts will be

---

123. See Group of Thirty (1988), CPSS (1992), and ECB 1998.

124. See CPSS and IOSCO 1997.

used in this chapter. Securities accounts require an institutional infrastructure to handle their administration, known as the depository system. The main economic function of a depository system is the provision of settlement services. Securities accounts, depository systems, and settlement arrangements are closely intertwined.

The major policy issues involved in developing a government securities settlement system to particular country circumstances concern the central depository, subdepositories, and settlement procedures. Central depository questions include use of automated securities accounts; whether the central depository should be placed in the central bank and, if so, what independence within this structure it should enjoy; and whether membership should be wide or narrow. Subdepository issues include why subdepositories may be necessary, how transactions in subdepositories may be linked to settlement in the central depository, and the need for proper supervision of subdepositories. Settlement procedure questions include what kinds of transactions need to be registered, how to progress toward prompt DVP and allowing same-day settlement, and what other steps must be taken to minimize settlement risk in a range of market environments. Finally, there is a question about using information in depository facilities for price discovery in what may be an otherwise opaque OTC market for securities. Related to all these issues is the use of electronic technology.

It is not possible to give a good answer at once to all these questions. The first step must be central depository accounts, organization, membership, and procedures. If these are in good order, questions about subdepositories can be more easily faced.

8.2 Securities Accounts

8.2.1 Need for Securities Accounts

Authorities worldwide have moved away from securities issued in the form of paper certificates to securities issued as securities accounts, kept with a special depository institutions. Important reasons favoring securities accounts over paper certificates include lower costs, elimination of delays in admission to trading, administrative simplicity, and protection against destruction, loss, theft or forgery. However, the main contribution of securities accounts has been to open the way to affordable and efficient settlement procedures, both in the primary and the secondary markets for government securities.

8.2.2 Legal Features of Securities Accounts

For a settlement system to be effective, a number of legal questions concerning the holding of securities must be answered. Almost every country has long had a set of specific legal rules concerning paper securities, and there are entrenched legal views based on this tradition. The basic elements of such rules and views can be easily transferred to securities accounts, but they are seldom directly applicable. There has usually been an intermediate stage, based on the immobilization of paper certificates in depositories, which started to recognize ownership rights through some equivalent of a security account.

Transfers of ownership started to take place by registration of the ownership of the accounts, skipping any attendant delivery or movement of paper certificates. In some cases, complex identification of the accounts mimicked the numbering of paper certificates. In others, securities accounts implied just a generic entitlement to a fungible amount of securities. As securities started to remain immobilized for their whole life, issuing few certificates for very large amounts started to take place, reaching in extreme cases a jumbo certificate for a whole issue. These systems all worked under legal systems based on the principle that physical possession of paper certificates was a requirement for proof of title and delivery of certificates a proof of changes in ownership. In practice, they functioned because most investors, for convenience reasons, accepted the alternative solution provided by the depositories and because investors' need for paper certificates, always envisaged as a last resort, was exceptional.

Given the movement away from securities issued in the form of paper certificates to securities accounts, the legal backing for securities accounts should support ownership based on inscription in the appropriate register and changes in ownership or pledges based on the corresponding transfer or blocking entries in the register. The legal backing should also cover electronic payment orders or other binding instructions. The traditional distinction between bearer and registered securities becomes inapplicable to securities accounts, which are registered by definition. At the same time,

8

securities accounts can, if supported by law and administrative provisions, open the way for an alternative distinction between explicit registration of the beneficial owner and registration of a nominee representing the beneficial owner. Although a small set of articles in the appropriate legal code may be the only modification needed to deal with these legal questions, in many countries the paperless system is characterized by a lack of adequate legal coverage for securities accounts. (See Chapter 9, Legal and Regulatory Framework.)

8.2.3   Transition Issues

Beyond legal or administrative difficulties, policymakers may find that the introduction of securities accounts may meet the reluctance of investors accustomed to paper certificates, particularly to bearer certificates. The transition to securities accounts may be facilitated by previous familiarity with the custody of paper securities by banks,[125] by a centralized registration of paper securities,[126] or by systems in which a significant volume of non-negotiable securities owned by small investors are distributed and managed by banks.[127]

Authorities in some countries have used a gradual approach to the introduction of securities accounts. Such accounts have been used for some new type of securities (Treasury bills in many countries) or only for newly issued securities, while paper certificates have been retained for others, in some case for only a transition period. Alternatively, securities accounts may be offered on an optional basis, at least temporarily or for certain types of securities, with the expectation that as investors recognize the advantages of securities accounts they will select that option. Another option is to allow the conversion of paper certificates into securities accounts or the reverse.[128] Finally, a complementary approach has sometimes been used, where securities accounts are paperless, but paper

---

125. Spain is a notable example, where bank custody of paper certificates was a generalized practice, in contrast to the tradition in other countries (e.g., the United Kingdom).

126. Bangladesh and Kenya, for example, in recent years have employed this method.

127. Bangladesh and China are examples of countries that follow this procedure.

128. Spain, during 1987–91, offered this option, and hardly any use was made of it.

notification of transactions (the equivalent of bank statements) may be offered or required.[129]

There are also transitory operational reasons for the concurrent use of paper certificates and securities accounts. Policymakers in countries lacking a valid legal foundation for securities accounts may resort temporarily to some scheme of voluntary immobilization on which to base securities accounts. Modest scale schemes for Treasury bills associated with the interbank money market may be particularly feasible and have proved to be a fitting starting point.[130]

8.3   Depository System for Securities Accounts

8.3.1   Registration Function of the Depository System

Owing to the inseparable legal and economic functions of the depository system, requests for registration will be, with few exceptions, requests for settlement. To simplify, registration instructions and settlement orders will be treated as equivalent in the discussion that follows.

The main policy issue concerning the registration of transactions is defining the different categories of transactions to be recorded by the system. Government securities can change hands due to many reasons and under various legal forms. Keeping track of all potential transactions in government securities would involve unwarranted costs and would create administrative complexities. All depository systems for government securities have, therefore, opted for a simplified categorization of recorded transactions.

---

129. Some countries have required a standard format notice for transactions involving a transfer of ownership to nonfinancial investors, with features more akin to a paper security than to a normal bank statement, to be sent to a new owner of a security. Such notices have very limited legal value (at most proof of an initial acquisition) and, being nontransferable, are definitely not a proxy paper security. Statements, however, can be important for the credibility of the depository and are reassuring for investors.

130. The early precedents of the Spanish depository system (1973–82) involved such a scheme, based on central bank securities and on some special short-term Treasury paper. Similar schemes have recently been implemented for Treasury bills in Bangladesh and Kenya.

Transactions in the primary market must be separately identified, because they all involve the Treasury as a counterpart. There are three major transactions types: the issue of new securities, by which they are initially registered with the depository system; the redemption of outstanding securities, by which they are removed from the depository system; and explicit interest payments.[131]

Concerning secondary market transactions, the depository system should be able to register the transfer of securities without payment. Since there is no settlement complication, newly developed depository systems have often started by being able to do little more than register the transfer of securities, while taking time to add or expand the necessary settlement facilities. The transfer of securities without payment takes explicit care of transactions, including donations, inheritance, and execution of collateral, which do not fit easily into any of the general categories enumerated below. The depository system does not take care of a counterpart payment, which must be made through channels external to the regular settlement facilities of the depository system. Additional transfers without payment include transfers for the management of subdepositories' accounts with the central depository, transfers among subdepositories, and transfers to engage in securities lending. Temporary transfers, to be reversed on a predetermined date and based on a single initial instruction, should also be envisaged.

Blocking securities from trading is another essential feature of a depository system.[132] This is essential in order to facilitate the numerous possibilities for using government securities as collateral for other transactions. By immobilizing securities held as collateral under a repurchase agreement, when such blocking is agreed by the trading partners or mandated by the authorities, the depository can help ensure that these will be available should the party that provided the collateral default. The depository

8

---

131. A number of complexities could be associated with the three types of transactions. These include disbursement in several installments, payment with other securities due to mature, redemptions through quarterly or annual quotas, optional redemptions under specific circumstances, frequent interest payments, or special premia attached to particular conditions, even lottery features. Modern debt management has given up most of these practices, both to increase the transparency of securities management and to simplify their administration.

132. Nearly all countries with advanced depository systems have procedures to block securities from trading. Mexico, among countries with developed depository systems, does not offer this possibility.

system will not keep track of all the reasons for blocking securities, and would normally only distinguish between decisions mandated by judicial or administrative authorities and those authorized by the owner of the securities.[133]

Spot trading, implying an immediate exchange of securities against a cash payment, is the cornerstone of a depository system. In fact, a depository system capable of settling spot trading would be an almost fully functional final settlement system. (Final settlement may be "real time" or at the end of the day, depending on the settlement system. See below.) The same facility would serve to settle any forward trading (introduced on the settlement due date and unidentified to the depository system as a forward deal), as well as repurchase agreements (introduced as two successive spot deals, and again unidentified to the depository system as a repurchase agreement). This situation has sometimes emerged in depository systems that did not envisage an explicit treatment of forward transactions and repurchase agreements.[134]

Dealing with forward trading involves registering on any date standing instructions for execution on some specified future date. Trading for same-day settlement should ideally qualify as spot and other trading as forward. In practice, regulations on trading may take a different approach, influenced by historic precedents stemming from longer settlement delays used to define spot trading transactions.[135] The same facility can be used to register advance trading in securities due to be issued on a known

---

133. Some depository systems envisage the possibility of issuing special certificates as proof of ownership, with standing validity until explicit cancellation. This also implies the blocking of securities until cancellation of the certificate.

134. This situation emerged in Slovenia in 1999. This was also the case, and recently modified, for repurchase agreements in Poland. This is a typical situation in many markets based on paper certificates and traditional settlement facilities.

135. Under currently accepted accounting standards, participants in any forward transaction are required to record explicitly in their accounting statements (either above or below the line) any forward commitments as of the date they are entered. Such commitments entail several risks, and ignoring them may distort the assessment of the true financial situation of the trading partners. Registration by the depository system of forward trades as of the date they are entered (based on irrevocable settlement orders) is an added guarantee to the trading partners. It leaves with a third party a useful record of the contractual agreement between the trading partners, thus converting the depository system into some sort of informal notary. Advance issue of standing irrevocable settlement orders is a safeguard usually welcomed by trading partners.

date (when-issued trading), which may become relevant as the market develops.

Similar to forward trading, special procedures to register repurchase agreements should be an additional essential feature of a well-functioning depository system. This should take notice, as of the time the initial spot transaction is registered, of the standing instructions to carry out, on the agreed date, the reverse forward leg of the transaction. This will be useful to cover the possibility of forward repurchase agreements, agreements in which the two legs are forward transactions, a transaction practice that may become relevant in a developed market for government securities.[136]

Although securities lending is an important activity in developed markets for government securities where short selling is an essential instrument for dealers in government securities, special procedures to register loans of securities may not be necessary. Repurchase agreements offer an ideal and frequently used channel for collateralized lending of securities, and temporary transfers of securities without payment can be used to this effect.

Swaps of securities may be an occasionally relevant trading technique. This can be recorded by allowing for the possibility of registering simultaneous and opposite transfers of securities.

Futures and options are increasingly common transactions in developed markets. They can take many forms, traded and netted through a special exchange. The central depository will not be involved in such trading until a future involving a security becomes due or an option is exercised. At this point, ordinary spot transactions will take place to cancel the claims stemming from the trading in derivatives. The central depository can also become involved in the recording of securities held as margin collateral and changes thereto.

---

136. The justification for the explicit recording of repurchase agreements, unnecessary on strictly settlement grounds, is similar to that for forward agreements. Internationally accepted accounting standards require that repurchase agreements be recorded as lending operations rather than as two independent, outright transactions. Advance recording of the forward leg offers added guarantees to the trading parties. Furthermore, only one initial set of instructions is sufficient to carry out the two-stage settlement of the spot and forward legs of the transaction. Lacking an explicit registration by the depository system, it would be extremely difficult to gather reliable statistics on repo trading.

8.3.2   Organization of the Depository System

8.3.2.1 Layered Structure

The degree of centralization of the settlement system will depend in part on country circumstances. For an emerging-market country, a single register, where all individual holdings are listed, may be sufficient. This could include all individual holdings, including those of retail customers. Alternatively, it could include only financial institution participants that would distinguish their holdings at the single register between their own account and the account of their customers. These institutions would, in effect, be acting as implicit subdepositories for their clients. With modern communication and computer facilities, a single register should be technically feasible.[137] As the number of investors and their transactions in government securities rise and a variety of privately issued securities become tradable, a fully centralized depository may become unwieldy, justifying the introduction of subdepositories.

Most countries end up adopting a two-tier structure, consisting of a central depository complemented by a number of financial institutions acting as subdepositories. Only a select set of financial institutions is allowed to hold securities with the central depository, while nonfinancial investors and even some financial investors are allowed to hold securities only with subdepositories. Subdepositories, in turn, hold global nominee accounts with the central depository. These global nominee accounts must be a precise counterpart of the accounts they have opened to their clients.

This two-tier basic structure may have some variants, based on special factors or country-specific arrangements. International depositories (e.g., Clearstream, EUROCLEAR) may be linked to the system, either at the

---

137. Among countries with efficient settlement facilities, Sweden approaches the single depository model. Any investor is entitled (but not obliged) to hold individualized accounts with the central depository, and many of them do, though management of such accounts requires using some bank as an agent. Denmark has a similar model, and Finland is planning to add such a possibility to its two-layer depository system. Other countries with a single depository include mainly small countries with an emerging primary market for a limited set of securities and a narrow secondary market. Lithuania and Slovenia, for example, fall in this category. Argentina has had a large single depository, with millions of accounts, but it does not provide settlement services, except indirectly, for stock exchange trading. The situation in Argentina is in the process of changing.

central depository or the subdepository level, thus introducing an additional layer. In some countries, authorities may allow subdepository institutions to hold the counterpart of their clients' accounts with another subdepository. This may lead to a three- or more-tiered structure.[138] Sometimes, despite the tiered framework, some investors holding securities with a subdepository are allowed, under specific circumstances, to have their holdings also identified separately at the central depository.[139] This rather atypical solution is apparently to reduce investor fear about the trustworthiness of subdepositories. The reverse situation may also emerge. There may be a single depository, but direct access to it is only permitted to select financial institutions, while other investors have to link with the central depository through these institutions.[140]

8.3.2.2 *General Versus Specialized Depository Systems*

Regardless of its actual layering, a depository system for government securities is usually a fully integrated structure with a single central depository.[141] Policymakers must decide whether such a system should be specialized for government securities or should encompass many types of securities, with government securities as a specific segment.

Almost all successful depository systems for government securities were initially set up as independent systems devoted only to government securities.[142] There are precedents for depositories specialized in government securities that have expanded their activity to cover bonds issued by

---

138. The United States offers the most significant example of a multi-tiered depository structure.

139. Mexico offers this possibility to some financial institutions not allowed as direct participants.

140. The depository systems of Denmark, Slovenia, and Sweden operate under this principle.

141. Single central depositories for government securities are common in most countries. As exceptions, France formerly maintained, and Poland still maintains, separate central depositories for Treasury bills and for bonds.

141. Systems born as specialized include Brazil, Canada, Colombia, Mexico, and the United States in the Americas; Japan in Asia; and Belgium, Bulgaria, France, Greece, Italy, the Netherlands, Poland (one of the facilities available), Portugal, Russia, and Spain in Europe. Germany, Switzerland, and the Scandinavian countries have tended to an integrated system.

regional or local governments, local issues by international financial organizations, and nongovernment bond issues, many of which may correspond to large public financial intermediaries.[143] There are also examples of initially separate systems that have tended to become single depositories, mainly in countries with well-developed financial institutions.[144] Attempts to start with a single unified depository system in countries where a range of securities is traded have usually encountered difficulty in integrating government securities with other securities or in developing efficient settlement procedures.[145]

8.3.2.3 Automation

An adequate depository system for government securities accounts becomes feasible with automation, both at the central depository and the subdepository levels. In some cases, central depository automation has begun with a simple personal computer application and software developed in-house or by the International Monetary Fund. An important requirement in software development is central depository interface with secondary market transactions. Complications may arise from development by each subdepository of its own software and with the subdepository's interface with the central depository.

Good communication facilities are essential for an effective government securities depository system. Sophisticated computer-to-computer

---

143. In the U.S. depository system, municipal bonds and bonds issued by some financial public agencies are included. The same is true for China's central depository. In the Spanish system, regional governments are eligible, and most of them have taken advantage of this option. There is, however, no known case in which nonfinancial public enterprises are included.

144. A move toward an integrated depository system for all securities has recently emerged among members of the European Monetary Union. Only Belgium and Spain still retain a separate arrangement for government securities. Those EU countries that have moved toward a single unified depository system, however, still have a way to go beyond the formal institutional shell. Mexico is an example of a country outside Europe where the move toward an integrated depository system has also recently taken place.

145. The experiences of Argentina, Ecuador, Hungary, Panama, Poland, and Slovenia illustrate the difficulties that countries have encountered in integrating government securities with other securities or in developing efficient settlement procedures.

communications are being introduced in many countries, which may be unwarranted for some emerging-market countries. There are many examples of depository systems for government securities that have managed to function efficiently with rudimentary communications facilities (telephone, fax), provided necessary equipment and staff were assigned to cover communication needs.

8.3.3   Depositories

8.3.3.1   Central Depository Organization and Membership

Many central banks have found it desirable to play an important role in setting up and running central depositories for government securities. Central banks have encouraged development of a market for government securities as a means to eliminate the need for central bank lending to the government, as an important vehicle for the conduct of their own monetary policy operations, and as a way to improve the monetary policy transmission mechanism. Setting up and managing efficient settlement arrangements for government securities is relatively easy and inexpensive when the securities accounts and the deposit accounts of the main market participants are held with the same institution, i.e., the central bank. The central bank may already have a depository system in place for its own instruments, the required expertise and resources for expanding this facility, and a reputation for professional competence and honesty. Another significant advantage of central depositories associated with the central bank is the ability of central banks to resist the pressure of vested interests and to draw on their supervisory capabilities.

While it is desirable for the central bank to play an active role in establishing and managing a central government securities depository, the depository function need not be a direct central bank responsibility. Organizing the central depository as a separate public agency, even if located within the central bank, allows a more transparent delineation of functions and responsibilities and more easily allows for independent official oversight than if the facility were a direct central bank responsibility. A related policy question is oversight of the central depository. The central bank itself, the Treasury, and the supervisory authority for securities markets might be included on the central depository board of management.

There must also be a mechanism for close interaction with market participants. Inclusion of market participants on the board is debatable. On the one hand, their participation would provide practical market perspectives to the design and operation of the depository arrangements. On the other hand, their participation could lead to a conflict of interest since they may represent their personal pecuniary interests rather than those of the public at large. If market participants are not included on the depository management board, procedures, formal or informal, for regular consultation with market participants are essential.

An alternative to a central depository associated with the central bank is a self-standing institution that could perform the same depository functions and provide similar settlement efficiency, although it would not have the above-cited advantages of the central bank. Needed for a self-standing institution are excellent electronic communications with the central bank, where the deposit accounts that will finally support settlement are held, and efficient procedures to coordinate transfers of securities accounts in the depository and transfers of money at the central bank, so as to ensure DVP. Reasonable communications of the central depository with market participants would also be necessary. Some countries that have recently transferred the depository function for government securities to a general depository for all securities have proved the feasibility of this approach. The recent attempt to do so and the limited number of countries involved indicate, however, that this route is not easy to pursue. In most cases, the depository for government securities started at the central bank and was moved at a later stage to a separate agency.

A central depository must determine the type and number of institutions allowed to hold government securities accounts with it. In a two-tier depository system, all subdepositories would be account holders at the central depository for securities belonging both to their own and to their clients' accounts. From a market development perspective, many other financial institutions actively engaged in the market for government securities might also find it desirable to hold accounts with the central depository.

Restricted participation in the central depository leads to an enlarged role for subdepositories. The difficulties associated with setting up a reliable and efficient subdepository system may be an additional reason to favor direct participation of financial intermediaries in the central depository.

Whether or not a financial institution allowed to hold securities accounts with the central depository should be entitled to hold money accounts with the central bank opens a host of related issues, from an efficiency and risk standpoint. Widening central bank account holders beyond banks to private financial institutions raises questions of central bank exposure to a greatly enlarged safety net and of enlarging central bank facilities providing liquidity to the market.[146] Limiting central bank exposure to the market through real-time gross settlement or other procedures (see below) and netting outside the central bank makes opening central bank accounts to institutions other than banks more feasible. This may well be desirable from a market development standpoint.

While holding deposit accounts with the central bank need not necessarily mean that these institutions should have access to the central bank lending facilities available to banking institutions, excluding institutions that conduct similar business from such access raises questions of equitable treatment and fair competition. Institutions excluded from the central depository would settle their transactions at the subdepository level. Exclusion may or may not have adverse implications for market development. Some markets, notably in the United States, have thrived despite the exclusion of nonbank financial institutions from accounts at Federal Reserve Banks. One reason for widespread bank participation in the securities markets in the United States was, for years, a large, implicit intraday overdraft allowed on banks' deposits with Federal Reserve Banks. The overdraft facility enabled a bank to authorize deductions from its Federal Reserve account before expected receipts were transferred to the account. The bank, in turn, had lower administrative costs and could offer its customers money transfer facilities at reasonable

---

146. There are rather generalized conventions, often incorporated in laws concerning the central bank, which limit the type of financial institutions entitled to hold deposit accounts with the central bank to those considered as "monetary institutions," namely banks and other deposit-taking institutions (savings banks, credit unions and credit cooperatives). These institutions are usually subject to reserve requirements and provide general payment services. Normally, these are the only financial institutions with access to central bank lending facilities. Nonbank financial institutions, such as insurance companies, pension funds, securities firms, or managing companies of investment funds, which may all be significant participants in the wholesale market for government securities, may be deprived of direct access to deposits with the central bank.

8

prices. The Federal Reserve recognized this exposure as unwarranted and has since greatly restricted it, but U.S. banks have continued to offer competitive payment services to clients.

In addition to private financial institution participants in the central depository, there are other potential participants in the central depository. First is the central bank itself, which will normally trade in government securities as part of its monetary policy functions. The Treasury may be an additional likely candidate, to the extent that it may engage in trading activity. It may also be appropriate to open Treasury accounts to handle the issue and redemption of securities. Some subnational government agencies might also be considered, if they issue securities or are significant holders of government securities and are entitled to hold deposit accounts with the central bank. (See Chapter 11, Development of Subnational Bond Markets.) International depositories are another category of potential participants.

Policymakers will need to set explicit and transparent rules for membership in the central depository and establish clear criteria and procedures for application and decision. All decisions concerning membership should be published immediately, and a public register of members of the central depository should be available. A standard regulatory measure to limit settlement risks in the central depository is an on-going screening of the creditworthiness of participants. Restrictions based on prudential grounds are always difficult to formulate. Obviously, any financial institution not subject to an effective (rather than simply formal) control by some supervisory authority should not be admitted to the central depository. Effective compliance with capital adequacy rules should be required, as well as with other objective and transparent criteria formulated in each particular context. Who sets the rules and who takes the decisions regarding membership in the central depository (the government, the minister of finance, the central bank, or the central depository) depends on many local factors, and it would not be meaningful to generalize.

8.3.3.2 *Subdepositories*

Setting up an efficient and reliable system of subdepositories has proved to be, in many countries, a more difficult task than introducing a central depository. The presence of subdepositories has strong implications for market development, as the government's capacity to place securities with any investor lacking access to the central depository will otherwise be limited.[147]

The authorization of subdepositories should be subject to formal conditions stricter than those for selecting other members of the central depository, since subdepositories can introduce new risks, including fraud.[148] Complex technical interactions with the central depository will be required to ensure the integrity and coherence of the whole depository system, based on the matching of clients' accounts with the subdepository and the subdepositories' nominee accounts with the central depository. Authorities in some countries starting a new depository system have preferred a relatively regulated approach to subdepository activity, contrary to the rather loose rules prevailing in other countries. This allows scope for subsequent relaxation of the system, as the depository gains experience and expertise.

Dealing with a limited number of subdepositories simplifies the administrative and regulatory tasks of the central depository. Opting for too small a number of subdepositories, however, can lead to complaints of unequal treatment, and may run contrary to the development of a competitive market for government securities.

Where the number of subdepository accounts is limited, those excluded may have to avail themselves of depository account facilities through other institutions that provide that service. The larger commercial banks often manage such subsidiary accounts for smaller institutions.

Basic rules and regulations should be set on the status of securities accounts held with a subdepository to ensure segregation from the subdepository's own accounts, to establish the status of accounts in case of

8

---

147. China offers a remarkable example. With a central depository in place since 1996, it has not yet finalized subdepository arrangements. As a result, nonfinancial investors are excluded from the market for government securities in book-entry form, which comprise by now all marketable securities. Similar situations prevail in many small emerging economies.

148. For instance, a subdepository may sell and retain under custody securities that do not really exist (i.e., the subdepository may "create" government securities without holding the corresponding counterpart account with the central depository). Such fraud may be perpetrated by a subdepository cheating its clients by pretending to sell and maintain under custody government securities while, in fact, diverting the client's proceeds to other purposes. The subdepository might also dispose of securities entrusted to its custody without the investors' knowledge.

subdepository bankruptcy, and to fix the status and responsibilities of sub-depositories as account holders with the central depository. Regulations for subdepositories should also include principles of good practice, free-dom to transfer securities from one subdepository to a different one in order to encourage competition, operating relations with the central depository, firewalls that separate a bank's subdepository business from its other activities, and statistical reporting requirements. The regu-lations should envisage sanctions for noncompliance. These should include, for extreme cases, the cancellation of the privilege to offer sub-depository services.

Similar to other financial activities, the provision of subdepository ser-vices and the attendant settlement obligations should be subject to super-vision. The responsible authority may be closely linked to the authority responsible for overall market supervision, though it may be argued that the tasks are far from comparable. In any case, supervision should include reporting requirements and on-site inspections,[149] as well as an easily acces-sible service to which customers may address complaints.

Policymakers will find little scope to plan for gradual implementation of a subdepository system. Regulations, both on substantive and procedural matters, should be in place, even if the subdepository system is small. It is unlikely that satisfactory regulation will be reached from the start, and experience with the system will be extremely valuable in improving the ini-tial rules. Special efforts should be made to achieve a careful and detailed drafting of regulations to facilitate development by the institutions con-cerned of the software necessary to run their subdepository business. Changing the rules may imply a need to change the software, which, in addition to being costly, will be a source of delay. In countries where candi-dates for providing subdepository services may lack the minimum technical standards and skills required to coordinate with the central depository, it might be necessary to implement a subdepository system gradually and introduce such a system selectively. For example, involving only headquar-ters offices in the financial center might be a viable interim solution for some countries.

---

149. In Spain, immediate supervision of subdepositories is performed by the central deposi-tory, which has a small team of inspectors. Action on observed inadequacies may be shared between the central bank (for deposit-taking institutions) and the securities commission (for securities firms).

Some alternative mechanisms are no direct substitutes for subdepositories, but may contribute to reducing the need for them. One is, of course, a more comprehensive central depository. This can be the most economic and practical approach in countries where the frequency of transactions, the number of securities account holders, and the number and variety of securities issued are not yet large. In addition, the Treasury or central bank in some countries has offered limited subdepository facilities to nonfinancial investors.[150] Almost invariably, these services have been set up as mechanisms to facilitate the participation of small investors in the government securities market. In some cases, these facilities offer only the possibility of buying newly issued securities, to be kept until redemption or to be transferred elsewhere for sale. In others, the agency involved may also be selling and repurchasing outstanding securities. Such arrangements normally face the constraint that the number of physical outlets the Treasury and central bank are able to provide may be limited.

Mutual (open-end) investment funds specializing in government securities or just holding a significant volume of government securities in their portfolio provide a useful alternative to retail investment and trading in government securities (and, in the process, an enhanced scope for the wholesale market). They also offer an alternative to the custody and settlement problems at the subdepository level, assuming, of course, that they hold their portfolio with the central depository and rely on its settlement facilities.

8.3.3.3 Integration in Depository System of Nonresident Participants

Countries allowing nonresidents to invest in domestic government securities have to provide the means to integrate nonresidents in their depository system and to give them access, to the extent possible, to the same settlement facilities as domestic investors. There are only rare and atypical precedents of a country allowing direct holdings of final nonresident investors with the central depository.[151] Most nonresident participants in government securities markets rely on some intermediate subdepository.

Domestic subdepositories should be allowed, in any case, to hold securities accounts belonging to nonresidents. Local branches of well-established

---

150. The U.S. Treasury and the central banks of Hungary and Spain manage such facilities.

151. The case of international financial organizations is one example.

foreign financial institutions may be in a particularly favorable situation to offer such a service.[152] For such an arrangement to be successful, however, excellent trading and settlement facilities should be in place. It is, thus, unlikely that this will be a promising arrangement in emerging markets. Domestic subdepositories do not normally provide services to all final non-resident investors, but rather to a limited set of well-known international dealers in government securities (including the parent house of local branches of such institutions). These international dealers have accounts for final foreign investors and thus act as an ad hoc third layer of the depository system.

More direct involvement of the central depository with nonresident investors may also be considered. A convenient solution would be to allow well-established international depositories like EUROCLEAR or Clearstream (formerly CEDEL) to become participants in the central depository. These agencies would thus reach a status similar to that of domestic subdepositories, except that the rules under which they would operate would be special bilaterally agreed rules.[153] As an alternative, some international dealers in government securities might be accepted as ad hoc subdepositories linked to the central depository. For obvious reasons, only a select set of well-known institutions should be granted this right.[154] In either case, the issue of allowing these institutions to hold deposit accounts with the central bank for settlement purposes would need to be addressed.

---

152. Spain offers a good example of this development, with some domestic subdepositories having specialized in providing services to nonresident financial institutions. As a result, direct links of nonresidents with domestic subdepositories have tended to become more important than links channeled through Clearstream and EURO-CLEAR, whereas prior to doing so the links of nonresidents were channeled through these settlement systems.

153. International depositories are not always keen to accept the possibilities offered by the central depository. Spain is an example where both Clearstream and EUROCLEAR are linked to the depository system through two important, separate domestic subdepositories (see previous footnote). A paradoxical reverse situation exists in Mexico. For Mexican Brady bonds, Clearstream is acting as the central depository and the domestic central depository as a subdepository.

154. Mexico offers such possibility, but with limited settlement facilities.

8

8.3.3.4 *Fees of Depositories and Subdepositories*

Policymakers may need to set parameters for central depository fees. Ideally, a central depository should be a nonprofit venture, though, to the extent possible, the costs of maintaining it should be identified and recovered through fees, either on transactions or a periodic fee.

Fees on transactions should be low per transaction, irrespective of volume. This approach, typical of modern payment systems, departs from the historical tradition, still ingrained in many countries, of fees proportional to the size of transactions. Fees on transactions have to be paid, inevitably, by the trading parties. As most transactions involve two parties (one paying, the other delivering securities), the fee should be split between them. This refers to secondary market transactions (including those in which the central bank is a party), since transactions linked to the primary market are usually free for investors, though not necessarily for the Treasury. It has become a general practice to charge the fee only once for transactions involving two successive opposite flows, such as in repurchase agreements and securities loans.

Periodic fees could conceivably be applied to the number of accounts maintained, though it is usual to base them on the volume of securities. In the latter case, the fee may be charged to the holders of the securities, to the issuer of the securities (the Treasury), or both. The frequent combination of fees on transactions and fees on holdings is justified, since the former reflect variable costs and the latter fixed costs.

In any case, it is essential that fees for use of the central depository and its settlement services should be kept low so that they do not have a significant impact on the yield for the securities transacted. This is consistent with cost recovery if the number of transactions or the volume of securities is large. Many emerging markets may not meet this condition. Consequently, the Treasury or the central bank may have to incur costs that significantly exceed the price for the services provided to them by the depository. The implicit subsidy by the Treasury or the central bank to other beneficiaries of the depository services would most likely be transitory, and can be justified as a way to develop the market for government securities.

Policymakers should leave subdepositories free to determine their fees or price differentials in response to market forces. Markets with low activity levels, however, do not favor price transparency, and limited competition

8

may be prevalent in highly concentrated banking systems. The best medium-term solution in this case may be the adoption of general policies to enhance competition and price transparency. Subdepositories should, in any case, be required to be explicit and transparent toward their customers concerning prices and fees. Any temptation by the government to regulate the pricing of securities traded through subdepositories should be resisted as contrary to market-oriented financial policy.

8.4   Settlement Procedures

In developed economies, the settlement of transactions in the primary and secondary markets for government securities may be the largest single component of the payment system, and by far more important than nonfinancial payments.

Settlement of transactions in the OTC market for government securities involves balancing efficiency, implying speed of execution, low cost and risk, including credit risk, liquidity risk, operational risk, and systemic risk. Settlement procedures will be identical in both wholesale and retail markets, and usually stricter and more regulated at the central depository level than at the subdepository level. All transactions in securities involving cash payments should in principle follow DVP, implying that delivery of securities must be simultaneous with payment, although this may not be possible at the retail level. Settlement orders must be possible for execution on any desired date, including future dates and on the same day, the latter being especially important for repurchase agreements.[155]

8.4.1   Settlement in the Central Depository

Transactions to be settled through the central depository include primary market and secondary market transactions. The former includes the first round of transactions associated with an issue, redemption, and financial servicing of government securities. The latter includes transactions of participants in the central depository acting on their own account.

---

155. Same-day settlement is indispensable for overnight repurchase agreements and is highly desirable for spot trading.

8.4.1.1 Settlement Orders and Matching

Secondary market transactions to be settled by the central depository will be unknown to the central depository until the trading partners deliver the settlement orders to the central depository for processing. Since there are always two parties to every transaction, the standard procedure is that each party issues a settlement order, one corresponding to the payment of cash, the other to the delivery of the securities. The central depository matches them before proceeding to later settlement stages.

Matching transactions before proceeding to final settlement, real-time or at the end of the day depending on the system, is a standard requirement in an efficient settlement system. Matching validates the authenticity of settlement orders, detects errors, determines the point when settlement orders must become irrevocable, provides trading partners with additional proof of the contractual agreement they have entered, and, most importantly is an absolute requirement for controlling implementation of the DVP principle and for keeping track of pending settlement claims. These features are relevant for any transactions to be settled, but they become particularly important when settlement flows on future dates are involved.[156]

To facilitate matching, settlement orders must be complementary, highly standardized, and as simple as possible. Both orders should contain the same basic elements identifying the transaction, though one will be an order for a cash payment and the other an order for the delivery of securities. Data included should only be limited to full identification of the transaction to be settled, using predefined codes for most items to facilitate automated processing. In cases involving future reverse flows (notably repurchase agreements, but also other securities lending or transitory transfers without payment), the initial settlement order should include all the necessary data for settlement of the reverse flow. It should be considered as a standing

---

156. Matching of transactions exists in most modern central depositories for government securities. Surprisingly, an exception is the U.S. central depository. In the U.S. case, transactions are settled on a real-time basis upon a single order issued by the seller of securities, but the counterparty is entitled to order the cancellation of such entries any time before the daily close of settlement hours.

and irrevocable order issued in advance to carry out the transaction.[157] As a by-product, a well-designed settlement order would contain all the necessary data to produce relevant statistics on trading.

For central depositories associated with the central bank, the collection of settlement orders will normally be based on whatever general communications facilities and procedures are already available for other large-value payments facilities (central bank transactions, interbank unsecured loans, interbranch transfers, or other general interbank payments). The facilities need not be particularly sophisticated. Online electronic communications may be highly desirable, but it must be stressed that quite efficient settlement systems have been based on rather rudimentary communications facilities. Even the physical delivery of paper orders could suffice at an early stage, though normally telephone, telex, fax, or Internet could be used, as has been the case in the past in most countries that now rely on more advanced technology. Appropriate security procedures (validation rules, encryption, and authentication of messages) should be introduced. Matching itself provides a security check. Since orders will always be for transfers among a limited set of known participants, the affected party should be able to detect unilateral fraud. Protecting the secrecy of the parties involved in individual transactions may be a more important issue in countries with a record of administrative corruption.

Settlement orders should reach the central depository as soon as possible after trade execution, to speed up further processing. This need is more obvious in real-time settlement systems, but is also important for those relying on settlement at some end-of-day point to allow for same-day settlement and avoid any workload accumulation at the close of business. Poor back-office arrangements of trading parties are the usual cause of delay.

The working hours of the central depository must be tailored to the pattern of prevailing banking hours. Settlement hours set limits to normal trading hours for same-day settlement. Too short a time schedule for settle-

---

157. This is a point worth emphasizing, as there have been examples of countries setting up otherwise efficient settlement facilities that have ignored this fact. Besides the inconvenience of having to handle a duplicate number of payment orders, the advantages of advance registration were lost, including any knowledge about developments in the markets for repurchase agreements, since each of these was handled as two independent outright transactions belonging to the spot market.

ment may unjustifiably constrain the hours available for such trading. The strong interaction between the market for government securities, the inter-bank money market, the foreign exchange market, and the intervention operations of the central bank call for coordination of the trading and set-tlement schedules in each market. Settlement facilities should be available for necessary late-hour adjustment.

In order to simplify the workload, some central depositories require a minimum size for settlement orders to be processed through the normal communications channels. Small transactions do not play a significant role in the market, and flat settlement fees per transaction discourage the possibility of breaking a single underlying transaction into various settle-ment orders.

The matching of received settlement orders by the central depository should be recorded on a computer to expedite matters and eliminate further sources of error. Suitable backup facilities should always be in place. Matching should take place on an on-going basis, immediately following the receipt of settlement orders. A record should be kept of the exact time at which each pair of settlement orders is matched. The trading parties should also be informed, as soon as possible, of successful-ly matched transactions.[158] Some end-of-day batch communication should in any case be envisaged for transactions due for settlement on future dates. Matched settlement orders should be integrated in a database (including separate records for the second leg of repurchase transactions and similar two-sided transactions) of transactions pending settlement, which will be the basis on which settlement decisions will rest. A proce-dure is needed to cancel unmatched orders and to inform as soon as pos-sible the involved parties so that they may submit revised orders. Only fully matched orders would go for further processing by the central depos-itory. With a proper matching procedure in place, transactions could be handled on a DVP basis.

---

158. Where online communication facilities exist, there is a more efficient alternative to the procedures so far described. Only one party (say the seller of securities) is required to submit the necessary settlement data to the central depository, which takes care of relay-ing the data to the other party, asking for confirmation. The positive or negative result is reported back to the initiating party. Thus communication of payment orders, match-ing, and confirmation of matching become a single process. Among newly developed markets, Mexico is an example of a country that has adopted this system.

8.4.1.2 Net Versus Gross Settlement

Most payment systems with a predefined set of participants, including those involving securities settlement, have traditionally operated on a multilateral net basis. On this basis, payment obligations are accumulated over some period (normally one day), and at some point (normally the end of the day), the net balance of payments to be made or received by each participant against the whole set of other participants is calculated. These net balances, adding by definition to zero for the whole system, are actually paid to/by the agent in charge of running the system. Payments are, therefore, pending until they reach what is known as "finality," namely, the legal assurance that the payment obligations/rights have been legally satisfied. For ease of reference, such systems will be referred to as multilateral net settlement (MNS).

As participants usually have both in- and out-payments, netting reduces the amounts finally due for settlement and allows participants to operate with comparatively small balances (both money and securities) in a securities settlement system. MNS, however, raises some difficult issues, since at the end of the day some participant may not have the necessary cash or securities balances to satisfy obligations. All MNSs envisage the possibility that, in such case, all or part of the transactions involving such a participant will be excluded from settlement, and a new set of multilateral net balances will be calculated. After excluding some participant, however, it is likely that other participants will suffer the effects of not being credited the payments due to them by the initial defaulting participant and will also fall into default, thus requiring further rounds of readjustment. More importantly, when default is partial, only some transactions of the defaulting participant need to be excluded. Which ones are excluded and which ones are settled may be hotly debated by the affected parties. If the defaulting party is an institution that is on the verge of bankruptcy, the implications of such discretionary decisions may become very unpleasant. Therefore, unwinding of trades due for settlement takes place, in fact, very rarely in MNS. Several alternative solutions, based on covering imbalances through lending, are normally followed.

Because of MNSs' potential problems, a consensus has emerged in recent years favoring a different approach to settlement. This is the so-called real-time gross settlement system (RTGS). This approach is based on very good, online communications. Under it, transactions are settled bilaterally, on an on-going basis and as soon as possible. Transactions that cannot be settled for lack of funds or securities are queued, to be settled as soon as this deficiency is resolved. After some pre-established time without execution, transactions may under some systems be canceled. In case of several pending transactions, priority rules (established in advance by the parties or the system) may be applicable. Participants are kept continuously informed of their settled and pending claims.

Intermediate solutions exist as well. MNS systems may operate with more than one daily settlement cycle. A frequent formula—used by some countries in their transition to an RTGS system— involves just two cycles: one at the end of the day, and one at the opening of business, the latter for settlement of orders introduced at earlier dates for value this date.

8.4.1.3 Risk Management Provisions of Settlement

Given the potential systemic risks involved in the settlement process, policymakers should be especially attentive to various sorts of risks that require minimization. Careful screening of participants in the settlement facilities should be a major consideration in the initial selection of members of the central depository. Supervisory authorities should monitor settlement performance and be ready to exclude any institution failing to maintain a satisfactory record. Risk avoidance would also include application of the DVP principle, an active money market including, for the settlement of government securities, a market for very short-term repurchase agreements (see Chapter 2, Money Markets and Monetary Policy Operations), and allowance of a short time (normally not more than half an hour) between provisional closure of the netting procedures and final closure of the settlement cycle. Participants with deficient balances are individually informed and requested to go to the market and try to close some special transaction with other market participants to cover the cash or securities balance shortfall. Risk avoidance may also include reserve requirements allowing averaging of daily balances, thereby allowing banks to temporarily draw on these reserve balances for settlement if needed.

Most MNS arrangements rely, one way or another, on some end-of-day, last resort cash-lending facility by the central bank. It may be discretionary or automatic, with the latter possibly subject to limits. Usually, central bank lending for this purpose is based on overnight, secured loans (mainly repurchase agreements), for which a penalty rate is charged and which may

8

incorporate other restrictive conditions to discourage frequent use.[159] The purpose of a cash-lending facility by the central bank is to avoid the need for unwinding transactions due for settlement, while strongly encouraging participants to use alternative means, including the recourse to other participants through money market transactions, in order to avoid or deal with settlement difficulties.

The central bank can create unlimited amounts of cash by granting credit, but the central depository cannot create securities.[160] A standard method is to create a voluntary pool of securities, contributed by participants, but also sometimes the central bank, which can be lent automatically (normally through overnight repurchase agreements for which a penalty rate is charged) to any party that has not otherwise been able to obtain them.

Special risk management considerations are also involved in an MNS system allowing for more than one settlement cycle. Taking as a reference systems that allow for one additional settlement event at the opening of business, the possibility that some member may not be able to meet its obligations at this point must be faced. Contrary to arrangements for end-of-day settlement, in this case the usual procedure is to resort to gross bilateral settlement. Settlement of transactions for which there is a lack of securities is postponed to the end-of-day cycle. To settle transactions for which there is a lack of money, the seller receives payment based on central bank intraday credit to the purchaser, the central bank retaining a pledge on the securities as collateral, or, alternatively, the operation can be done through the use of repos. This combination of very transitory unwinding of some transactions and settlement of others based on collateralized intraday credit is usually a smooth operation, and it may provide, in some countries, early finality to a large volume of transactions.[161]

---

159. In some cases, the central bank may even be authorized, failing other arrangements, to seize securities in the central depository belonging to the failing institution and to sell them in the market.

160. A central depository should not "create" securities. Some stock exchanges or their attendant settlement facilities have been notorious for facilitating settlement procedures by delivering securities they have not yet received, thus "creating" securities. The counterpart cash balances received but not delivered have been a non-negligible source of income for the agents of such settlement arrangements.

161. This was the case in France, which resorted to this system in its recent transition to a full RTGS system. It now remains, with little change, part of their RTGS system.

As regards RTGS, many of the above risk management considerations for MNS systems may also be applicable. However, the main problem is to minimize the need for excessive balances of settlement means. This is usually done through intraday credit provided by the central bank. This raises, in turn, complex technical and policy issues that are too complex to be covered here.[162]

The choice between MNS or RTGS systems must consider market demand, technical requirements, and relevant risk management provisions. Market demand for RTGS in securities markets has been associated with highly developed financial markets, such as the special needs of monetary and financial integration in the EU. Technical and cost considerations do not favor RTGS systems for emerging markets, and the same applies to their risk management requirements. Despite the superiority of the RTGS system, most emerging-market countries are not in a position to implement RTGS. For these countries, the MNS system seems likely to remain the best choice in most instances, with the possibility of expanding it later with some additional daily settlement cycle.[163]

8.4.1.4 *Linking Delivery of Securities with Payment*

Processing settlement orders with DVP implies (irrespective of the MNS or RTGS character of the settlement system) checking the availability of securities in the central depository and the availability of funds, wherever they may be maintained, to ensure that matching changes in the funds and securities take place nearly simultaneously. The standard approach (ignoring for simplicity any settlement difficulty) consists in executing first the

---

162. See Furfine and Stehm 1998.

163. This conclusion on RTGS for securities need not apply to RTGS for other large payments. In fact, if the European experience can be generalized, introducing an RTGS system for other payments may be a prerequisite or at least the normal way to proceed later to RTGS for securities. Some countries have implemented (e.g., Slovenia) or are in the process of implementing (e.g., China) some RTGS facility for interbank or other large payments. However, caution may also be required here. Central banks in some countries with very narrow financial markets maintain, paradoxically, some large-value interbank payment facility working on an RTGS basis, even based on the physical delivery of paper payment orders (e.g., Bangladesh and Kenya). Given the very small number of daily transactions involved, these are hardly relevant precedents.

transfer of securities on a provisional basis, then the transfer of money, and finally lifting of the transitional condition to the transfer of securities. This may involve simple or complex procedures, depending on the depository arrangements.

For a central depository run by the central bank, the linking of delivery of securities with payment is an internal affair, and there may be no significant difference between running an MNS or an RTGS system. In fact, an MNS system may in practice be managed like an RTGS system if transactions are immediately entered in the corresponding accounts, on the assumption that only rarely will there be a need to undo them at the end of the day. This would be a different matter from considering them final from a legal perspective.[164] This approach may facilitate the monitoring of settlement developments, and be helpful in avoiding the risk of misjudging developments in securities settlement that may result from considering it isolated from other segments of the payment system.

For a separate depository, this may instead be a complex issue. With ideal online computer links between the central depository and the central bank and maximum compatibility of computer systems, the procedures might be equivalent to any system fully managed by the central bank. Without a good communication system, an external depository might have difficulties in running an RTGS system.[165] Difficulties should be smaller, however, for an MNS system, since such a system might require linking with the central bank only at the end of the day.

8.4.1.5 *Settlement of Primary Market Transactions*

Settlement of transactions associated with the primary market is a comparatively simple task. The first round of any such transactions must take place in the central depository, where the total outstanding amount of any security must appear, either under the own or correspondent accounts of direct members or of subdepositories.

---

164. This is how MNS securities settlement worked in the Spanish central depository, run by the central bank, until the recent introduction of RTGS, which was in fact facilitated by that practice.

165. These difficulties explain the delays experienced by some European countries involved in the parallel move from the central bank to a self-standing agency and from MNS to RTGS systems.

Redemption of securities is equally straightforward. Without any need for intervention of the involved account holders, the Treasury should issue an order, for value on the redemption date, to cancel the outstanding securities and to pay the corresponding amount (including, in many cases, implicit interest) into the deposit accounts of the securities accounts holders. The central depository knows the cash amounts to pay to the direct members and the global amounts of securities to take out of their own or correspondent securities accounts. Subdepositories would, in turn, make the detailed allocation of redemptions to their own clients, following a similar procedure. Interest payments would imply a similar, but even simpler, procedure, since only cash payments would be involved.

Settlement of newly issued securities should also be a simple matter, if placement procedures are adjusted to facilitate settlement. For auction and syndicated placements in which the participants are institutions holding securities accounts with the central depository and acting either on their own account or on account of a third party, the solution should be simple. The Treasury would deliver the securities to the central depository and would simultaneously issue a debit payment order to obtain the counterpart funds. The Treasury could do this for the whole amount to be issued, leaving to the central depository any allocation of securities and funds to the involved agents, or could itself make this allocation (usually involving only a limited number of institutions). Securities might be fully allocated to the own accounts of subdepositories, leaving to them the task of transferring the necessary amounts to their correspondent accounts.

Since DVP should prevail, if funds are not available the standard procedure is to postpone the issue of the corresponding securities and settle the disbursement at the next feasible opportunity. Cancellation of such claims (as happens in some countries) should never be envisaged. Most countries have complementary measures (managed by the Treasury rather than the central depository) to penalize, economically or otherwise, such disbursement failures.

8.4.2   Settlement in Subdepositories

Settlement of transactions through subdepositories is far more complex than that for the primary market. Transactions settled through subdepositories may be numerous, with small transactions typical of a true retail market, or may include a large volume of transactions typical of a wholesale market, which for some reason are not settled at the central depository level.[166] Two separate settlement processes must be distinguished: direct settlement between the trading partners, and a counterpart settlement at the central depository where the securities accounts are represented through global correspondent accounts.

Transactions between two parties holding securities with the same subdepository do not imply any change in the subdepository's accounts with the central depository. Transactions in which one of the parties is a subdepository, acting against its own portfolio, and some customer of the same institution, will require transfer of securities within the subdepository's account at the central depository, but will have no payment implications for the central depository. Besides secondary market transactions, all transactions resulting from issues and redemptions in the primary market would fall under this category. For each type of security, the subdepository must order a transfer to/from its own portfolio account from/to its correspondent accounts. Since many transactions of opposite sign may be involved, the usual approach is to require subdepositories to report daily to the central depository the net movements for each type of security. There is then a daily reconciliation of correspondent accounts at the central depository and client accounts at subdepositories. For transfers resulting from repurchase agreements, standing instructions for reversal on maturity are normally allowed or required. Since the central depository may have no alternative means to identify erroneous reporting, on-site inspections may be required to ensure adequate compliance.[167]

Transactions involving two subdepositories, covering both transactions between customers of different subdepositories or between customers of one subdepository and another subdepository acting on its own account, require a movement of securities in the central depository between the accounts of two subdepositories. Such a movement also has a payment counterpart. Since many underlying transactions may be involved, but only global net

---

166. Spain offers a relevant example of the second possibility, with transactions settled through subdepositories exceeding the volume of transactions settled through the central depository. This results from a significant direct market participation of nonresidents and a large number of nonbank financial institutions holding securities with subdepositories (in some cases, despite the possibility of using the central depository).

167. On-site inspections also include cross-checking subdepository data with a sample of investors.

amounts are relevant for the central depository, subdepositories may be encouraged or required to lump transactions together, even to net them bilaterally, to bring only the net cash and securities balances to the central depository. This may require time, and subdepositories may be in a difficult position to offer same-day settlement to their customers. A procedure may be allowed to register exceptional transactions individually, on the same on-going basis applied to wholesale market transactions.[168]

In the first stage of settlement, directly between subdepositories and customers, general good-practice regulations may be the rule. Same-day settlement in secondary market transactions may be difficult as a rule, but some maximum settlement delay should be established.[169] For primary market transactions, however, same-day settlement should not be a problem and should be mandatory. DVP is unlikely to prevail in trades between partners of unequal standing. Financial institutions will often not deliver securities without advance payment, and will not pay without earlier delivery of securities. This will not normally imply a relevant risk to the affected customers, and the cost implications may be contained through the timing rules noted above. Depending on the size, solvency, and reputation of the customer, as well as on the size and overall volume of transactions, settlement will increasingly approach DVP.

8.4.3 Settlement of Stock Exchange Transactions of Government Securities

Stock exchange trading in government securities plays an insignificant role in many developed markets for government securities, with trading taking place in the over-the-counter markets.[170] Policymakers in many emerging markets, on the other hand, may find a more active niche for stock

---

168. Such a procedure is available in Spain for transactions exceeding some large, but not exceptional, amount. Mexico follows an alternative approach, where such a procedure is available for any transaction, though subdepositories are allowed to group homogeneous transactions as they wish.

169. Who sets the rules and who takes the decisions (the government, the minister of finance, the central bank, or the central depository) depends on local factors, and it would not be meaningful to prescribe a common procedure.

170. Spain and the United States are two countries that do have stock exchange trading of government securities, but their activity in this area is insignificant.

exchange trading in government securities because of failures to set up conditions for development of OTC markets. Over time, it is unlikely that stock exchange trading will remain important relative to OTC trading (as OTC markets in these countries take hold), given some inherent weaknesses involved in stock exchange trading of government securities (e.g., inferior settlement facilities, inadequacy for trading repurchase agreements, and higher intermediation costs).

The potential advantages of centralized stock exchange trading of government securities are offset by inherent disadvantages from a settlement perspective. In developing countries in particular, stock exchange membership has been limited to a restricted set of individuals or to small, poorly capitalized institutions that do not hold to any significant extent clients' deposit accounts nor custody of clients' securities. Consequently, complex transfers of money and securities are required for settlement. The ideal solution is to allow stock exchange members to run a subdepository holding account with the central depository system. The stock exchange would take care of trading, as well as matching and netting any resulting settlement obligations, and then communicate such net settlement obligations to the central depository. Unfortunately, this solution often faces the difficulty that many stock exchange members fail to meet the solvency and technical eligibility criteria required from subdepositories or other direct members of the central depository.

8.5   The Depository System as Source of Data

Although there may be no substitute for real-time price transparency, a depository system and its settlement facilities offer an excellent basis for compiling frequent, detailed, and reliable ex-post trade reporting information, as well as data on outstanding claims. Such data can also provide an audit trail for market investigation and indicate potential problems for market surveillance. With one exception, all the potentially relevant information on trading would be contained in the coded data included in settlement orders. For the central depository, no other data would indeed be necessary. For subdepositories, irrespective of the forms they might use for client settlement orders, it should be required that they should keep a register of transactions based on the same codes used in the settlement orders of the central depository. In fact, this may be advisable on supervisory grounds alone. In addition, and this is the exception mentioned above, sub-depositories should be required to apply some simple coded classification of the intervening parties (e.g., different types of financial institutions, if relevant, nonresidents, government agencies, enterprises, and households), based, where available, on identification codes already in place (e.g., tax ID numbers). This would allow the compilation of relevant statistics on holdings of government securities and on outstanding repo agreements or other future commitments.

8.6   Conclusion

A well-structured securities settlement system contributes to the development of an active and liquid secondary government securities market. In addition, an effective securities settlement system provides a reliable record of securities holdings and minimizes risk by allowing for DVP and same-day settlement.

A securities settlement system can take varying forms. In an emerging-market country, a single, centralized depository, without subdepositories, located at the central bank may be sufficient. Wide membership of financial institutions in the centralized authority should be encouraged, although care must be taken by the central bank to limit its exposure. As the market expands and becomes more sophisticated, subdepositories may become necessary. Authorities should establish a frame of reference for subdepositories that minimizes risk and encourages competition.

Settlement procedures will depend on country circumstances and the degree of automation. A wide range of technology is possible. At one extreme, a simple PC at the central bank automating securities accounts and connections with account holders by telephone or fax may suffice. At the other extreme, the central depository and subdepositories may be interconnected electronically so that RTGS is possible. In between, there are many possibilities. Whatever approach is suitable at a given time, authorities should strive to minimize potential risks in the system and to improve it.

8

Bibliography

CPSS (Committee on Payment and Settlement Systems). 1992. *Delivery Versus Payment in Securities Settlement Systems.* Bank for International Settlements, Basel, Switzerland. Available at www.bis.org/publ.index.htm.

CPSS and IOSCO (International Organization of Securities Commissions). 1997. *Disclosure Framework for Securities Settlement Systems.* Bank for International Settlements, Basel, Switzerland. Available at www.bis.org/publ.index.htm.

ECB (European Central Bank). 1998. *Assessment of EU Securities Settlement Systems against the Standards for Their Use in ESCB Credit Operations.* Frankfurt, Germany. Available at www.ecb.int.

Furfine, C. H., and J. Stehm. 1998. "Analyzing Alternative Intraday Credit Policies in Real-Time Gross Settlement Systems." *Journal of Money, Credit and Banking* 30 (4): 832–48.

Group of Thirty. 1988. *Clearance and Settlement Systems in the World's Securities Markets.* Washington, D.C. Available at www.group30.org.

8

Chapter 9

Legal and Regulatory Framework

An appropriate legal framework is a key underpinning of an effective government securities market. The legal framework should set out clear government borrowing authority and establish the process for issuance of government securities. The legal framework should also provide investors with certainty as to process, rights, and responsibilities. It should include appropriate regulation of market participants, market conduct, and rules for clearing and settlement.

9.1   Introduction

Government debt securities must be supported by a clear legal framework that grants government the authority to issue debt, binds it to meet its repayment obligations, and governs the rights and responsibilities of those who purchase and trade in government debt securities.

Because a government issuer is a public body, the process through which it issues debt should be set out in law. This law, or laws, should include (i) clear authority to issue debt and, if the issuance of debt is to be made by a government agency, ability to delegate that authority to the appropriate agency; (ii) a description of the process by which the legislature enables the government to issue debt, including any limitations on borrowing; (iii) a description of the internal management process and legal authority with respect to issuance of government securities and management of the debt portfolio; and (iv) the legal status of the different types of government securities.

The secondary market in government securities should be supported by effective regulation through a securities regulatory authority, and rules

9

related to market intermediaries, market conduct, transparency requirements, and clearing and settlement.

9.2   Government Borrowing Authority

Governments should have an explicit and well-defined authority to borrow, with such authority to be granted in the constitution or in legislation. Box 9.1 provides examples of borrowing authority for several countries. The law in some countries grants the capacity to borrow directly to the legislature, while in others the government is granted the authority subject to approval from the legislature. The law may impose prior legislative authorization on the issuance of government securities as a check against abuse of the borrowing authority.

By setting out clear authority to borrow, the law establishes explicit parameters for the government in borrowing and serves to connect the debt obligation to the government or state, thereby providing investors with the assurance of repayment when the government changes hands.

For a number of historical, political, and sometimes technical reasons, the law of some developing countries either does not expressly allow or prohibits the government from borrowing in the domestic market. This limitation has serious implications for the development of government securities markets and the creation of a viable domestic capital market. Policymakers should carefully review whether the original reasons for imposing this limitation on government authority remain relevant.

As part of its authority, the government should also have the legal ability to delegate borrowing authority and debt management policy to the public agency or department that carries out the debt management work. The law should set out debt management objectives and guidelines for the debt manager, balancing the flexibility to efficiently structure the government's debt portfolio with accountability.

Lack of clarity in the borrowing authority (as between the legislature and government, for example) can increase the cost of debt financing because there is uncertainty as to the government's control over repayment. Credit-rating agencies, for example, focus on the clarity or ambiguity in legislative control of government borrowing activity as a way to measure the prospects of the government servicing its debt or government bailouts.

Box 9.1: Examples of Borrowing Authority

United States

The Congress delegates general responsibility for Treasury debt management to the Secretary of the Treasury. A ceiling on the outstanding stock of debt is set by the Congress (although the ceiling has been made flexible in historical practice). United States Code Annotated (USCA), Chapter 31, Section 3102–3104. (a) With approval of the President, the Secretary of the Treasury may borrow on the credit of the United States Government amounts necessary for expenditures authorized by law and may issue bonds of the Government of the amounts borrowed and may buy, redeem, and make refunds under section 3111 of this title.

Sweden

Constitution Chapter 9, Section 10: The Government may not, without authorization by the Riksdag (i.e., the Swedish people's assembly), borrow funds or otherwise assume financial obligations on behalf of the State. Act on State Borrowing and Debt Management, Section 1: Following specific authorization by the Riksdag for each individual fiscal year, the Government or, following resolution by the Government, the Swedish National Debt Office, may borrow funds on behalf of the State in order to: (1) finance current deficits in the National Budget together with other expenditures incurred pursuant to Acts of the Riksdag; (2) provide such loans and fulfill such guarantees as resolved by the Riksdag; (3) amortize, redeem and repurchase state debt; and (4) fulfill the central bank's requirements of currency reserves.

United Kingdom

National Loans Act 1968, Section 12, "Power of Treasury to Borrow": Any money which the Treasury considers expedient to raise for the purpose of promoting sound monetary conditions in the United Kingdom and any money required — (a) for providing the sums required to meet any excess of payment out of the National Loans Fund over receipts into the National Loans Fund, and (b) for providing any necessary working balance in the National Loans Fund, may be raised in such manner and on such terms and conditions as the Treasury thinks fit, and money so raised shall be paid into the National Loans Fund.

Japan

Constitution, Article 85. Expensing the government budget or the government's incurring a liability shall require approval of the Diet.

Hong Kong, China

Exchange Fund Ordinance, Section 3 (3): Without restricting the generality of the powers of the Financial Secretary…, the Financial Secretary may borrow for the account of the Fund either in Hong Kong, China or elsewhere, on the security of the general revenue. (4) The aggregate amount of borrowing under subsection (3) outstanding at any one time shall, subject to subsection (5), not exceed fifty thousand million dollars, or if held in foreign exchange, the equivalent at the current rate of exchange. (5) The Legislative Council may from time to time, by resolution proposed, with approval of the Governor in Council, by a designated public officer required and directed by the Governor to attend a sitting of the Legislative Council for that purpose, determine some other amount to be the amount which the aggregate amount of such borrowings outstanding at any one time shall not exceed.

9

9.3   Details of Legal Borrowing Authority

The legislation governing government borrowing may establish details of borrowing authority, including issuance limits, internal procedures, transparency, and accountability. These details might also be contained in guidelines, policies, or regulations that accompany the legislation.

9.3.1 Borrowing Limits

Limitations on the government's authority to issue debt securities can be established in legislation with a specific ceiling on total debt or minimal net increment limit or by requiring specific approval of the issuance by the legislature (either through the annual budget law or through a specific law approving a particular issue). If such limits are contained in the legislation, it is important to establish a system of legislative authorization consistent with modern practices for the issuance of government securities. A system that calls for a case-by-case authorization may be inefficient because the legislative process is usually time consuming and has an uncertain outcome.

The system should balance accountability to the legislature with flexibility. For example, the authorizing legislation in some countries sets out general legislative authorizations to issue government securities for every fiscal year (corresponding to the budget cycle) and requires the government to report annually to the legislature. This system provides a check on government authority (legislative approval and annual reporting), but it gives the government the necessary flexibility to manage debt (by granting the terms of authority for a year). Other systems grant the government authority to issue securities up to a certain amount within the fiscal year.

The legislation may also impose limitations on government guarantees or allow the legislature to set such limits. The legislation should also allow for requests to be made to the legislature for additional borrowing outside of prescribed limits.

9.3.2   Internal Management

The authorizing legislation should be set out in the authority to delegate debt issuance responsibility and may also define the administrative process for debt management.

Whether in the form of a government agency, the central bank, or within the finance ministry, a debt management office's role, function, and organization need to be defined in appropriate law and regulations along with record-keeping and reporting requirements. To eliminate any doubt by potential creditors, the law should clearly indicate that financial obligations incurred by a delegated agency fully and wholly bind the state.

The administrative organization for the management of public debt must have a sufficient degree of functional autonomy to fulfill its mandate without undue political interference. The debt manager must be given sufficient latitude to allow him or her to execute debt management effectively. Such autonomy, however, carries with it the requirement that the debt management office be accountable and transparent in its operational activities, procedures, and results.

9.3.3 Transparency and Accountability

The legislation should include record-keeping and reporting requirements for the debt management office in addition to the means by which transactions are recorded, to whom they are reported (for example, the legislature or cabinet), and the frequency with which they are reported. The government debt issuance practice should be transparent and accountable in order to assure investors that the contract (repayment of the debt and payment of interest) is a secure investment. When governments report to the legislature on public-debt management, such records provide a basis for the legislature to exercise its control. Of course, a balance between accountability and transparency, which are desirable, and excessive bureaucracy, should be struck. In addition, the issuance and management of public debt must be subject to audit and internal control procedures.

9.3.4 Disclosure

Government securities are generally exempt from disclosure obligations (such as prospectus requirements) applicable to private sector issuers. This practice has developed because of the unique position of government as a public issuer. A public parliamentary approval and budget process provides information to investors, and, as a matter of choice, the government may disclose its financial condition, its future plans for borrowing, and other information of interest to the investor in a manner similar to conventional

9

private issuer disclosure. Indeed, many debt managers now publish comprehensive annual reports outlining debt operations and debt strategies.

Should the government decide to issue debt in international markets, substantial additional disclosure may be required, since the foreign market will treat the government as it would any private issuer. Even in those cases, because of the special status of most government debt obligations, the market concedes some special treatment for these bonds, which are called sovereign and subsovereign bonds. The same is true of obligations to establish bondholder committees; while normally exempt from such requirements, the government may have such an obligation in a foreign market.

9.3.5   Access

The law should contain a clear basis for the distribution of government securities in the primary market and, as a general rule, there should be fair and equal access. Detailed terms of access may be set out in guidelines or policy. Exemptions to the general rule of equal access may also be set out in such guidelines or policies; for example, in (i) allocations restricted to institutional investors, (ii) allocations for market makers, (iii) allocations for financial sector entities that assume special commitments with the government as part of financial restructuring operations, and (iv) limited allocations to facilitate the dispersion of government securities in the market.

9.4   Terms of the Instruments

The government should have the authority to issue bonds in a wide variety of forms and should not be proscribed by legislation. Government bonds can be (i) issued as nominative or bearer bonds; (ii) represented in physical or book-entry form; (iii) have short-, medium-, or long-term maturities; and (iv) have an explicit interest rate or an implicit (discount bonds) or explicit interest rate, or be zero-coupon bonds or even indexed bonds (indexed to inflation or the floating rate, for example). Diversification of the terms of instruments can be a tool for effective management of debt service and profile, especially when the secondary market is not well developed (see Chapters 3 and 4).

Because of their characteristics as public-issued financial instruments, government securities may have some terms and conditions that differ from those applicable to private sector securities. This is true in the case of securing government securities. As a rule, governments do not pledge or create any mortgage or secured interest over public assets or resources to secure their issues of bonds and bills. Government assets and revenues are protected, sometimes even at a constitutional level, by rules prohibiting seizures, attachments, embargoes, and the like. At the same time, in some circumstances, governments can assign government-owned resources or the proceeds of their sale (for example, gold or petroleum) to service or back special-issued securities.

9.5. Legal and Regulatory Framework for the Secondary Bond Market

9.5.1 Regulation of the Secondary Bond Market

In most countries, government securities trade in the secondary market along with all other securities and are, therefore, subject to secondary market regulation. Effective secondary market regulation is necessary to support a viable secondary market. Since government securities are often defined as "exempt securities," that is, exempt from regular prospectus requirements, it is important to ensure that this status does not undermine the integrity of the secondary market.

Regulatory functions may reside with different authorities, and practices may vary across countries. A typical structure may involve the central bank or Ministry of Finance regulating the primary market and primary market dealers, while the securities regulatory authority regulates market intermediaries in the secondary market. It is important that all aspects of regulation are covered and that the various authorities coordinate their regulation of the bond market. Harmonization and coordination of regulation will avoid gaps that may result in increased risk. A lack of harmonization can result in different treatment of market participants undertaking the same activities, which may give rise to regulatory arbitrage and a distortion of market activity.

Effective regulation of the secondary market should include (i) regulation of market intermediaries, (ii) market conduct regulation (including trading rules) and market surveillance, and (iii) transparency requirements, which will vary according to the choice of market structure.

9

9.5.2   Authority to Establish a Regulator

Government should have the legal authority to establish a securities regulator. In turn, the securities regulatory authority should have the legal authority to make and enforce rules and regulations related to market and business conduct, market intermediaries, and trading systems. The IOSCO Objectives and Principles of Regulations state that the securities regulator should be operationally independent from government, preferably with autonomy over its budget and "accountable for its functions and the exercise of its power." The regulatory authority's powers should be clearly set out in legislation along with provisions for its accountability, such as transparency of rule making, transparency of enforcement proceedings and reporting requirements. The securities regulatory authority should have all necessary authority and resources to carry out its mandate and enforce compliance with its rules.

9.6   Market Structure and Regulation

Regulatory issues related to trading and trading systems and transparency requirements will depend on the type of market structure.

The market can be organized in a number of ways: (i) as an exchange with an order book and post-trade reporting, (ii) as a dealer-driven market with some transparency provided by market intermediary reporting, (iii) as an OTC market with some electronic reporting or information sharing with or without the use of interdealer brokers, or (iv) through a combination of these trading systems. The market may also be open to ATSs, which may set up their own electronic systems independent of or in conjunction with the principal bond market. Market structure choices are discussed in detail in Chapter 7.

The regulatory authority should have the ability to monitor trading and enforce trading rules regardless of the market structure. Most bond markets are OTC or dealer markets, and in this case the regulator may impose post-trade reporting, record-keeping, and audit trail requirements on market intermediaries. If the bond market is an exchange, the securities regulatory authority should have the ability to license exchanges and impose requirements for reporting, record-keeping, fair access, and risk management on exchanges. Similarly, if ATSs feature trading in bonds, the regulatory authority should have jurisdiction over ATSs. The regulator should have the ability to request information from the exchange or ATS, perform an examination of the ATS or exchange, and review and approve any regulations made by an exchange.[171] Exchanges and ATSs should be required to maintain an audit trail, conduct effective market surveillance, and have adequate capacity to assist the regulatory authority to detect market manipulation, misleading conduct, and other fraudulent or deceptive conduct that may distort price discovery and unfairly disadvantage investors.

9.7   Market Conduct

Fundamental rules pertaining to market conduct should be included in securities regulation. These rules should address fraud and misrepresentation, duty to clients, market manipulation, and self-dealing. The securities regulatory authority may rely on the exchange to carry out market conduct regulation and market surveillance, but should maintain appropriate oversight of the exchange's regulatory functions (including reviewing and approving rules). The securities regulator should consider setting out minimum market conduct standards in its own rules in order to ensure consistency across trading systems.

In an OTC market, the securities regulatory authority should develop market conduct rules and should have access to necessary trading records (to be kept at the market intermediary or at a reporting location, if applicable) in order to investigate compliance with the rules. A front-running rule, for example, would prohibit the market intermediary from using information obtained from a client placing a trade on its own behalf ahead of the client, profiting from the client's trading information. Investigation of the violation of this rule would require access to trade tickets (recording the

---

171. Authorities in many countries are currently contemplating the regulatory treatment of ATSs. ATSs have fallen under either exchange or market intermediary regulation in most jurisdictions. Some systems have been intentionally left outside the regulatory framework. In the United States, the SEC has issued "Regulation ATS" as a comprehensive framework for ATS regulation. In Canada, ATSs have only been allowed to operate on a restricted basis, either as members of an exchange or in trading foreign unlisted securities. A proposed new regulation has been published, but implementation is still pending. In Europe, deliberations on EU-wide regulation of ATSs are just starting (see FESCO).

details and time of the client and market intermediary trades); the identity of employees taking and placing the trades, respectively; and the record of trade executions (trade tape) showing times of trade execution.

9.8   Regulation of Market Intermediaries

The effective regulation of market intermediaries is important to investor protection and to systemic risk, but it is particularly important to the functioning of the secondary market if the market structure relies on market intermediaries (as market makers and in the OTC market).

Market intermediaries should be subject to entry or licensing standards, including proficiency and capital requirements. Market intermediaries should be subject to ongoing capital adequacy requirements and to internal control requirements to ensure sound risk management. In particular, margin and credit rules and rules regarding segregation of customer assets are important. Market intermediaries should be subject to business conduct rules and required to have standards for professional conduct. The regulator should have full authority to conduct examinations of market intermediaries, impose conditions on them, and enforce compliance with regulations.

9.9   Role of SROs

Industry associations and formally recognized SROs and exchanges can assist effective market intermediary regulation and market regulation.

An industry body of market intermediaries active in the bond market may assist the securities regulatory authority to develop a proper regulatory framework and standards. An industry association might establish appropriate dealing or transaction conventions and standards of business conduct and provide expert commentary and advice during policy formulation and rule making. An industry association can also develop transaction standards, such as a Master Repurchase Agreement (MRA) or pricing or yield calculation formulas. These standards may be consistent with similar international standards (for instance, those established by the Bond Market Association in the United States and the International Securities Market Association in London). Consistent transaction standards will facilitate participation of international dealers and investors in the domestic market. An industry association may also consider offering trade execution services when the market is still thin and trading volume does not warrant entry of IDBs. As the market grows and the formation of IDBs becomes warranted, however, the industry association's trade execution services may conflict with those of the IDBs, which may be members of the association.

While an industry association can contribute to standard setting and policymaking, a formally recognized SRO can assume regulatory responsibility for its members. The securities regulatory authority should have the ability to recognize and delegate authority to SROs. The regulatory authority should have an effective oversight role over the SRO, including the right to conduct examinations, impose conditions, and review and approve rules. In order to be effective in its role, the SRO should have the authority to enforce compliance with its established rules.

9.10 Legal and Regulatory Framework for Payment and Settlement of Government Securities (see Chapter 8, Developing a Government Securities Settlement Structure)

While a principle of safe and efficient payment and settlement applies to the settlement of any securities, trading of government securities requires exceptionally safe and efficient settlement arrangements because of the large value of the transactions and the need to enable active trading. Poor management of settlement risks in government bond trading can generate major systemic risks to the financial system. The legal and regulatory framework must provide clear rights and obligations of parties in government securities transactions in settling executed trades. There should be clear legal treatment of, and effective regulatory enforcement against, failure to pay upon receipt of securities or vice versa in both primary and secondary markets. Given the trend to dematerialize securities in order to effect transfer by electronic book entry, proper legal foundation for recognition of electronic government securities as evidence of obligation and transfer of its legal ownership without (paper) documentation should be provided.

Private sector entities in many countries play a central role in conducting the day-to-day payment and settlement arrangements for both the

9

government and private sector bond markets.[172] A government supervisory or oversight role for these activities is nevertheless common in nearly all countries. The agency responsible for the supervision and oversight for the payment and settlement arrangements of government securities varies among countries. In many countries, these responsibilities are handled by the central bank.[173] In others, the central bank and the government agency responsible for the regulation of the securities market share the responsibilities. The regulatory agency with oversight responsibility should have clear authority over the clearing and settlement system, including the ability to conduct examinations, impose conditions, and review and approve rules.

The rules and operating procedures governing the payment and settlement arrangements for government securities should be available to market participants. Payment and settlement organizations should be required to have a framework that allows the oversight or regulatory agency to ensure accountability of the systems and to monitor developments in the payment and settlement systems. Finally, the payment and settlement organizations should be required to report periodically to the oversight or regulatory agency and, if necessary, submit periodic audits and examinations.

9.11   Conclusion

Sound government securities market development requires the underpinning of a coherent legal and regulatory framework.

The principal elements of a legal framework are:

- Clear borrowing authority
- Rules for the issuance of government securities
- Clearing and settlement system rules

---

172. In many countries, the government securities market is supported by a dedicated settlement infrastructure operated by the central bank. However, there are a gradually increasing number of cases in which the government securities custody and delivery function has been transferred out of the central banks and consolidated with central securities depositories serving all types of securities.

173. Some central bank laws include a clause(s) that authorizes the central bank to be the sole registrar of government securities.

- Rules governing the organization and functioning of the primary and secondary markets
- Rules setting out the legal status of government securities

The focus of regulations for the regulatory and supervisory framework for government securities markets should be to ensure equitable, smoothly functioning, and transparent markets, as well as protect investors and consumers of financial services, particularly in the payment and settlement area. Which government agency or agencies are assigned the regulatory and supervisory responsibilities and accompanying powers must be clearly defined and publicized.

In their role as regulators and supervisors, the authorities should prevent improper market conduct such as market manipulation and insider trading. A requirement that information potentially affecting prices is released expeditiously and to all market participants at the same time will result in fair and transparent markets. Requiring intermediaries to comply with minimum capital requirements and internal control procedures will contribute to reducing systemic risk. Also important for minimizing systemic risk are reliable systems for settlement of cash and securities transactions. Lack of standards in these areas have led to substantial problems and often set back the development of government securities markets.

9

Bibliography

BIS, Basel Committee on Banking Supervision. 1997. *Core Principles for Effective Banking Supervision.* Bank for International Settlements, Basel, Switzerland. Available at www.bis.org.

IMF (International Monetary Fund) and World Bank. 2000. *Draft Guidelines for Public Debt Management.* Washington, D.C. Available at www.imf.org/external/np/mae/pdebt/2000/eng/index.htm.

IOSCO (International Organization of Securities Commissions). 1990. *International Conduct of Business Principles.* Resolution 16 and Report of Technical Committee, International Organization of Securities Commissions, Montreal, Canada.

————. 1994. *Operational and Financial Risk Management Control Mechanisms for Over-the-Counter Derivatives Activities of Regulated Securities Firms.* Report of Technical Committee (35), International Organization of Securities Commissions, Montreal, Canada.

————. 1996. *Report on Cooperation between Market Authorities and Default Procedures.* Report of Technical Committee (49), International Organization of Securities Commissions, Montreal, Canada.

————. 1997. *Towards a Legal Framework for Clearing and Settlement in Emerging Markets.* Report of Emerging Market Committee (73), International Organization of Securities Commissions, Montreal, Canada.

————. 1998a. *Objectives and Principles of Securities Regulation.* International Organization of Securities Commissions, Montreal, Canada. Available at www.iosco.org.

————. 1998b. *Methodologies for Determining Minimum Capital Standards for Internationally Active Securities Firms Which Permit the Use of Models Under Prescribed Conditions Report.* Report of Technical Committee (77), International Organization of Securities Commissions, Montreal, Canada.

————. 1998c. *Risk Management and Control Guidance for Securities Firms and Their Supervisors.* Report of Technical Committee (78), International Organization of Securities Commissions, Montreal, Canada.

9

Development of Government Securities Markets and Tax Policy

Tax policy has significant impact on financial decisions of investors and firms. Certain tax policies, such as transaction tax, can stifle the development of capital markets. New financial products, such as mutual funds and asset-backed securities, will have difficulty in competing against traditional substitutes without proper tax treatment. Thus, a well-developed financial system requires a well-designed tax policy.

The development of the secondary market and an investor base for government securities will be influenced by the tax treatment of the earnings of interest or capital gains on government securities holdings. Similarly, the tax treatment of different financial instruments used in government securities markets and of holders of these instruments, including tax exemptions for government securities, will affect the manner in which government securities markets evolve.

10

10.1   Introduction

Taxation of financial instruments has significant implications for financial market development. Taxation of capital gains and income from securities affects consumption-saving and investment decisions, influencing the general level of savings, the demand for financial assets, and investment. It also strongly affects the allocation of savings.[174] If the effective tax rate is higher for equities than for bonds, corporations would prefer debt financing to share issuance, resulting in a more leveraged corporate capital structure. If the interest from bonds and bank deposits is subject to different tax rates, the competitive relationship between banks and financial institutions dealing in securities is affected. In some countries, favorable tax treatment for long-term savings has led to a rapid growth of pension funds and mutual funds, which has transformed the structure of the financial industry. Pension and mutual funds have become major holders of government securities.

Poorly designed tax policies, prevalent in many developing countries, can be a major impediment to well-functioning financial markets. The absence of an appropriate tax system could stifle the emergence of new financial instruments and financial institutions such as asset-backed securities and mutual funds. The development of robust government securities markets, therefore, is also inhibited by the failure to take the adverse consequences of tax policies properly into account in the setting of tax policy.

The tax treatment of financial instruments has often generated intense policy debate between tax and financial officials, and even within the same government ministry. Authorities responsible for collecting taxes are primarily concerned about protecting the revenue base. Especially in developing countries, tax authorities frequently skew the tax regime to take advantage of a relatively well-institutionalized financial sector from which revenue can be raised with little administrative effort.[175] Authorities responsible for the development of financial markets, on the other hand, aim at developing a liquid and integrated capital market and favor a tax system that meets the needs of different market participants and does not severely discourage savings and investment.

Considering the importance of financial markets in the development of the national economy, it is essential to design a tax system that is compatible with financial market development without seriously violating tax principles. Good communication between tax and financial market officials and an awareness by officials of how new financial instruments work will assist in developing a balanced tax system.

---

174. See OECD 1994a.

175. Transaction taxes on financial transactions have been viewed by tax authorities as a convenient way to collect taxes from the financial sector.

Tax neutrality is a desirable tax system objective because it minimizes market distortions and promotes efficiency.[176] To achieve tax neutrality, it is important to avoid tax fragmentation, which is the different tax treatment of transactions taking different forms but having the same economic consequences. Tax fragmentation can take place across types of income, participants, instruments, and time. Fragmentation can create serious tax loopholes and tax avoidance opportunities. The introduction of new taxes to deal with the perceived consequences of previous taxes often leads to a more complicated and fragmented tax regime.[177]

To achieve tax neutrality, the government must equalize effective tax rates across various capital and income structures—between corporate and noncorporate capital, debt and equity finance, and capital invested at home and abroad. While this is not easy to achieve, good tax policy should, nevertheless, seek tax neutrality.

10.2   Tax Treatment of Capital Income

10.2.1   Taxation of Interest: Schedular Versus Integrated Approach

With some exceptions (e.g., Chile, Greece, Iceland, Poland, and Turkey), the majority of countries tax interest income or capital gains from government bonds to achieve fiscal equity between capital income and wage and salary income.

Many countries traditionally have taxed interest from government bonds under the comprehensive income tax (CIT).[178] The CIT is an integrated income tax system under which all sources of income (wages, rents,

10

---

176. Tax neutrality requires that taxpayers' economic decisions should not be affected by imposition of a tax. In relation to savings decisions, tax neutrality requires that the choice of where to save (the allocation of savings), when to save (the timing of savings), and how much to save (the amount of savings) be independent of all taxes.

177. The introduction of new taxes to deal with the perceived consequences of previous taxes has been the practice in the United States, the United Kingdom, and other common law countries.

178. See Norregaard 1997.

dividends, interest, and profits) earned by the same taxpayer are treated as a single income and taxed at a single (often progressive) rate. Proponents of the CIT maintain that it would, if properly designed, achieve both efficiency and distributive objectives (horizontal and vertical equities).[179] For this reason, tax reforms have often converted "schedular" ("compartmentalized") income tax systems into "integrated" ("comprehensive") systems.

Among the 30 OECD countries, 18 countries include interest from government securities in the CIT. Six of these countries also incorporate a withholding tax element into the CIT. In Belgium, France, and Portugal, taxpayers have an option between the CIT and a withholding tax on interest from government bonds. In Spain, Switzerland, and the United Kingdom, the withholding tax applied on interest earned on government securities is applied as a credit against the CIT.

In Scandinavian countries (Finland, Norway, and Sweden), interest from government securities like other capital income is taxed under the dual income tax system (progressive tax for labor income and proportional tax for capital income), where interest is taxed at a flat rate, although it constitutes global personal income.[180] Non-OECD countries, such as China and the Czech Republic, apply a flat tax rate on interest from bonds.

10.2.2 Withholding Tax[181]

One notable trend in taxation of interest earnings in general, including on government securities, during the past two decades, is application of a

---

179. Full realization of a CIT is not easy to attain. To achieve full tax neutrality, accrued income from intermediated savings (e.g., pension funds and life insurance companies) should be attributed to individuals, which can be difficult to calculate. The merits and limitations of the CIT are addressed in OECD 1994a.

180. Cnossen (2000) analyzes the tax reforms in Scandinavian countries. According to Cnossen, conversion to the dual income tax (DIT) can transform "nominally comprehensive, but factually concession-riddled income taxes into effectively more comprehensive, if nominally less progressive, DITs."

181. A withholding tax is a tax deduction at source (employers for wages and interest-paying financial institutions for interest). One needs to distinguish between two types of withholding taxes: creditable versus final. In the former, the withholding tax is creditable against the final tax liability of taxpayers when they file their taxes after the end of the tax year. For a final withholding tax, the final tax liability of a taxpayer for this source of income is cleared with the withholding or tax deduction at source.

withholding tax and/or a separate flat tax for interest earnings. The motivation for this is the administrative ease associated in raising tax revenue from this source. In four OECD countries (Austria, Finland, Italy, and Japan) and in some non-OECD countries (for example, Brazil, Egypt, and India), interest from government securities is excluded from the CIT but is liable to a final withholding tax.

A withholding tax has been favored in some countries because of its ease of implementation and low compliance cost. In addition, a withholding tax is effective in preventing tax evasion. From the perspective of tax authorities, a withholding tax guarantees a minimum level of taxation, even when taxpayers fail to report interest income in their regular tax returns. It advances the collection of revenue by tax authorities, since the tax is deducted when interest is paid and before income is reported in regular tax returns. In some countries, the act of withholding by the paying agent leaves an administrative track that tax authorities find helpful in detecting unreported sources of income and wealth.

A withholding tax is especially useful and warranted in countries where a central depository and a good reporting system for financial intermediaries are not in place. In some jurisdictions, including Germany, Luxembourg, Switzerland, and the United Kingdom, banking secrecy provisions prohibit tax authorities from obtaining information from financial institutions.[182] In such circumstances, tax authorities have had to rely on withholding taxes to detect tax evasion.

A withholding tax has shortcomings, however. First, it may inherently distort horizontal taxation equity in the sense that taxpayers subject to withholding tax may pay a higher proportion of income in taxes than those who earn nonwithholding income.[183] Second, a withholding tax is not easily applicable to newer financial instruments such as deep discount bonds and derivatives. Third, it impairs the country's ability to attract foreign savings if the withholding tax is applied to nonresidents.[184]

10

---

182. Developing countries suffering from pervasive tax evasion should consider granting tax authorities access to banking secrecy with strict anti-abuse requirements.

183. It is the final withholding tax that gives rise to possible distortions. The creditable withholding tax is simply a collection device and has no substantive economic consequences.

184. In Scandinavian countries, nonresidents are exempt from withholding tax.

10.2.3 Treatment of Capital Gains

10.2.3.1 Capital Gains Taxation and Bond Washing

Many countries, especially industrial countries, tax realized capital gains from company share transactions, either as ordinary income in comprehensive income taxes or as separate capital gains taxes.[185] A smaller number of countries tax capital gains realized from transactions in government securities. If capital gains are not taxed or are taxed at a lower rate than interest income, investors may try to convert interest income into capital gains through "bond washing"—selling bonds just before a coupon payment date and repurchasing them immediately thereafter. To counter such tax avoidance practices, most countries not levying a capital gains tax on bonds have adopted various anti-conversion rules.

10.2.3.2 Tax Treatment of Deep Discount Bonds[186]

Deep discount bonds are securities issued with a reduced or zero rate of interest. Those with a zero rate of interest are called "zero-coupon bonds." The yield on deep discount bonds is the difference between the purchase price and the redemption price. A conventional bond can be converted into a series of zero-coupon bonds by stripping.[187] In some countries, a capital gains tax—usually at a lower rate than ordinary income tax—is payable on the yield from a deep discount bond. In this case, investors could benefit from differences in the tax treatment of deep discount bonds and conventional bonds.

However, most OECD countries treat the discount on issue as interest income and as accruing over the bond's life. Thus, the holder of deep discount bonds pays tax on accrued income on a yearly basis.[188] In some

---

185. The taxation of capital gains has become one of the more controversial policy issues. Burman (1999) reviews various policy issues of the capital gains tax within the U.S. context (see also Gravelle 1994 and Cnossen 2000).

186. OECD (1994b) examines the taxation of new financial instruments, including deep discount bonds.

187. Stripping involves separately trading registered interest and principal of securities.

188. In calculating annual accrued income, most countries use a constant interest rate compounded annually. Others do not, recognizing the discount accrued evenly over the

countries, the discount is taxed on redemption or disposal of the bond, giving a small advantage to the holder.

Unintended distortions may sometimes result when tax legislation does not distinguish taxation of discount instruments from that of conventional bonds, but regards the implicit yields of the discount instruments as interest income rather than capital gains. Taxation of discount bonds may become asymmetrical and non-neutral when negative yields (which might reduce the value of the discount interest below its acquisition cost because of an increase in market yields after the discount instrument was purchased) can neither be considered capital losses nor be offset against positive yields earned by the investor on other assets.[189]

An additional administrative burden for holders of deep discount instruments is imposed when withholding taxes are declared to be applicable to all implicit yields earned on such instruments.[190] If withholding tax is imposed at redemption, the market prices of deep discount bonds should be adjusted to reflect such taxation as they are traded, complicating the trade and limiting the bond's liquidity. If some market participants are exempt from withholding tax, it is not easy to adjust market prices between two trading parties.

In some jurisdictions, withholding tax is imposed yearly on an accruing discount bond. The purchaser sometimes might be subject to withholding tax on the whole difference between purchase price and issue price, despite the seller not having acquired the bond at the time the bond was issued. This requirement may be in place when it is difficult to know the seller's purchase price. If the bond is traded frequently, the total amount of withholding could be greater than the total amount of ordinary tax due on the discount.

If the tax treatment of coupon-paying conventional bonds is more favorable than that of zero-coupon bonds, issuers may try to seize the

10

---

bond's life. The linear approach is less preferable to the holder because the discount will accrue more rapidly under the linear method of calculation than the compounded basis, resulting in a heavier tax burden during the early life of the bond. The linear basis is thus especially detrimental to deep discount bonds with long maturity.

189. OECD (1994b) shows that if a bond is sold before redemption, the difference between accrued interest at the time of disposal and the disposal proceeds is not regarded as taxable gain or deductible loss in 7 of 24 OECD countries.

190. OECD 1994b.

advantages applicable to coupon-paying conventional bonds by issuing them at a low rate (i.e., a coupon-paying deep discount bond). To prevent that possibility, some laws set ceilings for the maximum discount at which a coupon-paying bond can be issued. In the United Kingdom, for example, deep discount is defined as either more than 15 percent of the bond's redemption amount or 0.5 percent multiplied by the remaining years until redemption.

10.2.4 Accrual Versus Realization in Income Taxation

Particularly for personal income, tax systems do not normally tax interest income and capital gains as they gradually accrue, but only when they are realized—when bond coupons are paid or financial instruments are sold or redeemed. This may produce a so-called "lock-in effect" as investors postpone realizing losses or profits that incur taxes. A lock-in effect may also occur when tax treatment differs between long-term and short-term holding of financial assets. Such tax effects are sometimes compounded by accounting rules that do not require assets to be marked to market, which can affect the liquidity of some public issues. These treatments create deferrals of tax with various related distortions, such as favoring some assets over others or discouraging taxpayers from selling assets.[191]

To prevent problems such as the lock-in effect and bond washing, some countries have adopted an accrual basis for calculating the tax on interest paid or received. In an accrual system, securities are generally marked to market at the end of each tax year, and any accrued gain or loss (even unrealized) is taken into account for tax purposes.[192] In countries with an accrual system, prices are normally quoted "clean," with accrued income accounted for separately. This also simplifies the calculation of tax liabilities on an accrual basis.

---

191. In the case of mutual funds, a lock-in effect may significantly limit the willingness of investors to actively manage their portfolios. The mutual fund industry in many countries has recently responded to this problem by offering umbrella funds and other products that allow individual investors to shift funds without being subject to taxation.

192. New Zealand was one of the first countries to adopt such a policy in 1986. The United Kingdom moved from a realization to an accrual basis in 1995 and thereby significantly changed the substance of its tax system.

10.2.5 Tax Treatment of Inflation Adjustment of Government Securities

In countries with a relatively high inflation rate and a progressive personal income tax, if the entire nominal interest from bonds is considered taxable income, the real (i.e., inflation-adjusted) after-tax interest for domestic investors may easily become negative, thereby discouraging retail demand for government bonds.

Inflation adjustment and proper measurement of taxable income were major tax policy issues between the mid-1970s and mid-1980s, when high inflation swept the global economy.[193] During that period, many countries introduced various methods to reduce taxation of nominal increases in income and in the value of taxable assets. As inflation rates declined considerably thereafter and income tax schedules became flatter, those measures subsequently were discontinued or were no longer relevant in most countries.[194]

While inflation adjustments in taxation for income and capital gains from government securities may be justified even under moderate inflation, most countries do not apply them because of difficulties in administering such adjustments. Also, compensation in taxation for inflation for government securities may be seen as providing benefits for higher-income citizens who are often holders of such securities, and thus becomes more difficult to support politically. In a few OECD countries (Australia, Ireland, Luxembourg, Spain, and the United Kingdom), however, capital gains on financial assets are indexed for tax purposes.[195]

Even under moderate inflationary conditions, taxing nominal interest can push up nominal tax rates significantly. In this regard, inflation adjustments are as warranted on interest earnings as on capital gains, yet only a few countries (e.g., Brazil and Mexico) take inflation adjustments on interest earnings into consideration.

Inflation-indexed government securities provide investors with an effective method to guard against inflation risk by offering a nominal return that

---

193. Tanzi (1980) offers a comprehensive discussion of inflation adjustment in the context of personal income tax.

194. See Tanzi and King (1995) and Messere 1999.

195. See Tanzi and King 1995.

is adjusted with the inflation rate.[196] In countries prone to high inflation, a substantial share of the government bonds consists of inflation-indexed bonds.[197] Indexed bonds can be constructed in various ways. Two methods are widely used. The first is to index the principal: only principal is adjusted for changes in a selected price index during the life of the bonds with the coupon (interest) rate remaining fixed. Even though the coupon rate is fixed, nominal coupon payment also changes as principal is adjusted every period. At maturity, the principal repayment is the product of the face value of the bond times the cumulative change in the selected price index. In an alternative scheme, the coupon rate is indexed with the redeemable principal remaining fixed. Thus, all of the compensation for inflation comes through the coupon payment.

Although inflation-indexed bonds guarantee before-tax real returns, taxes re-expose indexed bonds to inflation risk. Because most tax rules do not distinguish nominal yield from real income, an increase in nominal yield due to inflation is subject to income tax and the after-tax returns are lowered. The indexing of the principal, which is the method commonly used in most countries, involves a further tax burden. In most countries, to keep the tax on index-linked government bonds equitable with other conventional bonds, the appreciation of the principal of indexed bonds, although received only at maturity, is taxed every year on an accrual basis. This means that in some inflationary environments, the tax liability for indexed bonds could exceed the principal-adjusted coupon interest income, causing a cash flow problem to taxable investors.[198] This problem increases the longer the maturity of the bond. This tax implication limits the demand for long-term inflation-indexed government bonds to tax-exempt investors such as pension funds and life insurance companies.

---

196. Price (1997) offers a comprehensive discussion of inflation-indexed bonds.

197. The share of indexed bonds in total government debt toward the end of the 1990s varied considerably (Israel 80.2 percent, Australia 29.5 percent, Turkey 24.3 percent, Brazil 19.6 percent, Sweden 12.5 percent, United Kingdom 12.0 percent, Mexico 8.4 percent, United States 0.8 percent, France 0.6 percent, and India 0.2 percent). See Kopcke and Kimball 1999.

198. Zee (1997) shows that, even though the tax is proportional, the taxation of income from indexing government bonds is not neutral between the principal indexation and coupon rate indexation methods as long as the accretion to principal is taxed on an accrual basis under the principal indexation method.

To solve this tax problem and boost the appeal of indexed government bonds, nominal principal adjustment due to inflation could remain tax exempt.[199] Alternatively, nominal adjustments could be taxed on an actual payment basis. However, these treatments would be favorable for inflation-indexed government bonds compared with conventional bonds and thus lead to distortions in the demand for indexed bonds relative to conventional bonds.

10.3   Tax Treatment of Different Financial Instruments

10.3.1   Favorable Tax Treatment of Government Bonds

In some countries, interest from government (and municipal) bonds is not taxed or taxed at lower rates than interest paid on private sector debt. Greece and Turkey, for example, exempt interest from government bonds but tax interest from bank deposits. Italy levies a modest 12.5 percent flat tax on government bond interest, which was tax exempt prior to 1987. In the United States, government savings bonds receive favorable tax treatment, and interest earned on state and local governments issues (municipal bonds) are exempt from federal taxation. Although favorable tax treatment of government securities is being eliminated or reduced in developed countries, it is still regarded as an acceptable and useful policy option in developing countries.

There are various reasons for giving government securities favorable tax treatment.[200] The most common seems to be a strong belief that tax-exempt government bonds have a marketing advantage and thereby widen the investor base for government securities. The United States utilizes tax exemption on municipal bonds as a federal subsidy to state and municipal governments.

There is, however, a growing consensus that the disadvantages of favorable tax treatment for government securities outweigh its advantages. First, in a competitive market, interest rate arbitrage will ensure that after-tax

---

199. In the United Kingdom, nominal gains on the face value of the Indexed Gilts from inflation are tax exempt, although capital gains are generally taxable.

200. The following discussion is drawn mainly from Norregaard 1997.

rates of return are equalized.[201] Second, tax-favored government securities are objectionable from the perspective of efficiency. To the extent that a government mobilizes a larger amount of capital through tax exemption for the securities it issues, it risks crowding out possibly more efficient private sector investment, thus reducing overall welfare.[202] Subsidization through tax exemption is also considered less efficient than an explicit budgetary subsidy.[203] Favorable tax treatment of government securities also raises questions about fiscal equity since in many instances the high-income group is the beneficiary of such favorable tax treatment, thus distorting distributional equity.

Finally, government securities have some advantages over private sector securities even without favorable tax treatment: they typically are risk free, diverse in maturity, and have a large market. Given these benefits, special tax advantages would give them an unfair competitive edge over private sector debt instruments and equity capital, thereby thwarting the development of the private sector capital market. The capital taxation in Italy, for example, characterized by broad usage of final withholding taxes and favorable treatment of government securities, is cited as an important reason for the country's poorly developed stock market.[204] To promote balanced financial market development, a government should seek to ensure a level playing field, where the government as a borrower competes equitably with private sector issuers.

10.3.2   Tax Treatment of Repurchase Agreements (Repos)

To establish an efficient repo market, the dual features of repos (sale and repurchase of a security or collateralized borrowing) should be clearly and appropriately defined in legal, fiscal, and accounting terms. From a legal

---

201. In a closed economy with a uniform tax rate, t, the interest rate on tax-exempt bonds (r_e) is lowered by the tax rate until $(1-t) \times r_t$ is equal to r_e, where r_t is the pretax rate of return.

202. Norregaard (1997) suggests that policymakers are affected by the fiscal illusion "that the normally lower borrowing costs associated with tax-exempt bonds also reflect overall or effective lower borrowing costs, and thus expand borrowing and public expenditures beyond what otherwise would have occurred."

203. See Norregaard 1997.

204. See Bargella and Castellucci 1998.

perspective, the sale and purchase characterization leads to better protection of the solvent party under most countries' bankruptcy laws. Otherwise, the solvent party is likely to be a creditor that is subject to a rigid insolvency proceeding. However, given the secured loan character of repos, both the seller and the buyer can enjoy the benefits of repo agreements—raising short-term funds at a cheaper rate than uncollateralized borrowing, and temporarily investing cash for collateral—while avoiding realizing a taxable gain or a transfer of assets on the securities involved.

If a tax law treats repos as separate sale and purchase transactions, both parties are subject to complex tax rules, generating extra transaction costs. In the Republic of Korea, for example, the seller (cash receiver) pays tax at the selling date for interest accrued during his holding period, and the buyer (cash provider) pays tax at the time of redemption for the interest accrued during the repo period. These tax burdens complicate repo transactions and deter market participants from entering into repos.[205] (See Box 4.6. in Chapter 4.) In Japan, repos are subject to a three-basis-point transaction tax—a factor considered a deterrent to the development of that country's repo market.

The tax treatment of coupons (interest payments) maturing during the repo period is singled out as a distinct irritant to market participants. Many countries that characterize repos as a secured loan apply a special treatment called "manufactured payment" on the coupon paid on the securities.[205] Under this system, the buyer (cash provider) that actually receives coupon or dividend payments will give to the seller (cash receiver) a "manufactured payment" equal to the coupon or dividend paid. The seller (the beneficial owner of the securities) is thus assured the same coupon or dividend stream as if no repo sale had been made. In France, a repo is legally treated as a sale and a purchase.[207] However, the law endows repos with a tax-neutral status, requiring the buyer to transfer the relevant coupon back to the seller. This unique combination of legal and fiscal frameworks—a very secure legal pro-

10

---

205. This problem has been responsible for the poor development of the domestic repo market in Korea. The Korean government recently committed to revise the tax law to treat repos as secured loans.

206. The system in the United Kingdom is discussed in Mouy and Nalbantian 1995.

207. The French government has successfully promoted the domestic repo market in recent years by providing well-balanced legal, accounting, and fiscal frameworks. Financial Times (1997) and Bainton 1995.

tection of repos and a removal of fiscal impediment—has led to the rapid growth of France's repo market.

10.4 Taxation of Different Government Securities Holders

10.4.1 Taxation of Nonresident Government Securities Holders

The taxation of income from foreign investments, and of investment abroad by residents, is very complex, as it is subject to interaction between two or more countries' tax systems and is dependent on specific tax provisions stipulated in both domestic legislation and bilateral tax treaties.

Regarding taxation of international capital flows, a country must choose between the "residence principle," whereby taxation rights belong to the capital holder's country of residence, and the "source principle," whereby these rights belong to the country in which the capital resides. Most countries, following the principles outlined by the OECD Model Tax Convention,[208] have double tax avoidance provisions that embody a combination of residence and source principles. In this regime, source countries apply a modest withholding tax to passive capital income, usually lower than the domestic tax rate.[209] Nonresidents typically receive credit for this withholding tax in the country of residence. In this way, double taxation is avoided and the tax is shared between the residence and source countries.

In the past two decades, an increasing number of countries have abolished—unilaterally or under tax treaties—withholding taxes on nonresidents. In addition, many countries are facing pressure to eliminate withholding taxes on interest earnings.[210] The principal reason for this trend is growing international tax competition to attract the funds of large

---

208. See OECD 2000a.

209. Article 11 of the OECD Model Tax Convention imposes a ceiling of a 10 percent tax on interest paid in source countries.

210. See OECD 1994a, Chapter 7. Alworth (1998) discusses the effects of withholding taxes in Germany, Italy, and the United States.

foreign savings institutions such as pension funds, investment funds, and life insurance companies. Such institutions, often tax-exempt in their home country, are particularly sensitive to source country withholding tax, which they are unable to reclaim in their home country.[211] Financial institutions that pay taxes in their home country may recover withholding tax, but administrative delays in this recovery create inconvenience and costs.

The reduction or elimination of withholding taxes on interest on financial instruments, on the other hand, raises a new concern, viz., the growing importance of tax evasion associated with international portfolio investment. Little or no withholding tax in a source country shifts the burden of effective taxation of cross-border capital flows to the residence country, which usually taxes foreign-source income under the personal income tax. With an increasing discrepancy between the withholding tax rate at the source and the corresponding personal income tax rate in the residence country, investors have a strong incentive not to disclose their interest income.[212] Furthermore, lack of an effective information exchange framework between the tax authorities of the two countries makes it difficult for a residence country to collect taxes due.

To address this potential tax abuse, proposals have recently appeared in the literature to raise withholding taxes at the source and enhance information exchange among national tax authorities.[213] As the present tax system inadequately catches cross-border capital income in the tax net, this alternative approach suggests that current, relatively low withholding taxes should be raised within a broad multilateral framework. This line of thought, although relatively new and requiring elusive multilateral agreements, represents a possible reversal of the trend to eliminate withholding taxes.

10

10.4.2 Taxation of Collective Investment Funds (CIFs)

The past two decades have witnessed rapid growth of collective investment funds (CIFs) in many countries. (See Annex 6.A in Chapter 6.)

---

211. For this reason, Alworth 1998 proposes that even countries continuing to levy withholding taxes on nonresidents should consider a zero tax rate for selected financial institutions.

212. For the practical difficulties of taxing international savings flows, see OECD 1994a.

213. See Zee 1998 and Tanzi and Zee 1998.

Considering the difficulties for individual investors to invest in government securities, CIFs provide an attractive vehicle for such investors, since they offer diversification of risk, quality asset management, and a variety of investment options.

To be competitive with other financial instruments, CIFs should be at least tax neutral; such funds—whether corporate or contractual, open or closed-end—should be no less attractive than the direct investment in the same assets.[214] This principle should be particularly observed for the corporate-form CIF. CIFs are sometimes wrongly treated as a regular company, subject to economic double taxation and thereby disadvantaged in relation to trusts and contractual CIFs which are not treated as taxable entities. This is often the case where CIFs are in the early stages of development and when the true nature of a corporate CIF, i.e., a conduit or a paper company for investment purposes, is not fully understood by policymakers.

In addition to securities transaction taxes, CIF earnings are subject to income and capital gains taxes. The International Fiscal Association's 1997 report identified five generic models for taxation of CIFs under two major fund tax regimes, the U.S. and European.[215]

The U.S. system of taxing CIFs is called "pass-through." All dividends and interest received by a CIF from its investments are given in gross form (i.e., no tax is levied at source) and passed through to CIF shareholders; all capital gains are also passed through. Under this system, all shareholders are responsible for their own tax calculation and payment.

Most European tax regimes require a tax deduction at the source (i.e., the payer of dividends or interest). The tax deducted and paid to the tax authorities is converted into a tax credit (as recognition of tax already paid). This credit passes through the CIF without further tax intervention

---

214. In some jurisdictions, CIFs enjoy a tax advantage relative to the direct investment in securities. However, special savings promotion schemes, such as individual retirement accounts (IRAs) and 401(k) retirement savings plans in the United States, and individual savings accounts (ISAs) in the United Kingdom, are generally believed to be more efficient and fiscally equitable (see St. Giles 1999).

215. International Fiscal Association 1997. The five main generic models of fund taxation are (i) not subject to tax, (ii) subject to tax but wholly exempt, (iii) subject to tax but not the object of tax, (iv) subject to tax and the object of tax with low or zero percent tax, and (v) fully subject to tax and the object of tax with integration at the investor level.

and is available to fund shareholders to offset their own tax liabilities. Since the deduction at the source is normally at the standard rate of personal income tax, most minority shareholders have no additional tax to pay. Only higher-rate taxpayers are subject to additional payments. For those jurisdictions having a personal capital gains tax, the CIF's shareholders will be subject to the capital gains tax when the shares are sold with gains.

In the U.S. model, tax effects occur at the level of the investor. Thus, this regime requires somewhat more financially sophisticated investors, along with a thorough and efficient tax collection system. The European system collects tax at the level of payer (corporate), and it mostly disregards capital gains so long as they are retained for reinvestment. This system is based on the recognition that taxation at the investor level is both costly and difficult to collect. Developing countries with weak institutional backgrounds may find the European approach appealing for its practicality and simplicity.

10.4.3 Taxation of Pensions

The tax treatment of pensions is important for the development of government securities markets. Contributions to private pension funds are a major source of national private savings, and hence represent an important source for institutional investment in the capital market, including for government securities.[216] Thus, policymakers should give careful consideration to designing a tax regime for pensions that is conducive (or at least not detrimental) to capital market development.

Most countries with well-developed pension systems provide favorable tax treatment for saving through pensions. The most common approach is to allow contributions to be deducted from taxable income, allow investment income to accumulate tax free, and tax benefits in full upon withdrawal.[217] Under this arrangement, taxes for contributions and investment earnings are deferred until withdrawal. Most tax legislation allows

---

216. This section is based in part on Dilnot 1992.

217. This approach is called EET, an acronym for *exempt (contribution)*, *exempt (investment income)*, *and tax (benefit)*. This tax regime ensures tax neutrality for consumption at different points in time.

expenditure-tax treatment only for pension funds, while other types of savings are subject to normal income taxation, which leads to enormous accumulations in pension funds.

Besides creating distortions among types of savings, favorable tax treatment of pension funds results in forgone tax revenue; i.e., taxes that would have been collected on contributions and investment earnings, less those paid on benefits.[218] In addition, high-income tax-payers benefit more from this preferential treatment. To deal with these effects, most countries with an EET tax regime set maximum limits for tax-deductible contributions.

Some countries, notably Australia and New Zealand, use an alternative taxation approach and tax both contributions into the pension plan and interest income, while allowing exemption of benefits.[219] Under this approach, pension savings are subject to the same tax rule applied to ordinary interest-bearing savings—a situation that constrains the development of occupational retirement plans.

In Germany, Japan, and Korea, pension liabilities held on the financial accounts of the sponsoring firms (book reserves) are, to some extent, tax deductible against the firm's corporate tax obligation.[220] For book-reserve plans, firms do not actually contribute to the plan, but each year charge prospective pension liabilities against the firm's financial statements. Despite alternative pension plans providing equivalent or better tax treatment, book-reserve plans are quite popular in these countries because firms can use money that would have been put into a pension plan as valuable working capital. In this sense, book-reserve plans thwart the development of private pension funds. Also, In the event of insolvency of sponsoring firms, employees are treated the same as other creditors. The vested benefits of employees, thus, could be severely jeopardized under the book-reserve system.

---

218. See Davis 1995.

219. This approach is called TTE, an acronym for *taxed, taxed, exempt*. This represents a comprehensive income tax regime and ensures tax neutrality between consumption and saving.

220. In Germany, contributions are fully tax deductible, with some restrictions; in Japan and Korea, only 40 percent of contributions are deductible.

10.5 Tax Incentives for Financial Instruments to Stimulate Savings

Tax incentives for financial instruments to stimulate savings have been criticized for various reasons.[221] Such incentives distort relative prices and lead to inefficient resource allocation, they create tax inequity because nonpreferred sectors must bear the heavier tax burden to compensate the government for forgone revenue, they promote unproductive rent-seeking behavior, and they undermine administrative simplicity of a tax system and impose substantial monitoring costs.

Nonetheless, both developed and developing countries have made extensive use of tax incentives for certain financial assets to stimulate private savings.[222] Box 10.1. provides a summary of targeted saving programs in selected industrial countries that have tax-saving incentives. Contributions to retirement savings and pensions are tax deductible in most countries; savings with life insurance companies also receive special tax treatment. Moreover, governments are providing various tax-exempt accounts and targeted savings promotion plans, such as the IRA and 401(k) in the United States and the *plan d'épargne populaire* (PEP) in France.

Empirical work on the relationship between tax incentives and overall saving levels shows mixed results. However, it is generally accepted that tax incentives have a strong impact on the composition of portfolios. In this regard, properly designed tax incentives, when used with care, can be effective in achieving certain economic goals such as the promotion of the long-term bond market. This is especially meaningful for developing countries in which the investors' time horizon is fairly short and short-term financial instruments dominate the bond market.[223]

10

---

221. See Chua 1995. Shah 1995 provides an extensive discussion of the pros and cons of tax incentives.

222. NBER (1994) analyzes in detail various types of tax incentives in seven industrialized countries.

223. Tanzi and Zee 2000 argue that most tax incentives in developing countries are cost ineffective and are often a recipe for corruption. However, they find that tax incentives targeted for rectifying market failure (and thus generating significant positive externalities) can be justified in developing countries.

Box 10.1. Targeted Saving Incentives in Industrial Countries

401(k) Plan

A type of defined contribution pension plan covered in Section 401(k) of the Internal Revenue Code of the United States of America. This plan allows employees to contribute pretax dollars to a qualified tax-deferred retirement plan. Employers usually match some of their employees' contributions to the plan to encourage employees' participation. Employees like this plan because they can defer income tax liability on the contributed income and their savings grow tax free until retirement. Employers like this plan because it limits the company's pension liability and shifts the responsibility of investment performance from the company's pension plan to employees.

Individual Retirement Account (IRA)

A tax-deferred, long-term saving program in the United States. Individuals could make tax-deductible contributions to IRAs limited to $2,000 per year. Filers with income above $40,000 (single) and $60,000 (joint) cannot make tax-deductible contributions, but still could make nondeductible contributions to gain the benefit of tax deferral. Withdrawals from IRAs prior to age 59 and 1/2 are subject to a 10 percent (of principal) tax penalty.

PEP

The tax-exempt individual savings plan (*plan d'épargne populaire*) offered since 1990 by banks and insurance companies in France. The duration of a PEP should be longer than eight years to be eligible for the tax exemption. At the end of a PEP, the subscriber can choose either the use of the tax-free lump sum capital or the payment of an annuity exempted from any income tax.

Personal Equity Plans (PEPs)

A policy measure introduced in 1986 to encourage wider share ownership in the United Kingdom.

Investors in PEPs are exempt from income tax on dividends arising from stocks held in a plan. In addition, there is no capital gains tax when stocks are sold. In January 1992, PEPs were split into two subplans—the "single-company PEP" and the "general PEP."

RRSP/RPP

The Canadian tax-deferred retirement savings program. Registered pension plans (RPPs) are occupational pension plans where contributions are deductible, income accrues tax free, and pension income is taxed when it is received. Registered retirement savings plans (RRSPs) are individual accounts similar to IRAs in the United States. The two systems have been implemented as an integrated system in terms of contribution limits. The RRSP is a more flexible system in which investors have great discretion over the types of assets they choose to hold and the methods of cashing out the funds. RRSP investors may either withdraw all of the funds at any point and include them in taxable income that year or purchase an annuity prior to their 71st birthday.

Vermoegensbildungsgesetz (Wealth Accumulation Program)

A German saving program introduced in 1961 in an attempt to partially equalize wealth distribution. Employees authorize the deduction of a certain amount of their salary, which is directly deposited into long-term (at least six-year) funds. Both the employer and the employee can make contributions. If the employee's income falls short of a certain limit, the government supplements the contributions at a fixed percentage until an upper limit is reached. Funds eligible for a subsidy include shares in the employee's own or any other company and savings at building societies.

Sources: NBER (1994) and Downes and Goodman 1998

If governments want to keep the effect of tax incentives to promote savings neutral as far as the choice of type of investment asset is concerned, the best way is to establish tax-favored savings accounts, which may be invested in any class of asset—certificate of deposit, bond, or equity shares. The choice of asset class would depend on the individual's risk preference, and would not be directed to any particular asset class because of tax considerations.

Where governments do use tax incentives, such measures should satisfy two basic criteria.[224] First, they should achieve their stated objectives. Second, they should be the most efficient means to achieve those objectives. It is not unusual to find tax incentives that fail to meet even the first basic criterion. With regard to the second criterion, only few tax incentives qualify. In designing tax incentives, tax authorities should, therefore, set clear policy objectives and rigorously check whether a tax incentive is the best means to achieve the set goals.

If a government manages tax incentives in an ad hoc and inconsistent manner, such incentives are subject to proliferate over time. If tax incentives are based on pressure from the business community on noneconomic considerations, other interest groups will also request special tax treatment. The tax system then will become more complex and inefficient. A sunset clause for tax incentives is a useful device against such proliferation by requiring policymakers to periodically review the efficacy and justification of tax incentives.

10.6   Transaction Taxes on Financial Instruments

Transaction taxes (especially stamp duties) have a long history in some countries, and many countries still rely on various types of transaction taxes.[225] Equities are typically subject to higher transaction taxes than bonds

---

224. See Institute for Fiscal Studies 1989.

225. Securities transaction taxes can be defined as any kinds of monetary obligation levied by public organizations on transactions (including issuance) of securities. Many countries impose a stamp duty (tax) on financial documents, including transfer of securities. In addition to the stamp duty, variations of securities transaction taxes include turnover tax, transfer tax, stock exchange tax, trading tax, transaction tax, and SEC fee. Spahn (1995) provides a good summary of financial transaction taxes worldwide.

and derivatives. Government bonds are usually exempt from transaction taxes. However, as financial innovation provides various close untaxed substitutes (including offshore transactions) the efficacy of transaction taxes has been eroded substantially. In addition, growing competition among international financial markets has put downward pressure on transaction costs. Consequently, during the past decade, several major countries have lowered transaction tax rates or removed transaction taxes altogether.

Given the high volume of financial transactions, many policymakers consider financial transaction taxes as a potent revenue source even at low tax rates.[226] Numerous discussions in the 1990s over securities transaction taxes (STT), especially in the United States, have been against a backdrop of this primary motive as a tax revenue source.[227] However, the revenue potential of transaction taxes could be significantly reduced by responses of market participants that lead to decreased transaction volume. In particular, transaction taxes on derivatives or short-term money market instruments could be harmful to markets that are characterized as high volume and low margins, resulting in severe contraction of trading with little tax revenue. Thus, static estimation of potential tax revenue from the imposition of transaction taxes based only on the current trading volume could turn out to be disappointing.

Some prominent economists, who maintain that financial markets absorb too many resources relative to their social benefits, have proposed transactions taxes to reduce excessive speculation by "putting sand in the wheels" of financial markets and thereby increase market efficiency.[228, 229] This proposal, however, has encountered heavy criticism from both academic circles and financial communities. Opponents argue that transaction

10

---

226. This is especially the case in developing countries, where financial markets are one of the few organized sectors.

227. See Catalyst Institute 1995.

228. See Tobin (1984), Summers and Summers (1989), and Stiglitz 1989.

229. Increased volatility in world financial markets has also spurred interest in levying a transaction tax on short-term capital flows to reduce volatility in foreign exchange and securities markets. The proposal to impose a tax on currency conversion (so-called Tobin tax), first proposed by James Tobin in 1984, has been widely discussed (see Raffer 1998). Along this line, Zee (2000) argues that a withholding tax, being more difficult to evade and administratively simple, is superior to some type of quasi-capital control measures such as a Tobin tax or nonremunerated reserve requirements.

taxes decrease the efficiency of financial markets by reducing liquidity and increasing transaction costs.[230] They also claim that transaction taxes increase the cost of capital, which could lead to lower rates of investment and output growth.

10.7   Conclusion

A tax system is inherently rigid. Once a tax rule is embedded in asset prices and creates associated interest groups, attempts to change it can become mired in political struggle. Furthermore, there are revenue consequences to any change. Tax authorities are generally reluctant to forgo existing sources of revenue unless forced to do so, which suggests that policymakers should make the extra effort to design an appropriate tax system, and should consider the possible adverse effects that a change might have on financial market development on a par with the revenue implications. For a balanced decision, close dialogue between tax and financial authorities is essential. A decision driven mainly by a myopic revenue objective is likely to unduly repress financial market development, including the market for government securities.

The taxation of earnings on government securities and any capital gains derived from transactions of government securities will influence savings and investment decisions in general, and, in turn, affect the development of the government securities market. An appropriate taxation system for interest earnings and capital income on government securities should be based on the three fundamental tax principles: tax neutrality, simplicity, and fairness. A tax system should collect tax revenue from interest earnings and capital income from government securities with the least distortions possible on the savings decisions of taxpayers. Although tax neutrality is a laudable objective, no tax system fully satisfies this principle. In designing a new tax regime or a tax reform strategy, tax authorities should properly assess the country's administrative capability and compliance costs to the public. It is sensible for developing countries to take an evolutionary approach: first, start with a simple tax system that

---

230. Shome and Stotsky (1996) offer a good explanation of adverse effects of transaction taxes.

requires little administrative resources and as the institutional infrastructure builds up, gradually transform the tax system toward a more sophisticated and neutral tax regime.

Finally, to achieve better efficiency and equity in taxation of interest earnings and capital income from government securities, two tax measures—favorable tax treatment of government securities and imposition of an array of securities transaction taxes—which are established in many countries and tempting to many policymakers, should be critically reviewed. It is difficult to find a convincing theoretical rationale for tax-exempt government securities. Poor institutional frameworks in developing countries could be a practical excuse for tax exemption of interest income altogether. However, so long as minimal tax collecting is feasible, tax authorities should consider introducing a tax system applicable to the earnings on government securities at terms that are comparable to other taxable income sources that can be administered with ease. A withholding tax could be a good stepping stone in this regard. With regard to securities transaction taxes, there is strong inertia to maintain existing transaction taxes or even attempt to introduce new transaction taxes when financial markets grow fast. However, in order to develop liquid and active government securities markets, governments would be well advised to eliminate securities transaction taxes.

10

Bibliography

Alworth, Julian S. 1998. "Taxation and the Globalization of Financial Markets." In P. Roberti, ed., *Financial Markets and Capital Income Taxation in a Global Economy*. Amsterdam and New York: Elsevier.

Bainton, Lyndsey. 1995. "The New U.K. Tax Regime for Repurchase Agreements." *International Financial Law Review* 14 (9): 43–44.

Bargella, M., and Laura Castellucci. 1998. "Capital Movements, Real Interest Differentials, and Taxation: Theoretical Issues and Recent Developments in Italy (1982–1994)." In P. Roberti, ed., *Financial Markets and Capital Income Taxation in a Global Economy*. Amsterdam and New York: Elsevier.

Burman, Leonard E. 1999. *The Labyrinth of Capital Gains Tax Policy: A Guide for the Perplexed*. Washington, D.C.: The Brookings Institution Press.

Casson, Peter C. 1998. "International Aspects of the U.K. Imputation System of Corporate Taxation." *British Tax Review* 5: 493–507.

Catalyst Institute. 1995. *Securities Transaction Taxes: False Hopes and Unintended Consequences*. Suzanne Hammond, ed. Burr Ridge, Illinois: Irwin.

Chua, Dale. 1995. "Tax Incentives." In P. Shome, ed., *Tax Policy Handbook*. International Monetary Fund, Washington, D.C.

Cnossen, Sijbren. 2000. *Taxing Capital Income in the European Union: Issues and Options for Reform*. Oxford and New York: Oxford University Press.

Davis, E. P. 1995. *Pension Funds*. Oxford and New York: Oxford University Press.

Dilnot, Andrew. 1992. "Taxation and Private Pensions: Costs and Consequences." In *Private Pensions and Public Policy*. Organization for Economic Cooperation and Development, Paris, France.

Downes, John, and Jordan Elliot Goodman. 1998. *Dictionary of Finance and Investment Terms* (5th ed.). Hauppaug, N.Y.: Barron's Educational Series, Inc.

Financial Times. 1997. "Repos and Strips." Financial Times Survey, Supplement (December 5), 1–6.

Gravelle, Jane G. 1994. *The Economic Effects of Taxing Capital Income*. Cambridge, Mass.: MIT Press.

Harris, Peter A. 1997. "Neutralizing the Imputation Systems." *Asia-Pacific Tax Bulletin*. Vol. 3 (June).

10

319

Hubbard, R. Glenn. 1995. "Securities Transactions Taxes: Can They Raise Revenue?" In Suzanne Hammond, ed., *Securities Transaction Taxes: False Hopes and Unintended Consequences.* Burr Ridge, Illinois: Irwin.

Institute for Fiscal Studies. 1989. *Neutrality in the Taxation of Savings: An Extended Role for PEPs.*

International Fiscal Association. 1997. "The Taxation of Investment Funds." In *Studies on International Fiscal Law.* 51st Congress of the International Fiscal Association, Vol. 82b.

Kopcke, R. W., and R. C. Kimball. 1999. "Inflation-Indexed Bonds: The Dog that Didn't Bark." *New England Economic Review.* January/February, Federal Reserve Bank of Boston, Boston, Mass. Available at www.bos.frb.org/.

Messere, Ken. 1999. "Half a Century of Changes in Taxation." *Bulletin for International Fiscal Documentation.* 53 (8/9).

Mouy, Stephane, and Edward J. Nalbantian. 1995. "Repurchase Transactions in the Cross-Border Arena." *International Financial Law Review* 14 (3): 15–19.

NBER (National Bureau of Economic Research). 1994. *Public Policies and Household Saving.* James M. Poterba, ed. Chicago and London: University of Chicago Press.

Norregaard, John. 1997. "The Tax Treatment of Government Bonds." *Tax Notes International,* Vol. 15.

OECD (Organization for Economic Cooperation and Development). 1994a. *Taxation and Household Saving.* Paris, France.

———. 1994b. *Taxation of New Financial Instruments.* Paris, France.

———. 1999. *Taxation of New Cross-Border Portfolio Investment: Mutual Funds and Possible Tax Distortions.* Paris, France.

———. 2000a. *Model Tax Convention on Income and on Capital: 2000 Edition.* Paris, France.

———. 2000b. *Model Tax Convention on Income and Capital: Condensed Version, 2000.* Paris, France.

Price, Robert. 1997. "The Rationale and Design of Inflation-Indexed Bonds." IMF Working Paper 97/12. International Monetary Fund, Washington, D.C. Available at www.imf.org.

Plasschaert, Sylvain R. F. 1988. *Schedular, Global and Dualistic Patterns of Income Taxation.* International Bureau of Fiscal Documentation, Amsterdam, the Netherlands.

10

Raffer, K. 1998. "The Tobin Tax: Reviving a Discussion." *World Development* 26 (3).

Shah, Anwar. 1995. *Fiscal Incentives for Investment and Innovation.* Oxford and New York: Oxford University Press.

Shome, P., and Janet G. Stotsky. 1996. "Financial Transactions Taxes." *Tax Notes International.* January.

Spahn, Paul B. 1995. "International Financial Flows and Transaction Taxes: Survey and Options." IMF Working Paper 95/60. International Monetary Fund, Washington, D.C. Available at www.imf.org.

St. Giles, Mark. 1999. *The Taxation of CIFs and Their Investors.* Processed.

Stiglitz, Joseph E. 1989. "Using Tax Policy to Curb Speculative Short-Term Trading." *Journal of Financial Services Research.* December.

Summers, Lawrence H., and Victoria P. Summers. 1989. "When Financial Markets Work Too Well: A Cautious Case for a Securities Transactions Tax." *Journal of Financial Services Research.* December.

Tanzi, Vito. 1980. *Inflation and the Personal Income Tax.* Cambridge, U.K.: Cambridge University Press.

Tanzi, Vito, and John King. 1995. "The Taxation of Financial Assets: A Survey of Issues and Country Experience." IMF Working Paper 95/46. International Monetary Fund, Washington, D.C. Available at www.imf.org.

Tanzi, Vito, and Howell H. Zee. 1998. "Taxation in a Borderless World: The Role of Information Exchange." In B. Wilman, ed., *International Studies in Taxation.* The Hague, the Netherlands: Kluwer Law International.

———. 2000. "Tax Policy for Emerging Markets: Developing Countries." *National Tax Journal.* July.

Tobin, James. 1984. "On the Efficiency of the Financial System." *Lloyds Bank Review.* July.

U.S. Treasury Department. 1992. *Integration of the Individual and Corporate Tax Systems: Taxing Business Income Once.* Washington, D.C.: Government Printing Office.

Zee, Howell H. 1997. "A Note on the Nonneutral Taxation of Indexed Government Bonds Under Alternative Indexation Schemes." *Economic Letters*, Vol. 56.

———. 1998. "Taxation of Financial Capital in a Globalized Environment: The Role of Withholding Taxes." *National Tax Journal* 51.

———. 2000. "Sending Short-Term Capital Inflows Through Withholding Tax." *Tax Notes International.* July.

10

Chapter 11

Development of Subnational Bond Markets

Decentralization of some governmental functions is taking place in many developing and transition countries. Decentralized entities are becoming responsible for undertaking various infrastructure investments required to meet basic needs at the local level, including utilities, water and sanitation, transportation, health and education, and environmental protection. Owing to fiscal constraints at the center, decentralized entities can rely only partly on capital grants from the center to fund these investments. To meet their funding needs, decentralized entities, therefore, need to broaden their own resource base, access subnational bond markets, and increase the efficiency of resource use. In emerging-market countries, these funding needs must be weighed against the prospect that multiple issuers of securities with varying claims to sovereign creditworthiness will fragment a nascent market and thereby reduce its liquidity and efficiency. On the other hand, properly managed subnational bond market can complement the national bond market.

Subnational entities have traditionally had restricted access to capital markets, partly due to central government's concerns on fiscal policy. If subnational entities are limited in their bond market access, they will need greater local resources or national assistance if they are to continue to meet their mandates.

11.1   Introduction

Efficient and well-regulated subnational bond markets are essential for financing local infrastructure investments. When they work well, these markets can be a powerful force for raising resources from savers, pricing subnational credit, and providing diversified financing products tailored to the needs of subnational borrowers. Financing can be through financial intermediation (i.e., through banks) or directly placed debt. However, the issuance of subnational securities in emerging-market countries presents significant challenges to policymakers concerned with bond market development.

Each country's constitutional and political framework and the condition of its financial system determine the feasibility and viability of a market for subnational bonds. The prospects for a market in subnational securities are a function of the degree of decentralization and devolution of government powers, especially regarding taxation. In addition, there are different levels of government (subnational, state or provincial, and municipal agencies), and the suitability of financing alternatives can differ. Furthermore, in many countries, the prerequisites needed for development of a subnational bond market do not exist or suffer from major shortcomings. These deficiencies hamper development of the market for both intermediated and directly placed subnational debt.

The overarching problem of subnational securities issues is that they generate moral hazard, i.e., the expectation by subnational bond issuers and/or market participants that the national government might be prevailed upon to assume the liabilities or the debt-servicing obligations of a distressed subnational borrower. This problem arises as a result of soft budget constraints in the fiscal decentralization system and deficiencies in the public debt framework. The problem of moral hazard is often compounded by lack of market transparency, weakness of market governance, distortions in the competitive framework among market participants, and weak capacity for financial management by subnational entities. An added and fundamental problem in emerging markets is the risk that issuance by subnational entities will fragment the debt market to the disadvantage of all issuers, not least national governments. The extent to which an active market in subsovereign debt is desirable is ultimately a question of whether the benefits of greater decentralization and their financing requirements outweigh the inefficiencies of moral hazard and market fragmentation. Careful

11

management of national and subnational bond market development can mitigate these concerns.

Even in countries where the fundamental prerequisites for subnational debt market development have begun to take hold, significant weaknesses often remain in the framework for developing the subnational bond market. These include weak linkages between development of the national and subnational bond markets, deficiencies in the regulatory and supervisory framework for subnational bond issuance and trading, and weaknesses in the relationships among bond market players and in instruments for credit enhancement and pooling.

This chapter discusses the importance of subnational debt markets in developing and transition countries, introduces some concepts that are useful in understanding subnational debt market development, and examines major policy issues in developing subnational debt markets, including fundamental constraints hampering the development of the market for both intermediated and directly placed subnational bonds. In addition, the chapter discusses the interrelationship of the domestic national and subnational bond markets and the regulatory framework of the subnational bond market. Finally, the chapter reviews the priorities for policy reforms required to strengthening the subnational bond market in developing and transition countries.

11.2 Subnational Bond Markets in Perspective

11.2.1 Importance of Subnational Debt Markets in Developing and Transition Countries

The trend toward decentralization has intensified in many developing and transition countries. In more than 70 countries where the World Bank Group is active, subnational entities—including states, regions, provinces, counties, municipalities, state enterprises, and local utility companies—are becoming responsible for delivering a wide range of local services and investing in local infrastructure. Many of these investments have become necessary as a result of rapid urbanization. However, because of fiscal constraints faced by central governments, many subnational entities can rely only partially on capital grants from the central governments to fund

11

these investments. In addition to improving the efficiency of resources and increasing the participation of the private sector in local services and infrastructure, they need to access bond markets to finance these investments.

The financing needs of subnational entities can be a stimulus for developing both the domestic and subnational debt markets. Subnational debt markets can effectively raise resources from savers, correctly price subnational credit, and efficiently allocate capital among competing subnational investments through diversified financing products tailored to the needs of subnational borrowers. These products can be structured flexibly. They range from instruments secured against the full faith and credit of the subnational entity, to instruments secured through a specific revenue stream, or a combination of both. Subnational debt markets can perform their role through delegated monitoring by financial intermediaries and through direct placement of debt with investors. At the same time, a multiplicity of subnational issues in a country's bond market that is still relatively undeveloped can fragment the market and make the establishment of national issue benchmarks more difficult. (See Chapter 4, Developing Benchmark Issues.)

While sizeable subnational debt markets have begun to emerge in such countries as Argentina and Brazil, where they account for about 5 percent of GDP, they remain embryonic in the vast majority of developing and transition countries. As such, in 1997 the stock of subnational debt in Argentina amounted to US$17 billion ($500 per capita) and $128 billion in Brazil ($800 per capita). In comparison, that of Germany totaled $69 billion ($800 per capita), Japan $322 billion ($2,500 per capita), and the United States $1,063 billion ($4,000 per capita).[231] The contrast is especially striking in the advanced transition countries of Central Europe, where subnational debt markets typically remain below 0.5 percent of GDP, despite considerable progress achieved in financial sector restructuring, privatization, and capital market deepening and diversification, and despite the growing demand for local infrastructure investment in light of possible EU accession. As a result, in many developing and transition countries there is a prospective gap between the rapidly increasing investment financing needs of subnational entities and the capacity of the domestic

231. Subnational debt as a percentage of GDP varies markedly among OECD countries largely as a function of constitutional differences, so that in the United States subnational debt is around 14 percent of GDP, while in the United Kingdom, it is essentially nonexistent.

11

subnational debt market to meet these financing requirements. The emergence of an orderly and efficient subnational debt market can address this potential development constraint.

11.2.2 Agency Problems and Subnational Debt Markets

In most developing and transition countries, subnational debt markets share a common distinguishing feature—a prevalence of agency problems.[232] One manifestation of the agency problem is that of "hidden action" in which subnational borrowers may have an incentive not to repay their lenders.[233] They may believe that they will be bailed out by the central government in case they default, thereby creating a problem of moral hazard. (See Section 11.3.1.) A second agency problem likely to appear is that subnational borrowers may have an incentive not to reveal certain characteristics about themselves to their lenders, resulting in "hidden information" and "adverse selection."[234] The incidence of these agency problems will vary

---

232. When a party, the "agent" is able to take actions on behalf of another, the "principal," agency problems arise where the interests of agent and principal are not aligned and the agent takes actions that the principal would not have chosen. These scenarios relate to subnational financial markets in that the subnational entity often is able to take actions that will have consequences for the national government.

233. "Hidden action" describes a situation whereby a party believes it will derive greater benefit from a given action if this action remains unknown. For example, if two countries agree not to pollute a shared lake, the willingness to continue to cooperate is a function of the performance of the other party. However, to the extent to which pollution has taken place does not become apparent until later, the reneging country that pollutes therefore benefits from this hidden action. In the case of subnational debt, hidden action describes the incentive a local authority has to incur greater indebtedness than recognized by the national government. As the national government typically picks up the debt of defaulting local governments, this is said to lead to moral hazard, a situation in which participants do not have to pay for the consequences of their actions.

234. The problem of hidden information occurs where a party believes it will receive better treatment if certain information is not disclosed. A classic example would be a person with a terminal illness who applies for life insurance and withholds information about his condition. If the life insurance company cannot distinguish who has ill health, the result is that the less healthy people, who know their own state, are more willing to buy life insurance. As a consequence, the insured population results in being less healthy than the population in general ("hidden selection"), which eventually will show up in the cost (premiums) of life insurance.

11

considerably depending on the structure of the subnational debt market in different countries.

At one end of the spectrum are countries with subnational debt markets in which the central government combines the functions of allocating capital grants and credit to subnational entities. Such centralized allocations are subject to conversion risk, which arises when these entities use part of the grant for purposes other than those intended. This risk is heightened when the central government has an inadequate monitoring mechanism. Centralized grant and credit allocations also are subject to inefficiencies in the use of funds, which result from the lack of incentives for the subnational entity to use its best efforts when undertaking a project, from imperfect information at the center about the local conditions where funds are allocated, and from the lack of a credible threat of no future financing.

At the other end of the spectrum are countries where decentralization is accompanied with a high degree of self-government and policy and project implementation on the part of the subnational entity. In these countries, the central government concentrates on capital grant allocation to subnational entities for projects for which private financial intermediaries and investors also provide financing, and loans to these entities compete with those from the private sector without an explicit or implicit guarantee for repayment from the central government. This market structure is still subject to the same conversion risk mentioned above, but the likelihood of inefficiencies in the use of funds inherent in the centralized allocation system is reduced because the decentralized credit system makes the threat of no future financing more credible. The decentralized structure also allows the central government to concentrate its resources on strengthening the efficiency of the grant allocation system by applying clear economic allocation criteria for grants and through effective monitoring and incentive systems for implementation of investment projects by subnational entities.

In the middle of the spectrum are countries with intermediate market structures. For such countries, the presence of multiple channels for grant allocation and for lending, both within the central government and among specialized agencies and state-owned financial intermediaries, amplifies the agency problems encountered in a centralized market structure. This results in multiple principal and multiple agent problems, and in implicit or explicit central government guarantees, which increase the risks of moral hazard and adverse selection. Additional agency problems may arise between state-owned financial intermediaries and private financial

11

institutions, particularly in an environment where state-owned financial intermediaries are protected by special regulatory provisions or fiscal privileges that result in a non-level market playing field.

11.3 Developing Subnational Debt Markets: Policy Issues

11.3.1 Moral Hazard

A major concern about the issuance of securities by subnational units is that they often lead to expectations that the central government might assume the liabilities or debt-servicing obligations of a distressed subnational borrower, thereby resulting in a moral hazard problem. Moral hazard in the subnational finance market has two fundamental sources—ex ante and ex post. Ex ante, moral hazard may stem from soft budget constraints in the system of fiscal decentralization, in the public debt framework, and in the financial sector itself. If a subnational entity defaults on a debt obligation, moral hazard arises through expectation of a bailout, or, indirectly, through expectation of intervention by the central government. Ex post, moral hazard may come from the modalities of actual intervention by the central government, in case of subnational entity default or in case of arrears on a nondebt fiscal obligation. In both cases, the way the central government structures its intervention, in terms of conditionality and of actual losses imposed on the parties concerned, determines the extent of a bailout or the degree to which moral hazard is increased as a result of intervention.

Another critical issue is the central government's political determination to stand aside when a subnational government defaults on its debts, or to impose a real cost on the subnational authorities as the price of government assistance. Ultimately, however, political constraints may limit the central government's willingness to impose the hardships of bankruptcy on the citizens of a subnational unit who form part of the national electorate.

In addition, to the extent that there is no assurance that the central government will assume the debt obligations of a subnational entity, the creditworthiness status that surrounds such debt obligations has implications for the development of subnational bond markets. If market participants are convinced that the central government will bail out a subnational entity,

11

and in a sense regard subnational bonds to carry an implicit central government guarantee, the attractiveness of subnational bond issues will be enhanced. On the other hand, if market participants have doubts about the central government's response in case of a subnational entity's inability to meet its debt obligations, it will make subnational bond issues a less appealing financial asset, thereby impeding the development of subnational bond markets. The ability of market participants to assess the likelihood of the central government's response to a subnational entity's debt-servicing difficulties for different subnational bond issues will determine as well the prospects of subnational markets to take hold.

The financial circumstances of subnational entities and the financial and political relationship between the central government and subnational units contribute to moral hazard in several ways. The limitations of fiscal autonomy of subnational bodies, the nature of the intergovernmental transfer system, and the character of the financial sector of subnational entities are the principal factors that lead to moral hazard.

The first channel of moral hazard within the fiscal decentralization system originates from limitations to the fiscal autonomy of subnational entities. On the expenditure side, these limitations pertain to mandated expenditures, such as civil servant salaries, or to regulations that limit the ability of subnational entities to adjust costs. A large share of local expenditures not being under the effective control of subnational entities generates moral hazard because it creates the expectation that the central government will intervene to support these mandated expenditures in case of an economic downturn. On the revenue side, these limitations originate from the small revenue base of subnational entities derived from subnational-collected taxes and fees, or from regulations limiting the ability of subnational entities to modify their tax bases and/or rates. A fiscal decentralization system in which local authorities have the authority to borrow independently, but have limited own revenues, encourages subnational borrowers to contract debt obligations against the anticipation of general transfers from the central government, thereby escaping the need to broaden their own revenue base to meet debt-service payments.

The second source of moral hazard originates from specific components of the intergovernmental transfer system, viz., deficit grants, capital grants, and transfer intercept arrangements.

Deficit grants are allocated by the central government to local governments facing an unexpected deficit "through no fault of their own." In theory, these grants will not generate moral hazard if their allocation rules are rational, transparent, and strictly respected by the authorities. In practice, allocation rules for deficit grants lack transparency and contribute to a softening of their budget constraint.

Capital grants may also be a source of moral hazard, depending on the type of grant concerned and on its implementation. To the extent that there are deficiencies in the monitoring system for these grants, subnational authorities may have an incentive to use the grant proceeds for purposes other than those intended by the central government. The likelihood of such diversions is intensified in cases where there is no distinction between capital and recurrent expenditures in subnational budgets, as is often the case in developing and transition countries.

Transfer intercepts are arrangements under which subnational borrowings are serviced directly by the central government, or under which a lender can seek payment from the central government for an overdue obligation by a subnational borrower. In both cases, payment by the central government to the lender is deducted from the transfer payment made to the subnational entity. These arrangements are appealing to lenders because they provide security for their loans to subnational entities. They also have shortcomings. In the presence of an intercept, lenders may relax their credit criteria and monitoring of subnational borrowers. If a large subnational entity defaults, the central government will be under strong political pressure not to apply the intercept, because the contraction of local services resulting from the intercept would be politically unbearable. However, if the central government suspends application of the intercept or applies it only partially, the credibility of the intercept system is damaged.

Specific types of fiscal or quasi-fiscal obligations of subnational entities to politically powerful constituencies, as in the case of pensions or social security payments, may also generate moral hazard. To the extent that subnational entities expect that arrears incurred on these politically sensitive obligations will eventually be covered by the central government, budget constraint is softened.

The absence of legislation stating unequivocally that subnational debt is not guaranteed by the central government, with possible exceptions to be approved on a case-by-case basis by the central government or by the legislature, is another source of moral hazard. Subnational entities and their lenders may be led to assume that the central government implicitly guarantees subnational liabilities. A bailout expectation is further reinforced by

11

absence of a clear framework for subnational bankruptcy. Even an explicit disavowal of central government support or the presence of subnational bankruptcy legislation may be insufficient to protect against moral hazard, if political pressure builds for the central government to provide support.

A third channel of moral hazard with the fiscal decentralization system is the financial sector channel. The existing guidelines for calculating bank capital, prepared by the Basel Committee on Banking Supervision (BCBS), imply a sovereign guarantee for subnational debt and, therefore, contribute to moral hazard. Under the existing International Convergence of Capital Measurement and Capital Standards issued in July 1988, national regulators allowed discretion as to the risk weightings to be attached to obligations of subnational entities held by banks under their supervision. According to these guidelines, a risk weighting of 0, 10, 20, or 50 percent can be applied for obligations of subnational entities issued in domestic currency. These percentage weightings reflect the amount of capital that a bank must hold for each such obligation relative to the capital that would be held for a corporate debt obligation. No adjustments are made to accommodate credit-worthiness, maturity, or other risk factors. As such, banks have a strong incentive to lend to subnational entities rather than to corporates.[235] By requiring a lower capital ratio for subnational debt versus corporate debt of a similar creditworthiness, the BCBS standard implicitly suggests that some other form of credit support (i.e., that of the national government) will be made available, thereby rendering the subnational obligations less risky than their inherent creditworthiness would suggest.

Hidden financing schemes, such as Treasury credit lines or specialized state agency credit lines that provide financing to subnational entities at subsidized rates, also contribute to moral hazard. Credit may be subsidized through recurrent budget subsidies and/or through blending of capital grants and loans, the latter originating mostly from international financial institutions. Because these subsidized lines are managed by a central government ministry or by one of it agencies, they are directly vulnerable to

---

235. According to the more recent BCBS proposal, The New Basel Capital Accord, January 2001, this discrepancy would be removed but not entirely eliminated. Under the new proposals subnational obligations rated less than A- would require a capital allocation of one-half to two-thirds that allocated to similarly rated corporate credits. In general, however, there is a closer association of creditworthiness and capital requirements.

pressure from large and politically powerful subnational entities or from powerful coalitions of municipalities. In many cases, repayment of these credit lines is poor because expectation of a bailout by the central government generates a culture of nonrepayment.

Lenders facing the threat of default by a large subnational entity, or of collective default by a group of municipalities, may exert pressure on the central government to intervene whether or not there is an explicit central government guarantee. In the case of external debt, pressure can include a fear that sovereign foreign debt will be downgraded if the central government fails to take over and service the subnational debt in default.[236]

Additional moral hazard can be generated ex post in the subnational finance market as a result of the modalities of central government intervention in cases of subnational default. For any given set of ex-ante incentives for market participants, additional moral hazard will be generated if these incentives succeed in pressuring the central government to provide support beyond what is stipulated in the legal and regulatory framework. The assumption of a subnational quasi-fiscal obligation by the central government can generate additional moral hazard on the subnational finance market if it is done without imposing a cost on the subnational entity. The transfer of provincial pension systems from the federal government to several provinces in Argentina in 1994 is a good illustration of the importance of specific types of government interventions in dealing with moral hazard. Argentina is the most decentralized country in Latin America, with 50 percent of public spending at the subnational level. However, the bulk of taxation is collected nationally, creating an imbalance that is met by giving provincial governments a "coparticipation" in certain tax revenues that cover, on average, 65 percent of provincial spending. Until 1994, all provinces administered pension schemes covering employees of the province and provincial entities. However, the economic downturn

11

---

236. This risk became vividly clear in Brazil in early January 1998, when, Itamar Franco, the newly elected Governor of the state of Minas Gerais and President Cardoso's predecessor, declared a moratorium on his state's US$5 billion debt to the federal government. Two other important states, Rio Grande do Sul and Rio de Janeiro, also declared moratoria. The action of the states served to undermine Brazil's position in international financial markets, and there was a marked flight of capital. Minas Gerias had a US$80 million Eurobond repayment due February 10, 1998, and the moratorium put this payment in doubt. The federal government paid the international obligation of Minas Gerais to maintain Brazil's market credibility.

following the Tequila Crisis of 1994–95 rendered many provinces unable to pay pensions and, due to the tax-sharing system, unable to generate additional revenues. As a consequence, it became necessary for the national government to assume the pension obligations.[237]

11.3.2 Fundamental Constraints in Developing Subnational Bond Markets

Weakness of the local government budgeting, accounting, and auditing framework undermines the quality and reliability of information available to the subnational finance market, thereby inhibiting the development of subnational bond markets. There may, for example, be a lack of distinction between current and capital expenditures in local government budgets. Without this distinction, it is impossible to ascertain whether long-term borrowings by subnational entities are for investment purposes only and whether the effectiveness of prudential rules for local government borrowing is undermined. In addition, multiyear budgeting is often absent at the subnational level.

An additional major shortcoming of subnational entities is an inadequate accounting and risk management framework for asset-liability management. Such a framework is necessary to enable informed judgments about the appropriate currency, interest rate, maturity, and structure of local government borrowings. (See Box 3.1. in Chapter 3.) Furthermore, local governments typically have limited knowledge of their assets, in terms of both ownership and valuation, which limits the feasibility of issuing securitized debt instruments.

Auditing budgets of subnational entities is often the weakest element in the budgetary framework. Local government budget audits are usually a responsibility of the central government's audit office, but the quality and frequency of these audits are generally low. To overcome these problems, some governments are moving to private sector audits of local government budgets, but broad coverage is often constrained by the limited development of the domestic auditing industry.

Another area of inefficiency may be hidden Treasury or special agency lines of credit, which often have a dominant role in the subnational finance market. This dominant position may be backed up by specific regulations,

---

237. See Nicolini et al. 1999.

such as rules restricting subnational entities to borrowing from the Treasury/agency line, or rules prohibiting them from borrowing from commercial banks. Such provisions undermine the emergence of a private subnational debt market. Treasury and/or agency lines may allocate credits to subnational investments at subsidized rates that do not reflect the underlying subnational credit risk. This distorts resource allocation among competing subnational investments and displaces private sector finance for subnational investments.

Transparency and reliable information are also essential for establishing a broad investor base for subnational bonds and for making pricing decisions for subnational issues. The information should include the financial condition of the subnational issuing entity, the intended use of the proceeds of the bond issue, the revenue sources for servicing the bonds, and the nature of any guarantees by the central government.

11.4 Linkages Between Government Securities Markets and Subnational Bond Market Development

11.4.1 Relationship Between the Domestic Government Bond Market and the Subnational Bond Market Development

The government securities market is the foundation for other components of the domestic debt market. In the private sector bond market, most market participants construct yield curves from observations of prices and yields in the government bond market. (See Chapter 4, developing Benchmark Issues, and Chapter 12, Linkages Between Government and Private Sector Bond Markets.) Government bonds have traditionally been considered default free, and the government bond market generally offers the most liquid and active trading environment.[238]

---

238. The assumption that government bonds in developing and transition countries are default free has been called into question since the Russian government bond default in August 1998 and the emerging practice of integrating government bonds into debt-restructuring agreements, as occurred with Ecuador in 1999.

Since subnational bonds carry a greater element of credit risk, and thus a commensurate higher yield, an appropriate comparison is probably with the private sector bond market.

The national government bond market's benchmark role can become less important as the subnational bond market gains in depth and diversity, or if tax or regulatory considerations play an important role in determining yield. Over time, prime-rated subnational issues may even become the dominant points of reference for establishing a yield curve for particular subnational issuers. Thus a subnational bond market may develop relatively independently of the evolution of the national bond market. For such an orderly outcome, development of both bond markets must be well managed.

Subnational bonds are likely to be smaller in size and less frequent than those issued by the national government and, therefore, less liquid. Subnational bond issues, thus, are likely to be more attractive for long-term investment purposes than short-term liquidity.

It is generally preferable that the payment and settlement of subnational issues become part of a broad system that covers private sector securities rather than be linked with an exclusive facility for government securities. While a dematerialized delivery versus payment system is invariably to be preferred for all securities settlement (preferably offering real time gross settlement),[239] the more practical solution is that the settlement system should be commensurate with the breadth and requirements of the investor base, taking into account the characteristics of the financial instruments. Thus, a market with many institutional investors, with diverse investment objectives, and large issues with a high-credit standing warrants a sophisticated payment and settlement system. However, such an

11

---

239. In a dematerialized settlement system, investors deposit their securities with one or more common depositories, and the depository becomes the owner of record. Subsequent security trades are then recorded as transfers in the investors' accounts with the depository. This lowers transaction costs and increases security. Delivery versus payment describes a settlement process whereby securities are transferred against receipt of cash, frequently through a dematerialized settlement system. Real-time gross settlement refers to a process whereby the seller receives payment at the exact time the trade settles so that the buyer must have funds available for each purchase (see Chapter 8, Developing a Government Securities Settlement Structure).

advanced arrangement might not be worthwhile or appropriate for small issues of lower-credit standing, for a more limited number of investors, or if the investors are homogenous.

11.4.2 Role of the Subnational Bond Market in Diversification of the Domestic Fixed-Income Market

Beyond the basic general obligation bonds issued against the full faith and credit of the issuer, the subnational bond market may provide a wide range of dedicated revenue bonds issued for project or enterprise financing and secured by revenues generated from operations of the subnational entity.[240] In most developing and transition countries, general obligation bonds still largely dominate subnational bond markets, and revenue bond and structured bond financing is emerging slowly.[241] As markets develop, however, local governments tend to diversify their borrowing instruments and rely more on revenue bonds. This diversification has been observed in several Latin American countries, as subnational entities reentered the national bond market in the wake of stabilization programs following the 1994–95 Mexico crisis. The change from general obligation to revenue bonds in these countries also met the demand from institutional investors for additional security in purchasing subnational bonds.[242]

---

240. In the United States, the municipal bond market is characterized by a wide array of internal and external credit enhancement structures, including refunded bonds (which are bonds that have been refinanced with an amount invested in government bonds held in escrow to meet all remaining payments), insured bonds (where an insurance company such as the Financial Guaranty Insurance Corporation [FGIC] or the Financial Security Assurance [FSA] guarantees the principal and interest on the bonds), and bonds backed by letters of credit or other forms of credit enhancement from banks.

241. A "structured bond" is a generic term referring to any obligation other than a conventional general obligation bond. Structured bonds include asset-backed or insured obligations, revenue bonds and other forms of limited recourse financing, and bonds incorporating derivatives. The term "structured" implies that the instrument encompasses a degree of "financial engineering."

242. See Darche, Freire, and Huertas 1998.

11.5   Issuance of Subnational Bonds

In contrast to government bond issues, which are often issued through an auction arrangement (see Chapter 5, Developing a Primary Market for Government Securities), auctions are used to sell subnational bonds only in a few countries. In India, for example, subnational bonds are sold alongside national government securities by the central bank, and are purchased in the first instance by primary dealers, commercial banks, and other participants in government securities auctions. The subnational bonds are then settled like other government bonds through the central bank clearing and settlement systems.

More typically, however, bonds issued by subnational entities follow the practices of the corporate (or Eurobond) fixed-income markets. Such issues take the form of public issues or private placements. In the former, bonds are sold to a wide range of investors, usually by a syndicate of several underwriters. In a private placement, the bonds are sold to a very limited number of investors by only one investment bank.

While individual circumstances vary, in a public issue it is more common for the issuer to be underwritten so that the issuer is guaranteed that a given amount of bonds will be sold at a given interest rate or at a given margin over a reference rate. This process can follow a competitive bid process, where a number of banks or syndicates of banks acting together are requested to give their best price (or yield) for a given amount of bonds, with the mandate to carry out the financing being awarded to the bank that guarantees the best terms. The situation whereby the final terms of an offering are determined before coming to market is also known as a "bought deal." Alternatively, a public offer may be in the form of a negotiated sale where the issuer chooses the underwriter(s) first and subsequently agrees to the terms of the bond. In a negotiated sale, the underwriter(s) may also purchase the bonds as a bought deal or may follow a book-building exercise whereby the investment bank(s) launch the issue and publicly take soundings from potential investors as to pricing. In a private placement the transaction may also take the form of a bought deal or may be on a best efforts basis whereby the investment bank is only required to purchase bonds to the extent that investors have been identified.

For both public and private issues, the subnational borrowing entity (for example, a municipality) may or may not make use of the services of a financial advisor. The financial advisor is typically an investment bank familiar with the securities markets, which, instead of buying bonds from the issuer, acts as an advisor to ensure that the terms and conditions offered by the underwriting banks are the best that could be obtained in the circumstances. The financial advisor will guide the issuer as to market conditions, the level of interest rate the borrower should expect to pay (the coupon), and the optimal bond maturity to meet investor demand. For more complex bond issues, the financial advisor may enter into details of the bond structure. The financial advisor may help the issuer select underwriters and also assist the issuer in the preparation of the bond documentation. However, the primary responsibility for documentation is assumed by the "Bond Counsel" lawyers retained by the issuer to prepare the documentation that generally consists of an underwriting and selling agreement, which determines the agreement between the issuer and the underwriter, an offering circular (or prospectus), which represents the basic terms of the transaction to potential investors, financial information on the issuer, and the trust indenture (or fiscal agency agreement), which contains the obligations of the issuer and the legal rights of investors and determines the processes through which investors can exercise their rights and the issuer communicates with investors, invariably through a trustee or fiscal agent.

Practices vary between countries, but typically a bond issue by a subnational issuer will close one to two weeks after the launch date. The launch date is the date the offering circular is provided to the investors, and the closing date is the date the issuer receives the funds.[243] The payment to the issuer is made by the underwriting syndicate against delivery of the physical securities, typically represented by a temporary global note, which is later exchanged for definitive securities. The securities are delivered to a depository system (such as the Depository Trust Company in the United States), and all payments are channeled through this system. The bonds may or may not be listed on a stock exchange. However, the listing does not mean that the bonds will necessarily trade on that exchange. The listing merely represents that certain standards of disclosure have been met.

11

---

243. The practices for public offerings and private placements, whether best efforts or bought deals, are essentially the same. A private placement may or may not be listed.

11.6 Development of the Secondary Subnational Bond Market

As an initial step in secondary subnational bond market development, subnational entities may issue bonds to banks, and the banks may decide to keep these bonds on their books and treat them as a de facto loan. Subsequently, banks and other underwriters may opt for private placements of such bonds with selected domestic investors, such as pension funds, insurance companies, or mutual funds. A market in subnational bonds then emerges, as rated subnational entities opt for a public placement and institutional investors may decide to trade the subnational bonds held in their portfolios.

A range of direct and indirect measures can support development of secondary markets for subnational bonds. In terms of direct measures, some countries are exploring ways to facilitate the listing of subnational bonds on domestic stock exchanges and to encourage the development of pre-indication posting of indicative price information (including coupons, yields, offer amounts) or other municipal finance information systems.[244]

To promote secondary market trading of subnational bonds, several indirect measures can be taken. Removing minimum requirements for institutional investors to hold government securities, including subnational bonds, eliminates the bias toward private placement inherent in the system and increases the incentives for institutional investors to trade such bonds. (See Chapter 6, Developing the Investor Base for Government Securities.) These techniques, however, increase issuance costs and may also increase debt-servicing costs.[245] Such measures also increase the risks of the portfolio. (See Chapter 3, A Government Debt Issuance Strategy and Debt Management Framework.)

---

244. Such systems (e.g., Blue List and Munifax) are used in the United States to support placement and sale of subnational bonds. Indonesia and Poland have given particular attention to rules for listing bonds on their stock exchanges, but any impact on secondary markets in these countries is not yet apparent. See Leigland 1997.

245. See Leigland 1997.

11.7 Regulatory and Supervisory, Legal, and Tax Framework for Subnational Bond Market

11.7.1 Regulatory and Supervisory Framework for Subnational Bond Market

The basic regulation for subnational bond markets is the securities law. Since subnational entities compete directly with corporations for scarce resources, the regulations pertaining to issuance, initial and continuing disclosure, and settlement that are applicable to private sector securities should apply to subnational issues. (See Chapter 12, Linkages Between Government and Private Sector Bond Markets.)

Ultimate supervisory authority for the subnational bond market should rest with the securities market regulator. The market regulator may be modeled as a self-standing body, such as the Securities and Exchange Commission (SEC) in the United States, or as a specific department within a banking and capital markets supervisory agency, such as the Financial Services Authority (FSA) in the United Kingdom. Given the high fixed costs of establishing an effective regulatory and supervisory capacity, centralized market supervision[246] would seem appropriate for developing and transition countries that have nascent subnational bond markets. As the regulatory and supervisory framework for the subnational bond market gains strength and as the market reaches a certain volume of transactions, the authorities may consider supplementing centralized supervision with self-regulation among market participants. One option is to establish a self-regulatory body, such as the Municipal Securities Rulemaking Board (MSRB), that regulates the municipal bond market in the United States. This self-regulatory organization is subject to oversight by the SEC and is comprised of representatives from the municipal bond industry, the public, and government agencies. It provides guidelines for the preparation, sale, disclosure, and secondary trading of municipal bonds. The MSRB has

---

246. Centralized market supervision is supervision by a statutory body with purview over a broad range of financial activities and instruments, such as fixed-income and equity markets, derivatives, and futures.

authority to make rules regulating the municipal securities activities of banks and securities firms only. It does not have authority over issuers of municipal securities.[247] Another option is to delegate self-regulatory activities to other players in the market, such as commercial banks or trust organizations.

11.7.2　Legal Framework for the Subnational Bond Market

All provisions of the commercial code establishing the rights and obligations of creditors and borrowers in the financial market should apply to the subnational bond market. Similarly, the judicial framework for the enforcement of creditors' and borrowers' rights and obligations, and for the settlement of commercial disputes, should also pertain fully to subnational bond market participants. Some investors and financial intermediaries may be reluctant to enter the subnational bond market because they fear that their rights will not be protected and that they will not be able to rely on the judicial system in case of commercial dispute with a subnational entity. Enforcing foreclosure on local government assets pledged as collateral and enforcing covenants on local government revenue collateral are particular areas of concern.

Market governance also suffers from lack of a subnational bankruptcy framework, which can help clarify the rights and obligations of creditors and borrowers in case of default. Several countries have attempted to rectify this shortcoming by introducing a Chapter 9–type procedure[248] to regulate debt clearance in case of default by a subnational entity.[249] However,

---

247. Another informal association, the Government Accounting Standards Board (GASB), promulgates voluntary accounting standards. Neither the MSRB nor the GASB have the legal authority to mandate changes in management of the municipal bond market. This function remains under the authority of the SEC.

248. Chapter 9 of the United States Bankruptcy Code refers to the bankruptcy of municipalities. The application and interpretation of this law has been fraught with difficulties, including conflicts with the 10th amendment to the U.S. Constitution (which establishes state sovereignty) and disagreements over the definition of municipality.

249. One example is Hungary, which introduced such a bankruptcy law in 1995. Since the law was introduced, eight small cities have gone through the procedure and are now in stable financial condition.

local government bankruptcy legislation is not a panacea. Its effectiveness depends on the degree of independence of the judicial body responsible for triggering the debt clearance procedure and overseeing its implementation, and the independence of the court-appointed public officer responsible for conducting the procedure. Legislation of this type does not address the fundamental agency problems of moral hazard noted in Section 11.3.1 above, and in all countries the application has been limited to minor entities unable to exercise leverage at a higher level of government.[250]

11.7.3 Tax Treatment of Subnational Bonds

In the United States, interest earned from municipal bonds is exempt from federal interest income tax, but such exemption is subject to criticism. Tax exemption narrows the market for subnational bonds and could increase bond yield volatility. It makes bond yields more sensitive to changes in the distribution of investable funds between individuals and financial institutions. It also introduces variability in the value of the capital-cost subsidy enjoyed by municipalities. Tax exemption is economically inefficient, in that it encourages overproduction of public services and overuse of capital by the public sector. In addition, tax exemption is inequitable, because it erodes the vertical equity in the tax system by allowing the high-income group to benefit from a special tax feature that is not of value to the lower-income group. Tax exemption is also financially inefficient, because it imposes greater costs on federal taxpayers than the benefits it confers to state and local governments. Empirical evidence from the U.S. market tends to support this latter claim. For example, in fiscal year 1990, savings from tax exemption for state and local governments were estimated at $17 billion, while the revenue cost to the Treasury was estimated at $22 billion.[251] (For a broader discussion of taxation issues related to bond markets, see Chapter 10, Development of Government Securities Market and Tax Policy.)

11

---

250. U.S. cities, such as Philadelphia and New York, have received support from the state rather than the national government.

251. See Fortune 1991.

11.8   Credit Enhancement and Credit Pooling in Subnational Bond Markets

11.8.1   Credit Enhancement for Subnational Bond Market

In addition to playing a central role in the issuance of subnational bonds, financial advisors can play a major role in helping subnational entities access the market. (See Section 11.5 above.) The Bond Counsel of the subnational entity also plays a central role in ascertaining an issuer's authority to issue bonds, raise taxes or fees, and attach collateral.

A credit-rating agency can also be important in establishing the credit standing of a subnational borrower. On domestic markets, rating regulations vary across countries.[252] The credit-rating process may also influence subnational entities' policies directly, as officials may avoid certain policies that might lower the entity's credit rating in the future. Some countries have laws that require a subnational entity that issues a bond on the international market to obtain an international credit rating.

In addition to tax exempting interest earnings from municipal bond holdings (see Section 11.7.3 above), governments have adopted several other measures to make subnational bonds attractive to investors. Refunded bonds are one such technique. Refunded bonds are bonds originally issued as general obligation or revenue bonds, but subsequently collateralized, either by direct obligations guaranteed by the central government or by other types of securities. Maturity schedules of securities in an escrow fund are structured to pay bond principal, interest, and any premiums on a refunded bond.

Bond insurance is another credit enhancement method that can play a major role in deepening the market for subnational debt issues in developing and transition countries.[253] This process is superficially attractive in that

---

252. In Colombia, ratings from nationally recognized credit-rating agencies are required for regulatory purposes, while in Argentina ratings are voluntary and are used as a disclosure gesture. In Hungary, ratings from domestic rating agencies are required for public issues but not for private placements on the domestic market.

253. This practice has been particularly common in the United States, where monoline insurance companies, such as AMBAC (American Municipal Bond Assurance Corporation), FGIC, and FSA, have specialized in guaranteeing municipal debt issues, complementing the credit support provided by commercial banks through letters of credit.

11

sophisticated financial institutions can assume the responsibility of reviewing the complex and opaque financial condition of a subnational borrower and convert a weak investment-grade credit into a higher-grade offering. Bond insurance can be particularly important for large bond issuers or less than high-quality bond issuers that need to raise money in weak market environments. It can be also be attractive for lower-quality bonds, bonds issued by smaller subnational units not widely known in the financial community, bonds that have a sound but complex security structure, and bonds issued by subnational entities that borrow infrequently and do not have a general following among investors. The improvement in marketability gained by bond insurance can provide a net interest cost saving to the issuer or access to the market.

However, the issuance of bonds through the use of credit enhancement is relatively inefficient in comparison with direct intermediation by a financial institution, such as a bank, insurance company, or pension fund, acting as an investor. Credit-enhanced bond issues can only be competitive in cases, as in the United States, when there is a tax (or regulatory) constraint that impedes direct lending by sophisticated financial institutions. Moreover, in practice, the use of bond insurance has not always overcome the problems of moral hazard.[254]

Over the past two decades, bond insurance has been supplemented by other forms of credit enhancements provided by banks, such as irrevocable lines of credit.[255] Other types of less formal credit support can also be arranged, such as a put option requiring the counterpart to purchase a bond under predetermined circumstances. These kinds of third-party guarantees can be purchased from banks in a large number of transition countries. In addition, a growing number of international companies that provide credit guarantees have been created by private investors and international financial institutions and are open to providing guarantees for bond issuance by subnational entities.

---

254. For example, during the financial difficulties of Philadelphia, bond insurers are understood to have played a major role in encouraging the intervention by the state of Pennsylvania.

255. An irrevocable letter of credit is a form of guarantee provided by a bank that is provided to the trustee for a bond issue so that the bank is required to pay principal and/or interest in the event that the issuer should fail to do so. Such an instrument is termed "irrevocable" if the bank is obliged to make such payments regardless of the financial condition of the issuer.

11.8.2 Bond Pooling by Subnational Entities

Despite the development of bond insurance and other forms of credit enhancement, market access remains limited for subnational entities with poor credit ratings or limited credit experience and for small issuers. Since the early 1970s, state bond bank initiatives have emerged in the United States as a possible way to address this problem. A bond bank is a conduit financial institution that issues a bond on the market equal to the sum of the individual issues plus a reserve fund, and uses the proceeds to purchase the bonds issued by participating subnational units. It is similar to a municipal development fund (MDF), but typically relies on market-based financing through debt issues. The primary security for the bank issue is the subnational entity's pledge to repay principal and interest on its share of the debt issued, which can take the form of a full faith general obligation or a dedicated revenue pledge. State bond banks review the applications of individual subnational entities until sufficient credit demands have been made to warrant a bond issue. Although most bond banks are self-supporting operations that do not receive direct state appropriations or the state's full faith and credit backing, many are secured by a moral obligation. Giving the bond bank the right to intercept state transfers to the subnational unit in case of default may provide additional security. Credit-rating agencies consider the state to be the ultimate source of debt repayment for bond bank issues. In the absence of state support, rating agencies have tended to rate the debt issues of bond pools according to the lowest credit supporting the cash flows, thereby eliminating any benefits of pooling.

Bond banks suffer from several limitations. Since the bank acts as a conduit for subnational issuers to access national credit markets, a permanent funding pool is not created. A moral obligation pledge by the state and/or the establishment of an intercept right may create the expectation of a bailout by the state and could be a moral hazard for the subnational finance system.

11

11.9 Priorities for Policy Reform for Subnational Bond Market Development

11.9.1 Establishing a Foundation for Subnational Bond Market Development: A Policy Matrix

This section presents a framework for policy reform aimed at establishing prerequisites for subnational bond market development. The framework is presented in the form of a policy matrix. (See Table 11.1.) The vertical axis is organized around the major policy objectives inherent in the development of subnational bond markets in developing and transition countries, while the horizontal axis is organized around types of financial systems, from closed systems (state-dominated financial sectors) to open systems (competitive, diversified market-based financial sectors), with intermediate systems between the two extremes. The policy matrix presents for each policy objective and market structure the principal policy reforms required to establish the foundation for the development of a sound subnational bond market.

11.9.1.1 Reducing Moral Hazard in the Subnational Bond Market

Reducing moral hazard requires hard budget constraints across fiscal decentralization, public debt and intergovernmental transfer, and financial sector channels. Within the fiscal decentralization channel and the associated limitations to the fiscal autonomy of subnational entities, the first priority in a closed system is to unify the capital grant allocation scheme in order to reduce agency problems associated with a multiple grant system. As the market structure opens and evolves into an intermediate system, the key priorities are to establish clear rules for capital grant allocation within the unified system and to introduce a monitoring system to limit diversion of conditional grants into general-purpose expenditures. In parallel with these steps, current transfer systems need to be stabilized by introducing a fixed shared revenue formula and establishing subnational authority over own-source revenue rate setting. As the market structure evolves toward an open system, the government can focus on developing diversified, market-based revenue sources for the subnational entity.

11

Table 11.1. Major Policy Reforms to Develop a Subnational Bond Market
(by policy objective and type of financial system)

Policy Area	Closed System (state-dominated financial sector)	Intermediate System (market-based financial sectors)	Open System
Reducing moral hazard	Establish tight limits on government lending to subnational entities	Establish fixed shared revenue formula	Diversify own-source revenue base
		Establish subnational authority over own-source revenue rate setting (taxes and user fees)	
	Unify capital grant allocation system	Establish explicit rules for capital grants allocation	Limit capital grants to cover cost of externalities that cannot be internalized
		Introduce monitoring system to guard against diversion of capital grants	
	Control quasi-fiscal liabilities of subnational entities	Limit government guarantees for subnational transactions	Integrate guarantees and other contingent liabilities in debt of subnational entities
		Establish provisioning rules for subnational guarantees and contingent liabilities	
		Remove preferential capital adequacy treatment for subnational debt held by banks	
		Control large subnational exposure by domestic financial intermediaries	Progressively relax prudential rules in line with opening of market competition
		Establish prudential framework for borrowing by subnational entities	
Improving market transparency		Introduce separate current and capital accounts in subnational budget	Introduce subnational accrual accounting system
		Establish central/subnational asset designation	Introduce subnational asset valuation

Table 11.1. (Continued) Major Policy Reforms to Develop a Subnational Bond Market
(by policy objective and type of financial system)

Policy Area	Closed System (state-dominated financial sector)	Intermediate System (market-based financial sectors)	Open System
Improving market transparency *continued*		Introduce subnational accrual accounting system	Define treatment of subnational guarantees and other contingent liabilities in concession legislation
		Strengthen subnational auditing	Develop domestic private auditing industry
		Define specific formats for debt disclosure by subnational entities	Review formats for debt disclosure in line with evolution of subnational accounting framework
Strengthening market governance		Ensure equal treatment for subnational entities in commercial code	Introduce subnational bankruptcy law
Establishing level playing field in market	Separate capital grants system and central government-run financing schemes	Phase out central government financing schemes	
		Phase out MDF protective fiscal/regulatory framework	Increase private sector participation in MDFs
		Phase out rediscount window	
Developing subnational capacity for budget, accounting, and financial management	Establish basic cash accounting framework		Develop accrual accounting framework
	Establish basic current/capital budgeting framework	Develop basic capacity for liability management	Develop advanced asset-liability management framework

11

Within the public debt channel, the first priority within a closed system is to establish control over quasi-fiscal liabilities of subnational entities and to introduce limits on central government and/or state agency lending to these entities. As the market structure evolves into an intermediate system, the key priorities are to establish an explicit limitation on sovereign guarantees for subnational transactions, clear provisioning rules for subnational guarantees and other contingent liabilities, and a prudential framework for borrowing by subnational entities. As the system opens further, the government can focus on developing market-based pricing of guarantees and other contingent liabilities, and it can relax prudential rules in line with general hardening of the budget constraint.

Within the financial sector channel, the first priorities within an intermediate system are to remove preferential treatment for subnational debt in calculating capital adequacy, to control large subnational exposures by financial intermediaries, and, where they exist, to phase out rediscount windows for subnational loans by domestic financial intermediaries.[256] Several measures essential to a level playing field are also critical to reducing moral hazard in the market. These include gradually phasing out hidden financing schemes, such as Treasury and/or specialized agency lines of credit, and the protective framework surrounding municipal development funds (see below).

11.9.1.2 Improving Market Transparency

To promote transparency in the subnational bond market, the first priorities are to establish a subnational accounting framework separating current and capital expenditures, a legislative framework clearly designating subnational assets, regular audit of subnational accounts by the state audit office, and procedures and formats for debt and debt-issuance disclosure and registration by local governments. As an open market structure takes hold, the key policy priorities are to strengthen the subnational accounting system through (i) introduction of accrual accounting, in addition to the tradi-

---

256. Subnational bonds are eligible for rediscount facilities at central banks in many countries, including, for example, Argentina, Brazil, and India. These rules, however, are subject to ongoing review.

tional cash accounting system; (ii) introduction of market-based valuation for subnational assets; (iii) regulation of subnational guarantees and other contingent liabilities in concession contracts, and the pricing and accounting of these guarantees in subnational budgets; (iv) establishment of the legal and regulatory foundations for a domestic private auditing industry; and (v) revision of formats for debt disclosure and registration, in line with evolution of the subnational government accounting framework.

11.9.1.3 Strengthening Market Governance

Within intermediate market structures, the main priority is to ensure that the legal framework provides the same protection to creditors in the case of claims against subnational entities as in the case of private corporations under the commercial code. As a competitive market develops, the government should focus on introducing an effective subnational bankruptcy framework, focusing in particular on establishing sufficient distance between competent courts and subnational governments.

11.9.1.4 Establishing a Level Playing Field

Establishing a level playing field for the subnational debt market requires taking measures early on in the process of market development and following them through as the market evolves to an open structure. Within closed structures, the key priority is separating the management of unified capital grant allocation and of central government run financing schemes.

11.9.1.5 Developing Local Capacity for Accounting, Budgeting, and Financial Management

11

Governments should put in place a framework to support development of subnational capacity in accounting, budgeting, and financial management. Initial capacity building efforts should develop liability management at the subnational level. As an open market emerges, further capacity building efforts may focus on advanced asset-liability management techniques and the use of derivative instruments for risk management.

11.9.2 Strengthening Subnational Bond Market Architecture in Developing and Transition Countries

11.9.2.1 Encouraging Synergy Among Various Bond Markets and Within the Subnational Debt Market

While developing the government bond market is rightly seen as essential to establishing a benchmark for the subnational bond market, this relationship tends to become less important as both subnational and private sector debt markets develop. Within the subnational bond market itself, debt issuance by highly rated borrowers increasingly drives development of the market and plays a critical role in setting the reference yield curve for this market. Competition between private sector and subnational debt issuers for scarce investor resources drives the structure of the yield curve for various market segments and powers market deepening and diversification. Beyond developing the government bond benchmark for the market, the key priority is to establish and maintain a neutral policy stance about market access by subnational borrowers and about competition among various non–central government issuers. The cornerstone of this policy is to replace implicit, unlimited government guarantees by explicit but limited guarantees that are adequately priced and accounted for in the national budget.

11.9.2.2 Developing Regulatory and Supervisory Framework for the Subnational Bond Market

Because subnational entities compete directly with private sector issuers for scarce investor resources, the overall regulatory framework for subnational bond issues should parallel that for private sector issues. As an integral part of bond market reform programs, governments should pay particular attention to specific elements of the regulatory and supervisory framework that may require special treatment to account for specific characteristics of subnational issuers. It is especially important to establish specific formats for disclosure of financial information by subnational entities in the case of public issues and to revise regularly these formats as subnational accounting evolves. A priority is to establish specific regulations that support market diversification, increase investor confidence, and foster development of a secondary market in subnational bonds. The regulations should require a legal opinion before subnational bonds are issued; support development of structured subnational bond issues, particularly revenue and asset collateralization; sustain the issuance of bonds by intermunicipal undertakings;[257] give institutional investors freedom to invest across a broad range of instruments, including subnational bonds; and construct a tax regime that does not distort investor choice among various classes of securities.

11.9.2.3 *Maintaining a Level Playing Field Among Market Instruments and Participants*

Once national bond benchmarks are established, governments should establish a legal and regulatory framework that supports development of a wide range of subnational debt instruments, both bank lending and directly placed bond issues. Bank lending plays a central role for subnational borrowers in the middle of the rating scale. As their credit reputation grows and the need for delegated monitoring lessens, subnational borrowers can diversify their financing strategies and seek to place bonds directly on the market. The subnational bond market is closely intertwined with bank lending to subnational entities. Governments should avoid introducing distortions in the system of incentives between subnational bonds and loans, particularly through introduction of fiscal and/or regulatory privileges that favor one type of instrument over another.

Governments should also avoid introducing fiscal, regulatory, or other forms of support that distort competition among various actors on the subnational bond market. They should be careful when providing government support to specific market participants in order not to distort development of normal competitive relationships. For example, providing financial advisory services for bond issuance to subnational entities on a grant basis carries the risk of distorting the choice between competitive and negotiated sales and, therefore, the competitive relationship between financial advisors and underwriters. Providing backup facilities for bond insurers carries the risk of distorting the choice between bank lending and bond issuance and, therefore, the competitive relationship between banks and bond underwriters. Providing sovereign or intermediate government backup for a bond bank reserve fund risks distorting the choice between bank lending and

---

257. In some developing and transition countries, intermunicipal undertakings have the potential to become important borrowers.

bond issuance for issuers with a limited credit record and the choice between individual issues by small local governments and a combined issue by an intermunicipal undertaking.

11.10   Conclusion

The increasing role of subnational entities in capital markets reflects the trend of decentralization of some governmental functions, particularly for infrastructure investment, from the central government to smaller political jurisdictions. In general, the greater the financial autonomy of subnational units of government, the greater the likelihood that a subnational securities market could develop.

The central government usually issues bonds and bills in the domestic capital market, whether rates are low or high, with the aim of minimizing cost over the long run. In contrast, many subnational issuers (provinces, states, municipalities, and state enterprises) are opportunistic issuers that often do not have a recurrent financing need. They can, accordingly, look for special opportunities in the market by issuing bonds when interest rates are low or by targeting specific segments with high investor demand. For these issuers, timing and flexibility in the design of bonds are essential.

Even with financial autonomy of a subnational unit, a number of concerns arise in developing subnational securities markets. The overarching problem of subnational securities issuers is that they often lead to expectations that the central government might assume the liabilities of a distressed subnational borrower, thereby resulting in a moral hazard problem. In addition, the development of a subnational securities market may fragment the overall government securities market. The extent to which a subnational securities market is desirable is ultimately a question of whether the benefits of the greater financial autonomy resulting from decentralization are outweighed by the inefficiencies resulting from moral hazard and market fragmentation.

A well-functioning government securities market supports the development of securities markets for subnational entities. Providing a relatively risk-free asset such as a government bond establishes a reference for pricing subnational bonds. The market infrastructure needed for an effective government securities market, and particularly payment and settlement

11

arrangements, should be able to serve the needs of the subnational securities market as well.

The lack of market transparency, weakness of market governance, and weak capacity for financial management of subnational entities, however, impede the development of subnational securities markets. To gain market acceptance, subnational units of government must strive to overcome these shortcomings. Moreover, to establish their market standing, subnational bond issuers must be prepared to provide the public with relevant credit information, including the revenue basis for servicing their obligations, and they must establish a reputation for financial integrity. Technology and the Internet may eventually play a role in the information infrastructure by facilitating the dissemination of pricing information from all potential providers of a financial service and relevant financial information about particular new issues and about the issuers.

11

Bibliography

Arrow, Kenneth. 1985. "The Economics of Agency." In J. Pratt and R. Zeckhauser, eds., *Principals and Agents: The Structure of Business.* Cambridge, Mass.: Harvard Business School Press.

Barbery, Nicole, Burcak Inel, and Michel Noel. 1998. "Reforming the Legal, Regulatory, and Supervisory Framework for Borrowing by Subnational Entities: Key Priorities for Europe and Central Asia." World Bank, Washington, D.C. Processed.

Begg, Ian. 1998. *Intergovernmental Transfers and Capital Formation in CEECs.* World Bank, Washington, D.C. Processed.

BIS (Basel Committee on Banking Supervision). 1998. *Convergence of Capital Measurement and Capital Standards.* Bank for International Settlements, Basel, Switzerland. Available at www.bis.org/publ/index.htm.

————. 2001. *A New Capital Adequacy Accord.* Bank for International Settlements, Basel, Switzerland. Available at www.bis.org/publ/index.htm.

Caluseru, Gabriela. 1999. *Romania: Municipal Development and Finance Program: Policy Assessment Paper.* World Bank, Washington, D.C. Processed.

Costain, Juan, and Michel Noel. 1999. *Supporting the Development of Subnational Finance Markets in Developing and Transition Countries: A Strategy for the World Bank Group.* World Bank, Washington, D.C. Processed.

Darche, Benjamin, Maria Freire, and Marcela Huertas. 1998. *Subnational Access to the Capital Markets: The Latin American Experience.* World Bank, Washington, D.C. Processed.

Dewatripont, Mathias, and E. Maskin. 1995. "Credit and Efficiency in Centralized and Decentralized Economies." *Review of Economic Studies* (62), 541–55.

Dexia Bank. 1997. *Local Finance in the Fifteen Countries of the European Union.* Brussels and Paris.

Diamond, Douglas. 1991. "Monitoring and Reputation: The Choice Between Bank Loans and Directly Placed Debt." *Journal of Political Economy* 99 (4).

Dillinger, William, and Steven Webb. 1999a. *Fiscal Management in Federal Democracies: Argentina and Brazil.* Policy Research Paper 2121. World Bank, Washington, D.C.

11

———. 1999b. *Decentralization and Fiscal Management in Colombia*. Policy Research Paper 2122. World Bank, Washington, D.C.

El Daher, Samir, Mihaly Kopanyi, and Michel Noel. 1999. *Developing a Competitive Subnational Finance Market in Hungary: Policy Issues and Challenges*. World Bank, Washington, D.C. Processed.

El Daher, Samir, Mihaly Kopanyi, Michel Noel, Anita Papp, and Deborah Wetzel. 1999. *Hungary: Subnational Modernization: A Policy Note*. World Bank, Washington, D.C. Processed.

Fabozzi, Frank, T. Dessa Fabozzi, and Sylvan Feldstein. 1995. *Municipal Bond Portfolio Management*. Burr Ridge, Ill.: Irwin.

Feldstein, Sylvan, and Frank Fabozzi. 1987. *The Dow Jones–Irwin Guide to Municipal Bonds*. Homewood, Ill.: Dow Jones–Irwin.

Fortune, Peter. 1991. "The Municipal Bond Market, Part I: Politics, Taxes and Yields." *New England Economic Review*. Federal Reserve Bank of Boston, Boston, Mass. Available at www.bos.frb.org/.

———. 1992. "The Municipal Bond Market, Part II: Problems and Policies." *New England Economic Review*. Federal Reserve Bank of Boston, Boston, Mass. Available at www.bos.frb.org/.

Hill, Larry, and Bill Simonsen. 1998. "Municipal Bond Issuance: Is There Evidence of a Principal-Agent Problem?" In *Public Budgeting and Finance*. Vol. 18, No. 4. Transaction Periodicals Consortium, New Brunswick, N.J.

Humphrey, Nancy, and Diane Rausa Maurice. 1986. "Infrastructure Bond Banks' Initiatives: Policy Implications and Credit Concerns." In *Public Budgeting and Finance*. Vol. 6, No. 3. Transaction Periodicals Consortium, New Brunswick, N.J.

Inel, Burcak. 1998. *Russia: Looking Beyond the Crisis: Establishing a Regulatory Framework for Sub-Federal Debt in the Russian Federation*. World Bank, Washington, D.C. Processed.

———. 1999a. *Subnational Credit Markets in the Czech Republic*. World Bank, Washington, D.C. Processed.

———. 1999b. *Local Government Capital Finance in Latvia*. World Bank, Washington, D.C. Processed.

Jokay, Karoly, Judith Kalman, and Mihaly Kopanyi. 1998. *Municipal Infrastructure Financing in Hungary: Four Cases*. World Bank, Washington, D.C. Processed.

11

King, Tim, Alan Roe, and Paul Siegelbaum. 1998. *Analyzing Financial Sectors in Transition*. Research Working Paper, World Bank, Washington, D.C.

Leigland, James. 1997. "Accelerating Municipal Bond Market Development in Emerging Economies: An Assessment of Strategies and Progress." In *Public Budgeting and Finance*. Vol. 17, No. 2. Transaction Periodicals Consortium, New Brunswick, N.J.

Moody's Investors Service. 1998. *Subnational Governments: A Rating Agency Perspective*. New York, N.Y.

Murshed, Mansoob. 1994. "Adverse Selection and Moral Hazard in Government Grant Giving." *Economic and Social Review* 26 (1).

Nicolini, Juan Pablo, et al. 1999. *Decentralization, Fiscal Discipline in Subnational Governments, and the Bailout Problem: The Case Argentina*. Inter-American Development Bank, Washington, D.C. Processed.

Peterson, George E. 1997. *Building Local Credit Systems*. Urban Institute, Washington, D.C. Processed.

Qian, Yingi, and Gerard Roland. 1998. "Federalism and the Soft Budget Constraint." *American Economic Review*.

Towfighi, Shah, and Kurt Zorn. 1986. "Not All Bond Banks Are Created Equal." In *Public Budgeting and Finance*. Vol. 6, No. 3. Transaction Periodicals Consortium, New Brunswick, N.J.

World Bank. 1996. *Argentina: Provincial Finances Study: Selected Issues in Fiscal Federalism*. Washington, D.C. Processed.

11

Chapter 12

Development of Private Sector Bond Markets

The issuance of debt securities by private sector entities has considerable public policy benefits. Such securities help the private sector contribute to economic development through more efficient reallocation of capital. In particular, they improve access to capital for housing and infrastructure at a time when privatization and deregulation in many developing countries are shifting the financing of these projects from public to private hands. Private sector securities also help diffuse stresses on the banking system by matching long-term investments with long-term capital. There is thus a strong public interest in a viable bond market for private sector issuers. Authorities can support private sector bond market development by maintaining a well-functioning market for government securities and by helping to establish disclosure procedures and a credit-rating system for private sector securities, bankruptcy laws, avoiding public sector crowding out, and limiting statutory restrictions on the issuance of private sector debt securities.

12

12.1   Introduction

Private sector debt securities generally include short-term debt instruments, such as commercial paper, and longer-term debt securities, such as private sector bonds (with maturity of one year or more).[258] These debt securities can be classified into floating rate and fixed-rate instruments, secured or unsecured, senior or subordinated to other liabilities of the issuer, and publicly offered or privately placed. This chapter focuses on policy issues associated with local currency bonds issued by private sector entities in developing countries, with an emphasis on the linkage between the public and private sector bond markets.

Development of a well-functioning government bond market in developing countries will often precede and facilitate development of a private sector bond market. At the same time, private debt markets need other elements to be successful, most notably a disclosure system, a credit-rating system, and bankruptcy laws. Authorities should also avoid possible crowding out and statutory restrictions that impede private sector bond market development.

12.2   Benefits of Private Sector Debt Issuance

The issuance of debt securities by private sector entities yields public benefits at the macroeconomic as well as at the corporate level. Governments are increasingly unable to finance the massive investment required for major infrastructure projects, utilities, and housing. Privatizations and deregulation have intensified the need for long-term investment.

---

258. In order to meet particular needs, investment banks have been developing a wide range of debt instruments in addition to fine-tuning parameters of individual instruments for specific clientele. These include commercial paper, certificates of deposit, floating rate notes, zero-coupon bonds, deep-discount bonds, perpetual bonds, secured or unsecured bonds, convertible bonds, bonds with equity warrants, mortgage-backed securities, asset-backed securities, index-linked bonds, medium-term notes, dual-currency bonds, reverse dual-currency bonds, and catastrophe bonds. Terminology varies among jurisdictions, with the precise definitions of commercial paper, notes, and bonds carrying different meanings. In this chapter, "debt securities" is used as a generic term, while "bonds" is used to describe debt securities with maturities of at least a year.

12

Securitizations are another source of increased issuance. The Asia crisis also demonstrated to corporations and governments the perils of relying on foreign currency or bank loans for long-term investments without proper hedging. All of these developments are creating a growing demand for well-functioning private sector bond markets.

12.2.1 Benefits to the Economy and Financial Sector of Private Sector Bond Markets

Corporate finance theory shows five categories of benefits from private sector bond markets. Private sector debt markets can (i) diffuse stresses on the banking sector by diversifying credit risks across the economy, (ii) supply long-term funds for long-term investment needs, (iii) provide long-term investment products for long-term savings and lower funding costs by capturing a liquidity premium, (iv) endow financial products with flexibility to meet the specific needs of investors and borrowers, and (v) reallocate capital more efficiently. These are all features that should emerge as an economy develops and grows. By providing longer-term, fixed-rate, local-currency funding, private sector debt bonds help reduce interest rate, foreign exchange, and refunding risk and contribute in mitigating the kinds of problems that brought about the Asian financial crisis.

12.2.2 Private Sector Financing—Equity Versus Debt and Bonds Versus Bank Loans

A proper mix of equity and debt is vital for efficient corporate growth under normal business circumstances. Corporate growth would be constrained without debt financing.

Private enterprises have two basic means of securing debt financing—indirectly by loans from banks and directly by issuing bonds in the capital market. Debt securities, especially bonds with maturities of greater than a year, are generally cost effective for long-term, large-scale, and opportunistic financing by issuers with a high credit rating, while bank loans are cost effective for short-term, small-scale, and recurring financing by borrowers with a lower credit rating or without a credit rating. Some of the major differences between these two types of debt financing are shown in Table 12.1, although many debt instruments are hybrids or do not fit this neat dichotomy.

12

Table 12.1. Distinctions Between Bonds and Bank Loan Financing

	Bond Financing	Bank Loan Financing
Size of financing	Substantially large; no particular limit; small issues are impractical	Smaller than bond financing unless syndicated; limited by a credit line available to a borrower, industry, country, and other category to which the borrower belongs
Term	Usually one year or longer	Usually shorter than bond financing and rolled over; limited by credit policy of a bank
Repayment	Bullet or limited prepayment patterns; generally inflexible	Generally flexible
Interest rate	Fixed or floating rates	Floating rates for long maturities
All-in cost	Normally cheaper than bank loan financing, depending on market conditions; very cheap for opportunistic deals	Normally more expensive than bond financing
Credit analysis	Standardized rating by rating agencies	Proprietary credit analysis by a bank
Security	Normally unsecured	Normally secured
Use of proceeds	Normally not restricted	Normally restricted
Listing	Either listed or nonlisted	Nonlisted
Creditors	"Unspecific," many investors, including individuals, corporations, banks, insurance companies, pension funds, mutual funds, etc.	A small number of banks and some other financial institutions
Transferability and liquidity	Readily transferable, and limited liquidity except for "major" issuers	Often not transferable and not liquid

Source: Endo 2000.

12.3   Overview of Corporate Bond Markets

12.3.1   Corporate Bond Markets in Developed Countries

When considering the development of private sector bond markets in developing countries, a review of bond markets in developed countries provides some perspective on the potential role of private sector bond markets

12

Table 12.2. Domestic Debt Securities by Nationality of Issuers in Selected G–10 Countries
(1997, in US$ Billion)

	France	Germany	Italy	Japan	Netherlands	United Kingdom	United States	Total
GDP	1,392.5	2,089.9	1,139.0	4,197.4	362.6	1,312.3	8,110.9	18,604.6
Total debt securities	1,113.2	1,730.0	1,471.7	4,433.7	227.8	767.8	12,412.6	22,158.8
% of GDP	79.9	82.8	129.2	105.6	62.8	58.5	153.1	119.1
Public sector	647.4	777.5	1,123.4	3,116.8	177.5	465.4	7,337.1	13,645.1
% of GDP	46.5	37.2	98.6	74.3	49.0	35.5	90.5	73.3
% of total debt securities	58.2	44.9	76.3	70.3	77.9	60.6	59.1	61.6
Private sector	465.8	952.5	348.3	1,316.9	50.3	302.4	5,077.5	8,513.7
% of GDP	33.5	45.6	30.6	31.4	13.9	23.0	62.6	45.8
% of total debt securities	41.8	55.1	23.7	29.7	22.1	39.4	40.9	38.4

Sources: Schinasi and Smith (1998) and World Economic Outlook database

in capital market development. Even in developed countries, there are few active private sector markets, and activity in private sector securities pales in comparison with that of government securities.

The United States has by far the largest corporate debt market, not just in terms of absolute volume, but also in terms of percentage of GDP. (See Table 12. 2.) Activity in corporate bond markets in developed countries is centered on the primary market. Except for a small number of major issuers, liquidity of secondary markets for corporate bonds in developed countries is generally thin.[259] Institutional investors, rather than individual investors, dominate developed-country corporate bond markets. The majority of corporate bonds, once purchased by institutional investors, do not change hands until maturity. In the U.S. market, for example, more than 95 percent of corporate bond issues outstanding have no trades in the secondary market.

The breakdown of corporate bond issuance varies greatly among developed countries. In Germany, corporate debt has been dominated by banks, with the nonfinancial sector totally absent from the bond market. In virtually all other developed markets, including Japan, the United Kingdom, and

---

259. Even in the large U.S. capital market, only 4 percent of about 400,000 corporate issues outstanding in 1996 traded even once that year (see *New York Times*, June 27, 1999).

Table 12.3. Debt Securities Financing by Nonfinancial Firms in Selected G–10 Countries
(As percent of total funds raised in financial markets)

	Germany	Italy	Japan	Netherlands	United States
1990	0.0	0.2	14.2	3.4	48.6
1991	0.0	1.0	10.4	-2.5	33.5
1992	0.1	0.2	4.6	-0.1	18.2
1993	0.0	-6.5	7.1	12.0	10.6
1994	0.0	-2.9	11.5	-27.7	

Sources: Table 3 in Schinasi and Smith (1998); OECD, *Financial Statistics:* Non-Financial Enterprises Financial Statements (Part III); R. Todd Smith, "Markets or Corporate Debt Securities," IMF Working Paper No. 95/67; and Deutsche Bank, *Kapital Market Statistik*

Notes: For Germany, does not include international issues of bonds. For Italy and the Netherlands, does not include commercial paper. Minus figures indicate that redemption exceeded issuance amount.

the United States, bond issuance by financial institutions has been greater than issuance by nonfinancial corporations. (See Table 12.3.)

Institutional investors, such as insurance companies, pension funds, and mutual funds, are the major buyers of corporate bonds issued in developed countries. Holdings of corporate bonds by households in Japan and the United States accounted for 12.2 percent of the total of corporate bonds outstanding at the end of 1998, and bonds of nonfinancial corporations amounted to only 6.9 and 1.5 percent, respectively.[260] Households and corporations generally find a better risk/return trade-off for their investment through the intermediation of institutional investors that specialize in collecting and managing funds with specific characteristics.

12.3.2 Corporate Bond Markets in Developing Countries

Most corporate debt markets in developing countries are fledgling and small, even relative to their own low GDPs. Of the 10 developing countries from which the IFC has been able to collect reliable bond market statistics, only in the Republic of Korea and Malaysia do corporate bonds exceed 10 percent of GDP. In Korea, a majority of corporate bond issues had

---

260. See Bank of Japan (1998) and Federal Reserve Board 1999. The corporate bonds in Japan are "industrial securities" (straight bonds, convertible bonds, and bonds with equity warrants) and bank debentures.

guarantees from commercial banks,[261] although the issuers were reasonably diverse. Such Korean corporate bond issues might be regarded as a form of bank loans. Another example of commercial banks' significant involvement in a corporate bond market is the Czech Republic, where bonds issued by commercial banks accounted for 77 percent of all corporate bonds issued between February 1997 and October 1999.

Table 12.4 presents data on the outstanding stock of equities, bank claims on the private sector, and government and corporate bonds for a select group of developed and developing countries. Even allowing for the limitations and inconsistencies in the data,[262] it confirms a clear disparity between developed and developing countries for all categories of financing.

In order to understand the functions of private sector bond markets, especially in developing countries, it is helpful to distinguish between "major" and "minor" issuers of private sector bonds. Major private sector bond issuers are those issuers that provide investors with a regular, sizable and stable supply of bonds of high quality and uniform characteristics through public offerings. Minor private sector bond issuers comprise the rest. The latter may be of high quality in terms of creditworthiness, but they tap the bond market only irregularly. Their bond issues tend to be either small in size or opportunistic in timing, or both.

The distinction between these two categories of bond issuers should make it easier for policymakers in developing countries to lay out a development strategy for their debt market as a whole. The two categories of issuers and their bonds differ substantially. If the market is properly designed and maintained, bond issues by major issuers are likely to be traded on the secondary market. The trading volume of major issuers'

---

261. In 1996 and 1997, 93 percent and 87 percent of Korean corporate bonds were guaranteed, with the remainder nonguaranteed. In 1998, these proportions had altered drastically, with 33 percent guaranteed and 67 percent nonguaranteed (Bank of Korea and Korea Securities Dealers Association).

262. Though corporate bond markets already exist in one way or another in many developing countries, it is difficult to gather reliable statistical data on them. More surprisingly, reasonably consistent data for corporate bond markets in developed countries are also not available (see notes to Table 12.4). BIS data do not include domestic debt securities in some developing countries (for example, Indonesia, Philippines, the Slovak Republic, and Thailand), and show amounts different from IFC data for the other developing countries. There are apparently differences in definition between the two sources.

12

Table 12.4. GDPs, Equities, Government Bonds, and Corporate Bonds in Selected Developing and Developed Countries

Country	GDP	Total Equities		Bank Claims on Private Sector		Total Bonds		Government Bonds		Corporate Bonds	
Developing	$ bln	$ bln	%	$ bln	%	$ bln	%	$ bln	%	$ bln	%
Czech Republic	56.0	12.05	21.5	35.20	62.9	6.62	11.8	2.33	4.2	3.72	6.6
Hungary	48.0	14.03	29.2	8.26	17.2	12.04	25.1	11.80	24.6	0.24	0.5
India	372.0	105.19	28.3	98.79	26.6	108.88	29.3	63.07	17.0	16.49	4.4
Indonesia	92.0	22.10	24.0	63.37	68.9	1.70	1.8	0.00	0.0	1.00	1.1
Rep. of Korea	321.0	114.59	35.7	264.67	82.5	277.78	86.5	178.46	55.6	99.32	30.9
Malaysia	72.0	98.56	136.9	74.92	104.1	37.78	52.5	19.74	27.4	15.13	21.0
Philippines	65.0	35.31	54.3	32.71	50.3	9.26	14.2	7.87	12.1	1.26	1.9
Poland	158.0	20.46	13.0	30.84	19.5	12.63	8.0	12.63	8.0	0.00	0.0
Slovak Republic	20.0	0.97	4.8	8.92	44.6	3.39	16.9	2.78	13.9	0.51	2.6
Thailand	113.0	34.90	30.9	144.44	127.8	21.02	18.6	9.67	8.6	3.46	3.1
Developed											
France	1,455.0	991.48	68.1	1,121.82	77.1	1,209.90	83.2	731.30	50.3	478.60	32.9
Germany	2,123.0	1,093.96	51.5	2,672.98	125.9	2,005.90	94.5	865.90	40.8	1,140.00	53.7
Italy	1,186.0	569.73	48.0	740.64	62.4	1,579.90	133.2	1,215.60	102.5	364.30	30.7
Japan	3,787.0	2,495.76	65.9	5,046.28	133.3	5,213.60	137.7	3,700.50	97.7	1,513.10	40.0
Netherlands	378.0	603.18	159.6	468.73	124.0	243.60	64.4	199.40	52.8	44.20	11.7
United Kingdom	1,399.0	2,374.27	169.7	1,690.47	120.8	852.80	61.0	464.30	33.2	388.50	27.8
United States	8,511.0	13,451.35	158.0	5,412.90	63.6	13,973.20	164.2	8,002.40	94.0	5,970.80	70.2

Sources: J. P. Morgan, *World Financial Markets*; Institute of International Finance (IIF); IFC, *Emerging Stock Markets Factbook 1999*; IMF, *International Financial Statistics*; IFC, Emerging Markets Information Center Bond Database; and BIS, *Quarterly Review: International Banking and Financial Market Developments*

Notes:

1. GDP figures are nominal GDP for 1998 from JP Morgan's *World Financial Markets* (except Slovak Republic).

2. GDP figure for the Slovak Republic is nominal GDP for 1998 from the Institute of International Finance (IIF).

3. Equities figures are for December 1998 and are from IFC's *Emerging Stock Markets Factbook 1999*.

4. Bank claims on the private sector are from the IMF's *International Financial Statistics* and are for end-1998 (except France and the Netherlands, end–first quarter 1999, and Hungary, end–third quarter 1996). Amounts shown are US$ equivalents for local currency–denominated bank claims. Bank claims are the closest available proxy for bank loans, although claims could also include other claims, such as equity securities. Claims on the private sector, therefore, should approximate bank loans to the private sector.

5. Bond figures for the 10 developing countries include only debt securities with initial maturities of at least one year and are from IFC's Emerging Markets Information Center Bond Database. All data as of December 1998, except India (March 1998) and the Philippines (December 1997). Figures for the Slovak Republic are estimates. Amounts shown are US$ equivalents for local currency–denominated bonds.

6. Bond figures for the seven developed countries are debt securities of all maturities, not just bonds, and are for December 1998 from BIS's *Quarterly Review: International Banking and Financial Market Developments*.

bonds on the secondary market may become large enough for their secondary market prices to form a benchmark yield curve. However, as noted above, even in developed countries, activity on the secondary market for corporate issues is limited.

Major private sector bond issuers issue their bonds on an almost regular basis—say, every quarter—so that investors can reasonably anticipate when bonds will be available for sale. Infrastructure and utility companies, housing finance companies, and development finance companies have become major issuers of private sector bonds in developing countries in recent years.[263] Under normal circumstances, the issue size of the major issuers is relatively stable and large enough to meet the demand for the bonds across the market. Major bond issuers typically are financially strong and competently manage their business operations, and investors thus have confidence in their ability to pay interest and principal in a timely manner. The high quality is conveniently expressed with a rating symbol such as "AAA" or "Aaa."

Minor private sector bond issuers tend to be opportunistic. Opportunistic issuers tap the bond market only when a very attractive financing window opens to meet the specific, short-lived investment needs of a specific type of investor. Their bonds are likely to be diverse and unlikely to be traded (frequently) on the secondary market after they are initially placed on the primary market. Despite the inherent illiquidity of minor private sector bond issues, the primary market of minor issuers has contributed significantly in supplying long-term funds to a country's private sector.

12.4 Changes in Public Policy and New Financial Technology and Development of Private Sector Bond Markets

Changes in public policy and new financial technology have broadened the scope for private sector debt securities. This is allowing the private sector bond market to satisfy the growing borrowing demand generated by the

12

---

263. Major corporate bond issuers in developing countries include ICICI in India, KDB in Korea, and Industrial Finance Corporation in Thailand. (All three are development finance institutions, i.e., quasi-statal development banks, and perhaps fall in a/the subnational category.) A true corporate issuer in a developing country is EGAT, an electricity company in Thailand.

increase in private sector initiatives. The changes in public policy include the decentralization of public finance, privatization, and deregulation. These developments are reflected most directly in private financing demands for infrastructure and housing. Securitization is an increasingly popular new financial technology applicable to infrastructure financing and housing financing.

12.4.1 Infrastructure Financing

An increasing pace of infrastructure building and a shift of the leading role of economic development from the public sector to the private sector have stimulated policymakers in developing countries to develop a private sector bond market.

Social infrastructure building has been critical to economic development and is heavily dependent on long-term financing because of large capital investments and long gestation periods. Traditionally, most social infrastructure was built, owned, and operated by the public sector. Even after completion, governments often subsidized the operation of social infrastructure projects. The pursuit of economic efficiency has shifted the driving force of economic development from the public to the private sector. The shift has been realized by the privatization of state-owned enterprises (SOEs) and by the deregulation of infrastructure activities. The majority of privatized SOEs have been in the utility sectors, telecommunications, energy, transportation, water, and sanitation.

There has been a marked increase in the number of privatization transactions in developing countries. (See Figure 12.1.) Private participation in infrastructure projects in developing countries increased at an average annual rate of 34 percent in real terms from 1990 to 1997. Even after a downturn of infrastructure investment in 1998, a result of the Asian financial crisis in 1997, the real growth rate was over 25 percent over the period from 1990 to 1998.[264] These high rates of demand growth compare with an average real GDP growth rate of 6.4 percent for developing countries over the 1990–97 period.[265] (See Table 12.5.) It is estimated that 10–20 percent

---

264. See Roger 1999.

265. See IMF 1998.

Figure 12.1. Privatization Transactions in Developing Countries

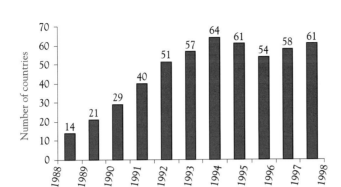

of these infrastructure project costs was locally financed by debt instruments issued in developing countries.[266]

The burden of infrastructure project financing is thus passing from the public to the private sector. Debt securities financing for infrastructure projects can be arranged normally through one of three routes: (i) long-term loans extended by development banks or development finance companies that are funded through issuance of their own bonds, (ii) bond issuance by project sponsors, (iii) non- or limited-recourse financing, such as build-operate-transfer (BOT) or build-own-operate-transfer (BOOT), which are innovative and increasingly popular.

Although many infrastructure projects are financed through syndicated loans of commercial banks, given the large investment sizes and long gestation periods of these projects, their financing through bond issuance in

266. According to the data on the 115 IFC-financed private infrastructure projects during 1967 to 1996, the financial structure of the projects was as follows: debt:equity = 58 percent:42 percent; local:foreign =33 percent:67 percent. If the debt and equity shares were the same in the foreign and local shares, the local debt share would be 19.4 percent (58 percent x 33 percent). The actual shares of local debt (local commercial banks) and local equity in 1996 were 10 percent and 26 percent, respectively. The range of 10–20 percent was estimated from the 19.4 percent and 10 percent figures (see Carter and Bond 1996).

12

Table 12.5. Investment in Infrastructure Projects with Private Participation in Developing Countries
(In 1998 US$ Billion)

	1990	1991	1992	1993	1994	1995	1996	1997	1998	Total	Average Growth Rate* (percent) 90–97	90–98
Sector												
Telecommunication	6.6	13.1	7.9	10.9	19.5	20.1	33.4	49.6	53.1	212.2	33.4	29.8
Energy	1.6	1.2	11.1	12.3	17.1	23.9	34.9	46.2	26.8	177.1	61.7	42.2
Transport	7.5	3.1	5.7	7.4	7.6	7.5	13.1	16.3	12.0	82.2	11.7	8.1
Water and sanitation	0.0	0.1	1.8	7.3	0.8	1.4	2.0	8.4	1.5	23.3	—	—
Region												
East Asia and the Pacific	2.3	4.0	8.7	15.9	17.3	20.4	31.5	37.6	9.5	147.2	49.1	19.4
Europe and Central Asia	0.1	0.3	0.5	1.5	3.9	8.4	10.7	15.3	11.3	52.0	105.2	80.6
Latin America and the Caribbean	12.9	12.3	17.1	18.0	18.4	19.0	27.4	45.1	66.3	236.5	19.6	22.7
Middle East and North Africa	0.0	0.0	0.0	3.3	0.3	0.1	0.3	5.2	3.6	12.8	—	—
South Asia	0.3	0.8	0.1	1.2	4.3	4.0	11.4	13.7	2.3	38.1	72.6	29.0
Sub-Saharan Africa	0.0	0.0	0.1	0.0	0.7	1.0	2.0	3.5	2.3	9.6	—	—
Total	15.6	17.4	26.5	39.9	44.9	52.9	83.3	120.4	95.3	496.2	33.9	25.4
Real GDP growth (in percent) (GDP vol. measure)	4.3	4.2	5.7	8.0	7.2	6.9	7.0	6.0			6.42	

Sources: World Bank, PPI Project Database, and IMF, International Financial Statistical Yearbook 1998.

*Growth rates are calculated on compounded basis.

12

the private capital market would be appropriate. The shift from public to private financing of these infrastructure projects has therefore led policy-makers to assess, plan, and implement the development of an efficient private sector bond market.

12.4.2 Housing Finance

The development of fixed-income securities markets would benefit housing finance. Housing represents the largest class of real assets in most emerging markets and is a major socioeconomic priority as well as an engine of growth. Affordable housing finance (with long-maturity loans at low spreads) requires a comprehensive housing policy and long-term mortgage markets that are well integrated with the financial markets. The size of residential mortgage markets often varies greatly among developed countries, and even more so between developed and emerging-market countries. In several high-income OECD countries, the value of outstanding residential mortgage loans exceeds 50 percent of GDP, while the average for Europe is 28 percent of GDP. In many emerging countries, mortgage markets represent less than 5 percent of GDP, although in Chile they approach 20 percent, and they are above that level in Colombia and Malaysia.

12.4.2.1 Types of Mortgage Securities and Mortgage Debt Issuers

A variety of securities can be issued by primary mortgage lenders, by special purpose vehicles often called "conduits," or by secondary mortgage companies purchasing mortgage loans with or without recourse from originators. For a housing finance industry in its infancy, a centralized liquidity facility issuing conventional bonds or enhancing mortgage securities appears fitting for many developing countries. Given an appropriate legal and regulatory environment, universal or specialized banks can also issue simple mortgage bonds as shown by the U.S. and European experience. Box 12.1. summarizes the range and variety of mortgage-backed securities in different regions of the world.

Debt issuers for housing finance can be grouped into three main types. First, there are bank and housing finance companies that originate housing loans. They can finance these loans by issuing long-term bonds rather than relying exclusively on short-term deposits and other short-term funding. Second, a centralized liquidity facility can purchase housing loans with recourse from the originators of these loans and finance the purchase by issuing general obligation bonds. Third, housing loan originators, or more typically a mortgage finance company, can buy housing loans from originators, securitize these mortgage loans, and sell mortgage-backed securities to

12

Box 12.1. Significance of Mortgage Debt Markets

The dynamics of mortgage bond markets and the growth of mortgage-backed securities varies considerably across regions of the world, and from country to country. The dynamics reflect the history and financial infrastructure of each market. In some OECD countries, mortgage-related securities have reached high levels of liquidity, performance, and market efficiency in relation to government bonds. A variety of debt products includes pass-through securities, collateralized mortgage obligations, mortgage bonds, uncollateralized bonds. Mortgage bonds proper provide no capital relief to lenders but reduce their liquidity, interest rate, and prepayment risks. Mortgage bonds are secured by a given pool or by the overall portfolio of mortgage loans, with seniority creditor status in the event of bankruptcy.

In Europe, mortgage bonds funded an average of 19 percent of residential mortgage loans in 1998, with much higher proportions in Denmark, Germany, and Sweden. In these three countries, property mortgage bonds fund more than housing and can also be collateralized with commercial property assets. In Denmark, for instance, corporations rely extensively on mortgage bonds, and this explains the small size of corporate debt in that market. In Germany, three-fourths of the *Pfandbriefe* are not property bonds ("mortgage" *Pfandbriefe*); they are debt obligations issued by state and local governments issued under a separate law ("Public" *Pfandbriefe*). The birth of the Euro and the growth of global markets favor the issuance of larger debt issues and more liquid debt securities.

In Latin America, inflation-indexed *letras hipotecarias* purchased by pension funds have financed the impressive growth of mortgage markets in Chile from less than 7 percent of GDP in the early 1980s to over 17 percent of GDP in 2000. These *letras* fund about two-thirds of the mortgage needs of the housing market.

In Asia, the National Mortgage Corporation of Malaysia (Cagamas) has catalyzed the growth of mortgage markets by funding the purchase with recourse to eligible mortgage loans through bonds and notes. Cagamas securities represented about 13 percent of the total fixed-income market in 1998 and about 40 percent of the funding of residential mortgages. Institutions comparable to Cagamas now operate or are being created in about a dozen of other emerging countries.

Measured in terms of outstanding debt, residential mortgages comprise the largest single sector of U.S. financial markets. Mortgage securitization has become a dominant component of mortgage debt markets. In contrast, mortgage securitization in Europe still represents less than 1 percent of total mortgage debt funding. U.S. mortgage-related securities are mostly issued or guaranteed by government sponsored enterprises (GSE) operating as private corporations with implicit government backing. The overall size of the mortgage-backed securities (MBS) market is now comparable to that of U.S. Treasuries. The annual issuance of MBS fluctuates over the business cycle, but MBS now fund about 50 percent of U.S. residential mortgage needs.

12

institutional investors interested in quality paper that offer better yields than Treasury securities.

12.4.2.2 Development Path of Mortgage Markets

Mortgage markets usually evolve gradually toward the more advanced securitization stage. Securitization refers to the pooling of normally illiquid assets and the issuing of new securities backed by cash flows from those assets. Such securities can take the form of bonds, shares, and unit trust certificates. Bonds are the most popular form, which is exemplified by the increasing popularity of mortgage-backed securities in developed countries. Of particular interest to governments is that securitization facilitates development of a secondary mortgage market through mortgage-backed securities issuance and at the same time helps improve the capital adequacy ratios of banks through the sale of otherwise illiquid mortgage loan portfolios. This assists and encourages banks to manage their balance sheets in a more sound and efficient manner.

Securitization helps to further reduce intermediation costs in a more competitive mortgage industry, allows for better management of balance sheets, and improves capital adequacy through the sale of otherwise illiquid portfolios. Reaching this advanced stage of market evolution, however, is demanding and requires having the appropriate legal and regulatory infrastructure prerequisites in place. The potential benefits of mortgage securitization, however, also carry the financial costs of new technology and information systems.

Mortgage debt markets benefit from the development of the market infrastructure built up for government securities, but they have their specific legal and regulatory needs. A sound retail (or primary) mortgage market is the cornerstone of housing finance. Basic requisites for mortgage markets include a land registry system, an effective bankruptcy law, efficient foreclosure procedures, reliable property valuation, proper mortgage loan underwriting, and modern technology in loan processing and servicing. Well-rated mortgage-related securities also require a comprehensive regulatory treatment for banks and institutional investors (pension funds, mutual funds, and insurance companies).

The development of government and mortgage securities markets is interlinked. As fixed-income securities markets expand in general, the supply of mortgage-related securities of various forms grows to represent one of the largest fixed-income markets. They offer quality securities with low spreads over Treasuries. As countries run sound fiscal policies with balanced budgets or budget surpluses, they will experience a relative shortage of government securities, making it more difficult to maintain bond benchmarks. (See Chapter 4, Developing Benchmark Issues.) In certain circumstances, mortgage bonds could assume this function. (See Section 12.5.1.1 below.)

12

12.4.3 Privatization and Deregulation

A major reason for increased private sector debt issuance is the greater involvement of the private sector in the economy as a result of privatization and deregulation. Some of the larger SOEs, with a correspondingly great need for debt financing, have been privatized and their industry sectors deregulated. The leading SOEs that have been privatized or deregulated have been the utility companies, such as telecommunications, electricity, and power. A motivation for privatizing these vital service providers could be their need for large amounts of investment and debt financing that are no longer available on the market or from banks unless their operations and balance sheets are radically rationalized through a private sector approach. In many developing countries, these privatized companies are becoming the most prominent issuers of private sector bonds.

12.5 Issues in Developing Private Sector Bond Markets

The government and private sector securities markets interact through many channels. Government actions can also hinder the development of the private sector securities market. Excessive government borrowing can "crowd out" the private sector, and transaction taxes can discourage trade in private securities. There are also other factors influencing private sector market development that are less directly in the hands of the government, such as sufficient supply of bonds by private sector issuers and demand for private sector issues by investors that are needed for deep and active markets. Capital markets need a critical mass of securities, investors, and funds for their efficient functioning. However, the size of the economy in which a private sector bond market is able to function appears to be more critical for the development of a private sector bond market than for the development of a government bond market. Therefore, a private sector bond market may be more difficult to develop in a small economy.

12.5.1 Linkages Between Private Sector and Government Bond Markets

A well-functioning government bond market often is the forerunner of a private sector bond market, and provides the institutional and operational infrastructure for the private sector market. The role of government benchmark issues, the experience of the dealer community, and the investor base for security purchases and trading all are valuable features of securities markets that could be drawn upon in the development of an effective private sector securities market. The government bond market also serves as a means of educating authorities, financial and nonfinancial institutions, and a wide portion of the populace about debt market operations. This will create a knowledge base about bonds that will be valuable when developing the private sector bond market.

12.5.1.1 *Government as Benchmark Issuer*

The government is by far the most likely issuer of debt securities that could serve as benchmarks. (See Chapter 4, Developing Benchmark Issues.) The benchmark yield curve is a basic benchmark for pricing other government or nongovernment bond issues of comparable maturities across the yield curve on the primary market as well as the secondary market. Other debt securities are priced by taking the corresponding maturity on the yield curve and adjusting for the (greater) credit risk of the nongovernment issuer. The government benchmark is an important tool for price discovery in other fixed-income securities markets, including the private sector debt market. Without that benchmark, it is difficult to price fixed-income securities, including private sector debt securities, in a rational manner.

The short end of the yield curve is important in the development of efficient money markets. The short end of the yield curve is a linkage to interest rates under the banking system. It is also where the monetary authorities can influence the general interest level of the economy through open market operations. The short end of the yield curve is, thus, the anchor to the entire yield curve. (See Chapter 2, Money Markets and Monetary Policy Operations.)

While government bonds work well as benchmark issues, countries with a small or no fiscal deficit, and those running budget surpluses after having run deficits in the past face, difficulties in supplying the government issues needed to constitute a benchmark yield curve.[267] (See Chapter 4,

---

267. The United States is facing the prospect of this situation, and this was also an issue in Australia in the 1990s.

Developing Benchmark Issues.) If government securities are not able to serve as a benchmark, it may sometimes be possible to use other bonds from major issuers, such as development banks, subnationals, or the major private sector issuers (such as mortgage bond issuers) as de facto benchmark issues. (See Chapter 11, Development of Subnational Bond Markets.)

With mortgage markets growing faster than government securities markets, consideration could be given to substitute mortgage debt benchmarks for government bond benchmarks. (See Section 12.4.2.2 above.) However, mortgage-backed securities other than bonds are not sufficiently homogeneous and free from various embedded risks for that purpose. In addition, the emergence of mortgage securities as benchmarks is difficult without a high degree of financial intermediation through a mortgage bank or a secondary market agency.

12.5.1.2 Dealer Community and Investor Base for Government and Private Sector Bonds

An efficient government bond market encourages, and even requires, the development of highly skilled fixed-income securities intermediaries. These intermediaries, in turn, can support the development of the private sector bond market. The government bond market can provide the experience needed to build skills in the fixed-income business, because it is more liquid than the private sector bond market and involves more issuance and trading—both of which also provide a strong profit base. Dealers need these skills and profits to support private sector bond transactions, which are riskier than government bonds because of the greater credit risk of private sector issuers and the lower liquidity of private sector issues (market risk). Two types of intermediaries where the government role is especially important are market makers and interdealer brokers (IDBs). (See Chapter 7, Developing Secondary Market Structures for Government Securities.)

Government securities also provide dealers with mechanisms to hedge their private sector securities market exposures. This could be done through repurchase agreements that are typically based on government securities, through government securities themselves that are lower risk and more liquid than private sector debt securities, or through interest rate derivatives that are often based on government securities.

12

12.5.2 Distinctive Characteristics of Private Sector Bond Markets

While government securities markets provide many elements needed for a private sector securities market to function, there are several components that a private sector debt securities market requires, and, if absent, could impede its development, regardless of how well developed the government securities market is. The most important components are attractive issuers, a disclosure and information system, a credit-rating system, and bankruptcy laws that are particular to nongovernment bond markets.

12.5.2.1 Disclosure System and Information

In order to attract and maintain investor interest, all bond issuers—whether government, subnational, or private sector—need to disclose objective, relevant, and timely information about themselves and about the securities being offered to the public. Disclosure issues relating to private sector bond development have some special aspects.

In contrast to a disclosure system, which depends on building investor awareness, regulators in developing countries sometimes use a merit system to oversee and guide private sector capital market issues. A merit system is one in which the regulatory authorities review the substantive merits of a proposed capital market issue in order to ensure that investors are protected and that the issue is compatible with national development objectives. Pursuant to laws, decrees, or directives, the authorities determine the participants that may enter the market and the terms of their involvement, including but not limited to the type of instrument that may be used and the substantive terms of the instrument (e.g., timing and pricing of the issuance). This gives regulators the ability to exercise considerable power over market outcomes.[268]

A merit system does not make regulators accountable for their decisions and can induce moral hazard among market participants and investors. A merit system will protract and even crush the development of a sustainable and efficient market mechanism. In private sector bond markets in developing countries, a merit system is exemplified by a queuing system, a

---

268. See Wong 1996.

coupon-rate control, eligibility criteria for issuers, restrictions on bond term, and the like. Use of a merit system is understandable in developing countries with major shortcomings in such essential market infrastructures as law enforcement and court systems, sophistication of investors, strong intermediaries, adequate credit-rating systems, proper accounting standards and auditing systems, and effective corporate governance. Even under such conditions, the use of a merit system should be considered as a temporary expedient, and it should be discontinued as soon as the market infrastructure is sufficiently strong to allow the private sector market to rely on conventional disclosure system procedures.

The extent of regulatory disclosure requirements for private sector debt instruments may vary by the issuing history of the issuer and the scope of targeted investors. The existence of an equity market is practically a prerequisite for private sector bond market development, as it often sets an example for disclosure practice. International accounting standards are a good model to follow to avoid accounting ambiguities in financial statement disclosure. Disclosure on private sector bonds should focus on the issuer's creditworthiness and the issuer's product information.

In addition to meeting regulatory disclosure requirements, the development of private sector bond markets could be aided by voluntary disclosure. Policymakers in developing countries should be aware of the important role that voluntary disclosure activities play in the functioning of developed-country capital markets, and should promote and facilitate proactive information dissemination by private sector entities. If not already mandatory, the voluntary public release of a credit-rating agency's rating of a private sector bond issuer could form an important element of a voluntary disclosure system. Voluntary disclosure is also achieved by improvements in corporate governance that focus on transparency of the issuer's activities and management,[269] public relations through the media, and investor relations.

---

269. In 1999, the OECD published, *Principles of Corporate Governance*. The five basic principles recommended for corporate governance are: (i) *The Rights of Shareholders:* The corporate governance framework should protect shareholders' rights. (ii) *The Equitable Treatment of Shareholders:* The corporate governance framework should ensure the equitable treatment of all shareholders, including minority and foreign shareholders. All shareholders should have the opportunity to obtain effective redress for violation of their rights. (iii) *The Role of Stakeholders in Corporate Governance:* The corporate governance framework should recognize the rights of stakeholders as established by law and encourage active cooperation between corporations and stakeholders in creating

12.5.2.2 Credit-Rating System

Credit-rating agencies perform a catalytic role in developing capital markets. The purpose of credit ratings is to provide objective and independent summary opinions of relative credit risk. Ratings give an indication of relative risk for a bond issuer's ability and willingness to make full and timely payments of principal and interest over the lifetime of the rated instrument.[270] Investors will demand a higher interest rate to compensate for investing in bond issues with a lower rating, which reflects higher credit risk. The differentiation of interest rates on the basis of risk has two beneficial effects—the efficient allocation of resources by investors and encouragement of companies to improve their financial structure and operations. Regulators can also use credit ratings when assessing fulfillment of capital adequacy requirements, with debt of a higher credit rating carrying more weight. More generally, credit-rating agencies encourage greater transparency, increased information flow, and improved accounting and auditing. For credit-rating agencies to be successful, they must be seen to be independent, and investors must understand and value the role of ratings.

While credit-rating agencies help in the development of capital markets, they also need a minimal degree of capital market development in order to be commercially sustainable. It is doubtful whether most developing countries have the minimal degree of capital market development to sustain a credit-rating agency under normal conditions. One alternative has been for credit-rating agencies to expand into other business lines such as providing general financial information services.

Some rating agencies have dropped the link between ratings and specific issues of debt. Instead, they have rated institutions that issue the debt. In the Philippines and Turkey, for example, domestic banks obtain ratings in

---

wealth, jobs, and the sustainability of financially sound enterprises. (iv) *Disclosure and Transparency*: The corporate governance framework should ensure that timely and accurate disclosure is made on all material matters regarding the corporation, including the financial situation, performance, ownership, and governance of the company. (v) *The Responsibilities of the Board*: The corporate governance framework should ensure the strategic guidance of the company, the effective monitoring of the management by the board, and the board's accountability to the company and the shareholders. (See OECD 1999.)

270. See Pinkes 1997.

order to establish relationships with foreign banks and even to raise funding on international markets.

Another, and more controversial, method to make credit-rating agencies willing to rate entities in developing countries has been to aid these agencies by public policy actions. In most developing countries with credit rating agencies, mandatory ratings by accredited credit-rating agencies have been introduced, and, often, a system is set up to license approved rating agencies. Mandatory ratings usually require private sector bond issues to be rated, and certain institutional investors may be restricted to purchase securities that have received a certain rating classification. For example, pension funds may be required to purchase only rated securities.

International credit-rating agencies, such as Standard & Poor's and Moody's, have advantages over domestic agencies in their greater expertise and credibility. They at times may lack, however, the qualitative understanding of local conditions, which is particularly important in developing countries where access to, and availability of, quantitative data is often lacking. A common approach has been for a domestic credit agency to form a joint venture with an international rating agency, with the latter providing technical assistance to the domestic rating agency. Fitch-IBCA Duff & Phelps,[271] a leading international credit-rating agency, has expanded its activities to lesser-developed capital markets through joint ventures. Often this has been with the International Finance Corporation of the World Bank Group helping to establish the new rating agency and taking a small equity share. Most of these projects are yet to be completed, and it is too early to assess the success of the local joint venture rating agencies that have begun operations. Their supposed catalytic impact on capital market development is far from demonstrated, especially as they almost all rely upon mandatory ratings.

Another issue is the optimal number of credit-rating agencies in a market. Too much competition in an undeveloped market may cause an inflation of ratings or lower quality of the rating process in an attempt to cut costs. Too little competition, on the other hand, raises concerns about slackening of standards and performance.

12

---

271. Fitch-IBCA and Duff Phelps Credit Rating (DCR) merged in March 2000.

12.5.2.3 Bankruptcy Laws

Bankruptcy laws are another essential element for developing private sector securities markets. Nongovernment bonds, typically private sector bonds, may default, whereas government bonds denominated in the local currency do not default, at least in theory.

The issuer's obligation to pay interest and repay the principal in a timely manner should not be a matter for issuer discretion. The investor is able to assess meaningfully the risk of investing in bonds only if the limit of the investor's legal ability to force the bankrupt issuer to service its obligations and the procedures for going to that limit are clearly defined. Bankruptcy laws define the limit and the procedures. A mechanism for efficient reorganization is vital to a smooth functioning of private sector bond markets in that it establishes the investor's right to recover investments and establishes the priority (seniority) or subordination of one investor's right to that of other creditors.[272]

The investor's ability to force a bankrupt issuer to repay its obligations under bankruptcy laws can be generally classified into three classes according to its security type—secured or collateralized bonds, senior bonds, and subordinated bonds.

12.5.3 Impediments to Private Sector Bond Market Development

The absence, deficiency, or ineffectiveness of the essential elements needed to develop and maintain an effective government or subnational bond sector discussed in other chapters of the handbook may impede market development and/or substantially impair the functioning of the market. While these considerations apply to the development of the private sector bond market, there are two specific government actions—crowding out and statutory restrictions—that can impair the development of private sector bond markets.

12

---

272. See Hakansson 1999.

12.5.3.1 Crowding Out by Public Sector Borrowing

Given the credit standing of government bonds, such securities, especially if priced competitively, will be the preferred investment choice for many market participants. Persistent large government budget deficits, financed by issuance of new government bonds, could absorb national savings, thereby crowding out the private sector from the bond market. Under such circumstances, the private sector will find it impossible to obtain investors for its bonds or will do so only at prohibitively high interest rates.

There are other ways in which the government may be crowding out the private sector. The government may be tempted to finance its fiscal deficit at the lowest possible cost before any nongovernment issuers tap the market. This could be achieved by offering special-issue bonds with a low yield but with other attractive features (e.g., tax exemptions, backing by proceeds of gold or oil, distinctive maturities) that other issuers are not able to provide. A variant is for the government to require financial institutions to purchase government securities to meet regulatory requirements (captive sources of government funding). (See Chapter 6, Developing the Investor Base for Government Securities.) There is not much that the private sector can do to contend with such government actions except to engage government officials and enlighten them of the undesirable consequences of their conduct and policies.

12.5.3.2 Statutory Restrictions

The primary private sector bond market is more subject to governmental interference than the secondary market because it is the entry point of securities into the market and thus the very first checkpoint for investor protection. Statutory restrictions are usually imposed around either the market participants' eligibility or product features, or both. Such government interference often ends up with a merit system. (See Section 12.5.2.1.)

Table 12.6 summarizes typical restrictions that the government in a developing country often imposes on the primary market for private sector bonds, possible motives behind the restrictions, and possible negative impacts of the restrictions on private sector bond market development. These statutory restrictions usually have plausible but ostensible policy objectives that often disguise their true intentions and/or negative

Table 12.6. Statutory Restrictions and Requirements Impeding Primary Corporate Bond Market Development in Developing Countries

Restrictive Areas	Restrictions and Requirements	Possible Motives	Possible Negative Impacts on Debt Market Development
Product features	No short term	To avoid conflicts with banking products	No reliable anchor for yield curve; will distort yield curve
	Cap on coupon rates	To keep general level of interest rates artificially low	Will hamper formation of yield curve; will dampen supply of, and demand for, long-term bonds
	No floating rate	To limit competition with bank deposits	Will limit hedging tools against interest-rate risks
	No/restrictive unsecured bonds	Unsecured bonds may undermine banks' demand for collateral to their loans	Will be disadvantageous to new, fast growing companies and noncapital-intensive companies
	Bank guarantee	To keep bond issuance under a bank's control	Will limit free risk/return trade-off
	No forex-linked bonds	Capital control	Will limit hedging tools against currency risks
Issuer's eligibility	Credit-rating-linked eligibility for bond issuance	To avoid conflict with banks in lucrative mid-market	Will limit free risk/return trade-off; disadvantageous to low-rated companies
	Cap on debt issue amount	To keep bond issuance supplementary to bank loans	Will limit free risk/return trade-off
	Queuing system	To keep room for government bond issuance	Will dysfunction demand/supply relationship
Underwriter's eligibility	Strict requirements or no license for new entrants	To protect vested interests of existing underwriters	Will limit competition and innovation
Taxation	Withholding tax and stamp duties	To compensate for weak tax collection system	Will fragment market and limit liquidity
Other	Ban on swap Ban on futures and options	Bureaucratic investor protection in absence of financial expertise and well-organized risk management systems at regulatory and corporate levels	Will limit hedging tools against interest rate risks; will limit arbitrage activities
	Vetting period of securities registration	Cumbersome and time-consuming; bureaucratic inefficiency. Banks may benefit from this inefficiency	Will reduce optimal financing opportunities; may raise financing costs to issuers

Source: Endo 2000.

12

effects. Possible motives behind those statutory restrictions can be categorized as:

- Protection of vested interests of market participants
- Preservation of the existing tax base
- Capital control
- Bureaucratic inefficiency

The development of private sector bond markets may erode some part of the business activity of commercial banks. Banks may feel threatened by an emerging securities industry, and often will attempt to use their political influence to foil or curb the development of such private sector markets.

Opposition to the development of a primary market for private sector bonds may also be found in a country's securities industry itself. Existing intermediaries, such as investment banks and brokerage houses, may have built up significant vested interests through a banking/brokerage business and may resist changes to existing market structures and environments. Pressure from these firms at times has effectively barred new entrants such as commercial banks and foreign investment banks from posing strong competition to them. In the process, the development of the private sector bond market is impaired.

As discussed in Chapter 10 (Development of Government Securities Market and Tax Policy), taxes on securities transactions and fees (stamp duties) are common impediments to the development of government securities markets. The same considerations apply to the development of the private sector bond market. Such taxes and fees reduce market turnover and thereby market liquidity in the secondary market for private sector bonds, and in this manner inhibit the development of the market.

Lengthy vetting of filed securities registration statements is in all likelihood not an intended restriction. It is a by-product of a statutory action to implement disclosure requirements. Nonetheless, cumbersome and excessive filing requirements can become a de facto statutory restriction in that it actually prohibits issuers from expeditiously availing themselves of timely financing opportunities.

In addition to making vetting operations at the regulatory authority efficient by periodic review of existing requirements and by staff training, a shelf-registration system may be helpful in this regard. A shelf-registration system allows for the sale of securities on a delayed or continuous basis. Once a prospective issuer registers for an amount that may reasonably be expected to be sold for a predetermined period (say, two years) after the initial date of registration, the issuer and its underwriters are allowed the flexibility to sell the registered securities when they think market conditions are most favorable during that period. The major security markets, including those in Japan, the United Kingdom, and the United States, have shelf-registration arrangements.

12.6 Conclusion

The issuance of fixed-income securities by private sector entities will contribute to economic development through more efficient allocation of capital to the private sector. New trends in public policy and financial technology broaden the application of private sector debt securities. They create new borrowers that arise from the growth of private sector initiatives, typically in housing finance and infrastructure building. Unlike government bonds, only a small number of private sector bond issues are likely to be liquid. A private sector bond market needs, among other things, a credit-rating system, a disclosure system including securities registration, and effective bankruptcy laws.

Development of a well-functioning government bond market in developing countries will often precede and facilitate development of a private sector bond market. A well-functioning government securities market provides the institutional and operational infrastructure for the private sector market. The government securities bond benchmark is an important tool for price discovery in the private sector fixed-income securities market. The experience of the dealer community and the investor base for security purchases and trading are valuable features of securities markets that could be drawn upon in the development of an effective private sector securities market. The government securities market also serves as a means of educating authorities, financial and nonfinancial institutions, and a wide portion of the populace about debt market operations. This will create a base of knowledge about bonds that will be valuable when developing the private sector securities market.

12

Bibliography

Aylward, Anthony, and Jack Glen. 1999. "Primary Securities Markets: Cross Country Findings." Discussion Paper Number 39. International Finance Corporation, Washington, D.C.

Bank of Japan. 1998. *Shikin Junkan Kanjo 1998*. Tokyo, Japan.

BIS (Bank for International Settlements). 1999. *Quarterly Review: International Banking and Financial Market Developments*. November. Basel, Switzerland. Available at www.bis.org/publ/index.htm.

Carter, Lawrence W., and Gary Bond. 1996. *IFC Lessons of Experience 4: Financing Private Infrastructure*. International Finance Corporation, Washington, D.C.

Darche, Benjamin. 2000. *Local Capital Markets and Private Infrastructure Development: Global Best Practice Review*. World Bank, Washington, D.C.

Endo, Tadashi. 2000. "Corporate Bond Market Development." IFC Working Paper. International Finance Corporation, Washington, D.C.

Federal Reserve Board. 1999. *Flow of Funds Accounts of the United States 1998*. Board of Governors of the Federal Reserve System, Washington, D.C.

Hakansson, Nils H. 1999. "The Role of a Corporate Bond Market in an Economy—and in Avoiding Crises." Working Papers RPF–287. Institute of Business and Economic Research (IBER), University of California at Berkeley.

Harwood, Alison. 2000. "Building Local Bond Markets: Some Issues and Actions." In *Building Local Bond Markets: An Asian Perspective*. International Finance Corporation, Washington, D.C. Available at www.ifc.org/publications/pubs/bond.html.

IMF (International Monetary Fund). 1998. *International Financial Statistical Yearbook 1998*. Washington, D.C.

Lee, Esmond K. Y. 1999. "Debt Market Development in Hong Kong." Presentation to the World Bank Group.

OECD (Organization for Economic Cooperation and Development). 1999. *Principles of Corporate Governance*. Paris, France. Available at www.oecd.org//daf/governance/principles.pdf.

Pettis, Michael. 2000. "The Risk Management Benefits of Bonds." In *Building Local Bond Markets: An Asian Perspective*. International Finance

Corporation, Washington D.C. Available at www.ifc.org/publications/pubs/bond.html.

Pinkes, Kenneth. 1997. *The Function of Ratings in Capital Markets*. Global Credit Research, Moody's Investors Service, New York.

Rhee, S. Ghon. 1998. "Institutional Impediments to the Development of Fixed-Income Securities Markets: An Asian Perspective." OECD/World Bank Workshop on the Development of Fixed-Income Securities Markets in Emerging Market Economies. Paris, France. December.

Roger, Neil. 1999. "Recent Trends in Private Participation in Infrastructure." *Private Sector/Viewpoint*. Note No. 196. World Bank, Washington, D.C.

Schinasi, Garry J., and R. Todd Smith. 1998. "Fixed-Income Markets in the United States, Europe, and Japan: Some Lessons for Emerging Markets." IMF Working Paper 98/173. International Monetary Fund, Washington, D.C. Available at www.imf.org.

Wong, Nancy. 1996. "Easing Down the Merit-Disclosure Continuum: A Case Study of Malaysia and Taiwan." *Law and Policy in International Business*. Fall.

12

Glossary

401(k). In the United States, a tax-exempt pension plan, similar to IRAs, available to self-employed persons and small businesses, covered in Section 401(k) of the U.S. Internal Revenue Code. Employers may match amounts contributed by employees.

Accrual basis of tax calculation. Tax system in which accrued gains or losses on a security (even if unrealized) are taken into account when computing the tax liability.

Accrual-based taxation. Tax on income that is earned in an accounting sense, but not received in cash.

Add-ons. Additions to auctions of Treasury securities for monetary policy purposes rather than for fiscal policy purposes. The proceeds from add-ons are often placed in a blocked account at the central bank.

ALM. See asset-liability management.

Alternative trading systems (ATS). See Electronic trading systems.

Amortization schedule. Timetable for paying down outstanding debt.

Annuities. Investments yielding a fixed periodic income during the holder's lifetime.

APEC. See Asia-Pacific Economic Cooperation.

Arbitrage trading. Exploitation of price or interest rate differences between markets.

Asia-Pacific Economic Cooperation (APEC). Organization of Asia-Pacific countries established in 1989 as an informal dialogue group to advance Asia-Pacific economic dynamism and sense of community.

Asset-backed securities. Securities that are secured by other assets. A well-developed asset-backed securities market is the mortgage-backed securities market. These securities are often in the form of certificates that channel, or pass through, the cash flow from mortgages to the certificate holder.

Asset-liability management (ALM). Risk management approach that examines the combined risks of assets and liabilities over time under different possible future scenarios.

ATS. See Alternative trading systems.

Auction-agency market. Form of order-driven market in which orders from traders are collected centrally in the order book of an auction agency, which traditionally has been an exchange.

Auctions. The sale of securities through an open bidding.

Autonomous transactions affecting excess reserves. Transactions affecting reserves held at the central bank over which the central bank has no immediate influence. Examples would be payments by the government from its account at the central bank and receipts by the government to its account at the central bank.

Back-office systems. Systems supporting actions that follow securities sales and dealing, such as confirmation of orders and accounting.

Bank debenture. Unsecured obligation of a bank.

Batch communication. Message grouping payment orders for securities transactions.

Benchmark issue. Issue of securities that is sufficiently large and actively traded that its price may serve as a reference point for other issues of similar maturity.

Benchmark yield curve. Yield curve formed on the basis of yields on benchmark securities of selected maturities.

Best execution. Fair execution of client orders of securities, so that no client has preference over another in terms of time of execution and price received.

Blind interdealer broker screens. Computer terminals provided by interdealer brokers on which bids and offers are placed without the name of the party bidding or offering.

Blue List. Service of Standard & Poor's that quotes prices on municipal and corporate bond offerings.

BMA. See Bond Market Association.

Bond bank. Conduit finance institution that issues a bond on the market equal to the sum of separate individual issues plus a reserve fund. It uses the proceeds to purchase bonds issued by participating localities.

Bond conversion (exchange). Purchase by the government of a particular series of government bonds using another series of government bonds as payment.

Bond Market Association (BMA). Founded in the United States, it represents securities firms and banks that underwrite, trade, and sell debt securities.

Bond pooling. Combination of separate bonds for the purpose of financing through an overall issue. See bond bank.

Bond washing. Conversion of interest income into capital gains by selling bonds just before a coupon payment date and repurchasing them immediately thereafter. This is done to avoid tax when capital gains are not taxed or are taxed at a lower rate than interest income.

Bond with equity warrant. Bond with the option of purchasing a proportionate amount of equity shares at a specified date and price.

Bondholders' committee. Group established to defend the interests of bondholders.

Bonds. Coupon-bearing securities, typically with a maturity of one year or more.

Bons du Trésor à taux fixe et à intérêts annuels. BTANs or negotiable fixed-rate medium-term Treasury notes with annual interest.

Bons du Trésor à taux fixe et à intérêts précomptés. BTFs or negotiable fixed-rate discount Treasury bills.

Book-reserve pension plans. Reserves for pensions held on the financial accounts of sponsoring firms. Firms do not actually contribute to the plan, but each year charge prospective pension expenses against the firm's financial accounts.

Book-entry securities. See paperless securities.

Book-entry system. System, often automated, for recording the ownership of securities.

BOOT. See build-own-operate-transfer.

BOT. See build-own-operate-transfer.

Brady bonds. Bonds of developing countries first issued in 1989 in exchange for restructured bank loans. Most are collateralized by U.S. Treasury zero-coupon bonds and interest collateral sufficient for one or two coupon (interest) payments. The bonds are usually settled through EUROCLEAR or CEDEL. The bonds were named after former U.S. Treasury Secretary Nicholas Brady.

Build-operate-transfer (BOT). Project in which an entity builds a facility, operates it temporarily, and then turns it over to the final owner.

Build-own-operate-transfer (BOOT). Project in which an entity builds, owns and operates a facility for a specified period of time and then turns it over to the final owner.

Buyback operation. Repurchase of bonds by the issuer prior to their maturity.

Call option. Contract allowing the holder to buy an asset at a preset price during the period the option remains valid.

Capital adequacy. Provision, typically imposed through regulation, of capital sufficient to cover the risks of doing business.

Capital gains. Increase in value of an asset between the time purchased and the time sold.

Capital grants. Grants allocated by national governments to subnational entities for capital expenditure purposes.

Captive sources of government funding. Purchases of government securities by banks or other financial institutions (e.g., insurance companies or pension funds) that are forced by law or regulation.

Cash management. Service responsible for managing short-term outflows and inflows related to debt management.

CEDEL. Cedel International was established in 1970 to reduce the costs of settling transactions in the Eurobond market. It has expanded to deliver clearing, settlement, and custody services in selected markets around the world.

Central bank liquidity management policy. Central bank policy regarding the management of the supply of bank reserves or settlement balance.

Central depository. The depository where final settlements of a securities transaction are recorded.

Certificate of deposit (CD). Certificate issued by a bank or thrift institution testifying that a specified sum of money has been deposited with that institution.

Chapter 9–type procedure. Refers to Chapter 9 of the U.S. Bankruptcy Code, which deals with defaults by municipalities.

CIF. See collective investment fund.

CIS. See collective investment scheme or collective investment fund.

CIT. See comprehensive income tax.

Clean quotation. Value of a fixed-income asset excluding accrued income.

Clearing. Matching of orders prior to final settlement.

Closed funds. Mutual funds whose shares are not redeemable, but are traded freely on the stock exchange.

Closed-end mutual fund. Mutual fund that issues a fixed number, of shares, which are then traded on a stock exchange.

Collateralized mortgage obligation. Security backed by a pool of pass-through mortgages, structured so there are several classes of bondholders with varying maturities. Principal payments from the pool retire the bonds on a priority basis as specified in the security's prospectus.

Collective investment fund (CIF). Publicly marketed, widely held portfolio investment fund investing in financial instruments. CIFs include authorized open-end funds and closed-end funds. Further, they include contractual investment trusts and unit investment trusts. Also called collective investment scheme.

Collective investment funds. Publicly marketed, widely held portfolio investment funds investing in financial instruments. They include authorized open-ended funds, closed-end funds, contractual investment trusts and unit investment trusts. Also called collective investment scheme.

Collective investment scheme. See Collective investment fund.

Commercial paper. Short-term, unsecured promissory notes issued by a corporation.

Committee on Payment and Settlement Systems (CPSS). Committee meeting under the auspices of the Bank for International Settlements to study problems and set standards relating to payment and settlement systems.

Compliance period for required reserves. See reserve maintenance period.

Comprehensive income tax (CIT). Income tax levied on all forms of income.

Comprehensive tax system. Tax system that is applied to the total of all forms of income.

Conduit or "paper" company. Company formed by an investor or group of investors as a vehicle for their placements.

Consumers' surplus. In the case of a sale of securities, excess between the price paid by purchasers and the (lower) price at which the issuer was willing to sell the securities.

Contingent liabilities. Liabilities that are conditional upon predefined events or circumstances.

Contractual CIF. Open-ended, noncorporate investment fund established by way of trust deed. In Britain, they are called unit trusts. Participating units in contractual CIFs may be bought and sold through the investment trust manager at proportionate underlying net asset value.

Contractual mutual fund. Mutual fund that operates on a contractual basis by which an investor agrees to invest a fixed amount regularly for a specified number of years.

Contractual savings industry. Insurance and pension funds that accept a variety of savings arrangements with a contractual payout commitment by an insurance company or pension fund.

Convertible bond. Corporate bond with a provision for its exchange into a set number of equity shares of the corporation at a prestated conversion price.

Corporate CIF. Investment fund that collects money from investors by selling shares in paper investment companies which are established solely to invest the pooled funds of small investors in financial assets. Corporate CIFs are divided into two types: (i) open end fund, or better known as a mutual fund, that will redeem their shares before the maturity on a continuous basis or periodically. (ii) closed-end fund whose fixed number of shares cannot be redeemed and are traded on the stock exchanges. Investors of closed-end funds have to sell them to retrieve the money before the maturity.

Corporate mutual funds. Mutual funds established as a corporation selling shares to investors.

Corporatize. Make an institution act like a privately owned entity.

Counterpart payment. Payment related to sale of a security.

Coupon washing trades. Securities transactions to exploit different tax treatments, such as between domestic and foreign investors, for particular bonds that may be taxable in one jurisdiction and not in another.

CPSS. See Committee on Payment and Settlement Systems.

Credit enhancement. Improving the creditworthiness of an instrument by some form of guarantee or security backing.

Credit-rating agency. A firm that rates the value of financial obligations or the creditworthiness of firms or countries.

Credit risk. Risk that a counterparty will not honor an obligation when due.

Crowding out. Causing issuance by non-government issuers to become more difficult due to a large issuing of government securities that absorb the bulk of national savings.

CSD. Central securities depository. See central depository.

Currency risk. Risk that a change in foreign exchange rates will diminish profitability.

Custody accounts. Accounts recording the holding of securities. See book-entry accounts.

Custody arrangements. Facilities for the safekeeping of securities and a record of their ownership.

Cut-off price. Lowest successful bid at an auction.

Dealer market. Market where dealers quote bid and ask prices to potential counterparties on request.

Debt management office. The government office that manages the public debt.

Deep-discount bond. Bond issued with a reduced or zero rate of interest. It sells for a deep discount from its face value, and the yield of this bond is the difference between the purchase price and the par value. Deep-discount bonds with no coupons are called zero-coupon bonds.

Default risk. Risk that the issuer will not pay principal or interest on schedule.

Deficit grants. Grants allocated by the central government to subnational governments in deficit.

Delivery versus payment (DVP). Link between the funds transfer system and the securities transfer system to ensure that securities will not be delivered until funds are received.

Dematerialized securities. See paperless securities.

Demutualization of exchanges. Shift of mutually owned exchanges to a publicly held, corporate form of ownership.

Depository system for securities. System that holds securities in safekeeping and records their ownership.

Derivatives markets. Markets for instruments whose value is derived from other underlying instruments.

Directed credit. Regulations that require banks to direct lending to specific sectors that the authorities deem to be in the public interest.

Disclosure requirements. Transparency requirements for entities issuing securities, to disclose information to the public related to the financial condition of issuing entities, terms of the securities, and other financial matters.

Discount window. Central bank lending facility, typically part of an accommodation lending facility. Discount window may lend by actually discounting securities from the borrower, but more often lends on such securities as collateral.

Discount. Difference between the issuing or purchase price and the value at maturity of a fixed-income security.

DIT. See dual income tax.

Dividend deduction system. System to avoid double taxation by allowing those receiving dividend income to exclude it from their taxable income.

DMO. See debt management office.

Double income tax (DIT). System in which the profits of a corporation are taxed twice, once at the corporate level and again as income tax levied on dividends to shareholders.

Dual income tax. Tax on income differentiated by two rates, used in Nordic countries, where there is a progressive tax for labor income and a flat tax on capital gains.

Dual-currency bonds. Bonds that pay interest in one currency and the principal in another.

DVP. See delivery versus payment.

EET. Exempt (contribution), exempt (investment income), tax (benefit). Tax regime allowing investment income to accumulate tax free, with benefits taxed in full upon withdrawal.

Electronic trading systems (ETS). Computerized trading systems that centralize, match, cross, or otherwise execute trades.

Emerging market funds. Funds that invest in the debt or equity of emerging-market countries.

E-trading. Trading of securities via electronic means.

ETS. See electronic trading systems.

EUROCLEAR. System founded in 1968 in Europe as a clearing and settlement system for internationally traded securities.

Ex-ante price information. Price information available before a trade is made.

Excess reserves. Deposits held at the central bank beyond those specified by reserve requirements.

Execution risk. Risk that the price of a security may change between the time a quote is made and the time it is acted upon.

Ex-post price information. Prices after a trade has been made.

FASB. See Financial Accounting Standards Board.

FESCO. See Forum of European Securities Commissions.

Finality at payment. Legal assurance that payment obligations/rights have been legally satisfied.

Financial Accounting Standards Board (FASB). Private group relied upon by the U.S. Securities and Exchange Commission for establishing financial accounting and reporting standards for publicly held companies.

Financial intermediation. Interaction of financial market participants, with a financial institution acquiring financial assets (savings) from individuals or businesses and making them available to other parties (investors—governments, businesses, individuals) at a fee (an interest rate).

Financial Stability Forum (FSF). Convened in 1999, the Forum brings together on a regular basis national authorities responsible for financial stability in significant international financial centers, international financial institutions, sector-specific international groupings of regulators and supervisors, and committees of central bank experts.

Fiscal illusion and tax-exempt bonds. Illusion that lower borrowing costs associated with tax-exempt bonds also reflect overall or effective borrowing costs.

Fiscal responsibility laws. Laws that define the responsibilities of different levels of government and the relationships among these levels.

Fit-and-proper tests. Criteria that must be met by individuals or institutions before they are permitted to enter business (usually in the financial sector) as a market participant.

Fitch-IBCA, Duff & Phelps. Global financial services company that rates credits.

Fixed-rate instrument. Instrument bearing a coupon that is fixed over its life.

Flat tax. Tax at the same rate on all forms of income, perhaps allowing for no deductions.

Floating-rate note. Note on which the interest rate is periodically reset in accordance with market rates.

Floating-rate securities. Securities on which the rate of return is periodically reset in line with market conditions at the time.

Floor-based exchange. Exchange where traders physically meet to trade on the floor in a trading pit.

Foreign-currency-linked instruments. Securities on which the return is indexed to the exchange rate of another currency.

Forum of European Securities Commissions (FESC). Organization of European securities regulators.

Forward leg. That part of a financial transaction scheduled to settle at a future time.

Forward transactions. Transactions to be settled at a date in the future.

Fragmentation of market. Presence in a market of too many instruments to support active trading of any one instrument.

Front-office systems. Systems that directly support the sales and dealing areas of a securities firm.

Front running. Intermediary, learning about a customer order, may first execute transactions for his own account.

FSF. See Financial Stability Forum.

Fungibility of securities. Substitutability between securities.

Futures contract. Standardized contract, traded on an exchange, for the purchase or sale of an asset in the future.

GASB. See Governmental Accounting Standards Board.

General obligation bond. Bond secured by general tax and borrowing power revenues.

Gilt-edged assets. Financial assets of very high credit quality.

Government bonds. Securities, usually of more than one-year maturity, issued by the central government on behalf of the nation for purposes of financing general or specific budget expenditures.

Government debt manager. Principal official of the agency that manages government debt transactions. This responsibility is normally assigned to the Ministry of Finance, which may appoint an agent for implementing all or part of this duty, such as a separate debt management office, the central bank, or other entity.

Government securities market. Market for tradable securities issued by a government.

Government securities. Securities (bills and bonds) issued by the government.

Government-sponsored enterprise (GSE). Private corporation with implicit government backing.

Governmental Accounting Standards Board (GASB). U.S. group organized in 1984 by the Financial Accounting Foundation (FAF) to establish standards of financial accounting and reporting for state and local governmental entities.

GovPX. GovPX, Inc., was founded in 1990 by major bond dealers and interdealer brokers to provide real-time prices of fixed-income securities.

Gross bilateral settlement. Settlement of funds or securities transfers individually (without netting) between two institutions.

GSE. See government sponsored enterprise.

Haircut. Percentage deduction from the market value of securities.

Hedge funds. Funds that manage positions in currencies or securities with minimal capital by financing these through offsetting transactions.

Hedging. Avoiding the possibility of loss in an asset or liability by a counterbalancing investment or borrowing.

Holding period tax. Tax levied on income accrued by the securities seller and interest accrued by the cash provider during the period a repo is outstanding.

Horizontal equity in taxation. Taxing of people in the same tax bracket at the same rate.

IASC. See International Accounting Standards Committee.

IDB. See interdealer broker.

IMLA. See International Municipal Lawyers Association.

Immobilization of securities. Storage of securities in a depository, with trade effected through a book-entry system.

Imputation system. System to reduce double taxation by giving the shareholder full or partial credit against liability on overall income for taxes paid by the corporation.

Index-linked debt obligations. Debt instruments on which the yield is linked to another rate, such as the inflation rate or the exchange rate.

Individual Retirement Account (IRA). In the United States, a government-allowed retirement account to which a specified amount of personal earnings may be contributed annually, with earnings allowed to accumulate tax free until withdrawal.

Individual Savings Account (ISA). In the United Kingdom, a government-allowed saving account on which taxes are deferred.

Inflation-indexed bond. Bond on which the nominal return is adjusted with the inflation rate.

Insider trading. Trading on the basis of information not available to the public.

Insured bond. Bond backed by commercial insurance policy.

Integrated tax system. See comprehensive tax system.

Interbank market. Market for short-term borrowing and lending between banks.

Interbank money market. Credit extended by one bank to another, usually on a short-term basis and often unsecured.

Interbank transactions. Short-term borrowing by one bank from another.

Interdealer broker. Broker that facilitates trading between dealers by providing information and matching orders.

Interest rate controls. Regulations that impose ceilings on interest rates a bank may charge on its credits or pay on its liabilities.

Interest rate futures. Futures contract on an interest-bearing security, such as a Treasury bill or Treasury bond.

Interest rate risk. Risk that interest rates may change and thereby reduce the value of an asset or raise the value of a liability.

Interest rate swap. Contract between two parties to exchange the cash flows from instruments held by each. Thus, one party holding a fixed-rate instrument might exchange the cash flows from it for the cash flows from a floating-rate instrument held by the other party.

International Accounting Standards Committee (IASC). Independent, private sector body formed in 1973 with the objective of harmonizing the accounting principles used by businesses and other organizations for financial reporting.

International Accounting Standards. Accounting standards developed by the International Accounting Standards Committee (IASC) and approved by the International Organization of Securities Commissions (IOSCO).

International central securities depository (ICSD). See central depository.

International Municipal Lawyers Association (IMLA). Nonprofit professional organization in the United States that has been an advocate and resource for local government attorneys since 1935.

International Organization of Securities Commissions (IOSCO). International grouping of securities market regulators that cooperate to ensure better regulation of the securities markets.

International Securities Market Association (ISMA). Self-regulatory organization that establishes rules and regulations for its member firms to observe when they deal with counterparties.

International Swaps and Derivatives Association. Self-regulatory global trade association of participants in the privately negotiated derivatives industry that tries to identify and reduce sources of risk.

Intraday overdraft. Withdrawals from an account greater than the amount of funds in the account that occur before the end of the business day.

IOSCO. See International Organization of Securities Commissions.

IRA. See Individual Retirement Account.

ISA. See Individual Savings Account.

ISDA. See International Swaps and Derivatives Association.

ISMA. See International Securities Market Association.

Issuing calendar. Dates at which debt will be issued, the maturities, and possibly the terms and amounts of the issues.

IT systems. See information technology systems.

Large-value payments. Payments in large amounts, usually transferred between banks or other financial intermediaries.

Layered structure. Settlement system where there is a central depository and one or more explicit or implicit subdepositories.

Letras hipotecarias. Spanish for mortgage securities.

Life cycle of a benchmark issue. Period between the issue date of a bond and the date it becomes off-the-run.

Limit order. Order contingent on its meeting a specified price target.

Limited-recourse financing. Financing in which the lender has limited recourse to the borrower's parent in case the borrower has financial difficulties.

Liquid asset requirement. Regulation that obliges banks to hold assets deemed as liquid. Such assets often include government securities and deposits at the central bank.

Liquid issue. Issue that is actively traded.

Liquid market. Market where buyers and sellers actively trade, so that individual trades are not likely to appreciably move securities prices.

Liquidity premium. Reduction in interest rates achieved in a liquid securities market.

Liquidity risk. Risk that a financial asset will not be able to be converted to cash quickly, and without a tangible loss of value.

Lock-in effect. Owner of a fixed-income asset of which the market value has changed since its purchase may prefer to wait for its maturity rather than sell it, in order to avoid loss or a tax on profit.

Loss-sharing arrangement. Agreement among participants in a clearing or settlement system regarding the allocation of any losses arising from the default of a participant in the system or of the system itself.

Manufactured payment. In a repo transaction, amount, equal to the coupon or dividend paid on securities held by the cash provider, paid by the cash provider to the securities provider.

Margin requirement. Contractual requirement to adjust for changes in market values. In a repo agreement, for example, if the market value of the securities held as collateral falls, the lender of the securities might be required to top-up the amount of collateral.

Marginal collateral. Additional collateral required by a contract because the market value of the original collateral has declined.

Market maker. Market maker quotes bid and asked prices for securities and normally is prepared to deal at those prices.

Market manipulation. Noncompetitive behavior to gain a market advantage. An example would be cornering the market in a security by buying such a large part of an issue that not enough would be available to others, who would then be forced to bid up the price.

Market order. Order to be filled at the best available price at the time of execution.

Market risk. Risk that changes in market conditions will adversely affect profits or the ability to manage a financial position.

Mark-to-market accounting methods. Accounting methods that regularly and frequently revalue securities or other assets in accordance with market prices.

Master Repurchase Agreement. A master agreement which governs the commitment by the seller (dealer) to buy a security back from the purchaser (customer) at a specified price at a designated future date.

Matching. Comparison of trade or settlement details provided by counterparties to ensure that they agree.

Maturity transformation. Borrowing at one maturity and lending at another, such as borrowing short and lending long.

MBS. See mortgage-backed securities.

Medium-term note (MTN). Noncallable, unsecured senior security of 3–6 years' maturity with fixed coupon rates and investment-grade credit ratings. MTNs have traditionally been sold on a best-efforts basis by investment banks and other broker-dealers acting as agents. Unlike corporate bonds, which are typically sold in large, discrete offerings, MTNs are usually sold in relatively small amounts either on a continuous or intermittent basis.

Merit system for securities. System in which the regulatory authorities review the substantive merits of a proposed capital market issue in order to ensure that investors are protected and that the issue is compatible with the national development scheme.

Micro-market structure. Structure of particular parts of markets, such as the issuing of government debt.

Middle office. The office of a debt management operation that is responsible for risk management.

Minimum capital requirements. Requirements to ensure capital adequacy of a financial institution by requiring the maintenance a certain degree of capital.

MNS. See multilateral net settlement.

Money market mutual fund. Mutual fund that invests mainly in short-term, money market instruments.

Money market. Market for short-term, near-cash-equivalent securities.

Moral hazard. The risk that the existence of a contract will change the behavior of one or both parties to the contract, e.g., an insured firm will take fewer fire precautions.

Mortgage bonds. Bonds secured by mortgages as indirect or direct collateral and containing embedded options giving the borrower the right to repay the bond at par before maturity.

Mortgage-backed securities (MBS). Securities backed by a pool of mortgages.

MSRB. See Municipal Securities Rulemaking Board.

MTS. MTS S.p.A., *Società per il Mercato dei Titoli di Stato*, and associated companies provide management and support for initiatives in Europe aimed at electronic trading for fixed-income securities.

Multilateral net basis. Sum of the value of all transfers a participant in the settlement system has received during a certain period of time less the value of transfers made by the participant to all other participants.

Multilateral net settlement (MNS). Settlement in which each participant settles the position that results from the sum of transfers made and received by it.

Multilateral trading. Trading between market participants, where there is sufficient price discovery for transactions between participants to be possible.

Multiple pledging of securities. Market malpractice of a market participant's employing certain securities held by him in more than one transaction at the same time. The market participant might, for example, pledge the same securities in two separate repurchase agreements.

Multiple-price auctions. Auctions in which each bidder pays the price it bid. Bids are placed in descending order, and the higher bids are accepted until the issue is exhausted.

Municipal bond. Bond issued by a subnational borrower, which in U.S. usage could be a state, county, or municipality.

Municipal Securities Rulemaking Board (MSRB). In the United States, board of 15 members, equally divided among public representatives, broker-dealer representatives, and bank representatives, which regulates municipal securities' dealers.

Munifax. Fax-on-demand service provided to members of the International Municipal Lawyers Association (IMLA) that covers ordinances, cases, regulations, articles and papers related to local government financing.

Mutual fund. Fund that manages a portfolio usually composed of a specific class of assets, such as money market securities, bonds, or equities.

Negative-binding theory. Governments can only do what the law explicitly allows them to do.

Net credit to banks and other financial institutions. Central bank claims on banks and other financial institutions less the central bank's liabilities to these institutions.

Net domestic credit to government. Sum of all credits extended by domestic entities to the government, in national and foreign currencies, less government deposits with the banking system.

Net present value. The present value of the expected future cash flows minus the cost.

Netting. Arrangement among two or more parties to net their obligations.

Nominal interest. Interest received or accrued without reference to inflation.

Nonbank financial institutions. Financial institutions other than commercial banks. These would include such institutions as savings banks, investment banks, insurance companies, mutual funds, and pension funds.

Noncompetitive auction bid. Auction tender, usually by retail investors or the central bank, that is not part of the competitive bidding process. Awards to noncompetitive bidders are usually at the average auction price of successful competitive bids or at the cut-off price.

Non-negotiable securities. Securities that cannot be traded.

Obligations assimilables du Trésor. OATs, or fungible Treasury bonds.

Off-off-the-run issue. Issue that is well seasoned.

Off-the-run issue. Issue that has been in the market, seasoned, or replaced by a new bond of similar original term-to-maturity.

On-the-run issue. Most recently issued bond for a certain term-to-maturity.

Open market operations. Central bank transactions with market intermediaries to affect general market conditions to meet monetary policy objectives. Such transactions may be outright sales or purchases of securities or repurchase agreements.

Open-end mutual fund. Mutual fund that may issue an unlimited number of shares to investors and that agrees to redeem its shares on investor request.

Open-outcry trading. Trading by oral cries or hand signals by traders meeting together, as in a trading pit.

Operational risk. Risk that breakdowns in internal controls, corporate governance, or computer systems and events such as major fires or other disasters could cause losses in securities transactions.

Opportunistic issuers. Irregular issuers of securities who await favorable market conditions or special needs to borrow.

Option-adjusted spread. The spread over an issuer's spot rate curve, developed as a measure of the yield spread that can be used to convert differences between theoretical value and market prices.

Options. Contracts that give the holder the right, but not the obligation, to undertake a specified transaction during a specified time.

Order taking. Response of a financial intermediary to a customer order. This is distinguished from market making, where the intermediary assumes a more active stance by quoting bid and asked prices to which a customer may respond.

Order-driven market. Market dominated by the placing of orders by customers.

OTC. see Over-the-counter market.

Over-the-counter market. Market for the trading of assets outside a formal exchange.

Paperless securities. Securities that are issued in the form of securities accounts, rather than as definitive pieces of paper.

Paris Club. International group of official creditors which lend to governments. The Paris Club may grant debt reorganization or other relief, usually associated with conditions for reform.

Pass through. No tax is levied at the source on dividends, interest, and capital gains passed on by a collective investment fund to its shareholders and taxed at shareholders' tax rates.

Penalty rate. A rate higher than that set for usual borrowing.

Perpetual bond. Bond that is not redeemable, has no maturity date, and pays interest indefinitely.

Pfandbrief. Mortgage in German, but can also be debt obligations issued by state or local governments.

Position limit. Limit on the number of contracts or share of a contract's open interest that a single entity may hold.

Positive carry. Financing a long-term security with a high interest rate by borrowing at a lower, short-term interest rate.

Price discovery. Process by which current market prices for securities become known.

Price risk. Risk that the market value of a security may decline below that of its purchase price.

Price taker. Seller who accepts the price offered for the amount of securities he is selling.

Primary dealers. A group of dealers in government securities designated by the authorities to play a role as specialist intermediaries between the authorities and the market, in government securities markets. Primary dealers usually have special rights to deal with the central bank in the open market operations and/or privileges in bidding at primary auctions of government securities. In exchange, primary dealers are usually obliged to participate in the primary market (which see) and perform market-making functions in the secondary market (which see), in addition to maintaining minimum capital and staff proficiency standards.

Primary market. Asset market where securities—government, subnational, and private sector—are first issued and sold, typically through some form of tender or auction process.

Principle of equality. Requirement for the government to give equal treatment to every potential bondholder, or at a minimum, every potential national bondholder.

Principle of generality. Requirement for a common set of rules to ensure equal access and fair competition in government contract tendering processes, including government securities issuance.

Principle of publicity. Requirement for the government to properly announce when and how it will open the tender process for securities.

Private placement. Direct sale of securities by the issuer to particular purchasers.

Privatize. Sell government-owned entity to private interests.

Progressive tax. Tax of which the rate rises with the amount of income.

Prudential regulations. Regulations that are designed as precautions against loss in financial activities.

Public debt management. The process of establishing a strategy for managing the government's debt in order to raise the required amount of funding, achieve its risk and cost objectives, and meet any other sovereign debt management goals the government may have set, such as developing and maintaining an efficient market for government securities.

Public debt. Stock of outstanding government debt obligations resulting from cumulative issuance of government securities.

Put option. Contract allowing the holder to sell an asset at a preset price during the period the option remains valid.

Quote-driven market. Market dominated by the reaction of customers to bid/ask quotations by dealers.

Real interest rate. The rate of interest excluding the effect of inflation; that is, the rate that is earned in terms of constant-purchasing-power currency.

Real-time gross settlement (RTGS). Continuous settlement of funds or securities transfers individually on an order-by-order basis (without netting).

Recourse loans. Type of loan in which the lender has a general claim against the parent if the collateral is insufficient to repay the loan.

Redemption profile. The schedule of government securities likely to be redeemed because of maturity or other reasons.

Refunded bond. Bond originally issued as a general obligation or revenue bond, but subsequently collateralized, either by direct obligation guaranteed by the central government or by another type of security.

Registered securities. Securities registered in the name of the owner.

Reinvestment risk. Risk that returns from a fixed-income investment cannot be invested at the same rate as the original investment.

Reopening operation. Issuance on more than one occasion of bonds with the same maturity and coupon of previously issued bonds in order to build the outstanding volume of the bonds to a desired level.

Repo. See repurchase agreement.

Repurchase agreement. Transaction recorded as the combination of an immediate securities sale with simultaneous agreement to reverse the transaction in the future. This combination is normally treated in practice as a lending of cash against securities collateral.

Reserve maintenance period. Period set by the central bank over which reserve requirements must be met.

Reserve money. Deposits held by banks at the central bank and cash in circulation.

Reserve requirement. The percentage of different types of deposits that banks are required to hold on deposit at the central bank.

Residence principle. In the taxation of international capital flows, principle that taxation rights belong to the capital holder's country of residence.

Retail investors. Smaller, usually individual, investors in securities.

Retail market. Market dominated by investors, often individuals, making small-size transactions.

Revenue bond. Bond issued for a specific project or enterprise and secured by revenues generated by that activity.

Reverse auction. Auction for the purchase, rather than for the sale, of bonds.

Reverse dual-currency bond. Bond that pays principal in the base currency, which is usually that of the investor, and interest in another.

Reverse tap purchase. Purchase by an authority of bonds from primary dealers or brokers in the secondary market by directly contacting them.

Risk management system. System to manage the various risks entailed in doing business.

Risk premium. Extra return demanded by investors because of risks associated with an issue.

Rollover risk. Risk that the issuer will have difficulty renewing an issue upon maturity.

RTGS. See real-time gross settlement.

Safety net. Possibility of official credit extensions to allay financial crises.

Same-day settlement. Settlement of a securities transaction on the same day that it is initiated.

Schedular tax system. Income tax regime in which each of various categories of income of the same taxpayer is assessed under different schedules (e.g., schedule A: income from land, schedule B: income from employment, schedule C: income from securities, etc.) and taxed separately. This compartmentalized income tax system is in contrast to a global income tax system under which all incomes, from whatever source derived, that belong to the same taxpayer are treated as a single set of income and taxed at a single rate.

SEC. See Securities and Exchange Commission.

Secondary market. Asset market where securities—government, subnational, and private sector—are traded after they have been issued or sold on primary markets.

Securities accounts. Accounts denominating the holding of securities, usually in automated book-entry form. See paperless securities.

Securities and Exchange Commission (SEC). In the United States, government agency that protects investors and maintains the integrity of the securities markets, primarily by requiring disclosure of financial information.

Securities lending. Temporary provision of securities by a securities creditor to a securities borrower.

Securities transaction tax. Tax on securities trading.

Securitization. The process of creating a pass-through, such as the mortgage pass-through security, by which the pooled assets become standard securities backed by those assets. Also, refers to the replacement of nonmarketable loans and/or cash flows provided by financial intermediaries with negotiable securities issued in the public capital markets.

Self-regulatory associations (SRAs). Groups of financial service entities, such as accountants and auditors, for self-policing.

Self-regulatory organization (SRO). Autonomous nonpublic body that regulates or oversees and monitors the behavior of affiliated participants in financial markets. Self-regulatory organizations may have formal powers delegated to them by public financial agencies, and often have some form of relationship with these agencies.

Senior debt securities. Debt securities that, in case of bankruptcy or other financial difficulty, would be given priority in payment of principal and interest.

Settlement cash. Cash balances held at the central bank that are available to meet settlement claims. See excess reserves.

Settlement risk. Risk that one party to a transaction performs, but the other party does not.

Shelf registration. Once an issue has been registered and approved, it may be sold on a delayed or continuous basis over a period of time.

Short selling. Sale of securities not in the seller's possession.

Short the currency. Sale of currency that is not held, in the expectation that it can be purchased at a lower price.

Single register. One set of accounts for all holdings of securities.

Sinking fund. Fund established for the purpose of paying interest and principal on a debt as these come due.

SOE. See state-owned enterprise.

Source principle. In the taxation of international capital flows, principle that taxation rights belong to the country in which the capital resides.

Sovereign bond. Bond governed by other than the national law of the issuer.

Special-purpose bond. Bond issued to finance specific projects.

Split-rate tax system. Tax system applying a lower tax rate for distributed earnings of a corporation than for retained earnings.

Spot transaction. Immediate purchase or sale of securities or other assets for cash.

Spread trading. Simultaneous purchase and sale of two related instruments, perhaps for different maturities.

SRA. See self-regulatory associations.

SRO. See self-regulatory organization.

Stamp duty or tax. Transactions tax on securities transaction paid by affixing a stamp to transaction documents.

Standby lending facilities. Central bank lending facilities available in case of necessity. A discount window could be one form.

Standing instructions. Agreed procedures for the handling of transactions that may occur in the future.

State-owned enterprise (SOE). Firm owned and controlled by the government.

Sterilized accounts. Accounts that cannot be drawn upon.

STP. See straight-through processing.

Straight bond. Bond with no special features.

Straight-through processing. Capture of trade details directly from front-end trading systems and complete automated processing of confirmations and settlement instructions without the need for rekeying or reformatting data.

Stripping. Separation of the interest payments from the principal of securities into two separately tradable instruments.

Stripped bond. Bond that can be subdivided into a series of zero-coupon bonds.

Structured bond. Bond tailored to the needs of the purchaser.

Subdepositories. Depositories for a group of financial institutions that do not qualify to be served directly by a central depository, which are in turn members of a central depository.

Subgovernments. Governments, such as states and municipalities, below the national government level.

Subnational government agencies. Government entities below the national level. These might include state and municipal governments and government corporations.

Subordinated debt securities. Debt securities that, in case of bankruptcy or other financial difficulty, would be less favored in payment of principal and interest than more senior securities.

Sunset clause. Clause in legislation for expiry of a program after a certain period. If deadline expires, legislation becomes automatically inoperative.

Swaps of securities. Trading of one security for another.

Syndication. Sale of securities through a group with which the issuer negotiates the price of the securities.

Systemic risk. Risk that the failure of one participant may lead to more general financial problems that could affect the stability of the financial system.

Tap sales of bonds. Sale of securities by the issuer over a specified period, the issuer fixing the price or setting a minimum price.

Tax avoidance. Escape from taxes by legal means.

Tax fragmentation. Multiple taxes on the same asset or type of transaction.

Tax loophole. Gap in tax law that allows taxes to be avoided.

Tax neutrality. Tax treatment that affects different transaction forms with the same economic consequences in the same way.

Tesobonos. Special securities issued by the Mexican government.

Tobin tax. Professor James Tobin's proposal to tax international currency transactions. This transaction tax, originally 1percent uniform tax on all spot conversions of one currency into another, was an effective means to mitigate excessive short-term international capital flows.

Trading and information system. System designed to disseminate price information and support transactions.

Transaction tax. Tax levied on transactions of securities.

Transactional liquidity. Availability of sufficient cash for market participants to trade securities. Refers to ease of trading in a market.

Transfer intercept. Arrangement under which subnational borrowings are serviced directly by the central government or under which a lender can seek payment from the central government for an overdue obligation of a subnational borrower.

Transfer of securities without payment. Shift of securities from one party to another without a cash counterpart.

Transfer risk. Risk that legal or regulatory barriers may prevent or inhibit transactions.

Transparency. Provision of the objectives of policy decisions and their rationale, data, and information related to monetary and financial policies, and the terms of agencies' accountability to the public in a comprehensible and timely manner.

Treasury bills. Securities issued by a Treasury, usually on a discount basis and for maturities of not longer than one year.

Treasury capacity in banks. Ability of banks to manage short-term cash and investment flows as well as attendant market and operational risks.

Underwriting. Form of syndication in which a selling group purchases securities from the issuer.

Uniform price auction. Auction in which each winning bidder pays the price of the lowest successful bid, which is the cut-off price.

Unitized pension fund. Pension fund for which monthly contributions are invested at a net asset value–based price and accumulated contributions are transferred at the same price.

Vertical equity. A tax fairness principle stating that those with a greater ability to pay should bear a greater tax burden, requiring the tax system to be progressive and instrumental in causing income redistribution.

When-issued security. Issue that has yet to be auctioned, but trades between the official announcement of a forthcoming auction and the date at which it is actually delivered to the market.

Wholesale investor. Larger, usually institutional investor in financial instruments.

Wholesale market. Market dominated by financial intermediaries typically making large investments in financial instruments.

Winner's curse. Problem faced by uninformed bidders. For example, in an initial public offering, uninformed participants are likely to receive larger allotments of issues that informed participants know are overpriced.

Withholding tax. Tax deducted from income as it is earned.

Yield curve. Relationship between the time to maturity of security issues and their yield to maturity.

Zero-coupon bond. Bond issued on a discount basis, so that all payment is deferred until maturity.